TEACHING ESL WRITING

JOY M. REID

University of Wyoming

REGENTS/PRENTICE HALL
Englewood Cliffs, New Jersey 07632

Library of Congress Cataloging-in-Publication Data

Teaching ESL writing / Joy M. Reid
p. ; cm.
Includes bibliographical references.
ISBN 0-13-888215-0
1. English language--Study and teaching--Foreign speakers.
2. English language--Composition and exercises--Study and teaching.
I. Title.
PE1128.A2R45   1993
428.2'4—dc20   92-39239
                                                                CIP

Publisher: **Tina B. Carver**
Managing editor, production: **Sylvia Moore**
Editorial production, interior design, and
        desktop composition: **Janet Johnston**
Electronic supervision and illustration on page 60:
    Molly Pike Riccardi
Acquisitions editor: **Anne Riddick**
Prepress buyer: **Ray Keating**
Manufacturing buyer: **Lori Bulwin**
Scheduler: **Leslie Coward**
Cover supervisor: **Marianne Frasco**
Cover designer: **Lundgren Graphics, Ltd.**

©1993 by Regents/Prentice Hall
A division of Simon & Schuster
Englewood Cliffs, New Jersey 07632

Printed in the United States of America

10   9   8   7   6   5   4   3   2   1

ISBN 0-13-888215-0

Prentice-Hall International (UK) Limited, *London*
Prentice-Hall of Australia Pty. Limited, *Sydney*
Prentice-Hall of Canada Inc., *Toronto*
Prentice-Hall Hispanoamericana, S.A., *Mexico*
Prentice-Hall of India Private Limited, *New Delhi*
Prentice-Hall of Japan, Inc., *Tokyo*
Simon & Schuster Asia Pte. Ltd., *Singapore*
Editora Prentice-Hall do Brasil, Ltda., *Rio de Janeiro*

with ESL students. The intent of this book is to provide essential background information, practices, and activities for a teacher who is becoming an ESL writing teacher, and to integrate those areas into a coherent whole. The book reviews a variety of information and perspectives, historical and current, and asks the readers to digest, integrate, and interpret the information, with the objective of formulating their own philosophies of and approaches to teaching ESL writing.

The first objective of *Teaching ESL Composition* is to review essential information concerning the field of composition for both NESs and non-native speakers of English (ESL students). Then, using this information as a knowledge base, the textbook provides specific information about planning a curriculum (programmatic considerations), developing syllabi for each level of language proficiency in an effective ESL writing program, and day-to-day lessons in basic, intermediate, and advanced ESL writing classes. Specifically, about a third of the text is historical/theoretical in its perspective, a third is directed toward curriculum and pedagogical issues in ESL writing classes, and a third is concerned with the actual teaching of ESL writing: implementation of the syllabus, sequenced activities and assignments that ESL writing teachers can adopt/adapt for their classes, and approaches to the response to and evaluation of ESL writing. Also included in this text are discussion questions and writing exercises about the contents of each chapter, and an annotated bibliography at the end of the book.

The book is not all-encompassing; it does not focus on immigrant and refugee non-native speakers of English, nor is it concerned with ESL students studying in elementary and secondary schools (often called Limited English Proficiency or LEP students). Instead, it focuses on (a) the student who is studying English as a second (or foreign) language in her/his own country with the intention of studying in a U.S. post-secondary institution and (b) the international student who attends an English for Academic Purposes (EAP) writing class in preparation for college or university work, or (c) the ESL student who is enrolled in a college or university undergraduate writing course in a U.S. post-secondary school.

A number of assumptions (one might say beliefs, others biases) underlie the planning of this book.

1. That effective, appropriate writing is teachable and learnable, but that teacher and student commitment, choice, and change are necessary for both;

2. That the teaching of writing, particularly writing for academic purposes, involves, at the very least, teacher- and student-

PREFACE

During her graduate work, my daughter Shelley was hired to teach two writing classes during the summer in the Intensive English Language Institute at the State University of New York at Buffalo. She had been working as a teaching assistant in the English Department, but she had never taught English as a Second Language (ESL) writing. That summer my telephone bill was enormous; almost every night, we would talk about the problems she was encountering, the lessons she was learning, and, eventually, the pleasures she was experiencing. I then decided to write this book so that other inexperienced teachers of ESL writing would have a sourcebook, a resource to consult before they entered the ESL writing classroom.

Students in training to become ESL teachers, and many relatively inexperienced teachers of ESL writing, have never had a course in writing beyond their undergraduate freshman composition course, and so, although they may (or may not) be successful writers themselves, they have little understanding of why they are (or are not) successful. Many of these same teachers (or teachers-in-training) have taken semester-long courses in grammar/syntax, the teaching of reading, and/or phonetics/oral skills. They are therefore more able to teach those skills than ESL writing, whether the skills occur separately or in an integrated skills curriculum. Only within the last five years have entire courses in teaching ESL writing been conceived, designed, and taught; only because the need for such courses has become clear, the knowledge to teach the courses (much of it adapted from NES—native speakers of English—composition) has become available. As a result, ESL composition teaching as a field of expertise, not a support skill, has begun to be recognized.

As many teachers trained for and used to teaching composition to NESs have found, the needs, backgrounds, learning styles, and writing strategies of most ESL students differ dramatically from those of NESs. Moreover, it is not simply a question of NES versus ESL students. Indeed, the differences between and among ESL students in terms of language and cultural backgrounds, prior education, gender, age, and ESL language proficiency make these students remarkably diverse in their needs and objectives. It is therefore essential for teachers of ESL students to learn about these needs and differences and to practice approaches and techniques—methodologies—that will be successful

CONTENTS

intervention in the drafting process, the revision process, and the presentation of a product;

3. That the teaching of ESL composition is not a single or a simple activity because writing itself is complex, and because the teaching of effective strategies and skills is an on-going, complicated, recursive process;.

4. That contrastive rhetoric, the belief that students from different language and cultural backgrounds present written material differently, is a valid and viable theory; therefore, the ESL writing class must address the questions of appropriate presentation of written ideas for a U.S. academic audience and for discipline-specific discourse communities;

5. That because of the diversity of students and their differing language proficiency levels, composition teachers must learn about cross-cultural issues;

6. That composition teaching should be student-directed and student-oriented, but that the teacher is responsible for structuring lessons and assignments that are designed to fulfill the needs of the students and the objectives of the syllabus;.

7. That the most successful ESL writing classroom occurs in an atmosphere of mutual respect and trust in which teacher responsibility is balanced by student responsibility;

8. That the teacher is responsible for establishing a classroom community in which students, as members of that community, help each other and learn together;

9. That the ESL writing curriculum should be planned (a) backwards, from overall exit objectives that are based on what the students will be doing when they complete the ESL writing program, and (b) with serious consideration to the parameters of the program: duration, student needs, and both internal and external environments;

10. That syllabus and lesson planning for the ESL classroom are based on function: that purposeful, authentic writing that fulfills the expectations of the identified audience forms the foundation of the class;

11. That response to and evaluation of student writing is an essential part of the ESL writing class, and that the processes are complex and ongoing;

12. That teachers themselves are classroom researchers, constantly investigating, reflecting upon, and interpreting the data of the classroom in order to make their teaching—and so their students—more successful.

Acknowledgments

Many people made this book possible. My students and colleagues, for the past quarter century, at the University of Kansas Applied English Center, at the Colorado State University Intensive English Program, and in the ESL classes at the University of Wyoming are ultimately responsible for the knowledge imparted here. I am especially grateful to the Department of English at the University of Wyoming for the time and support given me for the production of this text. In addition, my daughter has been an integral part of this book; she has read and edited the manuscript with care and love. Her suggestions ("Mother, don't be so pompous here—new teachers will never be able to do this successfully," "Why don't you give some failures as well as successes?") have improved the book exponentially; it was also her suggestion to name the "Blind Random" chapter and to focus on that analogy throughout. And my husband, Steve, who teaches composition to NESs at Colorado State University and who writes composition textbooks for those students, was my best sounding board and editor as well as a constant source of solace in my own writing process.

ESL teachers who deserve special mention for their contributions to this book include Diane Pollock and James Conger at the Western English as a Second Language Program (WESL) at Western Illinois University; Elizabeth Rodriguez at California State University, Sacramento; Edwina Echevarria, Mark Dorr, and Nathalie Bleuze at Colorado State University; and Ken Emery, Jodi Hill, Christie Stebbins, and Mark Walker at the University of Wyoming. ESL students who contributed their writing to this book include Saud Bin Al-Battl (Saudi Arabia), Brenda Alpizar (Puerto Rico), Gloria Arango (Colombia), Michel Camara (Senegal), Perlini Dandekar (India), Kuzuaki Goto (Japan), Sue-Lan Kao (PRC), Anna Lewan (Italy), Sue Leon Lim (Korea), Weoi-Choo Ong (Malaysia), Azmat Rahman (Bangladesh), Nidal Slaibi (Saudi Arabia), Yusef Vlanet (Indonesia), and Anne Waaden (Norway).

Writing a book about teaching writing is especially tricky business; my own writing is nowhere close to perfect, and the anxiety of making egregious errors is particularly prevalent when one's work should demonstrate the "form follows function" adage. Therefore, the reviewers of my original manuscript deserve special mention for their thoroughness and their encouragement: Kim Brown at Portland State University, Ann Johns at San Diego State, Constance Knop at the University of Wisconsin, Barbara Matthies at Iowa State, Ken Sheppard at Hunter College, and especially Barbara Kroll at California State University/Northridge, whose suggestions, perceptions, and expert editing skills helped with my revisions. My thanks, too, to Anne Riddick, Nancy Leonhardt, and Janet Johnston at Regents/Prentice

Hall, whose assistance and patience were remarkable, particularly when my hard disk blew up and I was frantic at the loss of several weeks' work.

Finally, during the preparation of this book, I corresponded with teachers of writing in ESL intensive language programs across the country. In response, many of those teachers mailed copies of their programs' writing curricula and syllabi and gave permission for me to use them in the book. I am grateful to the faculty in the following intensive language programs, and particularly to those people with whom I corresponded, for their generosity and assistance:

Colorado State University, Intensive English Program:
    Peggy Lindstrom, Charlie Brainer

English Language Services (ELS): Tay Lesley

Georgetown University, Division of English as a Foreign Language:
    Bill Norris, Margie Tegey, Abby Mason, Carol Kreidler

Georgia State University, English as a Second Language Programs:
    Patricia Byrd

Iowa State University, Intensive English and Orientation Program:
    Barbara Matthies

MacCormac Junior College, English Language Institute:
    Anne Nolan

Mission College, English as a Second Language: Jody Hacker

National Louis University: Julie Howard

Ohio State University, American Language Program: Bill Holshuh

Rutgers University, Intensive English Language Program:
    Guinn Roberts

Portland State University: Kim Brown

Sacramento City College: Elizabeth Rodriguez

San Diego State University, American Language Program:
    Bill Gaskill

State University of New York/Buffalo, Intensive English Language
    Institute: Barbara Campbell

University of California, Los Angeles, ESL Service Courses:
    Christine Holden

University of Denver, English Language Center: Norma King

University of Kansas, Applied English Center: Elizabeth Byleen,
    Betty Soppelsa

University of Ohio, Ohio Program of Intensive English:
    Connie Perdreau, Charles Mickelson

University of Illinois at Chicago, Tutorium in Intensive English:
    Betty Jacobsen

University of Maryland, Maryland English Institute: Les Palmer

University of North Texas, International English Language Institute: Rebecca Smith

University of Southern California, American Language Institute: Fraida Dubin

Western Illinois University, Western's English as a Second Language Institute: Lila Blum, Steven Kaesdorf, Diane Pollack, Marilyn Cleland

William Rainey Harper College, Programs in English as a Second Language: Jean Chapman

CHAPTER 1

Overview of Native English Speaker (NES) Composition

Although the development of composition as a field of teaching began nearly a century ago, it focused then primarily on the teaching of grammar and literature. As recently as twenty-five years ago in high school, college, and university English composition classes for NESs (native speakers of English), teachers taught literature and students wrote about literature. The main goal of such courses was "to introduce students to literary study and in the process to correct the writing in students' literary essays according to long-established standards of grammatical, stylistic, and formal correctness" (Bizzell and Herzberg, 1987, p. 3). English teachers designed, assigned, and evaluated **the product,** a piece of writing about literature the class had been studying. A typical assignment required literary analysis: "Compare the character of Nick Adams in Hemingway's short story 'Fathers and Sons' (from *The Snows of Kilimanjaro and Other Stories*) with the character of Dexter Green in Fitzgerald's short story 'Winter Dreams' (from *Babylon Revisited and Other Stories*)."

Some minimal information about parameters ("three to five typewritten, double-spaced pages") and evaluation criteria ("Two sentence fragments will lower your grade") were generally given. But teachers spent little or no time teaching the students how to write. They expected their students to plan and compose their assignments outside of class, and they graded the essays on the quality of the written analysis and the "style" of writing. The teacher's written comments on assignments often focused on grammar errors and syntactic "awkwardness" with vague references to content deficiencies such as "average work" and "support your ideas."

Today composition teachers and researchers are responding to what Maxine Hairston labeled "the revolution in the teaching of writing." Based on the research and classroom application of that research over a twenty-year period, Hairston proposed a new paradigm (a common body of beliefs and assumptions held by most practitioners in the field) that was a shift away from the traditional literature-based teaching of composition. She listed twelve features of the emerging paradigm:

1. It focuses on the **writing process**; instructors intervene in students' writing during the process.
2. It teaches strategies for **invention and discovery**; instructors help students to generate content and discover purpose.
3. It is based on rhetoric: **audience, purpose, and occasion** figure prominently in the assignment of writing tasks.
4. Instructors evaluate the written product by how well it fulfills the writer's intention and meets the audience's needs.
5. It views writing as a recursive rather than a linear process; the activities of **pre-writing**, **writing**, and **revision** overlap and intertwine.
6. It is holistic, viewing writing as an activity that involves the intuitive and non-rational as well as the rational faculties.
7. It emphasizes that writing is a way of learning and developing as well as a communication skill.
8. It includes a variety of writing modes, expressive as well as expository.
9. It is informed by other disciplines, especially cognitive psychology and linguistics.
10. It views writing as a disciplined creative activity that can be analyzed and described.
11. It is based on linguistic research and research into composing processes.
12. It stresses the principle that writing teachers should be people who write.   (1982, p. 82; emphases mine)

In short, the major changes involved in this shifting paradigm are

- an overall focus on the **process** rather than on the **product** of writing;
- concentration by classroom teachers on composing processes rather than on literary discussion;
- focus on the writer, and on the relationship between reader and writer;
- interest in research on writing processes and classroom teaching; and
- commitment to the idea that teaching effective, successful writing is possible.

Although researchers no longer think that writing processes can be fully described by a neat paradigm, the resulting emphasis on process has amounted to a revolution in the way teachers approach writing. As a result of this revolution, the study of composition is currently considered a serious discipline and worthy of advanced graduate work. By 1980, at least twenty major universities, including Carnegie-Mellon, Ohio State, Rutgers, and the University of Texas/Austin, offered doctorates in composition and rhetoric; many more institutions have full-fledged master's programs (Corbett, 1987). Undergraduate English and Education majors preparing to teach English in secondary schools are often required to take a class in the methodology of teaching composition. A great variety of textbooks for rhetoric and composition studies is available to help inexperienced teachers of writing examine their teaching philosophies, construct writing curricula, and investigate and solve classroom problems.* Among them are texts such as William Irmscher's *Teaching Expository Writing* (1979), Ericka Lindemann's *A Rhetoric for Writing Teachers* (1987), and Robert Connor and Cheryl Glenn's *The St. Martin's Guide to Teaching Writing* (1992).

In addition to current materials and degree programs, today's teachers of composition have access to networking and new research at annual regional and national meetings of such organizations as the National Council of Teachers of English (NCTE), College Composition and Communication Conference (4 C's), and The National Testing Network in Writing (NTNW). Professional composition journals include *The English Journal*, aimed at public school teachers; a variety of publications, such as such as *College Composition and Communication*, *College English*, *The Journal of Basic Writing*, and *Composition and Computers*, aimed at post-secondary teachers; and more theory-oriented publications such as *Written Communication*, *The Rhetoric Review*, and *Research in the Teaching of English*.

Beginnings

In 1963, to encourage research in and recognition of the young field of composition, the National Council of Teachers of English (NCTE) published its first, rather spartan survey of composition research. By the late 1960s, composition teachers were meeting, doing research, and writing about student writing processes, that is, the many complex, recursive steps (or phases) that writers move through as they construct a product (Berlin, 1990).

In *A Rhetoric for Writing Teachers*, Ericka Lindemann defines rhetoric broadly: "[W]hen we use language in more formal ways, with the premeditated intention of changing attitudes or behaviors, of explaining a subject matter, of expressing the self, or of calling attention to a text that can be appreciated for its artistic merits, our

---

*The annotated bibliography at the end of this book provides suggestions for a beginning research library and for other useful source material for each chapter.

purpose is rhetorical" (1987, p. 37). The seminal articles and books discussed below provided the basis for the development of the field of composition and rhetoric over the last quarter–century, a development that resulted in the shifting paradigm discussed by Hairston (above). Moreover, the developments in NES research outlined below function as a background for understanding ESL research and pedagogy.

The Expressive School

As pedagogy that would instruct students in the essentials of writing began to develop, practitioners in the emerging field of composition divided into two groups. Teachers of **expressive writing** focused on sincerity, integrity, spontaneity, and originality in composition classrooms; students were encouraged to "discover" themselves through language (Elbow, 1991a, 1991b; Faigley, 1986; Rohman, 1965). Teachers and researchers believed in expressive, self-actualizing writing in which students "discovered" ideas and themselves through freewriting and brainstorming (Coles, 1974, 1978; Elbow, 1973; Macrorie, 1970, 1976; Moffett, 1968). Focus in the classroom turned away from the final product, the structuring of essays and correction of error, to concentrate on creativity and self-discovery through the use of journals or daybooks, in which students wrote "freely," without the consequences of grammar evaluation, teacher-imposed topics and structures, critical comments, and, often, grades. The use of freewriting techniques that allowed students to use language as an aid to thinking and discovery supplanted impersonal prose, literary analysis, and the concentration on the product of writing that had existed in previous decades.

Peter Elbow is perhaps the best-known of the **"freewriting"** school. In *Writing Without Teachers* (1973), he encourages writers to put all their ideas on paper, quickly, without the revisions in word and sentence structure that can "interrupt" thought, and without lifting their pens from their papers. Through this freewriting, which Elbow considers a relatively risk-free way of transferring ideas into words and onto a page, students will discover both real meaning and what they want to say. This "unfocused exploring" is particularly useful in developing the writer's unique and authentic "voice," a genuineness in the author's perception of his/her subject. One variation of freewriting, also developed by Elbow, is "looping": freewriting for a short period of time, then re-reading and selecting the most important idea (a "center of gravity sentence") from that brainstorming to use as a beginning for another short period of freewriting. In a 1989 article, Elbow says that he values freewriting because

it can lead to a certain *experience* of writing or *kind* of writing process
. . . "getting rolling," "getting steaming along," "a door opening,"
"getting warmed up," "juices flowing," or "sailing." These all point to
the states of increased intensity or arousal or excitement. In these
states it feels as though more things come to mind, bubble up and
that somehow they fall more directly into language. (p. 60)

Donald Murray's books for teachers, *Learning by Teaching* (1982)
and *A Writing Teacher Teaches Writing* (1985b), and his many articles
(1978, 1985a 1988) have elaborated on freewriting techniques by
showing how to implement them in the classroom: by incorporating
paired student discussion and responses and, especially, by using
individual teacher-student conferencing outside of class, at each stage
of the writing process. Murray encourages teachers to limit the practice
of "authoritative teaching" and instead to practice "responsive
teaching"—that is, to *respond* to students' writing, discussion, and
questions rather than to proclaim answers.

The Cognitive School

The initial shift from product to process by the expressive school
also led to research from another group of composition practitioners.
During the 1970s, cognitivists began to investigate the **writing
process** and **process teaching**; they were particularly interested in
how these processes were related to cognitive psychology and to
psycholinguistics. Proponents believed in a research-based, audience-
focused, context-based approach to the processes of writing, in which
writers construct reality through language (Britton et al., 1975;
D'Angelo, 1975, 1980; Flower and Hayes, 1980; Young et al, 1970).
Cognitive researchers studied how writers approach tasks by problem-
solving in areas such as audience, purpose, and the situation for
writing. Research first focused on the early stages of composing:
invention (idea generation) and **arrangement** (organization of
ideas). In composition classrooms, teachers also focused on the initial
stages of writing, often called **pre-writing**; they began to teach **pre-
writing strategies** that allowed their students to generate ideas and
to arrange those ideas successfully. Students were encouraged to
experiment with a variety of pre-writing techniques, including
brainstorming, freewriting, outlining, cubing, clustering (see Figure
1–1, page 6), and listing. A student using cubing, for example,
visualizes a three-dimensional block. On each of the block's six sides is
a task that the student uses to generate ideas about her subject: *describe
it, compare it, associate it, analyze it, apply it,* and *argue for/against it.*

FIGURE 1–1 CLUSTERING

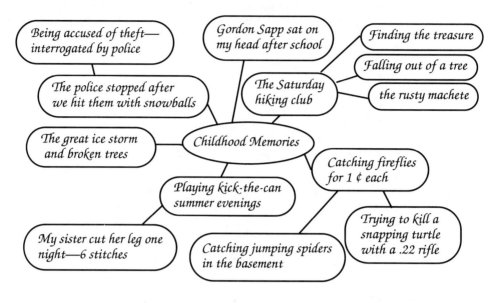

(S.D. Reid, 1992a, p. 106)

One contribution of the cognitivists to the field of composition was the use of "**invention heuristics,**" first pioneered by Kenneth Burke (1945). These organized lists of questions helped writers to generate, develop, and arrange their ideas. Such lists range from the relatively simple journalistic questions of *who, what, when, where, why,* and *how* to the more complex questions of Richard Young et al.'s (1970) multifaceted "tagmemic" theory that "asks writers to view their subject (whether it be an idea, event, or object) from three perspectives: as an isolated entity, as a dynamic process, and as a fully developed system" (Tarvers, 1990, p. 3). A third heuristic based on Aristotle's "topics" often appears in composition textbooks. The following table, from Elizabeth Cowen Neeld's *Writing,* illustrates how classical heuristics support students' invention processes.

TABLE 1–1 INVENTION HEURISTICS

<u>Definition</u>
1. How does the dictionary define _____?
2. What earlier words did _____ come from?
3. What do *I* mean by _____?
4. What group of things does _____ seem to belong to? How is _____ different from other things in this group?
5. What parts can _____ be divided into?

6. Did _____ mean something in the past that it doesn't mean now? If so, what? What does this former meaning tell us about how the idea grew and developed?
7. Does _____ mean something now that it didn't years ago? If so, what?
8. What other words mean approximately the same as _____?
9. What are some concrete examples of _____?
10. When is the meaning of _____ misunderstood?

Comparison
1. What is _____ similar to? In what ways?
2. What is _____ different from? In what ways?
3. _____ is superior to what? In what ways?
4. _____ is inferior to what? In what ways?
5. _____ is most unlike what? (What is it opposite to?) In what ways?
6. _____ is most like what? In what ways?

Relationship
1 What causes _____?
2 What is the purpose of _____?
3. Why does _____ happen?
4. What is the consequence of _____?
5 What comes before _____?
6. What comes after _____?

Circumstance
1 Is _____ possible or impossible?
2. What qualities, conditions, or circumstances make _____ possible or impossible?
3 Supposing that _____ is possible, is it also desirable?
4. When did _____ happen previously?
5. Who has done or experienced _____?
6. Who can do _____?
7. If _____ starts, what makes it end?
8. What would it take for _____ to happen now?
9. What would prevent _____ from happening?

Testimony
1. What have I heard people say about _____?
2. Do I know any facts or statistics about _____? If so, what?
3. Have I talked with anyone about _____?
4. Do I know a famous or well-known saying (e.g., "A bird in the hand is worth two in the bush") about_____?

(1986, pp. 46–47)

As cognitivist theories began to affect the composition classroom, teachers shifted to a more balanced combination of process and product. Instead of concentrating exclusively on the product, as the traditionalists had, or on the personal development of the individual student through expressive writing, teachers and students worked with the phases of the writing process that resulted in a final product.

Early Writing Process Research

Investigations by both Expressivists and Cognitivists into pre-writing processes expanded into more formal educational research that observed working writers. The method of data collection was often **case study research**: careful and detailed observations of a single case over a period of time and/or of a small group of writers during a single situation. The data were then categorized, interpreted, and reported. Many of the early studies used a "think-aloud" methodology, in which writers spoke their thoughts as they composed or planned their writing. Teacher-researchers such as Janet Emig (1977), Nancy Sommers (1980), and Sondra Perl (1980) used **"think-aloud" protocols** to study the composing processes—the writing behaviors—of students writing in secondary and post-secondary classrooms. In addition, their work examined the writing processes of both experienced and inexperienced adult writers. These researchers discovered that (a) there are many kinds of writing processes and that (b) composing is not necessarily linear. When writers are composing, they don't always plan, write, and revise, but they follow a recursive pattern, often going back in their prose to previous words, sentences, or paragraphs. They return to re-read, to remember, to add or edit, or perhaps to re-capture the momentum of their writing. For many writers, the process of putting words on paper is "two steps forward, one step back," a process of ebb and flow as they write.

The use of think-aloud composing protocols by Linda Flower (1979) and Flower and John Hayes (1980) focused on cognitive development and problem-solving. Flower and Hayes demonstrated that (a) because goals direct composing, there must be a purpose for writing; (b) simple cognitive operations produce enormously complex actions; and (c) successful writers often use a variety of composing processes, depending on the writing situation and the parameters of the task. In addition, Flower observed the differences between "writer-based" and "reader-based" prose. Writer-based prose is

> verbal expression written by a writer to himself and by himself. It is the working of his own verbal thought. In its structure, Writer-based prose reflects the associative, narrative path of the writer's own confrontation with her subject. [Reader-based prose is] a deliberate attempt to communicate something to a reader. To do that it creates shared language and shared context between writer and reader. It also offers the reader an issue-oriented, rhetorical structure rather than a replay of the writer's discovery processes. (1979, pp. 19–20)

Basic Writers

Late in the 1970s, social changes brought to universities many students whose first language was not English, or was not Edited Standard English (ESE). Studies of these writers by sociolinguists and composition teachers/researchers found that these new students were worthy of respect and care; they were not intellectually deficient, but were linguistically and culturally diverse. In particular, Mina Shaughnessy's seminal work, *Errors and Expectations* (1977), reported on her two decades of studying "severely underprepared" freshmen, whom she called **Basic Writers**, at the City University of New York. Shaughnessy studied 4,000 student essays, analyzed the errors, and posited that the cause of the error is more important than the fact of the error. Her book explained the developmental problems faced by such students, particularly those who had limited English proficiency (LEP), who were bidialectical (principally black students), and/or whose reading skills, as well as writing skills, were deficient.

> What has been so damaging about the experience of BW [Basic Writing] students with written English is that it has been so confusing, and worse, that they have become resigned to this confusion, to not knowing, to the substitution of protective tactics or private systems or makeshift strategies for genuine mastery of written English in any form. . . . Such was the quality of their instruction that no one saw the **intelligence of their mistakes** or thought to harness that intelligence in the service of learning.
>
> (1977, pp. 10–11; emphasis mine)

Shaughnessy recommended not only identification of student errors but also discovery of the linguistic and cultural reasons for the errors. In what was then a surprising innovation, she asked students to explain why they made the mistakes she found; she then designed her teaching around the misconceptions, misunderstandings, and lack of knowledge her students articulated. She encouraged the teaching of the conventions of academic prose, not so much because they were "correct" but because they fulfilled the expectations of the academic audience and were therefore necessary for successful communication. She focused her students' attention on **audience expectations**, and she demonstrated the necessity of teaching coping skills designed to meet those expectations and to build student confidence.

Another result of the influx of Basic Writers and LEP students to colleges and universities, particularly under some "open admissions" policies, was the development of "writing laboratories" or "**writing ,**" which provided additional assistance and resources for students. Writers from all disciplines began to use writing centers for help in identifying and recognizing the forms of ESE that would help them in effective writing (Kasden and Hoeber, 1980; Olsen, 1984). Areas addressed in writing centers ranged from strategies for identifying audience and purpose, to sentence combining to improve the sophistication of sentence structure, to building fluency and self-confidence, to working on grammatical correctness. Today, writing centers also provide opportunities for peer review and audience analysis (Dorazio, 1992). Although these resource centers have come under fire from those who feel that "remediation" should not be the function of post-secondary education, they have become an integral part of many institutions.

The continued influx of students whose native languages are not ESE will fuel additional research into their needs and their empowerment. More specifically, there will be research into the needs and problems of the overlapping categories of "underprepared" students, LEP students, and ESL students. Teachers will need educational experiences that will prepare them for multicultural classrooms so that they will be better able to help their students (Chaudron, 1988; Dean, 1989; Hyltenstam and Pienemann, 1985).

Current Research Trends

While study continues in many of the areas begun in the 1970s, some new or rejuvenated issues have appeared in the last decade: the social nature of writing, ethnographic studies of composing in the workplace as well as in schools, the use of computers in composition teaching, the work of James Kinneavy, the reading-writing connection, and composition classroom dynamics.

The Social Nature of Writing

In the 1980s, much research focused on the more theoretical area of the **social nature of writing**, of how cognitive processes function and are conditioned by social and historical forces, and how social circumstances shape the teaching—and the learning—of writing (Faigley, 1986; Fish, 1980, 1990; Lunsford, 1990). Patricia Bizzell (1982) and Kenneth Bruffee (1986) argue that knowledge itself is socially constructed, and they have examined in some detail how the situation and the social context in which writing processes are performed affect those processes. They found that any writing, whether about the self or reality, always develops in relation to previous texts and contexts, situations and experiences. In other words, the writing situation puts social and psychological, as well as rhetorical, constraints on the writer. For example, a writer involved in an automobile accident following a party would describe the accident differently for three different writing situations: (a) in a letter to her mother, (b) in a written report for the insurance company, and (c) in an essay for her freshman English professor. She would make different rhetorical choices precisely because each of these three social groups (the family, the insurance company, and the composition classroom) construct meaning differently.

In composition research, this awareness of writing situation in academic contexts has developed into the concept of "discourse communities" (Faigley, 1985). The term **discourse** refers to multi-sentence chunks of language; a community is a group of people with similar values, aims, aspirations, and expectations. Because texts are almost always written for persons in restricted groups or communities,

> within a language community, people acquire special kinds of discourse competence that enable them to participate in specialized groups. Members [of that community] know what is worth communicating, how it can be communicated, what other members of the community are likely to know and believe to be true about certain subjects, how other members can be persuaded, and so on.
> (Faigley, 1985, p. 12)

In his article "Inventing the University," David Bartholomae contends that different communities can be expected to have different perspectives and audience expectations, so many students have difficulty with the multiple communities' conventions of academic writing.

> Every time a student sits down to write for us, he has to invent the university for the occasion—invent the university, that is, or a branch of it, like history or anthropology or economics or English. The student has to learn how to speak our language, to speak as we do, to try on the peculiar ways of knowing, selecting, evaluating, reporting, concluding, and arguing that define the discourse of our community.
> (1985, p. 34)

In other words, because students lack the language, the experience, and sometimes even the awareness that the academic community has cultural, social, and rhetorical expectations, they are often involved in a constant struggle just to communicate.

In the examination of discourse that is socially constructed and evaluated, some researchers have called for the **empowerment** of students, and have argued vehemently against the belief that Basic Writers are cognitively deficient or "remedial" (Hull and Rose, 1989; Rose, 1985a, 1985b, 1989). Glynda Hull et al. suggest that teachers can "inadvertently participate in the social construction of attitudes and beliefs about remediation which may limit the learning that takes place in our classrooms" (1991, p. 300). Instead, these researchers view Basic Writers as unfamiliar with the discourse community that evaluates them, and their errors as systematic gaps in their knowledge.

To belong to a discourse community is to belong to a knowledge community. Teachers must therefore help students learn how to "search beyond their own limited present experience and knowledge

. . . to find ways to immerse writing students in academic knowledge/discourse communities so they can write from within those communities" (Reither, 1988, p. 144).

Ethnographic Research and Composing Processes

Many of the composition issues of the 1980s lent themselves to **ethnographic study**: observers enter a specific setting to collect data and to analyze writing processes and practices in specific work-related and culture-related communities—the job, the family, and the classroom (see Brannon, 1985; Crandall, 1981; Harrison, 1987; Scribner and Cole, 1981). Clifford Geertz (1973) called this kind of research "thick description": writing a detailed account of what ethnographers observe, then studying the accounts to discover and understand what happened in order to "reduce the puzzlement." Susan Florio and Christopher Clark (1982), for example, examined the functions of writing in one elementary school classroom, while Kenneth Kantor (1984) studied composing processes in a secondary school creative writing class from three perspectives: as a participant observer, an interviewer, and an examiner of student writing. In one of the best-known ethnographic studies, *Ways With Words: Language, Life and Work in Communities and Classrooms* (1983), Shirley Brice Heath reported on her ten-year study of working class families in two communities in the Carolina Piedmont. Among other areas, Heath investigated and interpreted the differences and relationships between attitudes and expectations concerning literacy—reading and writing— at school and at home. Another important ethnographic study by Lee O'Dell and Dixie Goswami (1982) examined literacy in the workplace; they studied eleven workers in a social services agency whose jobs required a substantial amount of writing.*

Ethnographic studies of the cognitive development of student writers and composing processes have produced much of the recent research in the field. Mike Rose (1985b) and Linda Flower (1989) examined cognitive and emotional problems in the composing process that result in "writer's block" and offered strategies for overcoming those problems. Peter Smagorinsky demonstrated the relationship between background knowledge and the composing process through the use of protocol analysis (1991). Other researchers and teachers focused on the effects of audience analysis on student writing and on

---

*Some ethnographic studies incorporate aspects of empirical research, which is distinguished from the *qualitative, descriptive, holistic* research of ethnography by its attention to quantitative data that are analyzed, often by statistical means. O'Dell and Goswami, for example, also statistically analyzed six textual features of their participants' writing.

the use of audience specification in writing assignments (K.Black, 1989; Redd-Boyd and Slater, 1989). Still others studied revision processes (Faigley and Witte, 1981; Flower et al., 1986), which they identified as being as recursive as composing processes. These researchers differentiated between experienced and inexperienced writers, and between surface changes, called **editing**, and the more significant text-based changes—**revisions**—that affect the content of the writing. Nancy Sommers, in a retrospective article on revising research, put it simply: "You can't just change the words around and get the ideas right" (1992, p. 26).

Computers and Composition Teaching

The use of computers in the teaching of writing was originally limited to word processing, which benefited students by providing easy correction and revision. Editing programs provided spelling checkers, diction flaggers, and readability scores that assisted students with textual errors.* During the past decade, the use of computers in composition teaching has grown dramatically. Software programs and teacher-designed computer exercises that prompt the writer to compose and revise and then offer suggestions for improvement have become available (Anandam, 1983; Bacig et al., 1991; Collier, 1983; Davis, 1984; Haas, 1989; D. Rodrigues, 1985). Comment files and networked computers allow students to review each other's drafts, and allow teachers to comment on and evaluate student prose (Daiute, 1985, 1986; Jansen et al., 1987; Joram et al., 1992; Mabrito, 1991; Marshall, 1985; Schwartz, 1985; Varone and D'Agostino, 1990).

Current software programs also analyze texts quantitatively by identifying discourse features such as word frequency and sentence length, and by providing information for statistical analysis concerning student use of language, changes from draft to draft, and number and type of revisions (Hull, 1987; Reid and Findlay, 1986; Smith, in press). Studies of computer-based revision strategies (Bridwell, Sirc, and Brooke, 1984; Daiute, 1986) reported the increased ease of revision with computers, and Dawn Rodrigues and Raymond Rodrigues (1989) demonstrated that using computers in the teaching of composition, whether in a full-time computer classroom or as a supplement to a writing class, changes the roles of both students and teachers. Computer conferencing and networked group work among students

---

*William Wresch's collection of essays, *A Writer's Tool: The Computer in Composition Instruction* (1985), Colleen Daiute's *Writing and Computers* (1984), and *Computers and Writing: Theory, Research and Practice*, edited by Deborah Holdstein and Cynthia L. Self (1990) give overviews of the early and current use of computer laboratories in composition teaching.

also changes the classroom environment, prompting classroom community and collaborative learning (Shriner and Rice, 1989; Thompson, 1989). Kate Kiefer and Charles Smith (1984), working with a Bell Laboratories series of text-analysis programs, the Writer's Workbench, empirically analyzed the number and types of revisions made by college freshmen working with and without computers. Kiefer and Smith reported that student editing skills increased as a result of computer-assisted instruction, and that students thought that computer use made revisions and writing easier.

With the expansion in the numbers and use of computer laboratories and computer classrooms in the teaching of composition, new research will continue to seek better ways to implement technology and to develop better writers through collaborative learning and individual teaching and learning styles (Schwartz, 1985; Selfe, Rodrigues, and Oates, 1989; Shriner and Rice, 1989). In a large-scale study of the use of computer classrooms in composition classes, for example, Stephen Bernhardt et al. (1989) assessed the broad, measurable effect of using computers to teach introductory college composition courses. Results paralleled prior research in two important ways. They indicated that the use of computers was favored attitudinally by the students and that students revised essays at levels substantially higher than the control group. Current computer network technology can create an interactive classroom that supports Murray's and Elbow's student-centered teaching methodologies and reinforces Bruffee's and Bizzell's notions that knowledge and discourse are socially constructed.

James Kinneavy and Traditional Rhetoric

For many teacher-researchers, the '80s offered an opportunity to reexamine the concepts of classical rhetoric, particularly as they were interpreted by James Kinneavy in his article "The Basic Aims of Discourse" (1969). Kinneavy organized discourse into four main types or **aims**: reference, persuasive, literary, and expressive. Each kind of discourse has a different aim and emphasis:

> **reference** discourse emphasizes the **subject**
> **persuasive** discourse emphasizes the **reader**
> **literary** discourse emphasizes **language**
> **expressive** discourse emphasizes the **writer**

In his determination of differing discourse purposes, Kinneavy also distinguished between **means** and **ends**. Methods of developing discourse, such as comparison/contrast, definition, and cause–effect, were, according to Kinneavy, means to the end (that is, modes) and should not be the aim of discourse. Instead, writers should identify the aims of their discourse—for example, to explain, to argue, or to explore—and then use the modes necessary for successful communication.

Applied by researchers, teachers, and textbook authors in the '80s, Kinneavy's paradigm has resulted in the virtual abandonment of the "comparison/contrast essay" and the "definition essay" in some composition classrooms because (a) these modes should be used as means, not ends in themselves, and (b) such discourse forms do not exist in the real world (Hagaman, 1980; Harris and Moran, 1979). Instead, students in Kinneavian composition classes may use several of these modes within a single essay (Cooper and O'Dell, 1978; Kinneavy, McCleary, and Nakadate, 1985; S.D. Reid, 1992a). Students in these classes also focus on the **purpose** of the discourse—the reason the writer decides to compose. Their aims discipline their purposes. When both aim and purpose are taught, the focus is on the social function of the product: explaining or reporting (referential discourse), arguing or problem-solving (persuasive discourse), or remembering or observing (expressive or literary discourse). The concepts of audience and purpose, of communicating competently, are paramount; composing processes are taught in a rhetorical context.

The Reading-Writing Connection

The proposition that reading and writing are integrally linked as skills and as makers of knowledge has been the focus of researchers for decades. Such investigation has been further informed by research that shows that reading is an active, not a passive, experience. In addition, research has shown that correlations exist between effective readers and effective writers (Britton, 1985; Salvatori, 1983; Tierney and Pearson, 1984); that reading is a form of learning (Bereiter and Scardamalia, 1984a, 1984b; Berthoff, 1985); and that reading and writing have common cognitive processes (Flower et al., 1990; Spivey, 1991). Marion Crowhurst demonstrated empirically the relationships between reading and writing persuasive discourse (1991). Louise Rosenblatt calls the relationship between the writer and the reader the "transactional paradigm": the human activity in which "the individual and the social, cultural and natural elements interfuse" (1988, p. 8). That is, in similar ways, the writer actively discovers and constructs meaning, interpreting and re-interpreting information for a reader, and the reader reconstructs and rediscovers that meaning by actively bringing her world knowledge and experience to the text (Horowitz, 1988; Smith, 1987; Spivey, 1987). In this paradigm, "text [is] no longer simply an artifact of the writing process but is the primary and essential link between writer and reader " (Huckin and Flower, 1990, p. 347).

In this constructivist view of the reading process, readers comprise "interpretive communities" that are analogous to the "discourse communities" of writers (Garrett-Petts, 1988). The reader brings to a text the sum total of all prior knowledge and experience—what some reading researchers call **schemata**: conventional knowledge structures that are activated under various circumstances, in the interpretation of what we experience (Hare and Fitzsimmons, 1991; Meyer, 1982; Meyer and Rice, 1982). "[R]eading of texts is an active event: it necessarily entails the bringing of prior knowledge to bear upon what is read. [Readers use this knowledge to enter into a] transaction with the text that makes the resulting understanding and interpreting individual and unique" (Purves, 1988, pp. 69–70). Interpretation is, then, a problem-solving process. More experienced readers may respond by using strategies that try to account for the writer's intentions and the writing situation as well as the meaning of the text (Comprone, 1986; D'Angelo, 1986; Haas and Flower, 1988). "Reader response" research, which investigates the cognitive relationships between reading and writing, will continue to affect the composition classroom (Clifford, 1991; Haas and Flower, 1988; Hansson, 1992; Kirsch, 1989; Rosenblatt, 1988; Sheridan, 1991).

Individualization and Collaboration in the Classroom

In the 1980s another area of research began that continues to have direct impact on the teaching of composition: the investigation into classroom dynamics and into individualization in learning styles, composing processes, and classroom interaction. Stephen Witte (1987) and Muriel Harris (1989), for example, describe differences between multidraft writers, for whom freewriting, drafting, discovering, selection, re-drafting, and dramatic revisions are crucial to clarifying their thinking and writing a quality text, and single-draft writers, who plan intensively before writing anything and "see" words, sentences, and paragraphs in their heads. Studies have also continued in the theoretical and practical bases for collaboration in the classroom:

1. cooperation between teacher and students in identifying processes, class objectives, and evaluation criteria for assignments (Bishop, 1992; Fleckenstein, 1992; Jensen and DiTiberio, 1989);

2. student group work and peer review of writing that provide the students with authentic audiences, discussion that leads to discovery, and necessary peer feedback (Freedman, 1992; S. D. Reid, 1992b; Tebo-Messina, 1989; Trimbur, 1989); and

3. metacognition—the raised and shared, articulated awareness of students and teachers about what they are doing and why they are doing it (Reither, 1988).

In a collaborative classroom, teachers are responsible for task setting, for classroom management, and for stimulating student learning; students, on the other hand, are responsible for the intellectual negotiation that results in their taking charge of their own learning (Weiner, 1986).

Writing Across the Curriculum (WAC)

This movement, which has occurred periodically in the field of composition for fifty years, has returned. Rather than confining the teaching of writing to freshman composition courses and other English department writing courses at the college level, writing across the curriculum advocates "writing-intensive" courses in all disciplines, with the recognition of writing as fundamental to discipline-oriented learning. "Write-to-Learn" programs stress the value of writing in chemistry and psychology as well as English classes. Students "pre-write" about upcoming topics in order to activate their schema (background knowledge) about that topic; they summarize assigned reading in their "learning logs" and synthesize lecture notes, then analyze in writing what they have learned. The newest movement toward writing across the curriculum is closely linked with vocational writing and the social movement in composition teaching. Proponents believe that students in all disciplines need intensive writing preparation for entrance into and empowerment in those discourse communities across the university and beyond (Bartholomae, 1985; Fulwiler, 1988; McLeod, 1986, 1989; Russell, 1987, 1990; Walvoord and McCarthy, 1991).

Testing and Assessing Writing

Testing the writing skills of NESs involves having students write about a topic (as opposed to discrete-point grammar testing). Issues of interest to both researchers and classroom teachers—topic design, directions, content-fair topics, purposes for testing, and evaluation methods—have been discussed for decades (Brossell, 1982; Cooper and O'Dell, 1977). Current research systematically describes holistic scoring procedures,* parameters for test design, the links between purposes for testing and purposes for evaluation, and statistical procedures for measuring valid and reliable test instruments (Greenberg, 1981; Huot, 1990; McKendy, 1992; Purves, 1992; Ruth and Murphy, 1984, 1987; E. White, 1986, 1990). New research will continue discussion in these areas and will include the social aspects for testing: the benefits of testing for students, respect for writers from differing backgrounds, and

---

* Holistic scoring involves the assigning of a single score to a piece of writing based on a "whole" reading of the essay. See Chapter 9 for further discussion.

the complexity of individual response and interpretation (Hayward, 1990; Hoetker and Brossell, 1989; Hourigan, 1991).

Classroom Implementation

Theory derived from research in an applied field such as composition should be applicable—and then applied—in the classroom. Nevertheless, the impact of research on the classroom has been incremental rather than dramatic, manifested most visibly in the decrease of literature-based freshman composition courses and the increase of skills-based courses with nonfiction essays and/or student essays as models and for discussion. Textbooks and syllabi have been developed that allow students to discuss composing ideas and strategies in the classroom that can then be incorporated into successful communicative prose. In many classes students work together, teaching each other and discussing the reading of texts and of peer drafts; teachers organize and facilitate those discussions. In-class pre-writing and revision processes, and a focus on what Wayne Booth (1963) called the conscious balance between *writer*, *subject*, and *audience*, has become more important. As a result, the concepts of **authentic purposes and audiences** have begun to dominate the composition class (Durrant and Duke, 1990; Shriver, 1992).

In keeping with the concepts of collaborative classrooms and shared responsibility for learning, teachers often ask for student input concerning writing tasks and evaluation criteria for those tasks. They require their students to identify not only audiences, purposes, and subjects but also their intentions: what they think they have accomplished in any writing task, what they consider weaknesses and strengths in any of their written products, and what revisions they think they need to make in those products. In other words, today's freshman composition teachers give students **ownership** of their writing and their learning, as well as multiple opportunities to discover and to articulate what they are doing and why they are doing it.

Conclusion

In the last decade, the roles of traditional product-bound teaching and expressive writing have begun to decline in composition classrooms. Although one or the other of these methodologies still prevails in some classrooms, many teachers and researchers have begun to implement a more balanced approach to the teaching of writing. In many composition classes, students are taught the essential elements and processes of writing and are encouraged to discover and extend their writing proficiencies. In addition, the concepts of audience and purpose as well as subject matter are stressed. The product, the final paper, will never again be the solitary focus of these composition classes, but it has assumed its rightful position—at the end of a significant number of intermingled, recursive writing processes. The curriculum in many composition programs includes all phases of the writing process, from the design of the assignment to individual generation of material, to issues of arrangement and presentation that fulfill the expectations of the audience, to the final product, with equal importance.

Discussion Questions

1 Consider the teaching of writing you have experienced personally as a student writer. Which approach(es) discussed in this chapter were used? The product approach? The expressivist? The cognitivist? The process? A combination? How successful was each approach?

2. In a small group of peers, discuss your writing and revising processes. Are you more a freewriter or an outliner in your idea generation process? Do you have multiple strategies for drafting? What *are* your strategies? Be specific.

3. In a small group of peers, share the evaluation or remembering paper you wrote in response to Writing Question #1 or #3 below. Take notes that might aid you as you begin to form your philosophy of teaching writing.

4. What are your attitudes toward small group and/or collaborative work? Discuss with your peers the reasons for your attitudes.

5. What new ideas about composition and rhetoric did you encounter in this chapter? Which of those ideas interests you? Which do you agree or disagree with? Why? Which of the ideas in this chapter could have helped your writing when you were in high school? Which might have been detrimental? Why?

6. Re-read Maxine Hairston's twelve features of the shifting paradigm in composition teaching at the beginning of this chapter. Which of these do you think are most important? Why?

7. What experiences have you had with computers and writing? What is your opinion concerning the use of computers in an ESL writing class?

8. Have you had any experiences with Writing Across the Curriculum (WAC) and/or with writing-intensive courses outside the English Department? If so, describe and evaluate those experiences. If not, predict what some of the advantages and disadvantages of a WAC program might be.

Writing

1. Think about several pieces of writing you have done during the past five years. Choose one that you thought was most successful or interesting or challenging or frustrating. Using the Kinneavian approach of "aims," write a brief "remembering" essay that details the process you used to write that piece and describes what made that piece of writing successful, interesting, challenging, or frustrating.

2. Choose one of the ideas or issues discussed in this chapter (such as collaborative learning, writing centers, writing across the curriculum). Read three of the relevant articles cited in this chapter. Make an annotated bibliography of the articles to share with your peers.

3. What kind(s) of writing tests have you taken? Choose one test and analyze its success or failure in terms of topic design. Was the topic interesting? Were you able to address it in the time assigned? Were you satisfied with the results of the test? Why or why not?

4. Write a brief essay that analyzes the group discussion you participated in Discussion Question #2 (above). What did you learn? How did you feel about the discussion? Was it beneficial? Why or why not? Be specific.

CHAPTER 2

Overview of ESL Composition

In general, the progress of NNS (non-native speaker)*—or ESL—composition theory and practice has followed NES composition, but often as much as a decade or more later. Even as recently as the 1970s many ESL composition teachers in intensive language programs used writing mainly as a support skill in language learning. Writing, for these teachers, meant doing grammar exercises, answering reading comprehension questions, and writing dictation. Writing was seen as one of a variety of techniques to add interest to a lesson, or as a testing device to diagnose grammar or comprehension errors.

Today ESL composition has begun to assume greater validity as a cognitive and a communication skill, in part because research in NES composition has influenced the growth of the field of ESL composition. In light of information about composing processes and university writing requirements, ESL writing teachers have reexamined their writing class objectives in intensive language programs. Various problems in teaching ESL students in freshman composition by teachers of NESs have emphasized the need for better pre-admission composition skills and for "sheltered" post-admission ESL composition classes designed for ESL students (Kroll, 1991). Recognition by ESL teachers and researchers of the need for second-language students to write for occupational or academic purposes has led curriculum designers and textbook writers to provide the necessary materials that allow the writing class to assume an equal role with other language skills (R. White, 1987).

Early ESL Methods

During the first three decades of the field of teaching English as a second language (TESL), the audio-lingual method (ALM) ("I say—you

---

*In order to avoid confusion between the acronyms for native English speakers (NESs) and non-native speakers (NNSs) in this book, the term English as a Second Language (or ESL) is used to describe non-native speakers of English even though English may be the student's third or fourth language and even though they may have studied or be studying English in their native countries (English as a Foreign Language, or EFL).

say") prevailed. The ALM is based on the behaviorist work of psychologist B. F. Skinner at Harvard University. Skinner taught rats and pigeons to form *habits* by rewarding correct behavior with food, and his **stimulus-response** research formed the foundation of the behaviorist movement in education. Skinner concluded that because "positive reinforcement" was an effective teaching method, students should be taught incrementally, in a series of small steps that allowed each student to succeed by responding correctly, and to receive positive reinforcement such as candy, praise, or approval. The ALM required the teacher to provide oral model language patterns (the stimulus) to the students, who would then repeat the pattern (the response) until the language structure became a language habit. The development of methods and materials for the ALM occurred at the University of Michigan; the so-called "Michigan method" was widely used in intensive language programs for thirty years (1940–1970) (Larsen-Freeman, 1986). It emphasized the teaching of **correct oral language** through the study of pattern practice, pronunciation, and grammatical structures.

Three major assumptions underlay the ALM. First, because positive reinforcement was vital for success, error had to be prevented and eliminated. Students were taught correct language usage, and mistakes were viewed as deviant. Second, habituation of language was seen as the foundation of fluent language; if students inculcated structures through drilling, they would be able to use the structures without difficulty, even without conscious struggle, outside the classroom. Third, oral language was seen as the pathway to language success, and fluency through reading, and particularly writing, were seen as tangential or "support" language skills. As a consequence, the ALM teaching in intensive language programs virtually excluded written English: students listened, then spoke, and eventually read. Writing was seen as even less critical to language competence. Until the early '70s, writing in many ESL classrooms was limited to the teaching of handwriting skills to students whose native language differed graphically from English, and to filling in the blanks of grammar and reading comprehension exercises.

Another factor that negatively affected the teaching of ESL writing was the lack of experience and knowledge about teaching composition among teachers and researchers. Most ESL teachers, untrained as writers or as writing teachers, entered the field from undergraduate majors in the humanities and the arts. In many cases, their only experience with the teaching of writing had been their participation in freshman composition classes. These teachers knew almost nothing about the theories and practices in the teaching of writing. If pressured into stating their philosophies about teaching ESL writing, they might have stated one or more of the following:

1. Writing is just another way of practicing grammar.
2. Just writing "a lot" will improve an ESL student's language.
3. You can't really teach writing.
4. The teacher's job is simply to design, assign, and evaluate writing.
5. If a student can speak English well, s/he will be able to transfer those skills to writing.

While each of these statements contains a small piece of reality, none encompasses the heart of teaching ESL writing; none speaks to the teaching of skills—heuristic, rhetorical, cognitive, and developmental— that result in successful progress in writing effective, communicative prose.

In addition, ESL teachers in training received little education about the teaching of writing. Until the last decade, most ESL methodology courses limited information on teaching writing to one to two weeks during a semester course. Considering the complexity of the writing task, it is little wonder that even trained ESL professionals often chose not to teach writing classes. And, when they were required to teach writing, teachers who had abandoned strict adherence to the ALM often continued to rely, in ESL writing classes, on sentence-level construction and on the teaching of grammatical sentence structures (Kroll, 1991).

Controlled Writing

As the need for writing skills for ESL students became apparent, and as research in the field of NES composition became accessible, ESL writing classes became a more integral, if not integrated, part of ESL curricula. In the 1970s, however, most ESL writing classes still focused on grammatical sentence structures that supported the grammar class and on **controlled writing.** Exercises consisted of pieces of discourse, which students were instructed to copy and in which to then make discrete changes or fill in the blanks, as in the following examples.

Model Paragraph:
The woman's a secretary. She's pretty. She's intelligent. She's happy. She's not sad.
The girls are students. They're pretty. They're intelligent. They're happy. They're not sad.

Instructions: Cover the Model Paragraph with a piece of paper. Copy the sentences below, in paragraph form as they are on the page. Add all necessary punctuation.

the womans a secretary   shes pretty   shes intelligent   shes
happy   shes not sad
the girls are students   theyre pretty   theyre intelligent   theyre
happy   theyre not sad

(Rainsbury, 1977)

Paragraph Puzzle: Complete the paragraph by choosing the right
word to fill in each blank. When choice is difficult, refer to
neighboring words or sentences for help.

How do we know that dogs (*have, show, are, is*) _____ color
blind? This has been tested in (*that, a, their, the*) _____ same
way that it has been (*discovered, heard, told, said*) _____
what dogs can hear. The attempt (*have, tell, say, has*) _____
been made to train dogs to (*whine, cry, bark, salivate*) _____ ___.

(Bander, 1983, p. 20)

Inwardly he was a disturbed being, a man of nerves, caprices, and
stubborn will. Accustomed to a set routine, he lived the disciplined
life of a hermit or ascetic. It was difficult to tell whether he had
adapted himself to this mode of life or accepted it against the grain.
He never spoke of the kind of life he would have liked to lead. He
behaved as one who, already buffeted and battered, had resigned
himself to his fate. As one who could assimilate punishment better
than good fortune.

(Henry Miller, *A Devil in Paradise*)

Situation: You are writing a descriptive paragraph about a woman.

Assignment: Rewrite the entire passage, changing *he* to *she* each time.
Change the nouns and pronouns wherever necessary.

(Paulston and Dykstra, 1973, p. 5)

The philosophy of controlled writing grew directly out of the
ALM: students are taught incrementally, error is prevented, and fluency
is expected to arise out of practice with structures. Journal articles and
textbooks defended those approaches (Dykstra, 1977; J. Ross, 1968),
principally on the basis that controlled writing allowed students to
practice and habituate correct structures and thereby learn to "write"
on their own. Christina Paulston extolled the virtues of controlled
writing for another reason: "[I]t will permit busy teachers to give daily
assignments of writing exercises—even in large classes—and at the
same time insure that the student's work will be substantially correct
and in acceptable form with acceptable usage" (1972, p. ix).

"Free Writing"/Guided Writing

In the late '70s and early '80s, as ESL writing teachers became more aware of current practices in NES composition, a movement from strictly controlled writing to "free writing" or guided writing occurred (Allen, 1981; Carpenter and Hunter, 1981; Raimes, 1978; Sampson, 1980). "Free" was essentially a misnomer, however; in general, the freedom was "guided." That is, free writing was limited to structuring sentences, often in direct answers to questions, the result of which looked like a short piece of discourse, usually a paragraph. Moreover, the exercises were language-based; they usually concentrated on vocabulary building, reading comprehension, grammar, and even oral skills that culminated in a piece of writing. Typical guided writing exercises in widely used textbooks included the following:

Model Paragraph

There are four seasons in New York City. The names of the seasons are winter, spring, summer, and autumn. In the winter it is very cold and windy, and in the summer it is very hot and humid. The weather in the spring and autumn, however, is very pleasant. For many people these are the only times that the climate is comfortable. There is one thing certain about New York weather. It never stays the same. Like a woman, it is very changeable.

Comprehension Questions

    1. How many seasons are there in New York City?
    2. What are the names of the seasons?
    3. How is the weather in the winter?
    4. How is the weather in the summer?
    5. What is certain about New York weather?

Vocabulary of Weather	Other Expressions
It is fair.	It always rains in the summer.
sunny.	It always snows in the winter.
mild.	
warm.	
cool.	It is always sunny.
windy.	It is usually rainy.

Oral Composition: Follow the model composition and answer the following questions in a paragraph about your country:

    1. How many seasons are there in your country?
    2. What are the names of the seasons?
    3. How is the weather in the winter?
                  in the summer?
                  in the spring?
    4. What is the best season of the year? Why?
    5. Is there anything certain about the weather?

<u>Written Composition:</u> Now write a composition about Weather in Your Country, following the model composition and answering the above questions.

(Baskoff, 1971, pp. 1–2)

<u>Model 1</u>

I am Mr. Baroni. My first name is Robert. I am twenty-five years old. I am a student. I am in the classroom now. I am at my desk. Mr. Peters is my teacher. He is in the classroom now. He is at the blackboard. He is busy now. The classroom is on the tenth floor. It is a small room. The classroom is in an old building. The building is downtown. The address is 234 N. Clark Street. The building is near the river. It is in the busy city of Detroit.

<u>Instructions:</u> Write one paragraph about yourself and your school setting on 8 1/2 X 11 loose-leafed notebook paper. Follow the model, but change all information that is not correct for you. For example: you are not Mr. Baroni; your first name is probably not Robert. Take as many structures and words from the model as you can use in your paragraph. Your paragraph should look like this:

_____
_____
_____
_____

(Blanton, 1979, pp. 7–8)

Today some ESL writing classes, particularly at the lower levels of language proficiency, successfully use controlled, guided, and "free" writing techniques to build vocabulary, sentence structure knowledge, and self-confidence (Cross, 1991). Some textbooks continue to be based on the principles of grammatical practice and even the ALM principle of accuracy. For example, in the series *Write Away: A Course for Writing English* (Byrd and Gallingame, 1990), the authors introduce their "system":

> The exercises in *Write Away* are **grammatically focused** and are always meaningfully contextualized. Students will be able to use their understanding of the content to sharpen their **grammatical accuracy**. . . . [T]he advantage of using *Write Away* is that these **grammatical operations** in writing and revising are anticipated and laid out in the sequence of each unit. The results of the **operations applied in sequence will produce a well-formed composition.**
>
> (p. xx; emphases mine)

The application of the principles of controlled, guided, and "free" writing may enhance students' grammatical awareness of a second language, particularly at the lower levels of language proficiency. The exercises closely reflect the behaviorist hypotheses: with constant practice of correct structures, students will learn the language and will therefore be able to transfer the repeated (controlled, guided) skills to original utterances. Research in second language acquisition, however, has demonstrated that language is not limited to stimulus-response behavior (Bialystok, 1990; Hatch, 1992; Krashen, 1981, 1982; Rivers, 1964, 1968). Rather than language being directed from the outside, learning is a process that the learner controls and to which the learner contributes (Fromkin and Rodman, 1988). Specifically, writing classes that stress repetition and accuracy while severely restricting composing and original thought serve more as grammar classes.

Language-Based Writing

Closely related to the focus on guided writing is the focus, by teachers and researchers, on teaching writing primarily as a language skill. In one of the first books written for teachers of ESL writing, *Techniques in Teaching Writing*, Ann Raimes gave the reasons for teaching writing: "We frequently have to communicate with each other in writing" and "Writing **reinforces grammatical structures**, idioms, and vocabulary." Teaching writing is "a unique way to **reinforce learning**" (1983, p. 3). An early section in the book is headed with the question "How Can Writing Help My Students **Learn Their Second Language Better?**" (p. 12; emphases mine). Many ESL writing textbooks of the early '80s reflected this language-based approach to writing (Bliss et al., 1985; Frank, 1983). Assignments like the ones that follow were based on the practice of language components—a specific verb tense, the use of adjectives, a particular sentence structure—that links them to guided and "free" writing classes.

> Purpose: to practice using conditional sentences in present tense.
> You are an art teacher. You want to introduce your students to the basic principles of mixing colors. You have decided to prepare a brief explanation to distribute to your students on the topic.
> (McKay, 1979a, p. 75)

> Chapter 1: Describing a Static Scene
> Focus on these syntactic structures
> sentence division and punctuation
> subject and predicate
> fragments and run-ons
> **yes/no** questions

prepositions of place
agreement: **there is** and **there are**
countable and uncountable nouns
determiners
    articles (**a, an, the**)
    quantity words **(some, much, many,** etc.)
-s inflection
sentence combining

<u>Core Composition</u>
1. Look closely at Magritte's **Portrait** and examine each object in turn. With a partner, discuss what you see in the picture.
2. Individually, write a short paragraph describing the picture as accurately and as fully as you can. . . .
3. Write your answers to the questions below.

<u>Questions</u>
What did you mention first?
What did you mention second? . . .

(Raimes, 1978)

Two other applications of language-based writing techniques are audio transcription and sentence-combining. The former consists of the use of **dicto-comps**, in which the teacher dictates short passages; after listening to the prose several times, students recreate the passage, partially or completely, as they remember it (Kroll, 1991). Some research suggests that dicto-comps may improve student fluency and sense of discourse coherence (Buckingham and Peck, 1976; Kleinmann and Selekman, 1980; Nation, 1991; Riley, 1975). The concept of **sentence-combining**, developed for NESs by Francis Christensen (1967) and William Strong (1973), was based on the ideas that (a) NES readers of prose prefer a style that is full of subordination and free modifiers and (b) writing sentences that are more syntactically complex encourages students to discover and demonstrate relationships between ideas. Sentence-combining techniques have been used with ESL writing students at all levels of language proficiency (Kameen, 1978; McKee, 1983; Pack and Hendrichsen, 1981; Shook, 1978). Advocates of sentence-combining activities believe that discrete instruction at the sentence level extends the cognitive strategies of students, improves the sophistication of their sentence structures, and eventually improves their compositions (K. Johnson, 1992). An example of a sentence-combining exercise:

1. The writer is young.
2. The writer is developing.
3. The writer works with options.

Possible "transformations" or combinations:

1. The young, developing writer works with options.
2. The young writer who is developing works with options.
3. The writer who is young and developing works with options.
4. Options are worked with by the young, developing writer.

(Strong, 1973, p. 4)

This language-based approach to the teaching of writing prevails in many ESL classrooms. For many teachers, however, the purpose of writing classes changed during the '80s. Raimes, for example, has stated that ESL writing teachers need what she calls "a new model for language teaching, one that acknowledges the value of writing for generating language, and that sees writing not just as one of the language skills to be learned, or the last skill to be learned, but as an effective way for a learner to generate words, sentences, and chunks of discourse and to communicate them in a new language" (1985, p. 252).

The Pattern/Product Approach

The shift from language-based writing classrooms to the study of composition techniques and strategies was gradual; it began with the recognition of the needs of ESL students in the academic environment. As writing placement examinations became common for university admission, and as ESL teachers and researchers examined the exit requirements from intensive language programs, they found that ESL students were unprepared for those proficiency examinations and for the written work required in academic classes. This recognition led teachers to bridge the gap between language-based writing classes that focused on sentence writing and writing-based classes that focused on creating compositions.

Several ESL teachers and researchers initiated writing-based pedagogy. Mary Lawrence (1973) was an early advocate of detailed problem-solving and invention strategies; Barbara Seale's *Writing Efficiently* (1978) gave ESL teachers and students a step-by-step approach that led to the production of what she called academic themes. Sandra McKay (1979a, 1979b, 1981) argued in both her research and her textbooks that grammatical accuracy in writing classes was a secondary concern; she then designed assignments in her textbooks that were audience- and purpose-specific (McKay, 1980, 1983, 1984). Thomas Buckingham (1979) applied theories developed by NES researchers to ESL composition teachers. Concentrating on the advanced language proficiency students, Buckingham compiled several goals for advanced ESL composition students:

1. to become **independent** of the controls imposed by the teacher or text,
2. to write for a variety of **communicative purposes**,
3. to extend and refine the use of vocabulary and sentence structures,
4. to write the conceptual paragraph (that is, paragraphs that were unified, arranged appropriately, and had sufficient detail),
5. to write longer units of discourse than the paragraph.

Many textbooks during the early 1980s focused on writing-based classes by approaching writing from a pattern/product perspective (see G. Barnes, 1981; J. Reid, 1982; J. Reid and Lindstrom, 1985; Rice and Burns, 1986; Wohl, 1985). Using **pattern-product techniques,** teachers focused on the concepts of the thesis statement and the topic sentence, paragraph unity, organizational strategies, and development of paragraphs by "patterns" or modes: process, comparison/contrast, cause-effect, classification/partition, definition, etc. Exercises to teach the logic of English organizational patterns included re-ordering deliberately "scrambled" paragraphs, identifying "irrelevant sentences" deliberately placed in paragraphs, identifying "suitable" topic sentences for specific paragraphs, and writing topic sentences for paragraphs from which the topic sentences had been removed. Writing assignments, which were generally modality-based (or pattern-based), frequently resembled the following:

Paragraph Writing: Cause-Effect (Focus on Effect)

Directions: Using cause-effect development, write a paragraph in which you describe the effects—negative or positive—that a teacher has had on your personality, your feelings about school, or your approach to life in general. Be specific:
    1. Mention at least three real effects;
    2. Explain each one, using examples, details, or anecdotes.
               (Arnaudet and Barrett, 1984, p. 111)

FORMAL WRITING

Choose one of the five topics below and write a classification paragraph. Remember to state your topic sentence in the introduction, to develop your discussion completely, and to summarize or restate your topic sentence in the conclusion. Try to use classification vocabulary. If you find it helpful, outline the three parts of the paragraph before writing. Write your paragraph on notebook composition paper.

    1. occupations
    2. sports

3. movies
4. your friends or family
5. any other topic of your choice

(Auerbach and Snyder, 1983)

The movement toward pattern/product teaching was a significant step forward from the language-based ESL writing classroom, and students in many writing classes today are still benefiting from this change. Current pattern/product-based ESL writing classes, both in intensive language programs and in freshman composition classes for ESL students, continue to concentrate on appropriate organization techniques for presenting written material in academic settings (Fazio et al., 1990; C. Shoemaker, 1985). Many of these classes also include idea generation and the concepts of audience and purpose in their curricula; teachers spend time on language issues related directly to writing (such as comma splices and verb tense use), but the focus is on the organizational conventions in U.S. academic prose.

The Process Movement

Nancy Arapoff (1968, 1969), Mary Lawrence (1973, 1975), and Vivian Zamel (1976, 1982) were among the first ESL researchers and teachers to begin stressing the value of **process writing** in the classroom. Research in the theory of process writing for ESL students paralleled the prior research with NESs: students were encouraged to explore a topic through writing, to share drafts with teachers and peers, and to use each draft as a beginning for the next. Vivian Zamel recommended process teaching as she castigated sentence-combining because it ignored "the enormous complexity of writing (pre-writing, organizing, developing, proof-reading, revising, etc.)" (1976, p. 89). In a direct commitment to the NES **expressive school**,* Zamel stated that "the act of composing should become the result of a genuine need to express one's personal feeling, experience, or reactions, all within a climate of encouragement" (1980, p. 74). In later articles (1980, 1982), Zamel followed Murray and Elbow in describing how writing can be taught as a process of discovery, and she encouraged researchers to investigate "what writing is, what it involves, and what differentiates the good and bad writer" (1980, p. 74). Barry Taylor, also reflecting the work with NESs by Peter Elbow (1973) and Nancy Sommers (1980), described writing as "a discovery procedure which relies heavily on the power of revision to clarify and refine that discovery" (1981, p. 8).

Since the middle of the 1980s, many ESL writing teachers have discovered, accepted, and implemented the approaches and

---

*See Chapter 1 for a description of the expressive school.

philosophy associated with process writing. Linda Blanton (1987) described the use of student **journal writing** that lowered the anxiety of her writing students and allowed them to discover interesting ideas. George Jacobs reported on the use of "quickwriting" as an invention device; his directions to students reflect Peter Elbow (1973): "Concentrate on ideas. Forget about mechanics, grammar and organization. Take care of those at another stage in the writing process" (1988, p. 284). Ruth Spack (1984) has written about using invention heuristics in the ESL freshman composition classroom; Spack and Catherine Sadow have described their use of "working journals"— ungraded, even unread, true "reader-based writing"—that allows students in a freshman composition class for ESL students to "become aware of writing as a way to generate ideas and to share them" in a non-threatening way (1983, p. 575).

Textbooks that focus on process teaching reflect the NES expressive writing school: they concentrate on personal writing, student creativity and decision making, and the development of narrative voice, sometimes downgrading or even eliminating the product. Using this philosophy, Ann Raimes, in her textbook *Exploring Through Writing*, describes the process to be used: "[S]tudents begin by gathering ideas from their own experience and knowledge, and then turn to other sources as they search for their own topic. [They] are given the opportunity to explore a variety of systematic methods of discovery while they read, write, and talk to each other"(1987a, p. vii).The following are typical writing assignments in process-based classes.

Part I. Getting Ready to Write

Exploring Ideas

1. What do you know about the handicaps that children have?
2. Do you know anyone with a serious handicap?
3. How do parents of severely handicapped children feel?
4. What kind of lives do you think children with severe handicaps lead?

In this chapter you are going to write an answer to this question: *Some children are born with severe mental handicaps. Should parents and doctors of these children be allowed to let them die?*

Your answer to this question will depend on what you know from personal experience or from your reading. Read these [following] accounts by parents of children with severe mental handicaps. Then in small groups discuss the questions. How do these accounts affect how you feel about the problem? What else do you know about this problem?

(Segal and Pavlik, 1985, pp. 126–127)

<u>Individual Assignments</u>

1. Take a few minutes to think about one of the following questions. (Your instructor will assign one or will let you choose your own).

    Question 1. What vivid memory do you have of a place in your past? For instance, think about a specific room, a house, a building, a town, or a national setting. Think about it as if you were filming it with a movie-camera, trying to capture all the details, so that someone else can see it as you saw it.

    Question 2. What details can you remember about a treasured possession you had when you were younger or a treasured possession you own now?

    Question 3. What do you remember about the events of one specific day of work? . . . etc.

2. Now, use section 1 of your notebook, the section reserved for class writing. Think for a few minutes of the important words that you will need to tell someone else about your memory. Then, list the words in your notebook on the second right-hand page (page 3).

(Raimes, 1987a, pp. 7–8)

Often process-writing textbooks are also, to a certain extent, language-based; they ask students to use certain grammatical and lexical features as they write. Trudy Smoke's advanced ESL textbook (1987), for instance, follows each reading with sections on vocabulary development, reading and thinking skills, word skills, and specific grammar foci: plurals, simple present tense, pronouns, modals, etc.

Certainly the process movement in ESL writing research and teaching has fulfilled the needs of some ESL students and furthered the field of ESL composition (Zamel, 1990, 1991). As teachers incorporated process teaching into their classes, writing became "freer" as a result of student discovery activities, journal writing, and lowered anxiety levels. Trudy Smoke echoes the expressive NES school as she explains to teachers in the Instructor's Manual for her textbook: "Students already have inside them much of what we are trying to teach, and our challenge is to find what is already there" (1987, p. v).

Current Trends and Research

During the past decade, the field of ESL writing research has expanded significantly, in many cases paralleling studies of NES writers. Some researchers have focused on writing processes—composing and revising strategies—while others have concentrated on the developmental processes of student writers. Studies in discourse analysis (the investigation of chunks of language, oral and written, that are greater than a single sentence) have sought to discover writing problems specific to ESL students and solutions to those problems. Following is an overview of some of that research.

Composing and Revising Processes

Many researchers of ESL **composing** and **revision strategies** have used a case study or descriptive approach (that is, ethnographic) rather than large-scale empirical studies (statistically based research) (E. Hall, 1991; C. Johnson, 1985a; C. Jones and Tetroe, 1987; Raimes, 1987b; St. John, 1987; Zamel, 1983). For example, JoAnne Liebman-Kleine examined composing strategies among her ESL freshman composition students (1986) and then organized a similar class ethnographically, asking her students to observe and interview each other concerning their composing processes (1987). Steven Ross et al. (1988) examined several techniques used in the process classroom, among them journal writing; results demonstrated that although increased opportunities for the practice of writing in a low-anxiety context may result in positive attitudinal changes, the results in the improvement of writing quality were mixed, with greater fluency evident only in narrative writing, not in more expository forms of writing. Tony Silva (1990, 1992) and Ana Frankenberg-Garcia (1990) studied the composing processes of both NESs and ESL students; they found that although the students had some composing strategies in common, there were important differences between them. Alexandra Krapels (1990) surveyed second language writing process studies and described the recurrent motifs and issues involved in case study research with second language writers.

Other studies of composing processes focus on cognitive load and language proficiency. One innovative study of composing processes, reported by Alexander Friedlander (1990), asked Chinese students to generate ideas and compose essays in both their native language and in English on two topics. The first essay, about a Chinese holiday, involved student knowledge and background experience acquired primarily in their native language; the second, about the U.S. university they attended, involved student knowledge and background experience acquired primarily in English. Friedlander found that for these students, the composing processes differed: they made many fewer notes when writing about a topic they had learned about in the language in which they were composing; that is, they used fewer overt planning processes when writing about Chinese holidays in Chinese or about computers in English. Another researcher, Alister Cumming, in a series of highly controlled, empirical studies, investigated the relationship between writing expertise (experienced, average, and basic writers) and second language proficiency (intermediate and advanced levels). He found that second language proficiency proved to be only "an additive factor, enhancing the overall quality of writing produced" (1986, p. 81), which suggests that second language proficiency and writing expertise are cognitively different. In addition, Cumming (1989) investigated the correlations between composing strategies, second language proficiency, and writing expertise. He found that composing strategies were related to writing expertise, but that second language proficiency was not directly related.

The importance of teaching and researching the **revision processes** of ESL writers has grown from the ALM objective of correcting all errors to the study of error as a necessary developmental process. Current research indicates that second language error is neither deviant nor random; instead, errors are often both systematic and reasoned (Kroll, 1991; Lennon, 1991; Scovel, 1988). Revision studies report on the ability of students to "monitor," to identify weaknesses and strengthen writing during revision and editing processes (Gaskill, 1986; Mittan, 1988, 1989; Wong, 1984). Chris Hall, for example, investigated student revision procedures in the ESL composition classroom (1987, 1990); he found that writing students with advanced language proficiency apply revision strategies used in their native languages. Others have looked at the response of teachers and students to error (Chappell, 1982; Davies and Omberg, 1987; G. Jacobs, 1989; T.Kobayashi, 1992; Nickel, 1985; Sheorey, 1986; Zamel, 1985). Raymond Devenny (1989) reported that, in a study of how ESL teachers and peers evaluated and responded to student writing, the dichotomy between teachers and students was not as strong as previous research had indicated. Instead of forming distinct evaluative or "interpretive" communities, the reader responses of teachers and students tended to be based on other factors such as content and overall readability.

Contrastive Analysis/Error Analysis

Early contrastive analysis research was essentially language-focused: linguists examined features of a native language (for example, English) that contrasted with features of a foreign language (for example, Spanish or Arabic) to determine what areas of second language learning would be most likely to cause difficulty for the students. Called "transfer" errors, these areas of second language learning often became the focus of the early grammar/writing classroom as teachers sought to anticipate errors before they occurred and to alert students to them. By the early '70s, contrastive analysis research had been extended to include error analysis, which examined the actual language performance of learners in order to determine whether the source of errors was "first language interference" or "developmental." In other words, researchers investigated the reasons that students made the errors: whether, for example, an error was a natural by-product of student risk-taking, an overgeneralization of rules, the transfer of a rule from the student's first language, or the level of difficulty of implementing the English language rule. Although error analysis studies have decreased in the last decade, early research results concerning the impact of native language interference or developmental error on ESL writing continue to influence the literature (Abunowara, 1983; Corder, 1981; Lee, 1976–77; Lowenburg, 1982; Nickel, 1989; Picus, 1983; Scott and Tucker, 1974; Thompson-Panos and Thomas-Ruzic, 1983).

Another research area links error identification to the revision process: "error gravity" studies view errors from the perspective of the academic reader. Researchers investigate the "irritation" or "acceptance" levels of native speakers—usually university non-ESL faculty—to specific second language errors. That is, researchers study the second language errors that interfere most with NES comprehension in order to help teachers and students edit more successfully. Such studies have shown that some discourse errors are more "grievous" than others (Janopoulos, 1992a; D. Johnson, 1985b; Neuman, 1977; Santos, 1988; Vann et al., 1992). For example, Roberta Vann and her colleagues (1984) investigated the responses of 164 faculty members to twelve typical ESL errors. They found that most respondents did not judge all errors as equally severe; incorrect word order was considered the most serious, and spelling errors the least severe. The data also suggested that the age and academic discipline of responding faculty members were important factors in their responses to the gravity of ESL errors; younger faculty members were more tolerant of error than older faculty, and faculty in the Social Sciences, Education, and Humanities were more tolerant of error than faculty in the Physical and Mathematical Sciences.

Coherence/Cohesion

From the seminal work of Michael Halliday and Ruqaiya Hasan (1976) to the present, researchers of both NES and ESL writing have studied the differences between **cohesion** and **coherence**, seeking to discover the bases for underlying organization and comprehension in academic prose (Carrell, 1982; Connor and Lauer, 1985; Johns, 1980, 1986; Koch, 1983; Scarcella, 1984b). Cohesion has been defined as the more limited term: specific words and phrases (transitions, pronouns, repetition of key words and phrases) that tie prose together and direct the reader (Connor, 1983; Connor and Johns, 1990). Coherence is the broader-based concept: it is the underlying organizational structure that makes the words and sentences in discourse unified and significant for the reader (Tannen, 1984a). This expected logical flow of ideas provides ease in reader comprehension (Halliday and Hasan, 1976).

Studies of coherence and the use of cohesion devices in ESL writing indicate that ESL writers of English use coherence and cohesion conventions differently than native-speakers do (Connor, 1984; Connor and Farmer, 1990; Gumperz et al., 1984; Hinds, 1987). Dean Brodkey (1983) and Kristie Fleckenstein (1992), for example, investigated the presence of coherence in written ESL prose by using an expectancy exercise with their students: starting with a single sentence or paragraph, they asked students to predict what the following text would be, then examined why those predictions were or were not correct. Ann Johns (1990) has maintained that the defined coherence or incoherence of a text is established through the fit between the knowledge and background experience of the reader, and the organization, content, and argument of the text. In a study of Japanese, Korean, Chinese, and Thai writing, John Hinds found that the samples he examined had a "delayed introduction of purpose" and a quasi-inductive style that "has the undesirable effect of making the essay appear incoherent to the English-speaking reader" (1990, p. 98). John Swales (1990b) studied the organization and use of coherence devices in the introductions to research papers and found that teaching ESL graduate students global coherence strategies helped them compensate for difficulties at the local level. Knowledge of the audience's attitudes, beliefs, and expectations by the writer is essential for coherent communication.

The Process-Product Classroom

Recent reexamination of the process approach and of academic expectations (Constantinides and Hall, 1981; Hamp-Lyons, 1986; Horowitz and McKee, 1984; Johns, 1985; Swales and Najar, 1987) suggests that the pendulum toward expressive and personal writing may have swung too far, particularly for ESL students who are neither familiar nor comfortable with the conventions and expectations of narrative and/or expressive writing. Researchers have investigated the parameters of specific assignments given by non-ESL academic faculty (Bridgeman and Carlson, 1984; Kroll, 1979). Horowitz (1986c), in his survey of university writing requirements, found that (a) academic writing assignments are usually carefully controlled, both in topic selection and in rhetorical organization, by the instructor, (b) that they rarely deal with personal or expressive writing, and (c) that they often call for some kind of research activity. Horowitz (1986a, 1986b) and Horowitz and Stein (1990) recommended the teaching of specific writing skills such as the synthesis of multiple sources, the connection of theory and data, the summary of and reaction to readings, and the report on a participatory experience.

In other surveys of non-ESL faculty, Grace Canesco and Patricia Byrd (1989) investigated the writing demands of business graduate student courses, and Grace West and Byrd (1982) looked at the technical writing assignments required of graduate engineering students. Both studies found that the production of written products is a major part of the requirements for graduate students, and both studies advocate instruction that "focuses on interpreting and responding to topics provided by instructors" (Canesco and Byrd, 1989, p. 314). George Braine (1989) analyzed assignments from ten undergraduate courses and concluded that all the assignments in the sample were highly controlled, and that science and technology majors in particular needed special composition sections to emphasize the skills of paraphrase and summary and to practice identifying audience expectations.

In other studies of graduate and undergraduate student writing, John Swales (1987) examined the use of secondary sources in research papers and described the problems that ESL writers have with those sources. Others (Jordon, 1989; Santos, 1992) have studied the differing perspectives of ESL student writers and academic readers of their academic essays and examinations. Ann Johns (1991) studied one student who had difficulty passing a university exit examination; she found that while he could write acceptable papers in his major field, the more personal, culturally bound topics of the essay exam required language, content, and rhetorical formats with which he was unfamiliar. As a result of such investigations, both researchers and teachers are turning more toward writing assignments and class objectives that consider the future academic writing needs of their students (Budd, 1989; Swales and Najar, 1987). None of this research precludes process writing; rather, Canesco and Byrd suggest that "the process approach to writing can occur within the context of the preparation of a rigorously defined academic product—if process is taken to mean that the writer goes through a process of thinking, selection of evidence, writing, and revision" (1989, p. 311).

Communicative Competence

The communicative approach to language teaching, first developed in Britain during the 1970s (Munby, 1978; Widdowson,

1978; Wilkins, 1976), holds four fundamental beliefs:

1. Materials in the language classroom should be **authentic**—or as authentic as possible—because the language of the "real world" is necessary for good language learning.

2. Activities in the language classroom should be "real" and **purposeful**: "With respect to teaching methodology, it is crucial that classroom activities reflect . . . those communication activities that the learner is most likely to engage in."
(Canale and Swain, 1980, p 33)

3. Language materials should be **contextualized**: instead of extracting or creating discrete pieces of language, materials must be presented in a meaningful context.
(Bensch, 1988; Schachter, 1990)

4. **Individual learner needs** are paramount in the language classroom; materials and activities should reflect those needs.
(D. Clarke, 1989; Shaw, 1992)

Although much of the research in communicative competence has focused on oral skills (K. Johnson and Morrow, 1981; Savignon, 1983; Schleppegrell, 1991) and to a lesser extent on reading (D. Clarke, 1989; Grellet, 1981), communicative teaching is certainly occurring in ESL writing classrooms. These communicative approaches stress the **purpose** of a piece of writing and the **audience** for it: authentic audience(s) and purpose(s). In specific ways, communicative writing classes employ:

1. the use of student writing samples in textbooks and of peer review of essays that allow fellow students to read, evaluate, and learn from "**authentic**" responses to academic assignments (J. Reid, forthcoming; Schenk, 1988);

2. the use of the ESL writing classroom to work on writing assignments from "real" academic classes, making the writing **purposeful**;

3. the integrating of skill-based classes in intensive language programs that allows students to write about what they speak and read about; this integration of skills gives students an **authentic, shared context** for writing (Purves and Purves, 1986);

4. the focus on **individual student needs** by teachers who encourage discovery writing and student-chosen writing topics.

ESL writing textbooks for academic purposes that genuinely reflect the communicative approach have as their goals (a) to assist students in the generation of ideas and strategies for identifying the purpose(s) of their written text, (b) to help students in developing strategies for the identification of audience expectations, and (c) to provide materials and activities for the consequent preparation and polishing of students' written texts to meet academic expectations. For example, Ronald White's textbook, *Writing: Advanced*, is based on authentic materials, individual composing processes, group work, and purposeful writing. He provides students with authentic advertising techniques for selling products, then asks students to write advertisements about themselves. He then gives the students the opportunity for authentic audience feedback and sharing:

> Bring your advertisement to class and put it together in a mixed collection with the advertisements written by other students. Select at random one of the other advertisements. Read it out to the rest of the class. Try to identify the person who wrote the advertisement. . . . When you have identified the subject of the advertisement, discuss whether the image you had as a reader was the same as the image the writer intended to promote. (1987, p. 33)

Ilona Leki's textbook *Academic Writing: Techniques and Tasks* (1989) also employs communicative approaches through the use of authentic professional and student essays. Each chapter is topic oriented and begins with "warm-up" journal exercises about the writer's thoughts and feelings concerning the topic. Following readings on each topic, students are asked to analyze the readings and apply that information to the writing assignment, which is purpose-based, not modality-based, and is directed toward an authentic audience:

WRITING ASSIGNMENT: EDUCATION

Your purpose in this assignment is to inform by examining an issue objectively, analyzing both its strengths and weaknesses or its advantages and disadvantages. You may choose to write on the pros and cons of the school system in your home country or some aspect of the school you are attending now, or you may write on any subject with two clearly opposing sets of features.

Invention

To prepare for this assignment, you may want to make two lists side by side. On one side, list the positive features of your topic; on the other side list negative features. . . . Or you might write an internal dialog in which one voice presents the virtues of your topic and the other voice insists on its vices.

After you have examined your subject through one of these invention activities, share the results with your classmates . . .

When you write your draft, keep in mind the needs of your audience:

Who will your audience be for this discussion?
Will these people already know something about the subject or not?
Will these people be more interested in the strengths or weaknesses of your subject? Why?
Does your audience have any responsibility for the subject as it is?
Or has your audience perhaps had first-hand experience with the subject?
What information will your audience need in order to understand and even agree with your analysis?

(1989, pp. 198–199).

The preface to Leki's textbook summarizes the communicative approach in ESL writing classes that strives to achieve a balance between process and product:

[S]tudents are taken through the writing process and given the opportunity to discover for themselves what kinds of approaches to writing are most useful to them. Students explore their ideas through journal writing, practice a variety of techniques for generating text, and learn how to elicit feedback on their writing from their classmates and how to respond to such feedback. Students are introduced to the rhetorical expectations of English-speaking readers on organization and development of written ideas, and they learn how to accommodate these expectations. Finally, students turn their attention to form, learning how to focus on technical and grammatical accuracy for writing situations that require such attention. (1989, p. vii)

Collaborative Learning

Closely related to the process movement and to communicative competence is the focus on collaborative teaching and learning. The movement toward individualization of instruction, the student-centered classroom, and the use of cooperative learning strategies in ESL classrooms parallels NES research and teaching. "Current approaches to writing instruction in a second language advocate the negotiation of meaning between student writers and their audiences, sequential processes of drafting and revising compositions, and the development of learners' abilities to diversify their capacities for written expression" (Cumming, 1989, pp. 82–83).

Collaborative learning and teaching strategies have been studied in order to determine how best to harness diverse strengths, energies, and personalities in the shared responsibility for education (Clark, 1987). The opportunities for collaborative learning in the ESL writing classroom include small group work for idea generation, cooperative work on gathering and organizing material, peer review and advice, and the presence of an authentic audience (other than the teacher) for the writer. The objectives of student independence in learning and student responsibility for learning are also met through such group interaction.* George Jacobs (1989) reviewed the NES research that validated the use of thoughtfully organized group activities as a means of enhancing both academic achievement and affective variables, and found that applications for ESL classrooms were viable. Roberta Vann and Roberta Abraham (1990), for example, studied two language learners to determine why their active use of strategies was unsuccessful; they found that often the strategies were inappropriately applied, resulting in limited learning. Classroom reports and research on collaborative and cooperative learning (Bassano and Christison, 1988; Christison, 1990; Nunan, 1989a; Scarcella and Oxford, 1992; C. Shoemaker and F. Shoemaker, 1991) indicate that the use of cooperative curricula and activities stimulate student participation and lead to language learning.

Although there is some resistance among teachers to implementing these theories, many teachers and researchers are investigating ESL collaborative classroom strategies (Bassano, 1986; Bialystok, 1985; Kral, 1992; O'Malley et al., 1985; Prapphal, 1987; Skehan, 1989; Wenden, 1985; Wenden and Rubin, 1987). Theresa Pica and her colleagues conclude that "To be effective, group interaction must be carefully planned by the classroom teacher to include a requirement for a two-way multi-way exchange of information. Thus the teacher's role is critical not only in providing students with access to grammatical input, but also in setting up the conditions for successful second language acquisition in the classroom" (1987, p. 323). In *Learner Strategies in Language Learning* (Wenden and Rubin, 1987), *Language Learning Strategies* (Oxford, 1990), and *The Tapestry of Language Learning* (Scarcella and Oxford, 1992), the authors help teachers translate insights from research on learner strategies into planning tools they can use to promote learner autonomy in their classrooms.

Computer-Assisted Language Learning (C.A.L.L.)

Computer-Assisted Instruction (CAI), or CALL, in ESL teaching has grown substantially since it was first introduced a decade ago. Although the use of CALL has stirred some controversy concerning cost effectiveness, the quality of existing software programs, and student and teacher resistance (Gueye, 1989; Hirvela, 1988), many teachers and

---

*See the activities chapters (Chapter 6 and Chapter 7) for collaborative and peer review activities.

researchers are firm proponents of the value of computer use with well-designed software in the ESL language classroom (Bickes and Scott, 1989; Clutterbuck, 1988; Cook, 1988; Cunningham, 1987; Higgins, 1988; Higgins and Johns, 1984; Rivers, 1990). CALL in current ESL writing classes involves much more than word processing programs and language drills; software programs, which are often designed or adapted for use by ESL writers, prompt students to improve their composing and revision skills. Gerald Dalgish (1984, 1985) and Hsien-Chin Liou (1991), for example, have designed software specifically for use in ESL writing classes, some of which track errors by student language background and help students monitor their own errors. Networking programs allow students to view each other's texts on their own screens and to communicate about those texts through their computers (Esling, 1991; Rinkerman and Moody, 1992). There are also computer text-analysis programs that can quantify text features such as word frequency and sentence length, and then offer writers suggestions for improvement of their prose (Hull, 1987; Kiefer and Smith, 1984; J. Reid, 1987). The advent of "user-friendly" course-authoring systems, coupled with continued teacher-training in the use of CALL, will make computers an active part of the learning process in future ESL classes.

Research in the use of computers in ESL composition is limited, but the results have paralleled NES research. Students react positively to CALL use; they find revision easier, they enjoy working with the computers, and they believe that the use of word processors, invention programs, and revision aids helps to improve their writing (Brownfield, 1984; Hanson-Smith, 1990; Kaufman, 1987; Neu and Scarcella, 1991; Parkhurst, 1984; J. Reid, Lindstrom, McCaffrey, and Larsen, 1983; Stall, 1988). Studies of student use of learning strategies in CALL indicate that ESL writing students use specific coping strategies in computer-assisted instruction, but that the strategies are in many ways inadequate (Chapelle and Jamieson, 1986; Chapelle and Mizuno, 1989; Jamieson and Chapelle, 1987, 1988). One solution to this problem is, of course, teaching appropriate strategies for using computers in an ESL class. Another, demonstrated by Doug Brent, indicates that teachers must not leave intervention solely to the computer programs; teacher feedback remains the most important part of the ESL writing class (1991).

Computer use in ESL writing classes will no doubt burgeon during the next decade "as teachers develop computer skills and greater understanding of the machine, and as they discover uses of the medium they could not have envisioned in their early encounters with the computer" (Dunkel, 1991, p. 26). Networked computer classrooms currently offer the most promise for enhancing collaborative and student-centered classroom learning. Continued research that examines the social and intellectual effects of CALL on language learning and, in particular, in the ESL writing classroom, as well as the development of better and more "user friendly" programs and intensive training of both teachers and students for computer use will be essential.

Proficiency Testing

The testing of ESL writing has undergone a radical change in the last decade. Previously, most student writing was evaluated on the basis of "indirect" discrete point grammar tests; however, the development of **direct tests** of writing in which students write in response to essay "prompts" (topics) has proved to be a more effective means of testing. Essay prompts, scoring guides, and holistic scoring for NES writing tests have gradually begun to replace multiple choice tests for ESL students (Peyton et al., 1990). In particular, the development of the Test of Written English (TWE) by the Educational Testing Service has influenced the teaching as well as the testing of ESL writing. The TWE began experimentally in 1986 (Kroll, 1990b; Stansfield, 1986), following rigorous reliability testing (Bridgeman and Carlson, 1984). It is now past the experimental stage, and is offered as an integral part of the TOEFL examination several times a year at TOEFL test centers throughout the world. The TWE is a separately scored and reported direct test of writing; students write 30-minute essays on a single given topic, and the resulting essays are scored holistically. That is, readers who have been trained to a carefully developed scoring guide read and then rate each essay as a "whole," without marking errors or counting essay traits. Each TWE essay is scored twice; each is assigned a score on a 1 to 6 scale, with 6 being the highest score.

Like many large-scale writing tests, the TOEFL Test of Written English has prompted some criticism directly related to the environmental conditions of the test: a 30-minute time constraint, a single topic, and an "unauthentic" testing situation. Other perceived problems are commonly associated with most large-scale direct testing: the use of generalized prompts, the lack of comparability of prompts, and the reliability of holistic scoring (Greenberg, 1986; Hamp-Lyons, 1990; Raimes, 1990). Research continues in the areas of rater training and scoring (G. Cooper and Hamp-Lyons, 1988; Janopoulos, 1986; G. Robinson, 1985b; Vaughn, 1992) and topic development (Hamp-Lyons, 1992; Hirokawa and Swales, 1986; Horowitz, 1986b; Tedick, 1990).

Alternative large-scale writing tests to the TOEFL have been and are being developed. Other large-scale direct tests of ESL writing include:

1. **Michigan English Language Assessment Battery** (MELAB)

A 30-minute impromptu essay, given as part of the English for academic purposes (EAP) battery of language proficiency tests, that is designed to measure proficiency at advanced levels. Students choose between two assigned topics. Two trained readers at the University of Michigan holistically score each essay on a 10-point categorical scale (English Language Institute, 1989).

2. **English Language Testing Service** (ELTS)

A test designed and administered by the British Council, primarily for post-graduate students applying for scholarships to British universities. The writing test section, introduced in 1980, consists of "two [discipline-specific] compulsory questions, each based on an input text which the candidate has previously read in another part of the test" (Hamp-Lyons, 1990, p. 79). The essays are scored on a 9-point scale by one reader only; there are five separate scoring traits, and the grading is carried out by large groups of well- trained readers without discussion.

3. **Australian Second Language Proficiency Ratings** (ASLPR)

Designed for overseas students entering postgraduate and vocational training courses and used by the English Preparatory Centre in Sydney, "The essay and report components require a response in terms of focus and style from generalized stimulus questions typical of university and technical course exams" (Williams, 1990, p. 61). Essays are scored on a 9-point scale by two readers who have been trained to a carefully developed scoring guide that characterizes performance at each level.

In an ESL writing class or program, testing can have various functions:

- **Admission** (or proficiency): These tests measure the test-taker's overall writing proficiency in English along a wide continuum. Proficiency tests like the TOEFL Test of Written English are generally independent of any instructional program and are highly standardized; universities usually set "cut-off" scores on the TWE as an admission criterion.

- **Placement**: The results of such tests determine the level of instruction for which a student is ready. The writing test, often developed and standardized "in house," should test the same types of knowledge or skills that are taught in the class in which the student is placed (such as use of verb tense or ability to develop ideas).

- **Diagnosis**: These tests are designed to measure specific aspects of writing ability (such as sentence structure, use of cohesion devices, or levels of specific support) (J. D. Brown, 1990). An effective diagnostic test enables the evaluator to identify strengths and weaknesses in writing and, most important, to be able to give students feedback about those findings.

- **Achievement** (or progress): These writing tests measure a student's success in learning some specific instructional content after teaching has taken place (Alderson et al., 1987). An effective test covers what has been taught (for instance, organization of material, overall coherence in a piece of writing) and can serve to evaluate teaching as well as learning.

Conclusion

The field of teaching writing to ESL students has changed dramatically in the last decade, and change continues to be the most predictable aspect of the research and teaching in this field. Perhaps the greatest change has been the relatively sudden interest in teaching ESL writing, particularly for advanced ESL courses. In their review article "Research in Applied Linguistics Relevant to Language Teaching," Rosamond Mitchell and Christopher Brumfit state: "The development of advanced writing skills in ESL is the predominant theme in the extensive current literature of L2 [second language] writing" (1989, p. 147). As a result, current classroom approaches appear to be following the trend in NES composition classes: a more balanced approach toward process and product.

In many educational areas, however, the results of research are often only gradually implemented in the classroom, and ESL is no exception. Perhaps because the field of teaching English as a Second Language is relatively new, theoretical approaches and methodologies abound (see Krashen, 1982; Larsen-Freeman, 1986; Long and Richards, 1987; Oller and Richard-Amato, 1983; Stevick, 1980). Many of them prove popular for a short period, then pass out of the literature without having made substantial effects on classroom teaching. Others, of course, remain, and some of those eventually make their way into second language classrooms. The focus on the expectations of **academic discourse communities** and the **writing process approach** appear to be lasting additions to the ESL writing classroom. At present, the research and teaching experience from the field of NES composition continue to influence the field of ESL composition, mostly in positive ways. In the near future, the information flow may become more reciprocal, particularly since research in such areas as collaborative techniques and discourse analysis can provide insights into the teaching of all composition students.

Discussion Questions

1. Have you studied a second language? If so, can you identify which method(s) your teacher(s) used? Were you, for example, taught using the ALM? In retrospect, which methods did you find most/least effective? Why?

2. If you have studied a second language, what memories do you have of learning to write in that language? What did you consider most difficult about writing in a second language? Why? In retrospect, what might have helped? With a small group of classmates, share your second language learning experiences.

3. Look at the statements from inexperienced ESL writing teachers about writing near the beginning of this chapter. Which do you agree, in part, with? Which seem to be least correct? Why?

4. In your opinion, why was writing the "forgotten" ESL skill for so long? Give reasons for your answer.

5. Based on your previous learning or teaching experiences, do you think that there are cultural differences in the organization and presentation of ideas? Why?

6. What specific information or ideas from Chapter 1 ("Overview of Native English Speaker Composition") might be useful for writing teachers of ESL students? Which have already been incorporated? Why? Which might be less helpful? Why?

7. Some citations in the reference list at the end of the book are not formally published, so they are not readily available. If you wanted to obtain copies of the references listed below, what process(es) would you use?

> Abunowara, A. M. (1983). Contrastive analysis of Arabic and English passive structures. Master's thesis, Colorado State University.

> Chelala, S. I. (1981). The composing processes of two Spanish speakers and the coherence of their texts: A case study. PhD dissertation, New York University.

> Connor, U. and Johns, A. 1989. Argumentation in academic discourse communities. Paper presented at the 23rd International TESOL Convention, San Antonio (March).

> Ney, J. W. and Fillerup, M. (1980). The effects of sentence combining on the writing of ESL students at the university level. ERIC Document, no. ED193 961.

> Walters, K. (1987). On written persuasive discourse in Arabic and English. Unpublished manuscript.

Writing

1. Select one of the composition textbooks discussed in this chapter or choose another composition textbook. Read the Introduction and peruse the Table of Contents. Then look through the textbook, at the exercises, the assignments, and the materials presented. Write an analysis of the textbook for other prospective ESL writing teachers: identify the language proficiency level, the focus, and the philosophy presented. Determine whether you think the textbook would be successful with an ESL writing class and, most important, why or why not.

2. Choose one of the authors referenced in this chapter (such as Patricia Carrell, Daniel Horowitz, Ann Raimes, Vivian Zamel). Read his or her articles on the reference list at the end of this book, and locate and read other current articles by that author. Make an annotated bibliography of the articles to share with your classmates.

3. Choose one article from the reference list. Read it carefully. Then write a two-page response to the article, summarizing and analyzing its main ideas for your classmates.

4. Many ESL language classes, and many ESL writing classes in particular, emphasize the teaching of culture along with language. Examine your attitudes about the teaching of language in a cultural context and write your reactions about the advantages and the disadvantages of doing so.

5. As you consider your philosophy of teaching ESL writing, brainstorm or make notes about your attitudes toward the following:
   a. collaborative learning in the ESL writing class
   b. CALL for ESL writers
   c. using reading in the ESL classroom

CHAPTER 3

Pedagogical Issues in ESL Writing

Research in both NES composition and ESL writing pedagogy suggests that writing itself is a form of learning, and that writing processes and rhetorical contexts for writing are crucial. However, since ESL classrooms are not culturally homogeneous, every pedagogical choice made by ESL teachers is governed in part by the multicultural needs of their students. If culture can be defined as "the overall system of perceptions and beliefs, values and patterns of thought that direct and constrain a social group" (Porter and Samovar, 1991, p.15), then teachers must understand how culture must necessarily inform their classroom pedagogy. In the process of developing a teaching philosophy to guide their teaching, ESL teachers need to know how culture affects communication in their classes, how research in contrastive rhetoric reveals cultural patterns of structuring prose, how individual students bring distinct learning styles to the classroom, how schema theory helps teachers understand connections between reading and writing, and how individual and cultural differences between speaking and writing will affect classroom pedagogy. What teachers know about these key cultural issues will determine what assumptions they make about their students, their classes, and their assignments. No philosophy of ESL teaching can ignore the dramatic effects that culture has on language learning in the ESL classroom.

This chapter presents and discusses issues in ESL teaching that arise from cultural differences. Some are controversial, some are directly focused on writing, and some are applicable in any ESL classroom. None of the sections below is definitive; each gives an overview of the issue. For further work in each area, see the annotated bibliography at the end of this book.

Cross-Cultural Communication

Language is one form of social interaction; therefore, knowledge of commonalities and differences in communication styles and strategies between cultures is worthwhile, even necessary, for both students and teachers. "[T]he better you understand and are prepared to deal with your own and other people's expectations, values, and desires, the more effective you can be in your interactions" (L. Tyler, 1985, p. 1). To communicate effectively within another culture, second language students must learn the social processes and the cultural conventions for that culture. Much empirical and experiential research has shown that differences in the strategies and processes of communicating interculturally can lead to miscommunication and misunderstanding (Cohen and Cavacanti, 1990; Maurice, 1986; Scarcella and Oxford, 1992; Tarone and Yule, 1989; Wolfson, 1986). It is, therefore, one responsibility of the ESL writing teacher to help students understand and participate in U.S. culture (P. Byrd, 1988) by teaching appropriate strategies for identifying and interpreting cultural background knowledge (G. Brown, 1990; H. D. Brown, 1991; Shen, 1989; Stevick, 1989). Anita Wenden gives a clear definition of strategies:

- what people *do* in order to learn a new language
- how they *manage* or *self-direct* these efforts
- what they *know* about *which aspect*s of their learning.

(1987, p. 6)

For ESL teachers, and especially ESL writing teachers, awareness of their students' cultures is essential, for only after coming to know, understand, and appreciate something of other cultures can one realize the importance of providing cultural clues to assist the language learner in a new environment (Valdes, 1986). By recognizing different world views and different ways of expressing reality, we can also recognize some universal properties that bind us all together in the world (G. Brown, 1986). Both learning and teaching in a cross-cultural or multicultural classroom demand more than just tolerance for cultural differences; they demand appreciation and respect for differences (M. Bennett, 1988; Wallace, 1988). In homogeneous classes, using cross-cultural sensitivity in teaching is a relatively simple process: sharing, comparing, and contrasting two cultures (the native and the target cultures) and providing opportunities for discussion, analysis, and practice. But even a seemingly homogeneous class is full of subcultures: differences in age, prior experience, gender, and other variables change perspectives and beliefs (Scarcella and Oxford, 1992). In more heterogeneous intensive English language programs, the variety of cultures represented often results in great diversity of values, attitudes, aims, and reactions (Valdes, 1986). An ESL writing classroom thus demands cross-cross-cross cultural education, for the students must learn not only about the target culture but also about each other if they are to function as peer readers and evaluators and members of a classroom community.

For reasons of ethnic, religious, economic, and developmental diversities, it is impossible—and dangerous—to make any generalizations about international students. All Saudis are not from the same tribe, family, or city; all Japanese do not come to the United States for the same purpose (H. D. Brown, 1992; P. Byrd, 1986). Nevertheless, although no culture is composed of clones who have been defined by their environment, "each culture is fashioned by pervading and prevailing tenets—whether they are conscious or subconscious, spoken or tacit" (Valdes, 1986, p. vii). ESL writing teachers have numerous opportunities to learn about their students' cultures through class discussion and, particularly, through writing assignments that encourage the students to investigate their own cultures, to identify values and expectations that they may not have consciously considered, and to communicate with their classmates about those cultures.

The Cross-Cultural ESL Writing Classroom

Several general areas of cross-cultural study are available for discussion and writing in the ESL classroom.* For instance, knowledge about non-verbal behaviors like the accepted distance between speakers (called proxemics), different gestures, and different behaviors can expand the horizons of writing students and can assist teachers in helping their students to be more comfortable. Here are some examples.

- Distance: in "high-contact" cultures (Arab, Latin American, Greek), people usually stand close to each other. In "low-contact" cultures (Northern European, North American), the comfort zone required is greater; people stand farther apart. Violation of these proxemics causes discomfort.

- Gestures: every language/culture employs gestures and body movements that convey meaning, and all cultures have taboo topics and gestures. In New Zealand and Australia, for example, the U. S. hitchhiking signal is taboo. The OK gesture (open hand raised, thumb and forefinger joined) is considered obscene in several Latin American cultures, while in Japan it is a signal that asks for change (coins) (Simons, 1989). In Paraguay, signs made with crossed fingers are offensive, but crossing legs is permissible as long as the ankle does not touch the knee (Morain, 1986).

- Behaviors: in Germany, people entering a row of seats in a theater face those already seated in the row as they pass in front of them; in Korea, making loud smacking and sucking sounds while eating is a compliment to the host (Morain, 1986).

*See Chapter 6 for specific cross-cultural topics and activities for the ESL writing classroom.

Identifying and analyzing the values and expectations of different cultures is also worthy of investigation in the ESL writing classroom. Understanding the widely differing cultural views on time and space, or about status and gender, for example, promotes tolerance and acceptance of differences in the classroom.

- In Mexico, a party invitation for 8 P.M. may produce guests by 9 or 10; if the invitation also indicates a time for leaving, it is an insult.

- The question "Do you fish?" to a high-caste Indian can be as offensive as "Do you steal?" In India, people who fish for a living generally belong to the low fisherman caste, and many Brahmins are strict vegetarians, for whom fish is taboo and distasteful (Nayar, 1986).

- For the Masai, there is always enough time; their lives are not governed by the clock, and they are never in a hurry (Skow and Samovar, 1991).

Information about and sensitivity to classroom behavior and classroom etiquette in other cultures may prevent misunderstandings in the ESL writing class. In the areas of what constitutes "cheating" and "plagiarism," for example, Phyllis Kuehn et al. (1990) found that attitudinal and behavioral differences exist between NESs and ESL students because of different values in their respective cultures. In many Latin and Arabic cultures, cooperation rather than competition is stressed; students are encouraged to help each other with assignments and even tests. An inexperienced teacher may mistake the high value placed on friendship and cooperation for the less worthy intention of cheating. Chinese students show respect for scholars by copying the words of teachers and writers; the idea that U.S. writers "own" words and that such copying is seen as stealing may seem absolutely foreign to those students. In addition, many students come from educational systems in which there is a great formality between students and teachers, where fifty or more students in a single class listen as one teacher demonstrates and uses English. Compared to this passive learning situation, an English language class in the United States may seem completely unstructured, anarchical. Other examples:

- In many Asian and African cultures, the roles of friend and critic are mutually exclusive; "constructive criticism" is therefore viewed as bizarre.
- A teacher standing with hands on hips can be interpreted as a hostile stance by an Indonesian.
- A teacher sitting on his/her desk may be seen as insulting by a Japanese student (Dunnett et al., 1986).

- Passing out papers with the left hand, rather than the right, may seem incredibly rude to some Arabic students.
- To touch a Thai student on the head is a major social transgression.

One valuable area of inquiry, particularly for students new to a culture, is the examination of culture shock: "[W]hen a person who has been nurtured by one culture is placed in juxtaposition with another, his reaction may be anger, frustration, fright, curiosity, entrancement, repulsion, confusion" (Valdes, 1986, p. viii). This phenomenon begins when the individual experiences excitement, happiness, even exhilaration on entering a new culture; however, within a period of weeks or perhaps months, the new experiences accumulate and then overwhelm the sojourner. Culture shock is characterized by feelings of frustration and anxiety that arise when familiar cultural cues are suddenly replaced by seemingly bizarre behavior. The student cannot make sense of the environment or predict the actions of others. Feelings of estrangement, anger, hostility, indecision, unhappiness, sadness, loneliness, homesickness, or even physical illness can result. Even mild culture shock can be debilitating: a depressed and alienated student does not learn well, and feelings of isolation and frustration can actually prevent learning. Teachers who are sensitive to the characteristics of culture shock can provide vital support for their students (Meloni, 1990; Scarcella and Oxford, 1992). Classroom opportunities for open discussion and sharing and writing assignments that allow students to express these feelings can go a long way toward mitigating the problems associated with culture shock. Writing class activities can increase awareness of typical patterns of adjustment, establish a support system, provide information about factors affecting those patterns, develop the capacity to manage the adjustment, and facilitate evolution in the new culture.

The ESL Writing Teacher as Cultural Informant

In addition to learning about the cultures of their students, language teachers must become cultural informants for the students, for only when students understand the target culture will that culture become an aid to language learning rather than a hindrance. As Shirley Brice Heath (1992) states, language learning is cultural learning. To become a cultural informant, teachers must be explicitly aware of U.S. culture; that is, they must study U.S. values and expectations in order to articulate those values and expectations to their students (Wanning, 1991). Bhaskaran Nayar offers valuable insights into the initial consciousness raising necessary for consideration of U.S. values and expectations:

There are several realities of the Third World which may not even occur to average Americans: that people don't get married just because they love each other, or that they may not have a choice in the matter; that relaxation is not necessarily on a beach, or under palm trees, or in the mountains, or at the other end of a fishing rod; that one could live and die peacefully without a social security number or without even being aware of Jesus Christ; that people do not necessarily have to eat meat, or use toothpaste, toilet paper, or deodorant; that one can have and retain love and affection without overt osculatory or other proxemic or tactile demonstration of it; that the right to privacy may not be fundamental; that a teacher's private life may affect his/her general credibility and acceptability; that students may not speak out even when they have a problem; that pursuit of personal material gains may only be of very low priority; that feelings of gratitude, obligation, indebtedness, appreciation, approbation, etc., do not have to be verbally expressed, but that such expression could even be taboo; that people do not need to have hobbies, or be conscious of their weight and figure; that life is not necessarily a race for achievement punctuated by weekends, holidays, retirement plans, etc. (1986, p. 13)

Observing one's culture through the eyes of an "outsider" is often a valuable way to analyze that culture. What follows is a description from *The Foreign Teaching Assistant's Manual* by Patricia Byrd, Janet Constantinides, and Martha Pennington (1989) in which the authors describe some of the nonverbal communicative gestures of U.S. teachers.

It is common for Americans to raise the eyebrows to emphasize a point while speaking. Raised eyebrows often accompany raised intonation as well. Sometimes, when another person is speaking, an American will raise the eyebrows to indicate special interest in what the other person is saying. In other cases, the listener's raised eyebrows indicate doubt, surprise, or disagreement regarding the speaker's words.

Americans will often show their attitude by either smiling or frowning openly. When speaking in front of a group, it is common for a person to smile periodically as a way to maintain good feelings with the audience. Frowning indicates various kinds of negative attitudes such as anger, distrust, or confusion, and so this expression should be avoided when lecturing. . . .

One of the most important social signals is eye contact. Americans prefer to establish eye contact with different members of the audience for several seconds each, moving the gaze around the room. A shorter period of eye contact or lack of eye contact will indicate nervousness, shyness, or lack of confidence to some Americans, while a prolonged gaze may indicate threat or aggression. (1989, p. 58)

Teachers who integrate cross-cultural communication activities into their ESL writing classes might consider Milton Bennett's (1988) assumptions: intercultural communication is an interactive process, a mutual creating of meaning. Any form of cross-cultural communication is subjective in its interpretations; that is, absolute judgments cannot be made. "Culture is an all-encompassing form or pattern for living. It is complex, abstract, and pervasive" (Porter and Samovar, 1991, p. 14). Therefore, the study of intercultural communication—what happens when people from different cultures interact face to face—is a lifelong endeavor for ESL teachers. As students and teachers in the ESL writing classroom open themselves to the knowledge of other cultures, the "filter" that prevents effective communication will be lifted and replaced by cross-cultural understanding.

Caveats

One problem the ESL teacher encounters in becoming a cultural informant is the thin line between informing and influencing. After all, second language learning in some respects involves the acquisition of a second identity (H. D. Brown, 1986). As teachers encourage students to maintain their individual cultural identity, they must also inform those students about the changes in thinking and behavior needed for moving from one culture to another (Althen, 1981; H. D. Brown, 1991, 1992). Stephen Bochner makes the distinction clear.

> "Adjusting" a person to a culture has connotations of cultural chauvinism, implying that the newcomer should abandon the culture of origin in favor of embracing the values and customs of the host society. On the other hand, learning a second culture has no such ethnocentric overtones. There are many examples in life when it becomes necessary to learn a practice even if one does not approve of it, and then abandon the custom when circumstances have changed. Americans will find that they have to stand much closer to an Arab during interactions in the Middle East than they would with fellow Americans at home. Japanese must learn to have more eye-contact with westerners during conversation than is customary in their own culture. Australians in Great Britain of necessity have to learn to drink warm beer, a habit they discard as soon as they depart. An English gentleman in Japan will learn to push and shove his way onto the Tokyo subway, but resume his normal queuing practice after returning home. The possession of a particular skill itself carries no value judgement—the act attracts notice only when the appropriate skill is not available, or the skill is used in inappropriate circumstances. (1982, p. 164)

Learning and Teaching Styles

In addition to the diverse cultural values and expectations in the ESL writing classroom, students have unique learning styles and strategies, and teachers have preferred teaching styles. Ideally, teachers need to know how students learn and then adjust their teaching styles to accommodate the range of learning styles present in the classroom. During the 1980s, educational research identified a number of factors that account for some of the differences in how students learn. Learning styles are described as cognitive, affective, and perceptual traits that indicate how learners perceive, interact with, and respond to their learning environment (Curry, 1990; Keefe, 1979, 1987). In most research, learning styles are described as points along a continuum between two opposing styles; while a few students occupy the far ends of the continuum, many others have multiple learning styles that allow them to switch styles according to their environment and the task at hand.

One kind of research in **cognitive learning styles** measures **field independence** and **field dependence** in learners. Field-independent students at one end of the continuum are analytic and prefer deductive, linear, sequential learning. Such students function best in classrooms where rules and highly specific instructions, discrete-point tests, and imitation are the focus. In contrast, field-dependent students at the other end of the continuum prefer cooperative and experiential inductive learning situations; they are most successful in classrooms in which teacher-student interaction and interpersonal feedback prevail (Chapelle and Green, 1992; Hansen and Stansfield, 1982; Witkin, 1976). **Affective learning styles** involve student-centered reactions to learning opportunities: levels of motivation, initiation of questions and reception of feedback, and levels of interaction and cooperation (Chamot and O'Malley, 1992; O'Malley, 1985; Oxford, 1992). Teachers are encouraged to provide their students with a supportive classroom atmosphere that is student-centered; materials that are interesting, authentic, and motivating; and cooperative and collaborative work that allows non-threatening interaction (O'Malley et al., 1986; Oxford, 1992; Scarcella and Oxford, 1992). In studies of NES **perceptual learning styles**, researchers (Dunn and Dunn, 1978; R. Dunn et al., 1989; Dunn and Griggs, 1988; Keefe, 1988) have demonstrated that visual learners may have difficulty learning from (auditory) lectures, while auditory learners may prefer them. Of course, most students are not at the ends of the continuum; many fall between and so possess the potential for using a variety of learning styles.

Research has also shown that teachers usually teach in the ways they preferred to learn (C. Bennett, 1986; Dunn and Dunn, 1978;

Simon and Byram, 1984). On the continuum of field-independent/ field-dependent teachers, for example, field-independent teachers prefer lecturing, structural activities, and print-oriented classrooms; they expect their students to follow directions and to see details clearly. Field-dependent teachers, on the other hand, often use discovery approaches and trial-and-error activities; interactive techniques, discussions, and intuition play large parts in their teaching styles (Garrott, 1984). It is unfortunate that many teachers—and ESL teachers are no exception—have little knowledge of learning styles or teaching styles. They develop and use methods and materials according to their own preferred learning styles and rarely consider the learning needs of their students. This mismatch in teaching/learning styles has often been cited as a major reason for poor performance by some U.S. minority students (Griggs and Dunn, 1989; Kleifgen, 1988; Peck, 1991) and for learning difficulties in second language classrooms (Ellis, 1989; McGroarty, 1991). As Patricia Furey (1986) indicates, ESL teachers would be wise to identify, investigate, and respond to differences in the emphasis students place on such modes of learning as inductive versus deductive reasoning, learning by doing versus observation before doing, and discovery learning vs. receptive learning. She points out that students from different educational backgrounds have varying preferences for rote learning, problem solving, creative thinking, and critical evaluation.

Research on the learning styles of ESL students is limited, but growing (Eliason, 1989; Kroonenberg, 1990; Willig, 1988). For example, Roberta Abraham (1985) and Jacqueline Hansen (1984) have investigated the impact of field independence and field dependence in two different ESL settings: the ESL grammar class and the testing of Pacific Island students. Studies in the cultural differences of learning styles have shown that different modes of thinking are characteristic of different cultures (Hainer, 1987; Heath, 1989; McGroarty, 1991). Rita Dunn and Shirley Griggs (forthcoming) indicate that there may be more field-dependent global learners in U.S. subcultures than in the mainstream population.

In a large-scale study that examined the individual learning styles of ESL students, J. Reid (1987a) showed that, in self-reporting surveys, post-secondary ESL students studying in intensive English language programs in the United States strongly preferred kinesthetic and tactile learning (that is, experiential, whole-body learning) and strongly rejected group learning (as opposed to individual learning) (see Table 3–1, page 58). In the same study, NESs preferred kinesthetic, visual and, to some extent, auditory learning. Yet, most secondary and post-secondary instruction in the United States is conveyed via lecture: teaching to an auditory preference (O'Brien, 1989). Moreover, analytic—that is, visual, field-independent—students tend to succeed

TABLE 3–1 MAJOR, MINOR, AND NEGATIVE LEARNING STYLE PREFERENCES BY LANGUAGE BACKGROUND

Native Language and Number of Students	Very Strong Learning Style Preference	Strong Learning Style Preference	Major Learning Style Preference	Minor Learning Style	Negative Learning Style
Arabic (193)	Kinesthetic Tactile	Auditory	Visual	Group	Individual
Spanish (205)	Kinesthetic	Tactile		Visual Auditory Individual	Group
Japanese (130)				Visual Auditory Kinesthetic Tactile Individual	Group
Malay 113)		Kinesthetic	Tactile	Visual Auditory Group Individual	
Chinese (90)	Kinesthetic Tactile	Auditory	Visual	Individual	Group
Korean (118)	Kinesthetic Tactile	Visual	Auditory	Individual	Group
Thai (47)	Kinesthetic	Tactile		Visual Auditory Group Individual	
Indonesian (59)			Kinesthetic Tactile Visual	Visual Individual	Group
English (153)			Kinesthetic Auditory	Visual Tactile Individual	Group

Source: Joy Reid, "The Learning Style Preferences of ESL Students" (1987a).

in school more often than interactive, field-dependent students; school validates the way field-independent students learn (McCarthy, 1987).

It is, of course, dangerous to stereotype various linguistic groups by learning style; age, gender, and the learning environment are among the many other complex variables that influence and individualize learning styles.

> {E]ven if we could accurately identify cultural tendencies in preferred perceptual or learning style, it would not mean that all members of that culture perceive, organize, or interpret information as culturally anticipated. While experiences within a particular culture, as defined by ethnicity, may contribute to the dominance of one style over the other, a given individual usually is a member of various groups (such as those defined by gender, socio-economic status, nationality), which also affects perception.   (G. Robinson, 1985, pp. 21–22)

Rather, successful individual language learners may be those who have identified and then practiced their preferred learning styles and strategies to make their learning efficient and satisfying (Oxford, 1990; Scarcella and Oxford, 1992; Wenden and Rubin, 1987). It is fortunate that learning styles and teaching styles can be developed and expanded (Guild and Garger, 1985; Pask, 1988); moreover, learning styles appear to shift and even change with age and environment. According to J. Reid's study, the longer ESL students were in the United States, the more their preference for auditory learning increased, probably because their listening skills improved and/or their university classes demanded more auditory learning. Many individuals can extend their learning strategies in response to the demands of instruction, context, and task (Kroonenberg, 1990; Skehan, 1991), but as Marion Tyacke indicates, bringing out the best in a learner can occur most successfully when the teacher makes processes of learning more transparent through strategy training (1991). In a truly successful ESL classroom, teachers must take into account how their students' varied cultural and linguistic heritages affect learning. It is the responsibility of the teacher to help students identify their preferred learning styles and to assist them to examine and extend their learning styles and strategies to better cope with the teaching/learning style mismatches they will encounter in U.S. classrooms. The Perceptual Learning Styles Survey and its accompanying informative material are found in Appendix X. Students (and teachers) can complete the survey, self-identifying their preferred styles, and then read about successful learning strategies associated with those perceptual styles.

Teachers, too, can learn to be flexible in their teaching styles, to expand their repertoire to accommodate student learning styles (C. Bennett, 1979; Goldstein, 1992; Peck, 1991). For example, the teacher who is most comfortable with a lecture approach and a structured classroom might experiment with collaborative group work and interactive tasks. Teaching students with multistyle techniques makes learning more enjoyable, improves teacher-student communication, and enriches instruction (Eliason, 1989; Stevick, 1989; Wederspahn and Barger, 1985).

Contrastive Rhetoric

ESL writing teachers also need to know how culture affects their students' preferences for certain rhetorical and organizational patterns. Just as ESL students have a variety of learning style preferences, they are also likely to have certain preconceptions about the formal features of culturally and rhetorically appropriate writing. Robert Kaplan first defined contrastive rhetoric when he sought to discover whether organizational patterns of written material vary from culture to culture (1966). In his investigation of 600 student expository paragraphs, written in English by native speakers of many language non-English backgrounds, Kaplan used philosophical, psychological, anthropological, and linguistic insights to describe the differences between the essentially linear English paragraph, which does not tolerate digression or repetition, and paragraphs that he classified generally as Semitic, Oriental, Romance, or Russian. He represented the differences graphically (see Figure 3–1); at the same time he cautioned that "much more detailed and more accurate descriptions are required before any meaningful contrastive system can be elaborated" (Kaplan, 1966, p. 12).

FIGURE 3–1 KAPLAN'S CONTRASTIVE RHETORIC PARAGRAPHS

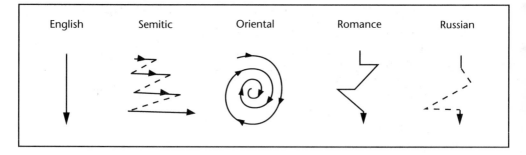

Since the appearance of Kaplan's article, the notion of contrastive rhetoric, along with the issues surrounding the transfer of cultural patterns in second language writing, has grown into an area of study. Kaplan himself has modified his original stance somewhat; what he initially explained as cultural patterns he now identifies as "preferential tendencies" (1982, 1983, 1988a, 1988b). Furthermore, he has become increasingly interested in the influences of oral culture and social values on written discourse, and on the distinctions among different types of written discourse. Kaplan has, however, remained committed to the pedagogical impact of contrastive rhetoric studies. Since he first began writing on the subject, his primary focus has been to describe rhetorical differences for the purpose of applying that knowledge to the ESL writing classroom.

During the last fifteen years, teachers and researchers expanded the notion of contrastive rhetoric. According to proponents of this theory, the style in which each culture organizes and presents written material reflects the preferences of that particular culture (Anderson, 1991; Carlson, 1988; Connor, 1983; Connor and Johns, 1990; Connor and Kaplan, 1987; Fagan and Cheong, 1987; Ostler, 1987). In one study, researchers analyzed meetings of the U.S. Security Council concerning the Arab–Israeli War (Glenn et al., 1977). They identified three general styles of presenting information: U. S. delegates used a "factual-inductive" approach in which facts were studied first and conclusions drawn from those facts. The Soviets' predominant style was "axiomatic-deductive," in which a general theory was first advanced and then facts were studied within that framework. In contrast, the Arab delegates were four times as likely to use an "intuitive-affective" approach, in which positions were expressed through personal appeals and emotions. As the researchers point out, when cultural styles of persuasion and thinking differ to this extent, effective communication is greatly reduced.

Specific differences in rhetorical organization have been examined for many non-English languages; researchers use a discourse analysis approach to examine overall organizational structures as well as the use of coherence devices and the frequency of discrete language factors. Studies investigate differences between English and Arabic (Anderson, 1991; Morcos, 1986), English and Chinese (Alptekin, 1988; Cheng, 1985; Scollon and Scollon, 1981); English and Spanish (Montaño-Harmon, 1988; Santaña-Seda, 1974); English and Thai (Bickner and Peyasantiwong, 1988; Indrasuta, 1988); and English and Japanese (Hinds, 1987; H. Kobayashi, 1984; Ricento, 1987). These and other studies have confirmed that many ESL writers do use different first language rhetorical patterns when writing English. For example, Shirley Ostler (1987), in a large-scale study, found that, on the oral to written continuum, Arabic students writing in English use language and organization that places that writing near the oral end of the continuum: long sentences joined by coordinate conjunctions, repetition, and syntactic balance. In another large study, Feng Chen-yu

(1981) found that, unlike NESs, Chinese writers are reluctant to take a stand, prefer moderate positions, and often conclude with a proverb or formulaic statement. Because "texts have schematic structures which are culturally variable" (Widdowson, 1987, p. iii–v), writers from one culture who write for readers in another culture often have problems with the identification of audience expectations and, so, with cross-cultural communication (Basham and Kwachka, 1992; Horowitz, 1986c; J. Reid, 1989; Scarcella, 1984a; Steele, 1990).

It is necessary to note that, although such differences may adversely affect communication with the U.S. academic discourse community, they should not be described as a stigma or a deficiency. Differences among rhetorical patterns do not represent differences in cognitive ability but rather differences in cognitive style. As Carolyn Matalene stated, "Invention, arrangement, style, memory and delivery can all be defined, practiced, and valued in ways other than our own" (1985, p. 804). To prepare ESL students for successful academic work in the United States, ESL writing teachers must give their students adequate opportunities to become aware of the constraints of U.S. academic prose and the expectations of the U.S. academic audience (Horowitz, 1986b; Silva, 1990; Swales, 1990a).

Schema Theory

Research into schema theory has helped many ESL teachers understand how their students' cultural, linguistic, and person experiences affect their learning. Patricia Carrell and Joan Carson Eisterhold have defined **schema** principally in relation to reading skills: "[P]reviously acquired knowledge is called the reader's *background knowledge*, and the previously acquired background knowledge structures are called *schemata*" (1983, p. 556). Because successful communication "rests firmly upon a common repository of knowledge and experience shared by writers and readers" (De Beaugrande, 1979, p. 260), students' prior knowledge will influence what, and probably how, they write. The writing of a text is an active event: it necessarily entails bringing prior knowledge to bear upon what is read. Carrell's seminal work (1984a, 1984b, 1984c, 1987a, 1987b) in ESL reading and schema theory has demonstrated that when non-native speakers of English read a second language, the patterns they have been enculturated to predict from reading and writing in their own languages can be quite distinct from those in English. Since ESL readers encode meaning in ways that are different from NESs, Carrell suggests that teaching ESL readers the text structure(s) of academic prose facilitates reading comprehension.

Carrell's more recent work reflects the increasing NES and ESL research concerning the link between reading and writing (1989, 1990,

1992). Applying schema theory to ESL writing, she indicated that, by providing necessary cultural information about the rhetorical organization of U.S. academic expository text and audience expectations of such text, teachers will make ESL writing more effective. Simply put, when form and content are familiar, reading and writing are relatively easy. But when one or the other (or both) are unfamiliar, efficiency, effectiveness, and success are problematic.

It is unfortunate that many ESL writing students have had no practice, either in their native language or in English, in identifying the expectations of their audience. Sybil Carlson notes that "Making a match between the expectations of the reader and the writer involves [a] complex interaction, since readers and writers have [each] acquired their idiosyncratic approaches to defining competent performance, largely through educational experience within their particular culture or sub-cultures" (1988, p. 233). For ESL writers whose schemata concerning U.S. academic expectations are at best limited, fulfilling those expectations is especially difficult. Moreover, Mina Shaughnessy (1977) characterized U.S. university professors the "least submissive of audiences": they expect the writer to make arguments and develop a case that meets their criteria for academic discourse. U.S. academic prose, then, reflects a certain core of cultural values: respect for individual autonomy, inventiveness, forthrightness and action, and regard for the individual personality. As a consequence of those cultural expectations, there may even be some bias of NES teachers and essay raters against culturally different discourse styles (Degenhart et al., 1988; Hamp-Lyons, 1987; Park, 1988).

ESL researchers (Grabe and Kaplan, 1989; Scarcella, 1986) have concluded that ESL teachers must become facilitators of the acquisition of appropriate schemata for their ESL writing students. Such information will prepare students to produce what Shaughnessy (1977) called the flow of information that any reader conditioned by U.S. literary custom expects to read. ESL composition teachers therefore need (a) to become informed about appropriate U.S. academic discourse patterns; (b) to inform their ESL writing students about discourse differences and audience expectations; (c) to provide practice with the imposition of appropriate patterns upon experience; and (d) to offer opportunities for practice and experience with the new schema. To accomplish these tasks, teachers can collect academic assignments from across the curriculum, analyze and describe audience expectations for each assignment, and plan lessons around the resulting information.*

*See Chapter 7 for sample academic assignments and Chapter 6 for cultural informant activities.

The Writing-Reading Connection

Closely linked to schema theory is the idea that reading and writing are integrally connected. All student writers read; they read about writing, they read the writing of others, and most important, they read and re-read their own writing as they write. And readers, particularly good readers, often write: they outline, they summarize, they respond to, and they synthesize their reading. Reading has always been a part of the ESL writing classroom. Students in grammar-translation classes read the text they were translating; ALM students read sentences in exercises and directions; language-based classes provided students with controlled paragraphs, and students also read the guided writing they completed. During the 1980s, however, research with both NESs and ESL students has resulted in a substantial change in perspective concerning the link between reading and writing.

First, research in the writing-reading connection has demonstrated that the two skills are cognitively similar: both writer and reader *construct* meaning from text and *interpret* meaning from text (Folman, 1988; Janopoulos, 1986; P. Johnson, 1986; Sarig, 1988). In addition, both reading and writing are multifaceted, complex, interactive processes that involve many subskills, and both depend on individual past experience (Horowitz, 1986c; Rosenblatt, 1988; Spivey, 1990; Sternglass, 1986). Furthermore, both writing and reading are interactive, recursive processes in which background knowledge (schema) plays an integral part; both activate schemata about the language, content, and form of the text, and both lead to the exploration of those schemata in discovering meaning. Both writers and readers have "drafts" of meaning in their heads as they begin, and both constantly revise these "drafts" in light of what Stanley Straw (1990) called "the emerging text." For ESL students, who have diverse cultural backgrounds and contrasting rhetorics, their schemata, and so their "drafts," may be inappropriate or insufficient.

As Martin Nystrand (1990) and Roger Shuy and David Robinson (1990) point out, teachers need to see writing and reading not merely as cognitive, constructive processes but also as social, communicative processes between writers and readers. Research with both NESs (Flower and Hayes, 1980; Meyer, 1982; Tierney and Leys, 1986) and ESL students (Carrell, 1987b; Johns, 1991; Krashen, 1984a) has shown the reciprocal relationship between reading and writing: good readers are often good writers, and good writers are often good readers. A review of NES studies of the relationships between reading and writing (Stotsky, 1983) found direct correlations between reading achievement and writing ability: better writers read more than poorer writers, and better readers tend to produce more syntactically mature writing than poorer readers. Another review of NES studies (Belanger, 1987) showed that direct instruction in sentence, paragraph, and discourse structures for writing results in significant improvement in reading. Harry Gradman and Edith Hanania studied 101 ESL students in an intensive language program; their research found that, of forty-four variables, the most significant correlation with TOEFL scores was active exposure to English through individual reading outside the classroom (1991). Readers discover ideas and form opinions about their reading, opinions and ideas they can write about; at the same time, they also accumulate schema—often unconsciously—about the formats of English writing and the expectations of the U.S. academic audience.

Although a substantial body of research currently exists in ESL reading and in ESL writing, exploration into the writing-reading connection for ESL students is still quite limited. Among the studies, Stephen Krashen (1988, 1984a, 1984b) and others (Datesman, 1990; Robb and Susser, 1989; Stuart, 1990; Susser and Robb, 1990) claim that ESL writing proficiency occurs only through the "comprehensible input" provided by <u>extensive</u> (that is, reading for leisure and pleasure outside the classroom), self-motivated reading.* Some course designers combine extensive with intensive (assigned, closely studied) reading: they use the link between literature, particularly American literature, and writing as a foundation for literacy and for the teaching of the "cultural particularities" of American values and culture (Bastürkmen, 1990; Carter and Long, 1987; Collie and Slater, 1987; McConochie, 1982; Murdoch, 1992a; Sage, 1987; Willoquet-Mariondi, 1991–1992). "Literature serves as a model and inspiration of language awareness. . . . the learners start from something they are engaged in and write from that interest " (Ibsen, 1990, p. 4). Applying the theory of the writing-reading connection, some textbook writers use literary texts and reader-response activities (LeBauer, 1992); others use professional and student essays with relevant topics that demonstrate typical academic writing (Blanton, 1992; Shih, 1992). In Ruth Spack's *Guidelines: A Cross-Cultural Reading/Writing Text*, essays from diverse fields of study are used to "foster critical thinking and to lead students toward developing ideas for their own essays" (1990, p. vii). The writing tasks grow out of and are supported by the readings as well as from individual student backgrounds and additional outside sources.

Reading and analyzing texts for successful communication

Research in Reading in English as a Second Language (Devine, Carrell, and Eskey, 1987), *Interactive Approaches to Second Language Reading* (Carrell, Devine, and Eskey, 1988), and particularly *Second Language Perspectives on Reading in the Composition Classroom* (Leki and Carson, forthcoming) present a thorough overview of current issues and research in reading and in the writing-reading connection.

patterns—that is, for what makes a passage unified and meaningful for readers in a specific discourse or interpretative community—should help readers plan their own written texts (Block, 1992; Lope, 1991; Meyer, 1982). Patricia Carrell distinguishes three kinds of cultural schema: linguistic (language knowledge), content (topic knowledge) and formal (rhetorical knowledge) schemata (1987b). Research by Robert Pritchard studied the effects of cultural schemata on reading process strategies and found that culture does influence both processing strategies and comprehension (1990). Fraida Dubin and David Bycina (1991) suggest that students need pre-reading activities to stimulate and extend schema, while-reading activities that allow students to interact with text and author, and post-reading activities that investigate the links between writing and reading to help students discover how to write within the discoursal demands of academic writing. For ESL writing teachers, having students write about reading and read about writing should lead to more effective written communication .

Differences Between Speaking and Writing

The differences between spoken and written language seem obvious: babies acquire their first language orally without effort, while school children must be taught to write. Speaking is most often a dialog, a conversation with a cooperative partner with whom we share some background, whose feedback is immediate and whose responses we can predict; writing more often seems to be a monolog, with the writer attempting to identify or create an audience, with only self-provided feedback (Schafer, 1981). Moreover, speaking techniques differ between NES and ESL speakers. Andrea Tyler and John Bro have demonstrated that ESL speakers, like ESL writers, differ from NESs in their use of coherence devices (1992).

Substantial research on the differences between oral and written language has, however, shown that, contrary to many previous assumptions, oral language is just as complex as written language, but that the types of complexity differ. Deborah Tannen (1982b, 1984b) asserts that both oral and written discourse can display features of the other, depending on the communicative environment—the situation, the objectives, and the discourse community. Indeed, the differences between oral and written discourse form a kind of discourse continuum, which is dependent, at the very least, on situation, task, audience, and function (Lakoff, 1981; Li and Thompson, 1982; Mangelsdorf, 1989; Tannen, 1982a). Douglas Biber (1988) has demonstrated, for instance, that the text (that is, the discourse) of BBC news broadcasts, which are given orally, closely resemble written prose, while informal letters to close friends often resemble oral discourse.

In general, however, written language often exhibits more "detachment" and a relatively greater degree of formality (Beaman, 1984; Chafe, 1982; Chafe and Danielewicz, 1987). Written prose usually has greater lexical (vocabulary) diversity, longer sentence length, and more subordination (Poole and Field, 1976; Thury, 1988). That is, speech has complex sentences with simple words, while writing has complex words in simple sentences. Wallace Chafe and Jane Danielewicz (1987) studied informal conversations and classroom lectures (which were transcribed) and informal letters and academic papers spoken or written by 20 professors or graduate students at two universities. In their detailed discourse analysis, the researchers found that:

1. Speakers tended to operate with a narrower range of lexical choices than writers, probably because the immediacy of the situation required quick articulation.

2. Speakers used fewer "intonation units" (a single, coherent group of words, usually a single clause) than writers, probably because writers are not constrained by a listener's short-term memory, and because writers have the time to construct, plan, and edit their prose.

3. Speakers used substantially fewer prepositional phrases and prepositional phrase sequences (two or more prepositional phrases together) than writers, probably because of listener overload and time constraints.

4. Speakers used significantly more coordination (coordinating conjunctions: "and," "but," and "so") than writers; speakers tend to "chain" clauses together with "and," and writers tend to sculpt their writing into a more complex, integrated whole.

5. Spoken sentences often consist of one or two words, while other spoken "chained" sentences are sometimes 100 words or more; in contrast, written sentences show a relatively normal distribution of sentence lengths centered around a mean of 24 words.

It is particularly important for the writing teacher to understand and impart the situational and social differences between writing and speech; inexperienced writers may be experienced talkers, but they must learn the conventions of written English. They must learn how to initiate a text, prolong it, and bring it to a close without help; they must be able to ask questions and answer them, pose problems and solve them, and perhaps present opposing views and refute them.

Conclusion

The cultural heterogeneity of the ESL writing classroom poses specific challenges for teachers as they decide on classroom pedagogy.

ESL writing teachers must realize, for example, not only that students from different cultural backgrounds present written material in different rhetorical and organizational modes, but that when they write in English, their discourse may reflect the patterns valued in their native cultures. Course syllabi and individual lesson plans should therefore reflect an awareness of and sensitivity to the students' diversity in native culture, learning styles, and schemata.

Josef Mestenhauser states that the word "professional" is integrally involved with the "possession of a body of theoretical and practical knowledge capable of being applied in ways of value to a significant number of people" (1988, p. 2). Only by examining the methodological issues in ESL writing can writing teachers make careful, considered, professional decisions concerning their philosophies of teaching. The information concerning pedagogical issues in ESL teaching in this chapter, and the extension of that knowledge through discussion, additional research, and application, form a part of the foundation for the professional ESL writing teacher.

Discussion Questions

1. Using the topics below, examine the cultural differences that exist among cultures. In small groups or pairs, discuss these differences; how might each affect successful classroom teaching?

General Culture	Classroom Culture
Differences in Cultural Values	
A. Individualism/ Group Orientation	A. individual competition, sense of privacy about individual work, striving for individual achievement
B. Attitudes toward use of time	B. notions of how much is to be covered at what rate, importance of efficiency of procedures, punctuality, correctness vs. speed, etc
C. Values relating to purpose of education in general and relative importance of different kinds of education	C. relative emphasis on learning an authoritative body of knowledge, on practical education, on political education, on acquiring the right credentials, on preserving the past vs. encouraging change, etc.
Differences in Views Toward the Teacher	
A. Views on status, prestige of teacher; norms of appropriate distance	A. rules of deference, propriety; degree of formality or informality between student and teacher

| B. Views on rights and obligations of teachers, i.e., teacher role | B. degree of authority invested in and expected from the teacher; degree to which teacher directs, dominates classroom activities; expectations of teacher as a)scholar, sage, (b)counselor, adviser, (c) personal tutor |

Source: Patricia Furey, "A Framework for Cross-Cultural Analysis of Teaching Methods" (1986).

2. In the U.S., how much someone weighs is not an acceptable question. Name five other taboo topics in U.S. culture. Discuss possible reasons for their inappropriateness.

3. The following aspects of American culture are frequently reflected, at least implicitly, in English language instructional materials. Which would you have believed are universal? common to all Western cultures? In what ways might people from other cultures view some of these beliefs and tendencies?

- the belief that each person is a distinct entity and ought to assert and achieve independence from others
- egalitarianism: the belief that all human beings are equal in their intrinsic worth
- a belief in action orientation: doing is more important that being
- a perception of interpersonal encounters primarily in terms of their immediate utility and downgrading of the social significance of such encounters
- universalism: the value attached to being guided in one's actions in a given situation primarily by an obligation to society, by general standards of conduct (laws, rules, etc.)
- a definition of persons (including oneself) in terms of their work and their achievements
- the belief that the collective wisdom of the group is superior to that of any individual
- the idea that the process of decision making requires evaluation of the consequences of alternative courses of action, and selection of the one that, on balance, seems most advantageous
- the belief that competition is a good way to motivate people
- the idea that there is usually a best way of doing something, which should be determined and then followed
- the idea that knowledge gained through observation is superior to knowledge gained in other ways
- the tendency to quantify aspects of experience
- the tendency to place higher value on utilitarian aspects of experience than on aesthetic ones
- problem orientation: the tendency to perceive "problems" in the world and in one's existence in it, and to look for "solutions"

- the belief that thought cannot directly influence events
- reasoning in terms of probability
- impatience: the tendency to be annoyed by the pace of the activities, if it is slow by one's own standard
- the tendency to make comparative judgments
- the willingness to offer one's services for the benefit of the "common good"
- the belief in the existence of a behavior pattern called "self-help"
- the use of absurd suppositions to communicate ideas or to elicit ideas from other persons (Kraemer, 1973)

4. Examine two commercial ESL writing textbooks to identify the inherent cultural aspects. Determine whether the cultural aspects in the textbooks could assist a teacher in meaningful cross-cultural discussion and writing. What aspects of culture are covered? Are the readings, exercises, and vocabulary items in a meaningful cultural context? Are U. S. or foreign cultures stereotyped?

5. Take the Perceptual Learning Styles Survey (Appendix 1) to determine your preferred learning styles. Discuss your results with others, and compare those results with the choices made by students in Table 3–1 in this chapter. In what ways might your learning styles influence teaching styles?

6. What are some other differences between oral and written communication? Compare and contrast some other types of formal oral communication or informal written communication.

7. Using the summary of results from the Chafe and Danielewicz study (see page 19, this chapter), consider the way an elementary school child might describe an experience during a "show and tell" time. What elements of oral language would be present in this description?

8. Re-read the summary of Alexander Freidlander's research in the composing strategies of Chinese students in English and Chinese in Chapter 2. How might schema theory play a part in his results?

Writing

1. Select a 300 to 400 word passage from an academic text. Then transcribe a conversation you have had or have overheard. Compare the two texts. In a short analysis, describe what elements of written and oral prose are demonstrated in the two texts.

2. Opponents of the theories of contrastive rhetoric argue that (a) no one who is not truly bilingual can possibly do research in the area (Krapels, 1990; Ricento, 1986); (b) contrastive rhetoric research that uses English as a "control" is a form of ethnocentricity and cultural imperialism (Kachru, 1982a; Kachru, 1982b; Kachru, 1985; Ouaouicha, 1986); and (c) differences in the written

presentation of ideas of ESL students are developmental, not cultural (Mohan and Lo, 1985; Zamel, 1976). How do you respond to each of these criticisms? Read one or more of the articles by authors who are opposed to contrastive rhetoric studies. Then write a brief analysis of one or more of these points.

3. Have you ever experienced culture shock? If so, describe that experience. What did you learn from it?

4. Read the passages below, each written by an ESL student. What language elements make each of the samples seem "foreign"? Consider not only the surface errors but also the oral language components and the expectations you have as the reader.

> My grandfather has lived in the end of the 19th and the beginning of the 20th century. I never saw him but I know much about his life and his time and I know enough about his behavior and habits because my father is like him. My grandfather was born, raised, and died in the mountain village which lack anything of modern society. He had to work hard early and to faith against nature for surviving and this way of life leads generally to wisdom, friendship, and peace of health and spirit. Now, this kind of life is called traditional, archaic, and sometimes miserable but I don't know if it is right or wrong.

> The teacher introduced two people in the class. First, the named are Mike and Justin and they are fifteen years old, and Mike is the son of the teacher and Justin is Mike's friend. They are studying in high school so they have a lot of classes like, geomotry, Spanish, political science, journal, band, health, choir, chemistry, alegebra, etc. After that, they brought two skateboards and one frisbee for their hobby, second we interview with them and they stayed very agreeable with us. They wore short pants, tennis shoes and blue or gray jackets. Justin dressed folkloric because he puts shoestrings green. However I had one surprise because Justin spoke with me in my language and I asked a lot of questions to him and he answered very good.

5. From your own experience, write a short personal essay that describes a time when your schema failed you: perhaps a silhouette that seemed frightening until . . ., a failure to understand a situation because . . . , humor that was not funny until . . . , etc. Think of examples in your own reading in which inadequate or inappropriate prior knowledge interfered with comprehension of the text. How did you/could you have compensated for the problem?

6. Examine the results of the Learning Styles Survey you took (#5 above). Then write a brief essay describing in what ways those results reflect (or conflict with) your growing knowledge of your ESL teaching philosophy.

CHAPTER 4

Curriculum and Syllabus Design

ESL writing courses must be carefully planned, each class a single piece of a complex design. The teacher should determine the goals for the course, then implement the materials in order to arrive at specific performance objectives (Nunan, 1989a). If the ESL writing class is one of a series in a writing program, it is necessary to know not only the performance objectives for the single course but also the overall goals for the writing program and the objectives for the other classes. If, in addition, an ESL writing program is part of an intensive language program, the curricula and syllabi for the other classes in that program should also be available to the teacher. Such an overview allows the teacher clear vision and direction; the teacher must then communicate that vision and direction to the students.

Developing and articulating the mission of the writing class or program results in the formulation of a **curriculum**: a general statement of the goals of the course that articulates the intended (and attainable) outcomes of the class/program (Dubin and Olshtain, 1986; Richards and Nunan, 1990). Those goals can be used to form the basis for specific descriptions of the intended outcomes. The specified objectives for the class (or for each class in the writing program) result in the development of a **syllabus**: "A syllabus is essentially a job specification, and as such it should set out clearly and precisely what is to be done, and the standards or criteria to be met by those who do it" (P. Johnson, 1981, p. 34). Since a curriculum and a syllabus are documents intended to guide teachers and learners, they should be in place and ready for use before the ESL writing class meets for the first time.

Vital preparatory work is necessary to gather detailed information before developing the goals of the curriculum and the objectives of the syllabi. Answers to the following questions are essential.

1. Who are the learners?
2. Who are the teachers?
3. Why is the writing class/writing program necessary?

Answering the first question will result in a description of the students in the class or program: their levels of language proficiency, their prior educational and cultural backgrounds, their general academic development, their ages and expectations, their learning styles and strategies. In answer to the second question, identifying the characteristics of writing teachers in the program will determine their level of knowledge and expertise in teaching ESL writing, as well as their experience, their attitudes toward classroom learning, and their philosophies of teaching writing. An examination of the rationale for the writing program and/or the class will result in information about the class setting (size, situation, resources) and the **language setting**—the situation outside of the ESL composition class in which the student will be expected to write.

Curriculum Development

A curriculum is a general statement that combines educational and cultural goals with language goals. The document contains distinct assumptions about the nature of language and language learning, and about the teaching of writing. Usually the curriculum statement is developed prior to the design of the class syllabus. Sometimes, however, decisions concerning curriculum goals and syllabus design occur simultaneously, and occasionally curriculum goals are articulated only after class syllabi have been developed, implemented, evaluated, and revised. Curriculum statements for writing classes fall into one of four broad categories: the language-based curriculum, the pattern-model–based curriculum, the process-based curriculum, or some combination of the first three.*

1. **The Language-Based Curriculum**. Goals for the language-based curriculum use the writing class as a context for consolidating students' oral command of English and for practicing grammar (Bowen and Madsen, 1985). The goals are centered around grammatical **accuracy** and **correctness**, and they focus on the ability of exiting writing students to use specific grammatical items such as verb tenses, articles, and coordinating conjunctions. An example of a language-based curriculum statement:**

> The writing curriculum of the Tutorium in Intensive English is
> designed to prepare students to communicate effectively in written

---

*To review these philosophies of teaching writing, refer to Chapter 2.

**Before writing this chapter, I asked colleagues to send me and allow me to use writing curricula and syllabi from their ESL writing programs. The materials used in this chapter are thus authentic examples. But it is the nature of curricula and syllabi to change—to be continuously evaluated and frequently revised. The materials in this chapter therefore represent curricula and syllabi at a specific point in time. This Language-Based Curriculum Statement from the University of Illinois at Chicago has since been revised. The revised statement is included later in this chapter.

English. Since most of our students will use their English in colleges or businesses, expository writing and real communication are emphasized. The program is centered around the **structure syllabus**, so that writing activities will **reinforce the grammar** being learned. In addition, the paragraph is the central focus of study at all levels, so that connected writing skills can be developed. (emphases mine)

> Tutorium in Intensive English
> (5-level writing program)
> The University of Illinois at Chicago

2. **The Pattern-Model–Based Curriculum**. Goals for the pattern-model–based curriculum focus on functional and situational writing, and on the expectations of the audiences for that writing. The goals emphasize the forms for writing, including thesis sentences and rhetorical modes such as the narrative, the comparison/contrast paragraph, or the expository essay. One example of a pattern-model–based curriculum statement follows.

The ELS writing curriculum has been designed to provide for the development of writing skills in a logical sequence beginning with a focus on sentence-level grammar and the writing of brief paragraphs at the 101 level and culminating in the development of organized, well-supported 2–3 page essays at the 109 level. Throughout this sequence, the instructor has two functions: (a) as a teacher of writing skills; and (b) as a tutor/editor who helps each student individually to improve his/her writing with respect to expression, content, logical organization, grammar, spelling, and mechanics. In accordance with this approach, the goals of the program for beginning, intermediate, and advanced levels are as follows:

Beginning (101–102)
Emphasis on developing paragraphs, though "true" 101 students may need a lot of sentence-level work. 101/102 students write on familiar topics and work from models. 103 students learn more explicitly about paragraph construction (**topic sentences, support, concluding sentences,** etc.) and develop paragraphs using narrowed-down topics, topic sentences, and outlines.

Intermediate (104–106)
Focus for intermediate students is on the short (3–5 paragraph) essay. Though students at lower levels may have already completed assignments in which they wrote more than one paragraph, the overt transition to the multiparagraph essay takes place in 104, where students learn how to expand a paragraph into a short composition. 105 students focus on specific features of the essay, including **thesis statements** and **introductory and concluding paragraphs**, and 106 students are introduced to argumentation and summary/analysis.

<u>Advanced</u> (107–109)
Advanced students concentrate on writing somewhat longer
(2–3 page) essays in various **rhetorical modes,** depending on level:
107—**examples** and **comparison-contrast**; 108—**classification
and process**; 109—**cause-effect** and **argumentation**. Students
complete individualized writing projects..   (emphases mine)

> English Language Services (ELS) Language
> Centers
> (9-level writing program)
> Headquarters Office: Culver City, California

✓   3. **The Process-Based Curriculum**. Curricular goals for the
process-based curriculum are based on the processes of communication
and negotiation. The goals focus on **fluency**, on discovery, and on the
individual unique development of each student. An example of a
process-based curriculum statement:

> The current ALP reading/writing curriculum places the ability to
> **communicate** and the development of language **fluency** as the
> primary aims of instruction, with practice of the traditional language
> skills simply a method of promoting the larger goals. In order to
> create the type of context necessary for such an approach, the
> majority of instruction in the reading/writing class is accomplished
> within the framework of thematic units that provide an engaging
> content base and allow for the integration of the **individual** reading
> and writing skills. In a content unit, students focus upon one broad
> content topic for several days, reading a number of different
> selections concerning the topic, discussing and relating them, and
> using them as a basis for a number of different writing tasks.
> Composition skills are explained as necessary to help students
> **communicate their ideas** more effectively within the context of
> the writing task.   (emphases mine)

> > American Language Program
> > (4-level reading/writing program)
> > The Ohio State University

✓   4. **The Combination Curriculum.** Many writing curriculum
statements merge two or even all three of the curriculum types
described above in an effort to meet the needs of their students and
their writing programs. In the two examples of combination
curriculum statements below, notice that the curriculum statements
incorporate <u>language</u>, *pattern-model*, and **process** foci (indicated by the
<u>underlined</u>, *italicized*, and **bold-faced** words).

> Goal: the effective communication of ideas in written form rather
> than the memorization of rules.

>   At each level, students will use both written and oral language as
> the means to developing a knowledge of <u>English grammar</u> <u>and</u>

<u>syntax</u>. Yet each level will have a specific focus and a set of skills to be mastered. Through techniques such as *scrambled sentences*, sentence combining, and error analysis, students can learn to recognize and <u>correct</u> their own writing errors.

English as a Second Language
(5-level writing program)
(Language- and Pattern-Model-based)
Mission College (Santa Clara, California)

* * * * * * * * *

Our primary task in the composition component of university ESL courses is to familiarize and equip students with strategies for approaching the academic writing tasks found in the university. In order to determine the most commonly assigned university writing tasks, many needs analyses have been conducted. Horowitz (1986b, 1986c) and Carlson and Bridgeman (1984) have pointed out that *university writing tasks have very prescribed forms*. Most essays require some type of analysis based on synthesis of information from multiple sources, selection of appropriate data, and connection of theory with data. The essays may follow any one of the following *rhetorical patterns*: descriptive process writing, research summaries, comparison/contrast essays, or argumentation.

Often, ESL students, either due to lack of understanding these rhetorical patterns or due to lack of previous academic composing experiences/instruction, must be familiarized with the *rhetorical structures and strategies* used in academic essays including paraphrasing, summarizing, *paragraph ordering, the movement from generalizations to specific supporting information,* the inclusion of information relevant to the analysis or argument being presented and the exclusion of irrelevant information, and the *framing of paragraphs around one concept or idea.*

In addition, ESL students' writing is stigmatized by <u>errors of syntax, grammar, and lexical choice</u>. It is our task to enable students to activate their <u>passive grammatical knowledge to edit for certain grammar errors</u> within their own written discourse and to develop strategies for increasing <u>lexical accuracy</u> and expanding their academic vocabulary.

This awareness of the needs of the students that we serve as well as an understanding of the academic writing tasks that they must master has led us to adopt a **process approach** to the teaching of composition. In this approach, writing for both native and non-native speakers is seen as a **recursive process,** composed of several interacting phases: pre-writing/planning, composing, revising and editing. Each of these phases can occur at any time during the production of a piece of writing.

While promoting **fluency**, creating meaningful opportunities to write, and **encouraging the drafting process** are important parts of the writing component, we approach writing primarily as a problem-solving activity. We advocate an instructional approach that will help ESL writers understand their own writing process while equipping them with specific strategies to solve the unique challenges that writing *academic expository prose* in a second language presents to them. We aim to promote student interaction and involvement in solving problems by having students write often and engage in various kind of writing tasks, including in-class writing, essays written under time pressure, and out-of-class papers taken through multiple drafts.

> ESL Service Courses
> (Language-, Pattern-Model-, and Process-Based)
> University of California /Los Angeles

Designing a Curriculum Statement

Designing an ESL writing curriculum statement usually begins with a brief **needs analysis** and involves both student and program needs. The formulation of goals in the curriculum statement for a writing program involves the concerns of the program and the institution. For example, in an intensive English program, curriculum development for the writing program might begin with a statement of the **exit goals**. If the exiting students will be required to take a freshman composition course, the exit requirements from the intensive language program might incorporate the skills needed to enter freshman composition. The resulting curriculum statement might be quite broad: "To provide the university with students whose writing skills meet academic standards." Or it might be more specific: "Students exiting the program will be able to successfully complete the freshman placement exam by reading the given passage and responding to it: summarizing, analyzing, taking a position, and supporting that position in the freshman placement essay." The curriculum statement may then describe the general processes in the writing course or program that are aimed at fulfilling the exit goals.

No statement of curricular goals is ever final. Consequently, curriculum designers must provide opportunities for adequate evaluation and for ongoing revision of the curriculum. Decisions concerning what to evaluate and how to evaluate should be made with the changing needs of the students, the program, and the institution in mind. (For one evaluation procedure, see Evaluating and Revising Existing Curricula/Syllabi later in this chapter.)

Syllabus Development

A writing program should provide not only general curricular goals but also objectives that make the goals possible. The syllabus provides guidelines for the effective, integrated organization of the writing class; it is an operational document that translates the philosophy of the curriculum goals into the course content. Each syllabus for a single course provides direction for the teacher in planning the class, and for students in setting their personal objectives.

The amount of detail in a syllabus depends on the philosophical assumptions behind the syllabus and on the experiences, the skills, and the styles of the teachers who will use it. Will the teachers using the syllabus be relatively inexperienced in the teaching of ESL writing? Will they need a highly developed and detailed syllabus that serves as a primary resource, or will they only need to consult the syllabus casually? Will they be free to adapt and supplement the syllabus? (Richards, 1990a). Many syllabus designers believe that a more detailed syllabus helps the teacher to clarify objectives and facilitate instruction. Explicit objectives make the evaluation process easier, since learners will be tested on the content of the syllabus. In short, a clear, well designed syllabus provides a foundation for both student- and teacher-accountability (Cross, 1991; Richards, 1990b).

Cumming (1991a) indicates that syllabus design is a surprisingly complex process that can include at least three planning models: the time-tabling model, which is concerned with scheduling course activities sequentially; the content model, which focuses on content components; and the social context model, which relates the syllabus to administrators, institutions, programs, faculty, and students. Syllabus design usually begins with the establishment of objectives that take into account the needs of the writing program and the needs of the students; it is often based on program history and teacher experience in the writing program. General questions in gathering information for a discussion of syllabus design parallel and extend those in curriculum statement development:

1 What should the role of the teacher be?

2. What should the role of the learner be?

3. What is the learner expected to know at the end of the course?

4. What is the learner expected to be able to do at the end of the course?

5. What materials will facilitate the learning experiences?

6. What activities will facilitate the learning experiences?

7. What are the criteria for deciding on the order of the elements, materials, and activities in the syllabus?

8. What techniques of evaluation will be used to assess course outcomes?

Syllabus Design for Writing Courses

Designing a syllabus is a multifaceted decision-making process. Particularly in intensive language programs, but also in other writing programs with a series of writing classes, initial decisions concerning the formulation of class syllabi must take into account the integration of syllabi within the writing program. In most cases, syllabus designers must include in their discussions not only exit goals but also consideration of the language setting, of the other skills classes or writing classes, and of the program's needs (Dubin and Olshtain, 1986). Next, working closely with the curriculum statement, syllabus designers should consider the basic assumptions in curriculum development: are the goals of the writing class or program **language based**, **pattern-model–based**, **process based**, or some **combination** of the three?

Horizontal and Vertical Syllabi

If the writing syllabi are intended for a multiskill, multi-level intensive language program, the resulting series of syllabi can be either horizontal or vertical, depending on students' initial program placement. In a **horizontal syllabus**, students are initially placed in all classes at the same level. For example, a student is assigned to the high- intermediate level, and s/he attends all classes (writing, oral skills, culture, etc.) at that level. Syllabus designers have as their primary function the integration of all skills at a single level, with the integrated writing syllabus (or any single skill syllabus) a secondary concern (Figure 4–1). For a relatively homogeneous student population,

FIGURE 4–1 HORIZONTAL SYLLABUS DESIGN (INTENSIVE LANGUAGE PROGRAM): CLASSES AT A SINGLE LEVEL INTEGRATED ACROSS SKILLS

	Reading	Writing	Listening	Speaking
Advanced	→	→	→	→
High Intermediate	→	→	→	→
Low Intermediate	→	→	→	→
Basic	→	→	→	→

the horizontal syllabus facilitates the integration of language skills because all students at that level are in the same classes. A student can read about a topic in reading class, discuss the reading in oral skills classes, and write about it in the writing class. The more heterogeneous the student body, however, the more difficult it is to implement a successful horizontal syllabus. Many Chinese students, for example, have advanced grammar and reading skills but low-intermediate oral skills; some Arabic students have advanced oral skills but only basic writing skills. In contrast, the **vertical syllabus** provides entrance and exit skills for each writing class in the program, but has only limited consideration of the entrance and exit skills in other skill area classes (Figure 4–2). Students are initially placed in writing classes according to their entrance skills in writing, and in other skill areas according to their placement scores on those tests. Such flexible placement procedures can result, for example, in a student being placed in a low-intermediate reading class, a basic writing class, and a high-intermediate oral skills class. The vertical syllabus, then, allows initial discrete placement of students according to their individual strengths and weaknesses, but it may hamper the planning of skill integration at single levels because students in the writing class may be in a variety of levels in other skill areas.

FIGURE 4–2 VERTICAL SYLLABUS DESIGN (INTENSIVE LANGUAGE PROGRAM): INTEGRATED CLASSES IN A SINGLE SKILL AREA

	Reading	Writing	Listening	Speaking
Advanced				
High Intermediate				
Low Intermediate				
Basic				

Examples of **horizontal** and **vertical syllab**i follow.*

HORIZONTAL SYLLABUS
BASIC LEVEL/LANGUAGE-BASED

Proficiency
The typical entering elementary student . . . lacks **control of basic structures**. There are few, if any, sentences where errors do not

*Portions of the syllabi cited in this chapter were selected on the basis of (a) their examples as syllabi types, (b) their possible use as models by readers of this text, and (c) the widest possible range of skill levels. Thus, in the first group of examples, I have used basic-level syllabi, which can be compared and contrasted, as well as a complete syllabus (from Colorado State University) in which the sequencing of syllabi is particularly clear.

interfere with meaning. Often what is written is no more than a list of ideas. The composition is rarely over 100 words long. The goal is for the student to reach at least an intermediate level with **control of simple structures** and generally comprehensible ideas.

Introduction and Goals
It is important for the writing teacher to view the elementary class as a foundation for the more advanced classes which will follow. It is a time to stress the basics, including legible handwriting, spelling, neatness, **basic punctuation and capitalization** rules, and carefully following directions. Students are working at both the sentence level and the paragraph level. In the former, which should make up a large percentage of all writing done, they are asked to answer **WH ques-tions based on readings** [guided writing], write sentences about stories they've read or about activities from Communication Situations class, or **write sentences from dictation** on familiar topics.   (emphases mine)

Elementary Writing Syllabus (Grammar + Reading; textbook is *Side by Side* by Molinsky and Bliss)

Item	Reading and Writing
Whose?	Reinforce: comprehension questions
But	Combining phrases and clauses
Simple past, irregular verbs	Paragraph of narration
How often?	Reinforce: comprehension questions
Comparison (nouns: the same as, different from)	Compare/contrast paragraph
Subject pronouns	Pronoun reference exercises
Polite request: May I, would you	Letters of request
Prepositions (time)	Introduce prepositions/dates
Present—habit, fact	Description of a holiday

Ohio Program of Intensive English
(3-level writing program)
University of Ohio

VERTICAL SYLLABUS
MULTI-LEVEL/PATTERN-MODEL–BASED

Basic Level:

Concentration: fluency through frequent in-class and out-of-class writing, journals, group writing projects
Objectives:
1. a knowledge (though not always accurate production) of punctuation, capitalization, subject-verb agreement, use of pronouns, correct spelling;
2. growing knowledge of varied sentence structures;
3. significant work in sentence combining, especially in the understanding of independent and dependent clauses;

4. introduction to pre-writing through class discussion;
5. understanding of the **rudiments of the paragraph**: what it looks like, that a **paragraph is about one   topic**, and that specific detail is part of a paragraph;
6. basic understanding (though not always accurate production) of **descriptive and narrative** (i.e., personal experience) writing in structured and free situations;
7. initial practice in revision.

Projects: handbooks for incoming students, recipe books, etc.

Low Intermediate Level

Concentration: the paragraph—conventional structures, development of information for an audience

Objectives:
1. growing accuracy in punctuation, capitalization, spelling, grammatical structures, and sentence structures;
2. focused work on the **topic sentence** and use of specific detail;
3. work on pre-writing strategies (e.g., brainstorming, cubing, looping, trees);
4. understanding and production of conventional methods of paragraph development **(modes**, e.g.,**cause-effect, classification, comparison/contrast)**
5. growing knowledge and practice of the use of connectors;
6. a basic understanding of the concept of writing for an audience;
7. introduction to peer editing, individual and group revision.

Projects: IEP newsletters

High Intermediate Level

Concentration: the essay; **conventional structures** and development of information for specific audiences

Objectives:
1. continued growth in accuracy in punctuation, capitalization, spelling, grammatical structures, sentence structures, and connectors (individualized remedial work)
2. understanding of the analogical link between paragraph and essay development and the expansion of paragraphs to essays;
3. understanding and function of and **production of topic sentences** and **thesis statements**, **introduction** and **conclusion techniques**, detail and development;
4. extended use of pre-writing strategies, group work, and peer editing;
5. focus on revision and monitoring strategies;
6. focus on the expectations of readers/audiences;
7. basic knowledge of reading/writing connections for investigating, explaining

Project: library module

<u>Advanced Level</u>

<u>Concentration</u>: academic writing and university writing assignments for the U.S. academic reader

Objectives:

1. continued growth in use of sophisticated sentence structures, coherence devices, and pre-writing and revising techniques;
2. analysis of academic writing assignments, relation of essay types to fulfill academic assignments;
3. continued work on **organization and development of essays** to fulfill expectations of U.S. academic audiences;
4. focus on reading/writing connection for effective writing in arguing, critiquing, persuading, exploring;
5. understanding of effective library research in individual major fields;
6. focus on persuasive and critical writing, research writing.

Project: research paper in major field   (emphases mine)

Intensive English Program
(4-level writing program)
Colorado State University

Sometimes a combination syllabus provides a workable solution to the problems raised by the horizontal and vertical syllabi. The combination syllabus requires that students entering the intensive language program be placed at the same level in two skill areas, such as grammar and writing, or reading and writing. In other words, in what is essentially a vertical syllabus, writing and grammar classes are integrated and planned horizontally as well as vertically. In another program, reading and writing classes are designed horizontally, perhaps with the classes being taught in a two-hour block by a single teacher or by two team teachers.

COMBINATION HORIZONTAL-VERTICAL SYLLABUS
INTERMEDIATE-LEVEL LANGUAGE AND PATTERN-MODEL–BASED

Review	**Teach in Depth**	**Introduce**
<u>Writing Objectives: Level 3</u>		
Paragraphs	Basic organization	Five-paragraph
narration	intro/body/concl.	compositions
description		
process	Three-paragraph	Argument
	compositions:	
	comparison	Summary
	classification	
	cause/effect	Paraphrase
	Transitions	Major mechanical errors:
	Outlining	frag, comma splice,
		run-on

Academic research skills
  book parts
  card catalog
  fact tools
  World Book
  researched composition

Grammar Objectives, Level 3

Tenses: present, past, progressives, future	**Present perfect**	Present perfect continuous
Questions: yes/no, WH, tag	**Passive**	
Articles	**Modals**	
Nouns: count/noncount		
prepositions	**Verbals**	

International English Language Institute
(6-level program, Grammar-Writing syllabus)
University of North Texas

Designing the Linear Syllabus

Whether the syllabus design is for an intensive language program or a single writing class, one more decision concerning overall syllabus design must be made before the syllabus is completed: whether the class syllabi will be linear or modular. In the **linear syllabus**, learners are expected to master a sequence of units of work; specific "microskills" or mini-competencies are learned, then integrated into "macroskills." Each writing class syllabus builds on the previous class, focusing on the "spiraling" of writing skills. Teachers and students work with the same skills more than once, but each time a particular skill reappears, it is at a more complex or difficult level, in different situations and for different purposes. In contrast, a **modular syllabus** integrates all skills under a thematic, topical, or situational context.

Perhaps the most widely used syllabus is linear: in either a single class or in a series of classes in a writing program, the objectives for each syllabus are arranged along a continuum. Sometimes the linear syllabus develops from a language-based curricular goal and is organized primarily around grammar and sentence patterns, or around skills and subskills. Other times the linear syllabus will be pattern-model based or process based. Developers of such linear syllabi believe that mastery of the distinct points (subskills, microskills, mini-competencies) along the continuum should result in effective macro-learning. Sometimes the sequence of learning is planned from the simple to the more complex: from word mastery to phrase mastery to sentence mastery to paragraph mastery to essay mastery. Other linear syllabi begin with the most frequently used forms (such as the *to be* verb in the basic writing class) or skills (for example, letter writing) and advance to the less frequently used forms of writing.

In designing such a syllabus, once the sequence has been decided, teachers need to focus on the **scope** (the amount of material to be covered in each course). Internal gradations of each unit and sub-unit are identified, analyzed, selected, and ordered over the period of time allotted by the class or the writing program (Dubin and Olshtain, 1986).

LINEAR SYLLABUS

MULTI-LEVEL/LANGUAGE-BASED

Course Descriptions and Objectives

Description: Basic Writing (Level 1)
Introduces kernel sentence patterns of written English for high beginning ESL students. Includes basic sentence transformations.

Objectives: The students will be able to
1. write the **four kernel sentence patterns** of American English in the affirmative statement, negative statement, and yes/no question form;
2. write such sentences with appropriate **sentence mechanics:**
3. demonstrate a familiarity with the basics of the American English spelling system.

Description: Intermediate Writing I (Level 2)
Focuses on the development of sentence-level writing skills. Emphasizes English punctuation, capitalization, and spelling for intermediate ESL students.

Objectives: The student will
1. **see 1 and 2 above**
2. significantly increase her/his ability to use **correct English spelling**

Description: Intermediate Writing II (Level 3)
Continues the development of sentence-level writing skills. Emphasizes English **punctuation, capitalization, and spelling.** Introduces English paragraph structure.

Objectives: The students will
1. **see 1 and 2 above**.
2. be able to write sentences using appropriate sentence mechanics
3. be able to write simple narrative paragraphs.

(emphases mine)

Programs in English as a Second Language
(8-level writing program)
William Rainey Harper College (Chicago)

Intermediate Composition

Purposes:

— To increase the students' fluency in written English—and their confidence so that they can communicate in written English
— To teach students to write the academic English combination of generalization and evidence
— To have the students learn to communicate using other types of written English—business letters, reports on interviews, **narratives** (of folk stories or legends or lives of known people from their countries)

Placement

Students who enter Intermediate Composition should have a basic understanding of English sentence structure; they should be able to write sentences of some complexity, using a variety of coordinating conjunctions and a few subordinates (e.g., because, although)

Objectives: Students will

— have many opportunities to write for communication; work within the writing process of pre-writing, writing, revising, editing, and production of final drafts
— the emphasis will be on revisions to improve and expand meaning so that students will come to recognize revision as a basic part of their expectations for their own writing
— learn a word-processing system and typing to make easier the revision of drafts and the production of attractive final products to provide examples to illustrate generalizations
— learn the **format and style of business letters** in the U.S.

Weekly Plans:

Week 1
— Assessment of the students' ability to **write sentences**— especially sentences on a particular topic
— Introduction of the students to the computer lab—word-processing and language-based software

Weeks 2–10
— Writing on a variety of topics and in a **variety of formats**, including **letter writing**, writing of **narratives**, etc.
— Work in the computer lab—writing and revising during a class with the teacher available to help—class could meet in the lab one day each week
— Study of ways to expand the kinds of sentences that they can write
— Introduction to the idea that academic writing combines generalizations with details
— Reading to seek information to use in writing

Grading:
— Assignments: 50%
— Final examination: 50%

High Intermediate Composition

Purposes:
— To teach students to write **multiparagraph compositions** that combine 3 or 4 paragraphs but that do not have full introductions or conclusions
— To introduce students to the selection and presentation of appropriate evidence through reading in various sources of information available through the university library

Placement
Students should enter the course with the ability to produce a short composition of paragraph length that combines a generalization with some type of support

Objectives: Students will learn
— to write using the process of pre-writing, writing, revising, editing, and presenting a final document—indirectly about **introductions/bodies/conclusions**—perhaps by writing business letters (salutation, body, closing) or narrative
— about reading as a source of information for writing a word-processing system and typing to make easier the process of revision and production of academic writing

Weekly Plans:

Week 1
— Assessment of writing ability
— Introduction to the computer lab
— Introduction/review of pre-writing strategies
— Writing

Weeks 2–10
— Practice in writing process
— Practice in **selection of evidence from reading**
— Production of many different types of written English, including business letters, narratives, reports on interviews, and **multiparagraph responses** to particular topics

Grading:
— Assignments   50%
— Final examination: 50%

Advanced Composition

Purposes: To prepare
— potential undergraduates for English 111 and for other undergraduate assignments
— graduate students for the writing required in their degree study

Placement
Students who enter Advanced Composition should be able to

write multiparagraph compositions, but are not expected to be able to write complete introductions and conclusions.

Objectives: Students will learn
— the process of pre-writing, writing, revising, and final preparation of **academic papers**
— to write academic papers made up of **multiple paragraphs** with introductions, middles, and conclusions
— about the appropriate selection and presentation of **supporting evidence for academic writing** in the U.S.
— to **analyze topics** presented by their instructors and to write appropriate papers in response to those topics
— about the meaning of "plagiarism" and ways to avoid this academic crime

Weekly Plans:

Week 1
— Introduction to the writing of **academic essays** through the study of sample essays and course syllabi
— Introduction to pre-writing tasks
— Writing of **first essay**
— Introduction to Computer Lab

Weeks 2–10
— Study of academic writing requirements
— Writing and revisions of own essays
— Writing and revision of other types of academic writing, e.g., written examinations

Grading:
— Along with other assignments, students should write at least 4 complete essays each term.
— The final examination will be scored by the teacher of the course and by another teacher of Advanced Composition.
— Students will be passed who can write an adequate first draft during the final examination period.

— Assignments: 50%
— Final examination: 50%   (emphases mine)

English as a Second Language Program
(3-level writing program/Quarter System)
Georgia State University

LINEAR COMBINATION SYLLABUS
MULTI-LEVEL/PATTERN-MODEL–BASED

Level 1 Writing Skills

- Sentence Level: write simple sentences using the acquired **grammar structures** based on answers to questions
- Paragraph Level:
    Content: write a short autobiography

write a short note, clear and legible, giving an explanation, request, information

Organization: chronological order
logical format for above assignments

Mechanics: **standard paragraph form**
center title, indent first sentence
basic conventions (capitalization, punctuation)

- Editing Skills: transformations in connected discourse
changing plural to singular
pronouns, affirmative to negative
proof-reading: subject-verb agreement, an/a, spelling

Level 2 Writing Skills

- Sentence Level: same as Level 1 + **generate a main idea sentence** and **write supporting sentences**, given a topic
- Paragraph Level:
  Content: same as Level 1 +
  write at least a one-paragraph passage describing themselves, their families, their country, etc.
  write letters to give autobiographical information, issue an invitation, thank host

  Organization: write a simple **process passage**, such as getting a driver's license, cashing a check, buying an airline ticket, taking a bus to the mall, doing the laundry
  use simple transitional words

  Mechanics: same as Level 1 + punctuate a series and punctuate a compound sentence
- Editing: using teacher-generated questions, make appropriate changes in the text; order sentences

Level 3 Writing Skills

- Sentence Level: Same as Levels 1 and 2 + **write main idea**, sentences and **outline sentences** based on picture uses
- Paragraph Level:
  Content: same as Levels 1 and 2 + write instructions on how to make a good impression at a party, how to use a copying machine, how to get to a particular location
  write letters to, for example, solicit information about housing, admissions, etc.
  complain to landlords, advisors, etc.

  Organization: write at least a **two-paragraph passage** using **classification, comparison /contrast, examples**; use transitional words

describe an accident, an event
analyze cause/effect, why, for example,
a college is popular/unpopular,
a person is healthy/unhealthy
the causes of famine
Mechanics: same as Levels 1 and 2 + punctuate complex
sentences, appositives, adverbials

- Editing: same as Levels 1 and 2 +
use an edit sheet to check for central idea,
sufficient development, appropriate arrange
ments of ideas:
practice group editing, peer editing, self-editing
(emphases mine)
Intensive English and Orientation Program
(5-level writing program)
Iowa State University

Designing the Modular Syllabus

The focus of the **modular syllabus** is on content rather than
form, on all skills rather than separate skills. In intensive English
language program writing classes, for example, the basic level language
proficiency classes may be integrated with grammar classes and/or with
oral skills classes; learners study language through a series of topics (for
example, food, health, clothing) and learn writing skills through the
content material or "topic areas" (Van Ek and Alexander, 1980). At the
intermediate level, in a theme-based module on automobiles, the
writing class may study a situation (such as an auto accident) and then
report on the situation from a variety of viewpoints (the victim, a
bystander, the policeman). In the advanced writing class, students
might read about a topic (such as solar energy, soccer, the elderly),
discuss that topic in groups, and then write about that topic.

MODULAR SYLLABUS
ADVANCED LEVEL/PATTERN-MODEL– AND PROCESSED-BASED

Advanced Reading/Writing Syllabus (Level 4)

Writing: Students at the advanced level of instruction should already
be fluent writers. The curriculum at this level emphasizes the ability
to **extract** and **manipulate information from various sources**
in order to effectively address a topic for a particular **purpose** and
appropriate methods of overall organization. To accomplish
this larger goal, the curriculum also stresses effective use of **thesis
statement, development of clearly stated main ideas** with
adequate and convincing detail, and **appropriate methods of
overall organization.** In the tutorial component of the class,

accuracy and appropriateness of lexical and grammatical choice are also emphasized. In addition, matters of tone and **audience** are considered in each individual writing task.

The majority of class time is devoted to **pre-writing discussion** (to establish background information for writing tasks), **peer editing activities,** examination of **models**, and review of composition notions. Class time should focus on grammatical materials only when a problem is common to the majority of the class members. The weekly student-teacher tutorial provides an opportunity to address **individual** student questions concerning grammatical accuracy as well as matters of content, organization, and lexical choice.

As at the intermediate level, writing tasks should emerge from the content of the reading component. The course is **organized around content themes, requiring students to explore topics of interest** and to relate information from several and varied types of sources. The focus of instruction should always center on the particular content theme, not on any specific compositional notions (e.g., thesis statement, supporting detail, transitions). These compositional notions are explicitly taught only in relation to the specific writing task, never in isolation.   (emphases mine)

American Language Program
(4-level reading/writing program)
The Ohio State University

Content-Based Syllabus Design

In practice, a combination of approaches to syllabus design is often used (P. Johnson, 1981). One approach to syllabus design that incorporates elements of many of the aspects of course development discussed above is the **content-based syllabus**. Designed for students at the advanced level of language proficiency, content-based classes are closely related to the tenets of the communicative approach (see Chapter 3). In the following paragraphs, syllabus approaches are shown within brackets.

May Shih (1986, 1992) defined **content-based approaches** to teaching ESL academic writing as writing connected to the study of specific audience **[pattern-model-based]**and subject matter that develops thinking, researching, and writing skills authentically. In addition, content-based instruction and its corollaries, English for Specific Purposes (ESP), English for Science and Technology (EST), and English for Academic Purposes (EAP), to some extent parallel the "writing across the curriculum" movement of NES teachers and researchers of the past decade (Brennan and Naerssen, 1989). The focus in content-based instruction is on the development of curricula and materials especially designed both to teach language **[language-**

based] and to meet the needs of students in future academic work and/or particular fields of study (Black and Kiehnhoff, 1992; Horowitz, 1986a, 1986c; Pearson, 1981; Schleppegrell, 1985, 1991) or areas of work (Mosallem, 1984; Svendsen and Krebs, 1984). Coffey describes the purpose of content-based instruction in EAP: to satisfy a student's need for "quick and economical use of the English language to pursue a course of academic study" (1984, p. 3).

Ann Snow and Donna Brinton (1988) stressed the integrative aspects of content-based classrooms in which students concentrate on reading, writing, and study skills concurrently, while studying a single topic [**modular syllabus**]. Shih (1986) and others (Spack, 1988; Stoller, 1990) described several types of content-based EAP/ESP ESL writing courses:

1. the topic-centered module or mini-course, in which graduate or undergraduate students of any language proficiency level read and discuss materials about a single topic and then write about that topic, either individually, in pairs, or in groups [**modular syllabus**];

2. content-based courses organized around sets of readings, films, and/or videotapes on selected topics, in which graduate or undergraduate students, usually at the intermediate or advanced levels of English language proficiency, read and write intensively about a single topic or a series of topics;

3. ESP courses that are field specific in which graduate students in a single field (such as economics or mechanical engineering) study together in a "sheltered" atmosphere, usually within an intensive language program, reading and writing exclusively about their subject matter courses;

4. "adjunct courses," in which ESL teachers and content-based lecturers collaborate in the teaching process; most often this collaborative teaching takes place with post-admission university undergraduates. In such courses, the ESL writing teachers work with the content teachers to develop writing assignments, and the ESL students work with their ESL teachers on those assignments [**pattern-model–based**]; and

5. writing resource centers staffed with ESL writing tutors or teachers who work with post-admission students, both graduate and undergraduate, on a walk-in or appointment basis, individually or in groups, on specific course-related writing assignments [**pattern-model** and **language based**].

Some controversy surrounds the content-based approach. Because the arguments are central to any discussion of syllabus design, they are briefly summarized here. In opposition to the proponents of content-based teaching, Ruth Spack (1988) argues that pattern-model–based ESL writing courses should not prepare students for particular writing tasks based on the requirements of their fields of study. Spack believes that the narrowness of teaching patterns and specific strategies for meeting audience expectations truncates student writing development. Rather, she insists that composition courses for NNSs should focus on general writing principles through the teaching of literary analysis and personal writing (process-based), leaving the application of the principles of writing to the future demands of student course work. Daniel Horowitz (1992) takes Spack to task for her conclusion that the study of literary analysis and personal writing by ESL freshman composition students will "transfer" to "other courses which demand logical reasoning, independent thinking, and careful analysis of text" (Spack, 1985, p. 721). He argues, instead, for an EAP, content-based approach, that is, a direct addressing of writing assignments, structures, and audience expectations that will better prepare students for their academic work.

Evaluating and Revising Existing Curricula/Syllabi

Evaluating existing ESL writing curricula and syllabi requires many of the same processes that are used in developing new curricula. Three reasons for such examination are (a) to inform ESL writing teachers about a class/program, (b) to involve ESL writing teachers in the formulation of curricula and syllabi, and (c) to evaluate the need for curriculum/syllabus revision. At the least, the existing **curriculum** should be examined for its current relevance; it should clearly identify and describe the student population; it should define the class, program, and institutional goals; and it should list exit criteria from the course/program. The existing **syllabi** should:

1. provide teacher, student, and class/program profiles;
2. define underlying theoretical and practical assumptions of the class/program;
3. give clear pedagogical guidelines for teacher and student performances;
4. provide adequate direction and materials for evaluation of the students, the teacher, and the class (Dubin and Olshtain, 1986; Richards, 1990b).

Identifying the philosophical assumptions behind the development and implementation of an existing curriculum or syllabus can be difficult. In the revision of the curriculum and/or syllabus, discussion of the following questions will help to articulate the philosophy of prior and current curriculum goals and syllabus objectives.

Language-Based Syllabus

1. What elements, items, or discrete units of language content should be included?
2. In what order or sequence should the discrete elements be presented in the syllabus?
3. How should elements be presented to facilitate language acquisition?
4. How should the materials contribute to language learning in the classroom? (Dubin and Olshtain, 1986)

Pattern-Model–Based Syllabus

1. What prose conventions are expected by the audience?
2. How can the students best learn these conventions?
3. What models of successful/effective writing can be used to assist students in learning the structures of English prose?
4. How should patterns/models of effective writing best be used to facilitate learning?

Process Syllabus

1. How can each individual in class be uniquely valued?
2. How can each student reach self-individualization through writing?
3. How can the teacher facilitate individual development and fluency?
4. How can the teacher establish the positive class atmosphere in which learning occurs?

An evaluation of a combination ESL writing curriculum/syllabus might include answers to questions from all three syllabi types above. For example, a combination curriculum or syllabus might stress grammatical structures and fluency at the basic levels of language proficiency, organization of patterns and audience awareness at the intermediate level, and idea generation and self-discovery at the advanced levels.

Investigating the possibilities for revision of existing curricula and syllabi should occur frequently: a writing program develops and improves by regular oversight and revision. Below are some remarks written in the margins of an existing curriculum and class syllabus by the teachers in one ESL writing program; note that the teachers had first examined the document carefully, then indicated specific areas that should be further evaluated and perhaps changed.

- I am not completely satisfied with this lengthy approach to major writing assignments at the 02 level that I am coordinating. My biggest concern is that students are almost always working on more than one different composition at the same time. For example, they may be brainstorming and outlining one, while writing another. I think sometimes both students and teachers feel they are getting lost in a paper maze. This semester I am trying to work on ways to streamline the process [designed in the original syllabus] in order to shorten it. I still feel, however, that students need to become acquainted with and practice the different steps one goes through when doing out-of-class written assignments. At the 02 level, because this is often new to students, I find the process to be somewhat slow, particularly during the first half of the semester.

- How do we emphasize the differences between using models and plagiarism? When [in the existing syllabus] do students learn when copying is and is not appropriate?

- What are the lengths of compositions? Should we have our students write longer (say 500 to 1000 words) papers at least a few times? [No long assignments existed in the original syllabus.] Very few KU courses require only 200–300 word essays except on essay tests.

- This book has no context: it's therefore hard to absorb. It was a good idea in theory to use it. However, the exercises/vocabulary were just too difficult for all sections but the highest writing classes.

- Let's consider a combination structure/writing course. This could be done at all levels or we could decide to try it out first at a few levels, realizing that scheduling may be more difficult to arrange at the advanced levels. These two skills could be integrated by one teacher, which would presumably result in greater continuity and progress for the students.

- How about an optional one-hour library research course which would combine library, reading, and writing skills and could be offered for advanced students? This course would not take away considerable time from the reading and writing courses which could then be used more valuably.

- How much progress are our students actually making in their writing courses? What statistics have been done? What kind should we do?

- We need a more effective approach to making textbook decisions. All of the texts, which are now selected in isolation, should be reviewed in relationship to each other. . . . We may also want to develop a textbook evaluation form which would stress our main course objectives and would help us compare books in a standardized way.

Applied English Center
University of Kansas

Planning Curriculum and Syllabus Revision

The first step in the evaluation process of an existing curriculum or syllabus is gathering information:

1. current and previous student and teacher evaluations;
2. experiential and observational information;
3. student data from diagnostic, placement, progress, and exit writing samples;
4. theoretical and practical documentation from the field (such as academic journals and other ESL writing programs).

Second, discussion should focus on areas that have changed since the initial implementation of the curriculum or syllabus:

1. student/teacher profiles
2. class/program objectives
3. institutional goals or entrance criteria
4. advances in the field of ESL writing, current class materials.

Finally, questions concerning the specific curriculum or syllabus should be investigated and answered:

1. Are the goals/objectives still realistic and appropriate?
2. Are the approaches and methods current? flexible? Do they meet student needs?
3. Are the materials compatible with the syllabus? contextualized? authentic? culturally sensitive? Do they meet student needs?
4. Are the class/program resources (time, equipment, class size, out-of-class opportunities) adequate to implement the goals and objectives? to provide alternatives?

Revision of the curriculum statements and course syllabi are so on-going in writing programs that the curriculum statement from the Tutorium in Intensive English (University of Illinois at Chicago) earlier in this chapter has already been revised. The revisions occurred as writing teachers in the program discovered that what they were actually practicing in their classes differed substantially from the original curricular goals. The revised curriculum statement follows.

As writing teachers, we should strive

(1) to prepare students for, but not necessarily simulate, the kinds of tasks they will have to perform in "real-life" ESL settings, which may include American colleges, universities, and professional work environments.

(2) to help students develop and refine their abilities to assert and substantiate through written expression their ideas, opinions, and observations by teaching specific methods of organization, support, and clarification.

(3) to reduce the self-defeating effects of writer's block by encouraging fluency of ideas, if not written expression, through in-class activities such as brainstorming, pre-writing, freewriting, and oral discussion.

(4) to remind ourselves that writing in a second language is a learning process, requiring varying degrees of personal adjustment on the part of individual language learners, and as such, the writing of our students will improve most profoundly when the focus of our feedback is on content as well as form.

(5) to get students to take increasing responsibility for each other's writing whenever possible by teaching and reinforcing the concept of constructive criticism through such activities as peer correction and review.

(6) to get students to share the responsibility for each other's writing whenever possible by teaching and reinforcing the concept of constructive criticism through such activities as peer correction and review.

(7) to help students develop their repertoire of English words by reinforcing through writing vocabulary encountered in reading, listening, and speaking classes or other situations.

(8) to exploit the relationship between reading and writing whenever possible.

At all levels of instruction, writing activities centered on particular topics or rhetorical forms should progress from controlled to freer tasks. Teachers should include grammar and vocabulary exercises as needed, but the primary focus should be on composition. Teachers should allow students ample opportunities to write, not just talk about how to write. There should be a balance between in-class and take-home assignments.

Tutorium in Intensive English
The University of Illinois at Chicago

Evaluating Textbooks

Textbooks for ESL writing classes are usually chosen to fit syllabus objectives. Often, teachers choose from an approved list of texts; sometimes they may use any text they choose. Occasionally, textbooks serve as the basis for the class syllabus. In each case, evaluating textbooks is vital to the success of the class. The best single criterion for textbook evaluation is the recommendations of previous teachers of the class. A simple form like the one on the next page can be used to elicit such information.

TEXTBOOK EVALUATION

Teacher _____Class:_____ Date:_____Textbook: _____

1. Textbook Description:
   Type:
   Level:
   Key Features:
   Writing Activities that are emphasized:
   Writing Assignments that are emphasized:
2. Did this textbook meet the needs of the student? Why/Why not?
3. Did the text help you meet the syllabus objectives? Why/Why not?
4. Did you find this textbook easy to use? Why/Why not?
5. Was the Teacher's Manual for the textbook helpful? Why/Why not?
6. How much supplementary material did you have to develop? Why?
7. Did the text fit your teaching style? How? Why not?
8. List the most successful part(s)/lesson(s) in the book. Why was it successful?
9. List the most severe limitation(s) of this book.
10. What is your overall evaluation of the textbook? Be specific.
11. What advice would you give future teachers of the class who use this textbook? Be specific.

In the evaluation of new textbooks, specific criteria should be developed that match the performance objectives of the class (Benson et al., 1992; Skierso, 1990). The process of evaluating textbooks for use in a writing class might include investigation and discussion of the following:

1. The <u>introduction</u> (preface, rationale) to the text, which should include:
   A. a description of the scope and sequence of the book
   B. a description of the teacher/learner audience for the book (age, language level, educational background, etc.);
   C. a description of significant organizational features of the text;
   D. statements about the author's educational and linguistic points of view.

2. The <u>pedagogical assumptions</u> of the textbook:
   A. language based? model based? process based? a combination?
   B. appropriate for a horizontal or a vertical curriculum?
   C. arranged linearly or modularly or in a combination?

3. The <u>Table of Contents</u>:
   A. as a timeline for use, does it fit the class or need much adapting?
   B. content: culturally sensitive? contextualized? authentic materials?
   C. is there an index for quick reference and cross-referencing?

4. The <u>layout</u> of the book:
   A. clear, aesthetically pleasing?
   B. for the students (not the teacher)?
   C. user-friendly, with attention to detail?
   D. well made, so that it will not readily fall apart?

5. A careful reading of some of the <u>materials</u> in the textbook: do they
   A. provide sufficient tasks and exercises for both in-class work and homework?
   B. provide alternative materials in terms of learner tasks, learning styles, and presentation techniques?
   C. provide opportunities to achieve expected and appropriate outcomes?

6. The <u>Teacher's Manual</u> (usually available from the publisher without cost):
   A. does it consist of more than answers to exercises?
   B. does it have additional and supplementary exercises, quizzes?
   C. are there suggestions for teaching and problem-solving?
   D. is there adequate support for the teacher?*

Conclusion

The decision chart below outlines the general processes in curriculum and syllabus design discussed in this chapter.

Needs Assessment Considers:	students class/program teachers institution
Curriculum Statement Investigates:	language-based assumptions pattern-model–based assumptions process-based assumptions a combination of the above
Syllabus Design Focuses on:	single class OR writing program (series of classes)

<u>Syllabus Type</u>	<u>Organizational Focus</u>
language-based	single class OR writing program syllabus
pattern-model–based	horizontal OR vertical syllabus
process-based	linear OR modular syllabus
combination	combination syllabus

*My thanks to the teachers who participated in the USIA-sponsored seminar at the University of Veszprém, Hungary, during the summer of 1991, for their assistance in designing this list.

No matter what approach to syllabus design is used, writing classes should have stated curricula and syllabi, with stated goals and objectives. If such goals and objectives are not made explicit, questions of content, methodology, and evaluation cannot be systematically addressed (Richards, 1990c). Donald Bowen et al. (1985) and Margaret Pusch (1981) suggest the following as the "bare bones" of completed syllabus content that should be available to teachers:

1. a general statement of course purpose (directly related to the goals of the curriculum)
2. a statement concerning selected approaches to syllabus design that fits the participants and the curricular goals
3. a student profile (academic, personal, and motivational)
4. a teacher profile
5. relevant, useful instructional objectives for teachers and students; organization of learning experiences
6. performance objectives: clear standards, specific outcomes of the course, rate of progress
7. exit criteria specifications
8. program profile: class size, calendar and hours allocations, time and resource constraints
9. recommended texts, supplementary materials, and available audiovisual aids
10. structured out-of-class activities (e.g., tutorial activities, conferencing, Learning Center/Lab time, assigned homework time)
11. minimal instructional standards (i.e., teacher responsibilities)
12. evaluation: the process, context, and content for testing and grading.

Discussion Questions

1. In small groups, read through the following examples of **curriculum goals** and **syllabus objectives**. Identify the philosophical basis on which each is articulated. For example, which is an example of a language-based curriculum or syllabus? pattern-model-based? process-based? Which appear to be combinations? Is the syllabus horizontal, vertical, or a combination? linear, modular, or a combination? What does each tell you about the attitudes toward teaching and writing? Use the criteria for evaluating existing curricula/syllabi in this chapter as a basis for your analysis.

Curricular Goals:

1. to reinforce written command of certain structures learned in current and previous levels.

2. to construct sentences according to grammatical and semantic rules.

3. to attain fluency and clarity in writing through the use of a variety of sentence types containing transitional words, phrases and clauses that indicate logical organization and relationship of ideas; to correctly punctuate the sentence types taught at this and previous levels.

4. to construct coherent paragraphs which contain a clear topic sentence and specific supporting sentences.

5. to master organizational patterns in order to serve particular writing functions.

6. to produce paragraphs that serve the functions most commonly used in academic writing and business correspondence, and to use a format appropriate to the type of composition.

7. to correct, revise, and rewrite own work with the aid of feedback from the instructor.

8. to write well-organized, informative essays of four or more paragraphs, including an introduction, body, and conclusion.

English Language Institute
(5-level writing program)
MacCormac Junior College (Chicago)

Objectives and Goals [Curriculum Statement]

Students in all writing levels learn to master academic skills required by universities. From paragraph to essay, instructors provide a thorough explanation of rhetorical organization strategies and encourage rhetorical applications. In all writing classes, students are required to revise their writing, which is an essential part of the writing process, revision being distinguished from pure editing.

The writing levels are broken down into three more general levels: Beginning, Intermediate, and Advanced. All levels are encouraged to use prewriting techniques (such as brainstorming, clustering, outlining, prediscussion of topics, prereading, analysis of models), to determine audience and purpose in writing, to revise and to incorporate the use of dialogue journals.

American Language Program
(6-level writing program)
San Diego State University

Class Descriptions [Curriculum Statement]

Fundamentals: For very low level students who lack both facility and fluency in writing. Emphasis is on basic sentence structure and increasing fluency through writing assignments and journal writing. Introduce idea of topic sentence and development.

Academic Writing I: Students have serious problems with structure errors. Class emphasis is on developing structural control. Rhetorical skills are introduced. Thesis statement, development, and progression.

Academic Writing II: Students continue to work on structure problems, but at a more advanced level. Work on various sentences types and embedding. Rhetorical skills developed. More emphasis on essay form, thesis statement, etc.

Academic Writing III: Advanced course for rhetorical skills with remedial structure work as evidenced by student needs. Introduction to library and research.

> English to Speakers of Other Languages Program
> (7-level writing program)
> National-Louis University (Chicago)

Intermediate Writing Syllabus

Pre-Writing: in addition to meeting the requirements for the beginning-level student, the intermediate student will be able to

identify and explain unity as an element in writing

identify and explain cohesion as an element in writing

identify and explain the point of view of a writer

identify and explain the point of view of a reader

explain how language structures can be applied to enhance the writer's information (e.g., selecting passive voice to write about a procedure)

Writing: in addition to meeting the requirements for the beginning-level student, the intermediate student will able to

identify and generate the three parts of an essay: introductory paragraph, body, and concluding paragraph or statement

identify and generate essays based on the following logical structures:

cause/effect, comparison/contrast

order of importance and classification

illustrative incidents and example

description of sequence of event

definition

Post-Writing: the student will be able to

identify and mark written errors in sentences and paragraphs

identify improvements and corrections in final written drafts

assess feedback for future writing projects

> Maryland English Institute
> (3-level writing program)
> The University of Maryland

Level 2 [Low Intermediate] Syllabus

Focus

Students are introduced to the writing process and are given specific strategies enabling them to write a coherent and well-developed paragraph.

<u>General Overview</u>

Students practice:
1. exploring topics and examining ideas
2. developing and organizing these ideas
3. writing the first draft of the paragraph
4. editing and rewriting the paragraph

<u>Methods</u>

1. Teach pre-writing strategies
   A. discussing
   B. freewriting
   C. outlining
   D. interviewing
   E. listing ideas
2. Work through the prewriting activities with the students at first make lists, charts, and outlines together.
3. Stress correct spelling, capitalization and punctuation rules,and paragraph format.
4. Give students clear-cut writing objectives with each piece of writing.
   A. Who is their subject?
   B. Who is their audience?
   C. What is their purpose?
5. Introduce topic sentences.
6. Write paragraphs in class: some prewriting activities can precede this at home.
7. Provide an alternate system of feedback besides the composition teacher: another teacher, classmates . . .
8. Have students keep a journal.
   A. Don't give letter grades, but points or credit can be given for motivation.
   B. Students should be encouraged to write at least a page each time.
9. Reinforce the grammar, grammar/writing, and vocabulary skills taught at this level.
10. Use the ESL correction symbols to lessen student confusion.
11. Encourage students to use only an English/English dictionary in class as much as possible.
12. Hold teacher/student conferences to discuss individual writing problems.
13. Have the student write more than one draft of a paragraph.

English Language Center
(5-level composition program)
The University of Denver

Level 3 [Intermediate] **Course Outline**

<u>Objectives:</u>

1. To teach students to write sentences and paragraphs;

2. To teach students how to connect sentences using and, or, but, because, etc.
3. To teach students different ways of writing, such as:
    A. describing a person, place, or object
    B. comparing or contrasting
    C. explaining how to do something
    D. telling a story.
4. To help students get ideas for writing compositions.
5. To teach students how to improve their compositions.

<u>In-Class Activities:</u>
1. write during class;
2. work on writing assignments in pairs and small groups;
3. have large group discussions;
4. correct compositions in class;
5. rewrite compositions;
6. meet individually with the instructor in order to go over writing errors.

Intensive English Language Institute
(5-level intensive language program)
State University of New York at Buffalo

2. Writing programs begin with a perceived need to which the program of instruction is seen as a partial or full solution. Bowen et al. (1985) suggest that writing is the most demanding of the language skills. Do you agree or disagree? In light of that answer, discuss the three critical steps in developing an effective ESL writing program: planning, evaluation, and revision.

3. Examine three commercially prepared ESL writing textbooks from the list below. Look at the introduction (or preface), the Table of Contents, and the first two chapters of each textbook. Use the process discussed in this chapter to analyze the philosophy of writing teaching and writing learning in each textbook:

Bander, Robert G. (1983). *American English Rhetoric* (3rd Ed.). New York: Holt, Rinehart, and Winston.

Blanton, Linda L. (1979). *Elementary Composition Practice: Book* I. Rowley, MA: Newbury House.

English Language Center, Brigham Young University. (1990). *Expeditions into English: Writing 1*. Englewood Cliffs, NJ: Prentice-Hall Regents.

Frank, Marcella. (1989). *Writing as Thinking*. Englewood Cliffs, NJ: Prentice-Hall Regents..

McKay, Sandra. (1980). *Writing for a Specific Purpose*. Englewood Cliffs, NJ: Prentice-Hall.

Prince, Eileen. (1990). *Write Soon! A Beginning Text for ESL Writers*. New York: Maxwell Macmillan.

Reid, Joy. (1987). *Basic Writing*. Englewood Cliffs, NJ: Prentice-Hall.

Reid, Joy. (1993). *The Process of Paragraph Writing*, 2nd ed. Englewood Cliffs, NJ: Prentice Hall.

Spack, Ruth. (1990). *Guidelines: A Cross-Cultural Reading/Writing Text*. New York: St. Martin's Press.

4. Select one of the curriculum statements in this chapter. What might the syllabi for that writing class/program look like?

5. Using one of the class syllabi in this chapter, discuss what the syllabus for another class in that intensive language program might contain.

6. Working with a small group of peers, look at the teachers' comments on an existing curriculum on pages 23–24 in this chapter; then examine the process that follows that explains the information needed for evaluating an existing curriculum and syllabus. Which of the teachers' comments are related to the process? What other questions should the teachers be asking, and what other suggestions could they make?

Writing

1. Write a 2- to 3-page review of one of the three commercial textbooks you examined in Discussion Question #3 (above) for a group of teachers considering the book for use in an ESL writing class. Use the criteria listed in this chapter as a basis for your review.

2. In a small group, prepare three plans to carry out a needs analysis for the following situations:
   A. a group of university-bound, recently graduated high school students from a single country who will attend a two-month summer intensive writing program;
   B. a group of recently arrived adult immigrants from several countries who need a semester-long course in basic writing skills;
   C. a group of foreign graduate students from several countries who need a three-week intensive writing course in writing engineering research papers.

3. With a partner, use the results of the needs analysis from the previous question to prepare a curriculum statement for each program and a statement of exit objectives for each imagined class syllabus.

4. Working with a small group of classmates, select one of the class syllabi in this chapter. Write a brief curriculum statement for that writing class/program.

5. Examine the original and then the revised curriculum statement from the Tutorium in Intensive English, University of Illinois, Chicago program. In a brief paper, analyze the changes in philosophy that are apparent between the two.

6. Select a curriculum statement or a syllabus for a writing class that you particularly like. Then write a brief analysis, indicating how the curriculum statement or syllabus "fits" your developing teaching philosophy.

CHAPTER 5

Blind Random: The First Weeks

[T]he teacher fleshes out the syllabus and makes it real. Guided by the syllabus, she makes final decisions about classroom management, a style of relating to students, the number of steps in each point, individualization, the adaptation and supplementing of materials for classroom use, in-class testing, a feedback system, record-keeping, collaboration with other teachers, and the involvement of students in planning. The teacher tries to make the syllabus unfold on schedule, while testing whether the schedule is appropriate in that particular situation. . . . She adjusts for unexpected changes, such as the inexplicable differences from one term to the next among groups of students who should be identical, judging by available measurement instruments.   (Bowen and Madsen, 1985, p. 348)

You know what the first week of teaching has been like? It's like the step machine at my health club. I can choose one of three settings on that machine: a steady hill which is shown on the display screen; a Random pattern, which changes speeds every thirty seconds, following the pattern displayed on the screen; and one called Blind Random, in which the speeds change rapidly but the display screen gives no indication of upcoming changes. The first weeks of teaching ESL writing were like the Blind Random setting: I was always having to change my teaching plans—speed up, slow down, march in place—with no advance warning, no way to guess what was coming up next, always feeling off-balance and out of control.

(Shelley Reid, a first-time ESL writing teacher)

The two quotes above represent the extremes on a continuum. The first describes the ideal experienced teacher, and the second gives the feelings of a less experienced ESL teacher. The "blind random" analogy is apt; most new teachers experience the seeming randomness of the classroom, when plans or expectations must change rapidly. Yet there is almost always some contextual clue from students that the lesson, activity, or objective is not appropriate. Because most teachers of NESs have been the kinds of students they are teaching, and because NES writing classrooms are more or less culturally homogeneous, the new teacher understands both the expectations of the students and the verbal and nonverbal clues when things go awry. Past experience as a student has thus conditioned the NES teacher. The new teacher of ESL students, however, has limited knowledge about and experience with the diverse cultures of the students. As a consequence, almost certainly that new teacher encounters periods of randomness—of surprising incidents, time frames, and rhythms. In addition, because of the cultural differences between the teacher and students and among the students themselves, the randomness is frequently preceded by no clues—it occurs "blindly." The results are frustration, shock, and perhaps even panic for the teacher. This chapter attempts to ease the difficulties of the new teacher by providing information that will allow him/her to anticipate and plan, by describing the typical problems encountered during the first weeks of an ESL writing class, and by offering a variety of solutions suggested by experienced teachers.

In the list of criteria of successful teaching below (Blum, 1984), each statement is followed by an indication of the "blindness" and/or the "randomness" inexperienced teachers may encounter.

1. Instruction should be guided by a preplanned curriculum.
   (blindness and randomness due to unknown student needs)
2. Teachers should have high expectations for student learning.
   (blindness due to unknown previous student experiences)
3. Standards for classroom behavior should be high.
   (randomness due to different student and teacher perceptions)
4. Personal interactions between teachers and students should be positive.
   (blindness due to possible cross-cultural misunderstandings)

5. Class time should used for learning.
   (blindness due to possible differences in the definition of "learning")
6. Students should be carefully oriented to lessons (and to how to learn).
   (randomness and blindness due to differences in learning styles)
7. Instruction should be clear and focused.
   (randomness due to differences in student learning strategies)
8. Classroom routines should be smooth and efficient.
   (blindness and randomness due to diverse student needs)

9. Learning progress should be monitored closely.
   (blindness due to lack of known contextual clues)
10. When students don't understand, they should be retaught.
    (blindness and randomness due to limited teacher strategies for determining the success of a lesson)

teacher's attitude

classroom community

11. Instructional groups formed in the classroom should fit
    instructional needs.
    (randomness due to diverse student expectations)
12. Incentives and rewards for students should be used to promote
    excellence.
    (randomness due to differences in student and teacher
    perceptions)

For inexperienced teachers, this list may seem initially overwhelming; fortunately, however, the first four of the criteria encompass work that can be accomplished or at least begun prior to the class. For example, although the curriculum and syllabus will be only an inadequate guide to information about class diversity and expectations, they will in fact help orient the teacher. Such information about the students and about the writing program will help the new teacher become more aware of the potential for both blindness and randomness in the classroom. While expectations for behavior and interaction may need modification even on the first day of class, the more information gathered by the new teacher before the first day of class, the greater the sense of self-confidence.

The next four criteria focus on teacher attitudes that are often formed before the class begins, partially from the preplanned syllabus, partially on information about the students, and partially on the theory of second language learning that the teacher is developing. Statements in this second group of criteria (items five through eight) are conceptually clear and simply stated, but in practice they are much more complex, in part because of the blind and random aspects of each. Even experienced teachers preparing for a new class keep these principles in mind as they develop lesson plans, class objectives, and daily activities for their students. Beginning teachers should not expect immediate or complete success in implementing these criteria; all teachers spend their professional lives striving to meet them.

The final four criteria (items nine through twelve) are directly related to the teaching-learning interaction between teachers and students. They define a classroom atmosphere in which learning can take place most successfully. The establishment of a **classroom community** is essential for successful interaction. Members of the classroom community articulate and share aims and values, among which are mutual respect and a clear sense of mutual responsibilities for learning.

Learning about Student (and Teacher) Styles and Strategies

Identifying and analyzing the students who will be in the ESL writing class (and the needs of those students) form the basis for teaching: for creating a relevant, useful syllabus, selecting appropriate methods, and developing useful evaluation procedures (Bialystok, 1990; Chapelle and Greene, 1992; Pusch, 1981; Scarcella and Oxford, 1992; Willig, 1991). Many students in ESL writing classes come from educational systems in which there is great formality between students and teacher. Typically, fifty or more students listen as one teacher demonstrates and uses English (Dunnett et al., 1986). Many cultures include a tradition of deference and propriety in which questioning a teacher is unthinkable and passive learning is the key to success. For example, the high respect for age, authority, perfection, restraint, and practical achievements that form the basis for traditional Chinese values (Kroonenberg, 1990) may seem to a U.S. teacher to be passive and inappropriately silent behavior in a U.S. classroom. In contrast, the strong cooperative values and high level of social responsibility of many Latin societies (Diaz et al., 1989; Kagan, 1989) make the highly individualized and competitive values of U.S. students seem quite foreign to many Spanish-speakers. A class of ESL writing students from these diverse backgrounds can result in substantial classroom imbalance and even cross-cultural tensions as some "good" students respond appropriately while others struggle to find appropriate behaviors.

Indeed, for a newly arrived international student, a class in the United States must appear to be a structureless, anarchical situation for learning. In the United States, students are expected to take an active part in the learning process—to ask questions, to challenge each other and their teachers, and to work (often loudly) in groups. ESL students entering a U.S. class are immediately put into situations where they must share responsibilities, make decisions, evaluate their own progress, develop individual preferences, and synthesize and critically analyze material. As a result, they must confront a variety of different assumptions about learning and teaching (Dubin and Olshtain, 1986; Heath, 1992). A substantial part of any ESL teacher's responsibility is thus to orient her/his students to the expectations of the U.S. academic culture, where students are expected to take responsibility for their own learning and become actively engaged in their learning and problem-solving processes.

In addition, teachers must identify and analyze the cultural, social, and affective dimensions of language learning: how their students view teachers, and the differences in student attitudes toward learning. Such differences in world outlook can create interesting classroom scenarios. For example, a traditionally organized ESL writing class consisting entirely of Japanese students may be a quiet classroom indeed. With strong "face-consciousness" and a culture that considers group consensus a virtue, an individual Japanese student who volunteers answers risks exclusion from his group, even after class has finished (Shimazu, 1992). In a class composed mainly of Spanish speakers, however, the classroom may never be quiet, except when the teacher asks an individual a question. The attitude about cooperative work that pervades many Latin American countries may spill over in the ESL classroom. A class comprised of half Arabic speakers and half Indonesian speakers may be imbalanced in any oral activities, including group work. The Arabic speakers, who consider overlapping or interrupted conversations a sign of interest (Leki, 1992; Porter and Samovar, 1991) may seem to overpower the Indonesian students, for whom courtesy is embodied in pauses that precede conversation, a sign that the speaker is taking the subject seriously. A class of Chinese graduate students may have great difficulty in writing analytic, critical articles, preferring instead to quote authorities in the subject area and to avoid any form of criticism. Presenting their own ideas and worse, criticizing the ideas of authorities, would, from their cultural perspective, insult tradition and bring shame on them for their grossly individualistic stand.

In describing classroom cultures, Patricia Furey (1986) discusses attitudes toward the use of time and the social distance between teacher and student. For example, students from diverse cultural backgrounds have differing ideas about how much time should be spent covering material in a class; they also differ in their attitudes concerning punctuality and the importance of efficiency in procedures. Furey indicates that the degree of authority expected from the teacher as well as the degree to which the teacher directs and dominates class activities also depend to a large extent on the social distance established by each culture. For example, should the teacher focus her lessons on the best students? Should she be friendly toward her students? Should she ever admit that she "doesn't know" something? Should she always have the right answer?

Fortunately, ESL writing teachers have numerous opportunities to learn about their students. An open investigation by teachers and students into student perspectives can spark discussion, and students can often write dazzlingly detailed essays about their cultural beliefs. In addition to observing, researching, and studying cultural differences, teachers can ask their students to write about differences in educational systems, student and teacher expectations, student and teacher responsibility, and the like. Students may also be interested in describing their surprise and frustration as they try to adjust their learning styles and strategies to the new cultural community.*

*See Chapter 3 for more information on cross-cultural differences, and Chapter 6 for more cross-cultural activities to use in the ESL writing classroom.

Finally, teachers must also know—or begin learning—about their individual teaching styles. Do they prefer authoritative, participative, affiliative, or supportive relationships in the classroom? What kind of classroom atmosphere is best for them? What kind of activities are they most comfortable directing? What student qualities are most appealing for them? What kinds of classroom management processes are most productive for them? What forms of evaluation do they consider most appropriate? (See Appendix 2 for a sample survey to determine individual teaching style.) As the less-experienced teacher begins to formulate a theory of second language <u>teaching</u>, s/he must also identify and articulate her/his theory of second language <u>learning</u>: how *do* students learn to write in another language? What problems do they face? How do they solve those problems? How can the teacher intervene in and facilitate the processes successfully?

Planning Ahead

The more a teacher knows about the class s/he is going to teach, the easier the job will be. Perusing the existing curriculum to determine the overall goals of the writing class or program will assist the teacher in focusing her/his energies; a clear, progressive curriculum statement such as the one below can be a great help to the less experienced ESL writing teacher:

> Writing is viewed as an essential component of our curriculum. It is the task of the writing teacher to instill an appreciation and understanding of the writing process. This can be accomplished by providing a positive atmosphere and carefully guided instruction. The philosophy of this program revolves around one fundamental principle: If teachers supply academic writing tasks frequently and give specific direction with constructive feedback, they will provide the university with international students whose writing skills clearly meet academic standards.
>
> Intensive English Language Institute
The University of North Texas, 1991

Studying the syllabus for the class (and the syllabi for other classes in a sequenced writing program) will provide an overview of the course and essential information about how to attain the course objectives. For example, are the writing assignments in the syllabus developmental, moving from the subjective self and personal experience ("writer-based" prose) toward integration with the world outside the self ("reader-based" prose)? Are the assignments serially organized (separate, discrete, and independent) or are they cumulative, in which the assignments build on one another and reinforce prior skills (Rankin, 1990)? Richard Larson describes the truly sequential writing class/program as not merely a chronological arrangement of assignments but as a structure in which assignments are closely related to each other in service of the goals of the program. . . . The goal of each assignment in a true sequence should be to enlarge the student's powers of thinking, organizing, and expressing ideas so that he can cope with a more complex, more challenging problem in the next assignment.

(1986, p. 212)

Another way to prepare for a class before it begins is to become familiar with the textbook and other materials to be used in the class. Although the textbook is only one resource, studying it ahead of time will allow the sense of panic that arises between the syllabus and the reality of the class, particularly during the first two weeks, to diminish. Most important, talking with another teacher who has taught the course with that textbook will provide invaluable information—and, often, additional ideas and materials—not always available in the printed syllabi and textbooks.

If a weekly or a daily syllabus is provided, the teacher should look carefully at how much students and teacher are expected to accomplish in a week's time. How many pages in the textbook will be covered? What writing tasks will be assigned and evaluated? What specifically will students be learning during that time? Following are parts of three weekly schedules for three writing classes that were given to the students in those classes. Notice that although the first gives more detail and perhaps a greater initial feeling of security, the others give fewer cues, which may be better for experienced teachers who have fully developed their philosophies of teaching, but which are "blind" for less experienced teachers

WEEKLY SYLLABUS: HIGH INTERMEDIATE WRITING CLASS

Textbook: *The Process of Paragraph Writing* by Reid and Lindstrom

In Class	Assignments
Week #3	
Sentence combining; business letters; pre-writing; audience; titles; narrowing subjects to topics	*POPW*: read Chapter 2, pp. 20–26; Daybook: p. 36, paragraph about library experience
Week #4	
Writing rituals; topic sentences; modified topic sentences; in-class writing	*POPW*: read Chapter 2, pp. 40–55; Daybook: pp. 38-39 (choose one), Daybooks DUE
Week #5	
Topic sentences; techniques of; support; unity and coherence; pair work	*POPW*: read Chapter 3, pp. 56–69; Daybook: Exercise 3H (p. 58); analysis paragraph, Chapters 1–3

WEEKLY SYLLABUS: INTRODUCTION TO COLLEGE WRITING

Textbooks: *Steps in Composition*, 4th ed., by Troyka and Nudelman
Mosaic II: A Reading Skills Book by Wegman
Communication and Culture by Gregg
Refining Composition Skills by Smalley and Ruetten

Weeks	**Units of Instruction**
1–5	Introduction to college writing
	paragraph development (review)
	paragraph practice
	topic sentences
	focus and direction
	supporting details (facts, examples,definitions, etc.)
6–9	Organization of the three-part essay
	thesis
	development of body paragraphs
	introductions and conclusions
Ongoing	Review of writing problems
	sentence structure and word order
	verb forms and verb tenses
	subject/verb agreement
	fragments, comma splices, and run-on sentences
	punctuation problems
Ongoing	Vocabulary building
Ongoing	Reading
	reading and discussing essays
	critical evaluation
	main idea (thesis)
	major details and uses of support
	inferences
	drawing conclusions
	drawing conclusions and stating opinions
Ongoing	Essay writing based on essays studied
	three-part expository themes
	personal journal (eight-week period)
	written surveys of assigned readings

Elizabeth Rodriguez, Learning Skills Center
California State University/Sacramento

WEEKLY SYLLABUS: ADVANCED WRITING AND READING

Textbooks: *Developing Academic Reading Skills* by Latulippe
The Process of Composition by J. Reid
Research Matters by Hamp-Lyons and Courter

Weeks 2–4   Introduction to course materials; readings from texts and supplemental materials; vocabulary enrichment; intensive work on basic reading skills, paragraph development, beginning library skills, typing intensive.

Weeks 5–7   Readings from texts and supplemental materials, introduction to essay writing, advanced library skills, two essays due.

Diane K. Pollock, WESL Institute
Western Illinois University

Finally, the writing program (or the intensive language program) itself may provide an orientation for new teachers in the form of meetings prior to the term and, perhaps, continuing meetings throughout the term. An orientation meeting should provide the participants with a question period, during which they might ask about certain parameters:

1. Who ARE the students? What are their needs? What are their expectations? Their ages? Their backgrounds? Their prior education?
2. Who are the faculty mentors for this class?
3. Are additional (dittoed/photocopied) materials available for this class? Where?
4. Is another teacher teaching the same class who might be willing to act as a mentor?
5. Are any program-wide tasks such as pre-tests, permission forms, or policy sheets to be completed the first day of class?
6. Are there program-wide activities (for example, field trips or TOEFL exams) that are likely to affect the class?
7. Is there a new teacher's manual or another source of program curriculum objectives, program procedures, and policies?
8. How—and why—are the students "placed" into this class?

If, in addition to a program orientation, there is the opportunity to meet with previous teachers of the class and/or of the students in the class, other questions can be asked:

1. What has been the rate of progress of these students?
2. How does that rate coincide with program expectations?
3. What activities or tasks seem most appropriate? Most effective?
4. What kinds of personal interaction are appropriate for this class? Why?
5. Are there students with particular problems? What are they? What are possible solutions?

Teacher-Student Responsibilities

There is a contract—whether explicit or implicit—in all classrooms that defines the parameters and responsibilities of teachers and students. The roles for ESL writing teachers and students must be identified before the class begins and then explicitly established early in the class. ESL writing teachers indicate that these roles might include the following (some of which may seem "blind" and/or "random" for both teachers and students at the beginning of the class):

An ESL writing teacher has a responsibility to

- arrive in class well prepared and eager to help students learn
- provide students with a list of course objectives, assignments, and grading policies
- provide for the development of a classroom community in which mutual respect and responsibility exist
- facilitate classroom activities by planning, intervening, and mediating
- develop meaningful, sequential writing assignments
- provide multiple opportunities for students to investigate and practice writing processes
- act as a cultural informant, identifying and explaining the expectations of the U.S. academic audience and the U.S. academic classroom
- respond to and evaluate writing products
- balance classroom activities that reinforce reading, listening, and speaking skills as well as writing skills
- develop and clearly articulate the criteria for evaluation.

An ESL student in a writing class has the responsibility to

- arrive in class well prepared and eager to learn
- participate fully in the classroom community
- establish individual and group short- and long-term goals
- observe and analyze prior and present writing processes
- identify and determine the purposes for their writing
- analyze and practice appropriate formats for U.S. academic prose
- organize and present ideas appropriate for successful communication with the audience
- diagnose and revise drafts
- receive and give feedback on writing
- monitor for conventions of grammar, sentence structure, and so forth
- reflect on <u>what</u> s/he is learning and demonstrate <u>that</u> s/he is learning.

Operating Procedures

In addition to becoming familiar with the textbook(s) and objectives for the class, ESL writing teachers should formulate a clear series of procedures that they can then articulate to the students during the first day of class. Areas of procedural concern include attendance and participation policies, late papers, office hours, and grading processes. Specifically, students deserve to know the objectives of the course and their responsibilities in the class. Giving students a course information handout the first day of class is essential. Barbara Kroll (1991) lists the required information on a syllabus sheet that is given to students:

1. the number and kind of writing assignments students are expected to complete during the term
2. the timelines and deadlines for working on and completing papers
3. how many of the writing assignments will be done in class as "timed" pieces and how many will allow for the full drafted process, including one or more rounds of revision
4. what aspects of the composing process the class will cover
5. what aspects of English grammar and syntax, if any, will be directly addressed in class
6. what will constitute "satisfactory progress" in acquiring improved writing skills as the term moves along
7. how much reading if any (and possibly what specific readings) and
8. how the student's grade or a decision of credit–no credit will be determined (p. 251).

Below are two examples of such course handouts.

COURSE INFORMATION: WESL INSTITUTE
WESTERN ILLINOIS UNIVERSITY

Course Name: University Preparation / Reading–Writing
Instructor: James F. Conger   Office: 205 Memorial Hall (298-2224)
Course Texts: *Reading for Academic Success* by Lynch
            From Paragraph to Term Paper by Lipp
            Sentence Combination by Pack and Henrichsen
            Research Matters by Hamp-Lyons and Courter

Course Goals:

To improve reading/writing skills to a level where students can successfully complete a full-time study course in the English-speaking university setting. Specifically, this includes the following goals:

Writing: 1. to learn how to select writing topics that are both specific and appropriate; 2. to develop topics that are logical and clear; 3. to write essays in a clear, communicative style which uses a variety of sentence structures; 4. to use vocabulary which is best for you, for the topic, and thus, for the reader; 5. to strengthen your skills at revising drafts (word choice, essay structure, and style) and editing your writing for "mechanical" accuracy (spelling, punctuation, grammar, etc.); 6. at the end of the semester, to write a research paper, using library research methods and standard documentation, that meets the expectations of the American academic community.

Reading: 1. using a 3-part reading technique that will be useful in university work (pre-reading by skimming/scanning, second close reading for specifics, post-reading reflection exercises); 2. practicing the identification of main ideas; 3. developing a sensitivity for vocabulary comprehension; 4. making inferences that will assist reading comprehension; 5. restatement of reading ideas as a means of "personalizing" information.

Areas/Evaluation

Attendance	20%	Mid-term Exam	10%
Tests	20%	Outside Reading	10%
Essays	20%	Research Paper	20%

COURSE DESCRIPTION: FRESHMAN COMPOSITION
UNIVERSITY OF WYOMING

Textbook: *The Process of Composition,* 2nd ed., by J. Reid
One folder and one spiral notebook

Office Hours: Hoyt Hall, Room 407 (Phone: 766–2146)
9 A.M.–11 A.M., 1 P.M.–3 P.M. Wednesday (and by appointment)

Requirements

Attendance (2 absences maximum)
Class participation
Satisfactory completion of all assignments
textbook reading as assigned
writing
3–5 daybook entries each week
textbook exercises
5–6 essays (500–700 words each)
research paper (2,000 words)
in-class writing (3–4 essays)
reading quizzes as necessary
Successful completion of the weekly Writing Tutorial

The First Day

About half of the first class period will be occupied by housekeeping chores: greeting the students, writing the title of the class and the teacher's name on the board, calling the roll, asking students to help the teacher pronounce their names correctly, asking which name each student prefers to be called, and asking for basic information from each of the students. It is important to learn the names of the students as soon as possible, certainly by the second week of class. Because students tend to lose their identity for the teacher when they change seats, a seating chart is useful. On that chart write a personal clue to help identify each student (tall, mustache, nice smile) and help personalize the name-learning process. Alternatively, the teacher might ask all students to sit in the same seats (or to wear the same clothes—an option that usually brings smiles) for the first two weeks; visualizing and recreating the classroom and practicing the names by rote outside of class can also be helpful. Some teachers take pictures of their classes, an activity that promotes social exchange as well as giving the teacher a record of the class. Asking the students to begin learning each other's names early (perhaps through interviews during the first week of class), as well as correct pronunciation and background information, will assist the teacher in learning about the students.

Following the roll-call, a careful discussion of the operating procedures of the class should take place, using the course description sheet as the basis for discussion. The teacher should show students the textbook(s), identify the location of her/his office, and describe the course expectations. And because many of the newer ESL students will not know how to ask questions or even what questions to ask, it may be necessary for the teacher to model and to encourage students to ask questions about the progression of the class. The teacher might begin by discussing the value of question-asking in U.S. academic classes; s/he might share with the students a handout that explains question forms and functions, as Patricia Byrd, Janet Constantinides, and Martha Pennington do in their training manual for foreign teaching assistants (1989):

Question structure by function:

1. the obvious question, seeking explanation: "Will you please explain more about the first writing assignment on the syllabus?"
2. the clarifying question: "Do you mean that the research paper we will write in this class will require library work?"
3. the information-seeking statement that is really a question: "I don't understand the attendance policy."
4. the indication of confusion in a hidden question: "I can't follow this."

5. the extension-of-meaning statement asking for confirmation (a hidden question): "So, if I add all my grades together at the end of the course, I should be able to figure out what my final grade will be."

6. the comparison/contrast statement seeking confirmation (a hidden question): "The objectives for this class are similar to the objectives listed in the textbook."

Near the end of the first class, the teacher should make an assignment for the following class in addition to the acquisition of the textbooks; reading the preface of the text, interviewing a classmate in the class, or writing a self-introduction are possibilities. The assignment should be written on the board as well given orally. Beginning each class by writing the next day's assignment on the chalkboard (consistently in the same corner of the board) will help students learn to look for the assignment.

As part of the discussion of the syllabus and operating procedures, teachers should begin setting the stage for student responsibility for learning. In order to take responsibility, students need to be able to anticipate what will occur in the class, what expectations the teacher has for each class, and what each student should accomplish during the class. In contrast, if the students never know what they will be doing in class, they operate in a kind of vacuum. As a result, they may feel insecure, and more important, take no responsibility for what happens in class. In his study of three experienced ESL composition teachers, Alistair Cumming found a "fundamental systematicity" (1992, p. 29) among all three teachers that centered on their uses of only six teaching routines: attracting students' attention (about 7% of class time); assigning tasks (about 20%); collectively constructing interpretation (about 20%); establishing criteria (10%–15%); providing individual feedback (20%–24%); and guiding individual development (about 20%). The teachers alternated the routines in short sequences of a few minutes' duration that appeared "to sustain students' attention while helping to model and scaffold individual or group task performance" (p. 30).

Students benefit from clear classroom structure, and the lower the language proficiency of the students, the more the students will depend on a clear set of principles that underlie the class. The organization of the class should therefore provide a pace or a rhythm that the students can understand and anticipate. For example, the course description and syllabus sheet might indicate that field trips will occur on alternate Mondays, or that each day will begin with a five-minute "warm-up" period of writing in the daybook, or that revisions of writing will be due each Friday. At the beginning of each class, the teacher should write a brief list of the order of the day's activities; at the start of each task, the teacher should announce the approximate allotted time for that activity. Some teachers begin each class with a greeting ritual as each student enters; others begin each class with a vocabulary word or a sentence structure than needs explanation. Still others ask that, near the beginning of each class, students take turns putting translated sayings from their cultures on the board and lead a brief class discussion of the meaning of each saying.

Several other teaching considerations have been delineated by Sharon Bassano and Mary Ann Christison (1988). Notice the "blind" and "random" qualities of some of the advice.

1. Establish good eye contact-—don't talk over the students' heads or to the chalkboard.
2. Try to teach to all areas of the classroom and all students equally.
3. Write legibly on the chalkboard, large enough to be seen by all the students.
4. Speak loudly enough to be heard by all students and enunciate clearly; avoid idioms and, in classes of lower language proficiency, speak more slowly.
5. Vary the exercises in class, alternating rapid and slow-paced, individual and group activities.
6. Be prepared to give a variety of explanations, models, or descriptions in the (expected) case that some students need further examples.

Lesson Plans

Even the most experienced teachers make lesson plans, although their plans may not always be written. Formulating objectives, selecting and sequencing materials, and deciding upon interactional patterns are essential to class planning. For less experienced teachers, written lesson plans offer three advantages: (a) they assist the teacher in preparing for class, (b) they focus the relationship between overall objectives and class activities, and (c) they provide a record from which assessment of the plans and improvement on future plans are possible. The length and detail of an individual lesson plan depend on the needs of the teacher; however, if teachers are to learn from their successes (and failures), they must have the essential data of a fairly detailed lesson plan.

A lesson plan structures a class period in which the teacher's intentions are clear and instructional activities are sequenced according to a logic and structure that students can perceive. "A well-managed class is one in which time is well used and in which there are few distractions resulting from poor discipline or a poorly structured lesson" (Richards, 1990a, p. 8). The basic question in lesson planning is this: "What learning opportunities can I give my students in class that they can't get (or get as easily) outside the classroom?" The answers to this question help to form explicit decisions; general answers might include accurate and appropriate feedback, concentrated opportunities for practice, explicit answers and explanations, strategy training, real world information, counseling and support, cross-cultural information, prioritizing of information, and/or focus and awareness of specific knowledge (Larsen-Freeman, 1990). Lesson plans are not just lists of topics the teacher will cover. Ideally, they are sequenced series of activities for the student—activities that will help the student actively learn the material covered in that particular class.

One teacher-researcher who has investigated the needs of student learners for more than a quarter-century, Bernice McCarthy, has formulated a teaching model called 4MAT. Her studies of diversity in NES students' learning profiles has demonstrated that the process of learning involves four stages, each of which reaches students with differing learning styles and strategies: experience, reflection, conceptualization, and experimentation (1987). While McCarthy's focus is more on the differences among right- and left-hemisphere learning in students, her teaching model is particularly helpful for lesson planning. Figure 5-1 is a simplified explanation of McCarthy's 4MAT.

Clearly, teachers planning lessons (classes, modules, or courses) must consider their students' needs. To carry this axiom a step further, McCarthy suggests that teachers develop teaching strategies that, in addition to relating information (ideas, skills, or knowledge), engage students so that they (a) enter the lesson easily with interest, (b) are aware of the benefits of the lesson, (c) can relate prior information to the new information, (d) have opportunities to practice the materials (skills, concepts) of the lesson, and (e) are able to apply the lesson to alternative (and future) situations. The strength of the 4MAT model is, as Nancy Kroonenberg points out, that it demonstrates the need for preparation before information, and for application after practice (Kroonenberg, 1992b). While it is perhaps easy for a teacher to identify lesson objectives, the preparation needed to achieve the objectives may not be as simple. So although "class objectives" generally occupy the first lines of a lesson plan, on McCarthy's clocklike model they are implemented at five or six o'clock, well into the lesson.

Prior to the "teaching" of the objectives, teachers are responsible for raising awareness and stimulating interest about the lesson in their students. The "scene-setting" helps activate the schema that students possess about the subject: that is, they introduce students to the material by determining what the students know. Next, teachers must demonstrate the relevance of the material to the students; this is the

FIGURE 5–1 USING 4MAT® TO PLAN LESSONS

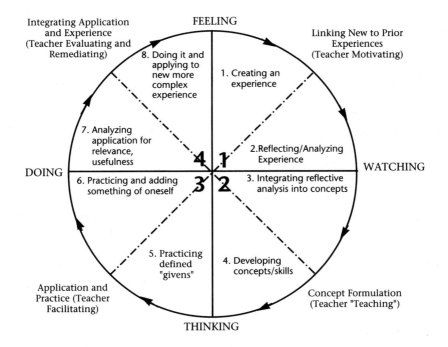

4MAT is a federally registered trademark of EXCEL, Inc.

Source: B. McCarthy, *The 4Mat System: Teaching to Learning Styles with Right/Left Mode Techniques.* ©1981, 1987 by EXCEL, Inc., 200 W. Station Street, Barrington, Illinois 60010. 1-800-822-4MAT.

"selling" part of teaching, what McCarthy calls "witnessing the value" of the material (p. 99), whether it be the study of poetry, a module on insect-collecting, or writing a persuasive essay. As the teacher explains the reasons for teaching, students are persuaded that learning will be beneficial for them (benefits, of course, can range from a passing grade on a test to a successful essay, from positive feedback from peers to feelings of self-satisfaction). Next, it is important to link the new information to prior knowledge, because it is easier to add to (and modify) existing information than to create entirely new information. Teachers extend the existing schema of their students by asking students to reflect on what they know and to integrate the new concepts into that previous knowledge. Finally, the "teaching" takes place; this information-giving stage is well known by teachers, and it is an essential part of the learning process. It is only one step in the cycle, however, and it is the final **teacher-responsible** stage.

While the early stages of learning are initiated and developed by the teacher, the second half of the learning process focuses on the growth of the independent learner. During these more **student-responsible** stages of learning, the teacher becomes more a facilitator who structures activities, intervenes when appropriate, and serves as a resource. As students practice, manipulate, and experiment with the new knowledge, they explore its usefulness individually and with others. They problem-solve and examine the information (or materials or skills), making necessary changes in their perspectives and accepting the new knowledge. It is essential that students have the time and opportunity to make the knowledge their own; only then can they make the cognitive change necessary for learning and growth. **Learning is change;** it can be imposed, but imposed change occurs only in the short term. Imposed change may force students to <u>perform</u>, but it will not motivate them to <u>become</u>. In the final stages of learning, students apply the knowledge to other assignments and/or other situations; the successful transfer of information or skills represents the last level of learning and change. The student who is able to evaluate knowledge and use it in alternative situations is indeed an independent learner.

Below are brief outlines of two lesson plans that incorporate the stages of learning described above. Note the movement from teacher-responsible to student-responsible activities.

TOPIC: USING SUPPORTING TECHNIQUES IN PARAGRAPH WRITING

Intermediate Writing Class (Time Frame: 3–4 class periods)

<u>Setting the Scene</u> (preparation, stimulating interest, raising awareness)	Teacher description of an elementary school classroom on Friday afternoon (Show and Tell). Difference between a six-year old saying, "Yesterday I went to the park, and I saw a snake" (telling) and "Yesterday I went to the park, and I saw a snake, and HERE IT IS!"
<u>Benefit to Students</u> (motivation, and reasons for teaching)	Discussion: need in U.S. academic writing for detail (facts, examples, personal experience, physical description) to support ideas. Readers find evidence (showing) more credible than simply stating (telling).
<u>Link Old to New Information</u> (extending knowl-edge)	Discussion: level of detail needed in students' cultures; use exercises with statements that range from straight facts (New Year's Day in the U.S. is celebrated on January 1st) to strong opinion statements (Acapulco is the best place for a winter vacation).

Presentation of New Material (information-giving)	Lecture: types of support used and valued in U.S. academic writing. Examples, models. Students ask questions, participate in discussions.
Practice (individual work and sharing with others)	Small group work; exercises; collaborative writing using techniques of support; experimentation, manipulation of new knowledge and problem-solving (growth toward independent learning).
Transfer (application to new situation)	Use of supporting techniques in individual writing assignment. Student samples on overhead projector, student collaborative paragraphs on chalkboard; spiraling of techniques of support in future modules.

PREPARATION FOR WRITING THE PERSUASIVE ESSAY

Advanced Writing Class (Time Frame: 4–6 class periods)

Setting the Scene (preparation, stimulate interest, raise awareness)	Warm-up journal entries: How to win a face-to-face argument; Why I chose this controversy; How I will refute the counter-argument; What I learned from the article I read about my topic
Benefit to Students (motivation)	Discussion: benefits of persuasion: in advertising, in personal arguments, in writing
Link Old to New Knowledge (extending information)	Discussion, board work: what is a controversy? Samples and mini-debates on board (living on or off campus; gun control; cigarette smoking)
Presentation of New Knowledge (information-giving)	Shaping persuasive discourse: connotative language, logical fallacies; pro arguments and support; counter-arguments and refutation
Practice (individual work and sharing with others)	Exercises (logical fallacies, connotative language, refutation techniques); board work with student topics, mini-debates; overhead projector for student samples, models of counter-arguments

Following are examples of class objectives and lesson plans. Notice the philosophy of teaching writing demonstrated in each, as well as the ways in which materials are selected and activities sequenced. Notice also the ways in which McCarthy's teaching model is implemented.

Lesson Plan Objective

Advanced ESL Composition Class

Textbook: *Academic Writing: Techniques and Tasks* by Leki

Objective: to present an incrementally more complex invention strategy than the Listing strategy from the previous class periods. Today's lesson involves following written and verbal instructions as an aid in generating ideas for composing essays. The students will also be asked to analyze their ideas to determine a hierarchical order as an aid for later English language paragraph organization.

(courtesy of Christine Stebbins)

Introduction and Lesson Plan Objectives

ESL Sheltered Freshman Composition Course

Textbook: *The Process of Composition,* 2nd ed., by J. Reid

The lessons I discuss below belong in the unit "Construction of the Essay," which serves as a two-week (six 1-hour sessions) introduction to the essay. Before this unit I will have conducted a grammar review based on student writing samples, and the unit following will fine-tune concepts discussed in this unit. . . . After a review period (of 10 minutes) on the importance of paragraph construction, I will show students the relationship between the paragraph and the essay, then discuss essay shape.

(courtesy of Ken Emery)

Often, the overall objective stated on a lesson plan is followed by a list of the activities to be accomplished during a class period; the amount of time for each activity is predicted on the lesson plan, and space on the page is left for the teacher's post-class comments. Below are three lesson plans. Each was written for a different level of language proficiency, and each was written to help the individual teacher. Notice that in every class period there is a variety of activities, and that often the teacher has planned work that involves students in **group work** and **pair/peer review** (printed in bold face) as well as individual work. Examine also (a) the sequencing of the activities in each lesson, (b) the spiraling of skills and information that works toward an objective, and (c) the use of *journals/daybooks* (indicated by *italics*) for informal writing and planning.

LESSON PLANS: BASIC WRITING CLASS

Textbook: *Basic Writing* by J. Reid

Objectives: plan and prepare for field trip to junior high school class; pre-writing and work on paragraphs about secondary schools in students' countries

Monday

Introduction: (15 minutes)
>review of coordinate conjunctions, sentence combining (last week)
>>*BW*, pp. 95–96, Exercises 4I, 4J
>>tell students this sentence combining will be on the quiz Wednesday
>>handout: review sheet and review exercises for practice

Discussion: plan for week—field trip to junior high school (15 minutes)
>mini-lecture: junior high school education system in U.S. (brief overview)
>students take notes
>**pair work:** students share notes, decide on questions to ask to obtain more information from the teacher/informant

Class discussion: (15 minutes)
>discuss elementary and secondary education systems in students' countries
>**small group work**—share differences in educational systems

Conclusion (5 minutes)
>assignment: make notes for paragraph about secondary schools in country

Tuesday

Journal Warm-up: (5 minutes)
>write about what you learned about other countries' secondary school systems in the last class

Whole-class planning for paragraph: Secondary School in My Country (10 minutes)
>discuss notes taken for homework
>boardwork (group brainstorming)

Writing (10 minutes)
>individual planning work and drafting
>mini-conferencing

Pair Work: Peer Review (15 minutes)
>read each other's paragraph drafts
>be prepared to tell what you LIKED about the paragraph you read: "I liked X's paragraph because . . ."

Review for quiz (10 minutes) (on the use of <u>and</u>, <u>but</u>, <u>so</u> to join clauses)
>go over questions on review exercise sheet
>answer questions
>calm and prepare students

Conclusion (5 minutes)
>assignment: study for quiz

Wednesday

> Introduction: finalize plans for field trip tomorrow (5 minutes)
>
> Quiz (20 minutes)
>> short quiz: paragraph about junior high schools in U.S. with
>> directions to combine the sentences
>> mark in class, discuss and review sentence combining
>> collect quizzes
>
> Revision: (20 minutes)
>> work on final drafts of paragraphs about secondary schools
>> mini-conferencing
>> **pair work**: ask partner from yesterday about possible changes
>
> Conclusion (5 minutes)
>> assignment (FRIDAY): finish paragraph for class booklet on
>> secondary schools

Thursday: Field Trip

Friday

> *Journal Warm-up*: (5 minutes)
>> write about the junior high school experience
>
> Class discussion (10 minutes)
>> junior high school experiences
>> differences, similarities, <u>surprises</u>
>
> Collect paragraphs for booklet: put into booklet form (10 minutes)
>
> **Small group work** (20 minutes)
>> compose thank-you notes to junior high school class
>> format on board (*BW*, pp. 172–173)
>> BE SPECIFIC! use details from class discussion, warm-ups
>> one person in the group does the handwriting, but . . .
>> everyone in each group signs name and country
>
> Assemble thank-you notes with booklet in envelope for junior high
> school (5 minutes)

Week's End Comments: Quiz showed that all students understood concept of sentence combining with coordinate conjunctions. Students excited about visiting a U.S. school; good questions about educational system in U.S. Field trip GREAT success (junior high students well prepared for our class visit—my students just lit up!). Paragraphs uniformly good and booklet a real treasure.

LESSON PLANS: LOW INTERMEDIATE WRITING CLASS

Textbook: *Interactions II*, 2nd ed., by Segal and Pavlik

<u>Objectives</u>: to have students learn the basics of writing and to express advantages and disadvantages

Monday

> check to see that homework was completed
> return *journals* and essays
> read pp. 79–80 and list info in paper; then class chooses the best ideas
> read composition and answer questions, p. 83 (best title?)
>
> assignment: rewrite essays, using my comments

Tuesday

> collect rewrites
> start Chapter 5
> anecdotes: "sometimes parents really do know best" (on board)
> do a quick-writing (10 minutes) in *journal* about this idea—a story
>   from your past
> look at p. 66: can you answer all the questions in your paragraph?
> read A, p. 6
>
> assignment: rewrite your anecdote using the ideas we've discussed

Wednesday

> collect anecdote
> discuss advantages/disadvantages of train travel/airplane travel:
>   examples on board
> generate on board lists of advan./disadvan. of bicycles (from pp. 79–
>   80 in text) (all students contribute)
> give a related topic: advan. and disadvan. of bicycle transportation in
>   Fort Collins
> give students a handout to use in **interviewing three people** for
>   their ideas on that topic
> **students ask a partner** in class to use as their first source
>
> assignment: ask two more people (native speakers of English) for
>   their input

Thursday

> return rewrites: work on sentence fragments (a big problem for this
>   class)
>   sentences on the board; students judge correctness
>   students state what they know about fragments; I fill in the gaps
> check interview sheet; discuss experiences students had with inter-
>   viewing
> discussion: decision-making process in their writing
> review of appropriate transition words for their advan./disadvan.
>   essay
> discuss titles: use the guidelines in the text; class chooses a title for
>   the sample essay
> 10-minute freewriting in their *journals* on the information they
>   gathered for their essay
>
> assignment: write the first draft of their essay based upon the infor-
>   mation they have gathered

Friday

continue work with fragments; textbook, pp. 87–88, exercises A, B (fragments)

peer editing of rough drafts: look especially for fragments, run-on sentences, digressions

collect drafts to make suggestions; use the form from the text for both the rough draft and final so they can see their improvements. I give a letter grade as well on the final draft only.

in-class pre-writing: Advantages and Disadvantages of Studying English in the U.S.A.

assignment: write the paragraph about studying in the U.S.A.

Edwina Echevarria
Intensive English Program
Colorado State University

LESSON PLANS: FRESHMAN COMPOSITION CLASS (REMEDIAL)

Text: *Academic Writing* by Leki

Objectives: topic sentence and paragraph development of a multiple example paragraph; successful workshop on the draft of the paragraph (peer editing)

CLASS #7

Daybook Assignment: prepare for multiple example paragraph assignment [on individual talents: what are you "The World's Greatest" or "The World's Worst" and why] make a 2-column list: Best   Worst
have at least 8 of each
pick two: cluster on reasons WHY

Return paragraph; collect Daybooks (in folders)

Topic sentence: what is it? what does it do?
—tells what's coming up
—writer's stance, argumentative edge (convincing readers that writer's perspective is right)

Identify topic sentences in paragraphs

How to support?

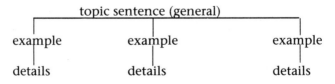

What examples does the writer use in each paragraph? Enough specific examples!
Which details best SHOW?

Why do we use personal examples?
>need to have topics broad enough and without specific information
>strategy similar in all types of writing: general sentence + developed support, with developing aspects of examples to illustrate the point

CLASS #8

Assignment: start drafting paragraph in the computer laboratory

Review: what is important for this paragraph? (Look at assignment sheet)
—focused topic sentence (e.g., 1 reason WHY)
—specific examples
—details, especially sensory, showing details
—AUDIENCE

Pair work: look at these two paragraphs and decide how well each meets the criteria

Discuss: what would make these paragraphs better?
draft a possible topic sentence: emphasize the five W's

Discuss topics: possible topic sentences
—what would you expect to read in this paragraph?
—what kind of examples does the author expect to use?
—what details would support this topic sentence?

Questions or problems

CLASS #9

Assignment: read Leki, pp. 122-134
Daybook: answer questions on p. 132
Rough draft due Thursday (typed on computer)
Workshop next class: don't be absent (or big trouble!)

Questions about paragraph?

Paragraph concepts handout, with samples

Unity: sample paragraph—what happened? How could this be fixed?

Coherence
—order (time, space, general to specific, most to least important)
—transition words, phrases (handout)
—repetition of key words and phrases
—use of pronouns in coherence

Practice: coherence exercises
take out prewriting: what will you do to organize examples and transitions?
do all examples, details relate to topic sentence?

CLASS #10

Assignment: revise paragraph in computer laboratory
Final draft due Tuesday, with all drafts and pre-writing, in folder

Problems or questions?

Importance of this **Peer Workshop**

Pairs: Nasir	Gerardo	Ulf	Yu-tsai	Souri
Tien	Bov	Lakshman	Trinh Park	Chien-cho

Read each other's paragraphs
  difference between editing and revising
  read paragraph aloud: listen for errors

What needs to be done?
  focus = what is it? how could it be improved? Check for split
    focus
  development: what examples used? relevant? do they SHOW
    focus?

Wrap-up: look over comments
  what suggestions were most helpful? what changes will you
    make?

Nathalie Bleuze
Department of English
Colorado State University

Troublespots

Each ESL writing class is unusual in some ways; the combination of cultures and goals, learning styles and strategies, ages and expectations gives each class a unique personality, but it also generates special problems and troublespots. Some problem areas are common in all ESL writing classes, particularly for teachers new to ESL writing. Below are six of those problems: student diversity, lack of community, mismatches in student-teacher perceptions, uneven pacing, student resistance to change, and levels of anxiety. Each is followed by suggested solutions and, when necessary, a discussion of "caveats"— issues within those areas that deserve special attention and caution.

Student Diversity

Even with careful placement testing, a single class of ESL students often includes a wide range of motivation and language backgrounds, due in part to the different educational experiences, ages, needs, and language proficiencies of those students. Some students are in class merely to mark time, while others expect the teacher to be the font of all learning. Graduate students study next to incoming freshmen; spouses attending the class have different motivations than do the businessmen; a student repeating the class has a different attitude from the newcomer; an immigrant or refugee student has vastly different English language background from the international "visa" students (Leki, 1992). Teaching might be easier in a writing program that is able to separate students into classes that will fulfill their individual expectations. Usually, however, the teacher must face a group like the one described above in a single class. It is distressing for both teachers and students for one class to include three disinterested teenagers who gossip in the back row, a lone student who dislikes writing even in his own language and stares out a window, a small group of students who do work at a task, and a very serious graduate student, who, having finished the task, waits impatiently for the class to move ahead.

There is, of course, no simple solution. Teachers can work to establish a feeling of community within the class by organizing group work methodically and by designing activities that will allow the strengths of one student to be shared with another. They can establish clear parameters for behavior, and they can plan activities that require the full participation of all class members. They can ask the students to discuss and write about their attitudes toward writing, and what effect those attitudes may have on their class performance. They can offer the students opportunities to discover their learning styles and strategies, to write about those styles and strategies, and to put those styles and strategies to good use. They can develop cross-cross-cross-cultural sensitivity in the writing class by having students share their cultures either in individual writing or in class/group projects. They can offer to the graduate students, or to students who seem ahead of the class, additional work, perhaps associated with their major fields, in return for which the students will use their skills to further the objectives of the classroom community. In short, they can encourage all students to perform at potential. And perhaps the most important decision the teacher can make—and clearly articulate to the students—is that both teacher and students must take responsibility for learning. Of course, adults can choose to fail or choose not to participate, as long as doing so does not interfere with the choices of others in the class, and as long as they understand that such choices have consequences.

Lack of Community

The first week of an ESL writing class is likely to be more or less chaotic, due in large part to the diversity discussed above and to the inevitable period of adjustment as teachers and students seek common ground. From the first day of class, however, the teacher must begin the process of forming a classroom community in which each student is a responsible participant. Teachers should explain to students that attendance and participation in the community are more important in a writing class than they are in other content area classes that emphasize acquiring information rather than learning skills. Therefore, attendance is essential because a missing community member results in more responsibility for other students; participation is essential for sharing the burden of learning writing skills. In this community, mutual trust and respect encourage progress; collaboration and cooperation among all members can result in positive learning experiences for all.

The theory of the classroom community, of course, is not always successful in practice; indeed, complete success might be only an ideal. Furthermore, a strong sense of community almost never occurs serendipitously, even in a NES class. The formation of a coherent community in an ESL writing classroom can be especially difficult: focusing diverse needs and personalities on common goals, cooperative learning, and trust is an enormous challenge. But the establishment of a functioning classroom community in which the students are committed to shared aims and values is the foundation for student-centered and student-responsible learning.

Shared responsibility is the key to building the level of comfort that is conducive to learning; this sharing should begin early and on a small scale. During the first week of class, or as soon as the class population is relatively stable, the teacher might assign "buddies": pairs of students (who are not friends), perhaps from different backgrounds, who exchange personal information and phone numbers. They then become responsible for each other: if one is absent, or has questions about an assignment, or needs some encouragement, s/he calls the buddy (note: not the teacher). Buddies might interview each other and then introduce each other to the class; they might write about each other for an early writing assignment. Buddies can be the audience for later writing and will therefore become peer reviewers for that piece of writing. Below are two descriptions of buddies by students whose essays were written for/to those buddies:

Audience: My audience is my buddy Tohka. She is from Malaysia. She is a short and thin person. She has black and straight hair that comes down to her shoulders. Her eyes are brown and her face has oriental features. Tohka has a very pretty smile which invites communication with others. I believe she is a little shy but when she speaks she is very distinct and open. I don't know her very well but she gives me a good impression by the friendly relationship we have.

Purpose: I expect Tohka to understand or have an idea of what forgiving and forgetting is. In our daily lives everyone faces situations where we are offended. Maybe after she has read my essay I will cause her to think or analyze if she is satisfied in the way she acts toward and judges people that have harmed or offended her in any way. I am not trying to persuade her. My essay is informative, but it may have an effect on her if she wants it to.

Brenda Alpizar
Puerto Rico

Audience: Michio, my buddy, is from Japan, and he's presently doing his graduate studies in Political Science. For me, Michio is the quiet type of Japanese, but he is quite active in sports, especially in tennis, and he also likes to play soccer.

Purpose: At the beginning, I asked Michio what he would like to know about my hometown, Kuantan. He mentioned quite a few things, and entertainment was one of them. Then I told him that I would write about soccer games and the Karaoka, and he agreed. Since he knew what I intended to write, I will expect him to make a comparison between the entertainment in his hometown and mine. Because he is also a soccer fan in Japan, I'm sure he would like to know about the way soccer fans in Kuantan cheer and support their team, and why the people in Kuantan like watching soccer games and singing in the Karaoka. So, my objective is to give an explanation on these two entertainments of the people in Kuantan, and why these entertainments have become popular in Kuantan.

Lee Lip Peng
Malaysia

To expand this seed of community, two pairs of buddies might, in the second or third week of class, form a small group for specific class activities and writing (see Chapter 6 for more information on the establishment, work, and activities of groups). Later, as the sense of community grows, groups or pairs of non-buddies can be formed for specific reasons: a trio of students whose latest essays indicated they needed to discuss, work on, and rewrite their conclusions; a pair of students identifying and analyzing the task for a shared university writing assignment; a small group debating two sides of an issue they will write about; a larger group generating ideas for an essay. The point of this collaborative work is that the end, the whole, is greater than the sum of its parts. Research (Keefe, 1989; Kohn, 1987; Scarcella, 1990; Scarcella and Oxford, 1992) has shown that students learn at least as well and as much from peers as they do from teachers. Oxford (1990) suggests that among the benefits of cooperative teaching are better student and teacher satisfaction, stronger language learning motivation, and more language practice opportunities.

Caveats: Group Work

The added elements of blindness and randomness in group work may discourage both teachers and students during the first weeks of class. Often a new teacher can feel overwhelmed at the grand potential for group work and then become distraught when her first attempt is far from the ideal. For example, selection of buddies and then of group members during the first two weeks of class is, by its very nature, random because the teacher does not know the students. Initial student reaction cannot be anticipated (that is, it is blind), except that some reluctance will be inevitable and some benign resistance will occur as well as some (perhaps silent) resentment. Some students may even view small-group work as a failure of the teacher to do his job. The mixed reactions may also result in one group (of the four or five) that does not function and becomes a source of frustration for all involved.

And there are other constraints with collaborative and group work: just assigning students to groups does not ensure a positive learning experience. Collaborative work can descend into pointlessness or busywork if it is not perceived by the students as authentic, goal-directed, and beneficial. It is, therefore the teacher's responsibility to plan carefully, facilitate, encourage, and in some cases mediate the communal class work. In addition, the teacher must direct the perceptions of the students: Why do you think we're doing this? What's the purpose of this exercise? What's the point of this work? How is this group work going to help your essay writing? In addition, teachers may feel a frightening loss of control even as they structure and facilitate relatively successful group work and as students begin to build their small-group communities. It is therefore wise to "start small" with group work, to establish pair work with buddies slowly, and to move into group work gradually as the sense of classroom community develops.

Mismatches in Teacher-Student Perceptions

A third potential problem or troublespot occurs because teachers may misperceive students' classroom behavior or responses. Because of differences in educational experiences and expectations, ESL students often do not provide their teacher with clear signs that indicate confusion, acceptance, understanding, or reluctance. These mismatches can result in enormous frustration for the teacher as well as the students. Clues that are obvious and expected in a NES classroom (nodding, presenting a "classroom face" to the teacher, taking a few notes, raising eyebrows, whispering with a friend, asking questions, raising objections, interrupting) may not exist in an ESL class. The expected protocols for question asking, teacher-student exchanges, and group work that seem normal in a class of NESs—and to teachers who have come out of NES classrooms as students—will probably not exist at the beginning of an ESL writing class. Teachers therefore need to be aware that, for example:

1. a student taking notes doesn't necessarily understand the material;
2. a student nodding, or even nodding in response to the question "Do you understand?" doesn't necessarily understand;

3. students not asking questions doesn't mean the material or assignment is clear;

4. immediate success in small-group work is extremely difficult to achieve, for both teachers and students; the gap between concept and practice is cross-culturally (and, in most ESL writing classes, cross-cross-cross-culturally) great.

The overall solution to these mismatches is (a) time for both teachers and students to make adjustments, (b) shared information, and (c) the establishment of a classroom community. Teachers must leave their expectations outside the classroom door and enter the class prepared to offer cultural and contextual information, in ways that will communicate effectively with students whose learning styles and strategies may be limited or simply different. For example, presenting the same material orally, writing it on the chalkboard, and asking students to take notes or role play the material will allow students with differing perceptual learning styles to better understand the material. A lecture can incorporate visual and hands-on materials simultaneously to meet student needs; in that way, students can develop concurrent strategies (Kroonenberg, 1990). And if students become aware of their learning styles and appropriate learning strategies, they will be able to take increased responsibility for their language learning (Oxford, 1990). In addition, teachers must devise several ways beyond a simple yes-no question ("Do you understand?") for students to demonstrate that they understand not only the class content but also the procedures. Asking students

- to re-explain for other members in the class,
- to perform the task,
- to write about their perceptions, and/or
- to transfer the information to another situation

will often more accurately indicate the level of understanding.

At the same time, teachers must begin educating their students about U.S. academic expectations in the classroom. For example, students should understand what questions are appropriate and necessary in a university class, and what expectations their professors will have concerning office hours, class participation, writing assignments, and group work. Role-playing exercises and small-group discussions concerning appropriate and inappropriate behaviors could center around appropriate verbal interchanges:

1. Asking a professor about a writing assignment:
   NOT (simply): "I don't understand."
   BUT NOT: "This is the first paper/review/report I have written at a U.S. university. May I make an appointment to talk with you during your office hours?"

2. Asking a librarian for help in researching a writing assignment:
   NOT (demanding): "Find these books for me."
   NOT (totally helpless): "I have to write a paper, and it's due tomorrow. What should I do?"
   BUT: "I've found three books about the topic of cellular coffer-dams, but I can't find this one. Could you please help me?"

3. Asking a native speaker peer in class about an assignment:
   NOT (abruptly): "What did he say?"
   BUT: "Hi. I'm [NAME] in your {x} class. Do you have the assignment for tomorrow's class?" (J. Reid, 1989)

Teachers might also arrange "What's wrong with this picture/conversation/scenario?" lessons in which role play and even videotapes play a part. For example, a videotape of an NES class (shot from the front of the classroom, a "teacher's view") might demonstrate native-speaker behavior, including contextual clues, question-asking, and teacher-student interaction patterns that ESL students can analyze and write about.

Uneven Pacing

In addition to the potential mismatches in perception, teachers accustomed to NES classrooms may also notice an immediate and serious problem with the seemingly arbitrary and unexpected "blind random" of the class rhythm. Even after careful assessment of class needs, perusal of the writing curriculum and syllabus, and formulation of lesson plans, a teacher in an ESL writing class can feel like a bumbling incompetent. For example, a lesson planned to cover a class period with three sequenced activities can result in (a) one activity being covered, laboriously, without positive response, (b) the entire lesson plan being completed in twenty minutes, or (c) the lesson plan being completed as planned but, in retrospect, ineffectively. In a worst-case scenario, the teacher presents new material and, by the middle of the lesson, becomes aware the students do not understand: some students might make initial attempts to participate but then lapse into puzzled silence, while others might seem lost from the beginning or completely disinterested in the process, and still others may actually seem wary or even hostile. There is, in short, "blindness" on both sides of the desk.

The most obvious solution is a combination of trial and error and an early focus on information gathering. Initially, the ESL writing teacher should probably plan lessons with several options: additional exercises for each section of the class and possible activities for each section—more examples and information than the teacher thinks necessary. Teachers may well discover that the students themselves are the best sources of information; soliciting feedback in as many ways as possible helps to overcome the mutual "blindness." For instance, the teacher might ask students to write about their perceived writing strengths and weaknesses, their opinions of writing, their objectives for the class, as well as their responses to specific lessons and tasks. At the same time, the teacher must evaluate the students based on what s/he observes and experiences early in the class: which student will need more assistance, who can function relatively independently, who will be able to help others? As the teacher strives for a sense of community in the class, s/he must, through observation, identification, and analysis, structure the class according to results—positive or negative—of the lesson plans during the first two weeks of class. And as the pace of the class settles, continued vigilance is necessary. At the end of the third or fourth week, the teacher will probably need to reevaluate and adjust to the class rhythm in another attempt to balance the needs of individual students with class objectives, and student needs with the writing program goals.

Student "Resistance" to Change

A fifth problem ESL writing teachers face is that their students are often unable—or perhaps unwilling—to process key concepts and information. For example, a formal or informal test may reveal that the concept of topic sentence or paragraph development is not demonstrated by students in their writing, even though class discussion and exercises have shown that the students understand the information. More advanced writing students may understand, intellectually, the concepts of contrastive rhetoric (see Chapter 3) but seem unable to adapt their presentations of written material appropriately for a U.S. academic audience. For the teacher, the realization that students are not "learning" can be frustrating and perhaps a personal affront, since student success often seems inextricably linked to teacher performance (Corder, 1989). For the students, the gap between understanding and performance can be equally frustrating. Often the problem is not that ESL writing students are recalcitrant or that teachers are ineffective. The "resistance" is not so much a function of conscious decision ("I will resist") as it is a function of (a) the learning curve and (b) the process of change.

Research about change (Leithwood, 1986; Miller and Gold, 1988; J. Reid, 1991a and 1991b; Schlossberg, 1987) indicates that change of any kind is a **process**, not an **event**. Change is time-consuming, initially frustrating and frightening, and only eventually satisfying and successful. The stages of change range through (a) initial awareness and information gathering concerning the change, to (b) suspicion and even resentment about the personal impact of the change, to (c) acceptance and implementation of the change, and finally to

(d) assessment and revision of the change. The following premises about change are true for teachers using a new textbook for the first time, employees learning a new assembly line technique, parents adjusting to children leaving home, and students learning about academic writing in the ESL classroom.

1. Change involves choice—it cannot be imposed successfully.
2. The decision to change is individual, highly personal, and complex.
3. No one changes unless that change is perceived as beneficial.
4. Change takes time and effort, and the more complex the change, the more time and effort it will take.
5. The more changes a person is involved in, the more difficult—and the more time-consuming—change can be.
6. Persons going through the change process can move linearly through the steps if the change is small and discrete, especially if they have multiple opportunities for practice and corrective feedback. More often, the process is recursive: persons will revert to previous stages as they move through the processes, depending on the complexity of the change and individual contexts.
7. Change is best accomplished through collaboration of the person initiating the change (such as the teacher) and the person entering the change process (such as the student).

Education is integrally related to the process of change, and learning about change is educational. The teacher in the ESL writing classroom can act as a cultural informant and a "change agent" by providing opportunities for the students to learn about the change process. For example, students can become aware of the benefits of changing the ways they present their written ideas: fulfilling U.S. audience expectations, communicating more successfully, and/or being viewed as better students. They should also understand the stages through which they will progress if they choose to adapt their writing strategies—and so their written products. If, for example, students are aware that their feelings of frustration, their reluctance to adapt their writing styles, and their fears about changing are normal, shared, and even expected, their progress may be quicker and easier. Valuable activities for the ESL writing classroom include discussions of the change process, written assignments about changes in students' lives, and identification by teachers and students of the stages of the change process students are working through.

Below is an overview of the stages in the change process, followed by typical comments of persons in those stages (Hord et al., 1987). In the classroom, the teacher is responsible for the first two stages:

interesting students and giving information about the change. Notice that the personal stage of change is <u>crucial</u>: it occupies the time between learning about the change and the time when the person commits to the change. Often this is a stage of reluctance and resentment, a time when the person needs the collaboration and support of peers and teachers.

Stages	Typical Comments	
Self		
Awareness	"I'm not very interested in X."	(teacher responsibility)
Informational	"I'd like to know more about X."	
Personal	"How will X affect me?"	
	"It looks really hard."	CRUCIAL STAGE
	"I don't really think I can do it."	
	"I don't want to do it."	
Task		
Management	"I'm spending all my time trying to do X."	(time and effort management)
	"X is taking too much time."	
Consequence	"How will X affect (my professor)?"	
Impact		
Collaboration	"How are others doing X?	(student responsibility)
	"I'd like to share what I'm doing."	
Refocusing	"I have some ideas about X that would work even better."	

Once the student has committed to the change, the next stage, the management stage, is important. During this stage, students may feel that the amount of work they are assigned is overwhelming; "You give too much homework" is a common feeling, even if it is not articulated. Teachers need to demonstrate time-management strategies and offer suggestions for prioritizing and streamlining processes that will permit the students time to adjust to the change, to practice the change, and to become proficient. Finally, while the last stages in the change process are the most rewarding for both teachers and students, as students approach independent learning, they almost never reach these stages during a single writing course. In fact, the students are often still struggling with the management stage when they leave the class, and some students, overwhelmed by their management problems, will have reverted to the personal stage and become increasingly unhappy with what they "didn't learn" in the course. Nevertheless, if the students have been educated about the change process, about their responsibilities for identifying and examining changes, and for decision-making concerning changes, the transition from one stage to another will be easier for them (J. Reid, 1991b).

Levels of Anxiety

Students studying English in preparation for university work often operate within extraordinary pressures. As well as the substantial problems involved in entering and surviving in a foreign country, many ESL students have very short timelines and/or funding for English study. Most are struggling to gain the necessary language skills to pass the TOEFL or some other type of entrance examination; many have external pressures from family obligations; and some have not studied formally for many years. In addition, ESL students are faced with the inevitable blow of immersion: the dramatic change from competence and confidence of the native speakers in their own countries to the fearful and infuriating feelings that result from trying to communicate and live in a foreign country.

For students encountering so many <u>changes</u> in their lives, the ESL writing classroom can be one more major hurdle. For students laboring under the shadow of the TOEFL examination, a writing class can be merely an additional burden. Or that class can be a haven, a place where students can feel comfortable as they rehearse, experiment, and practice increasingly fluent and accurate English. It can be a place where the demands of the TOEFL recede and the more long-term requirements of academic work are identified and practiced. If students can learn to leave some of their pressures outside the classroom, if they have opportunities to share their culture shock and anxieties, and if they are convinced that the work they are doing will benefit them in their future university work, hope rather than panic can pervade the class.

In order to mitigate the anxiety that so many ESL students face daily, teachers have to walk a narrow line between counseling and teaching, between supporting and educating. Teachers have found two specific ways helpful to establish a balance and enable students to participate fully in class. First, students can be given the first five minutes of each class to warm up by writing in journals or daybooks. For students with limited language proficiency, these "warm-ups" will be directive and similar from day to day (such as what I did yesterday, or Saturday, or Sunday), establishing language patterns and levels of comfort and confidence. For more advanced students who have been in the United States awhile, more open assignments can be an outlet for student expression:

Write about the worst thing that happened to you this week.

Write about something that surprised you about U.S. university students.

Describe what a good friend is.

Analyze the most difficult part of writing this essay.

Write what you know about the meaning of the word
  "investigating."
What are some ways to persuade someone?

Following the warm-up, the topic may be discussed or focus on other topics may begin.

Second, a source of comfort for many students is the ability to anticipate. Immersed in a new culture, their energy is spent trying to anticipate what will happen, what someone will say or expect, or what he, the student, should do. If, on the other hand, the students can anticipate what will happen during the class, what the teacher expects and what they will be doing, they can relax and direct their energies toward their writing. Classroom procedures, tasks and activities, and evaluative criteria should, therefore, be clearly articulated and consistent: "The ESL teacher should always expect to explain more about an activity, a lesson, a rule, or an expectation than she would in a native-speaker class, both to catch the 'I don't understands' which won't get said, and because there is less assumed communal knowledge" (S. Reid, 1991). Discussions of why students are doing tasks and what the benefits are for each activity help students see not only what they are learning but that they are learning. Teachers need to be aware that setting up classroom routines takes time and patience; moreover, any change to those routines can upset the tone and pace of the class.

In addition to the general pressures that ESL students endure, ESL writing students may feel particularly anxious about their writing. Shirley Marney (1990) discusses seven "panic points" for ESL writers; the feelings of blindness and/or randomness that accompany them are also listed, this time from the perspective of the students.

A. I've never been good at writing. [expectation of failure]
    blindness

B. I don't know what the teacher [unknown expectations]
    wants. blindness, randomness

C. I don't have anything to say. [limited information-gathering]
    blindness

D. I don't know how to start. [limited organizational skills]
    blindness

E. How do I make it longer? [limited development skills]
    blindness, randomness

F. I don't know anything about [fear of making errors]
    punctuation. blindness, randomness

G. I've got to hand it in. [fear of evaluation]
    blindness, randomness

In addressing the anxiety levels of their students, ESL writing teachers must face the affective as well as the intellectual needs of the students. They must plan group work that allows students to share their fears as well as their ideas, assign writing that focuses on the kind of communication they have been doing all their lives (such as "Warn someone about something"; "Describe a dream you had recently"; "Discuss one of your childhood pleasures"), and provide clear directions and expectations. These classroom techniques must be linked to the reassurance and encouragement that will foster a sense of confidence in the students and work to bring down the barriers to learning caused by insecurity and external pressures.

Conclusion

> Traditionally, the teacher has played the role of lead dancer in the second language classroom, actively leading the students through the various steps needed to tune their language skills to perfection. The students have passively accepted their role as dancing partner in classroom proceedings placing their dependence mainly in the hands of the teacher. . . . Granted, teachers generally adjust their steps in accordance with their students' level and ability; yet, it is the teacher who has taken, or has been given, the duty of deciding how, what, when, and where all of this will take place.   (Caprio, 1990, p. 17)

The focus of this chapter has been twofold: first, to show that the heavy responsibility on the teacher described by Caprio (above) is an unnecessary, and perhaps even harmful, burden, but a burden that probably parallels most students' perceptions of their teachers. In contrast, students in ESL classes must learn to take greater responsibility for their language learning, thereby gaining a sense of independence and control over their learning that will allow them to continue their development after the class has ended. In much the same way, ESL writing teachers must learn to take less responsibility for their students' learning and more for establishing and facilitating a classroom atmosphere that is conducive to learning; in that way, they allow their students to achieve independence in learning. The long-term question for the teacher is "What will they do after I wave goodbye?"

Second, ESL writing teachers must be aware that they empower themselves as they empower their students: "[W]e need to incorporate who we are . . . our own cultural, linguistic, experiential identities and authentic full selves—head, heart, and spirit—into our teaching experience. We become more empowered as we teach from our inner strengths, talents, and vulnerabilities, not from a 'role' of authority or expert, following externally and arbitrarily devised 'rules'" (Lundquist,

1990, pp. 2–3). The good teacher, then, is not so much one who adheres strictly to a "method," but one who is "cautiously eclectic" (H. D. Brown, 1987), one who recognizes that teachers, rather than methods, make a difference. Teachers must develop "their own individual theories of teaching, exploring the nature of their own decision-making and classroom practices" (Richards, 1990c, p. 9). As teachers recognize the tremendous variation among learners in aptitude, motivation, styles, and strategies, and as they work to establish a classroom community filled with independent, active learners, they will begin to understand that they can make the classroom atmosphere one of joy and celebration (Enright and McCloskey, 1988), worth and respect, appreciation and acceptance, safety and success, curiosity and challenge.

Discussion Questions

1. In small groups, describe a teacher who was, in your opinion, a great teacher. To what do you attribute the success of that teacher? What criteria do you think make a successful teacher?

2. In an article that described the "good language teacher," Prodromou (1991) listed the results of a student survey that described unsuccessful teaching characteristics. Among them:

very strict	believed students were all the same
shouted	didn't let us speak
talked and talked	made me feel anxious
rigid, sarcastic	gave marks all the time
not prepared	always above our heads
forced us to do things	gave a lot of difficult tests

What similarities and differences between NES and ESL perceptions do you find on this list? Discuss what characteristics you might add; give reasons for your choices.

3. How would you define a successful teaching encounter with a student? What kind of student do you think is the easiest for you to succeed with? Why? Describe the kind of student you think is the most difficult for you to succeed with. Why?

4. In her article "A Framework for Cross-Cultural Analysis of Teaching Methods" (1986), Patricia Furey suggests several areas of cross-cultural classroom differences: how students and teachers address one another; how much silence or participation in class are valued, and under what conditions they should occur; what kinds and how much factual information and personal opinion it is appropriate for students and teachers to reveal; and what specific gestures and expressions are appropriate for teachers and students to use. In pairs or small groups, discuss these areas of concern: How much do you know

about each? How might you handle each of these areas in the classroom? What problems could each cause in a class?

5. Below are several comments made by ESL writing students. Using the stages of change chart in this chapter, work within a small group to identify the stage each of the students below is in.

    A. I'm spending all my time doing the homework for this class.

    B. I don't understand how to get all my ideas organized.

    C. I tried brainstorming, and I think it's going to work for me.

    D. I don't think I'm a good student.

    E. Is this going to be on the test?

    F. I'm not very interested in writing.

    G. Maybe if you changed this assignment to X, it would be more interesting for the class.

    H. How can I get all this done?

    I. Why is this important?

    J. The way I do this in my language is better.

6. Analyze the lesson plans in this chapter. Can you infer differences in teaching styles among the teachers by examining their lesson plans?

7. Below are some extracts from the journals of graduate students in an ESL methodology course (each had participated in an ESL tutoring / teaching experience). Discuss their reactions with your peers. With which of these statements can you identify?

    A. "I feel like we're flogging a dead horse sometimes. Are we making any progress?" (courtesy of Christine Stebbins)

    B. "I am excited about meeting Margareth for the first time in quite a while because I feel ready. I have something wonderful to offer, and I'm anxious to see how it goes." (courtesy of Jodi Hill)

    C. "I was so mad that I couldn't get the equipment to work. I wasted a whole class." (courtesy of Mark Walker)

    D. "If only I can start over! I feel so much more aware of what I am doing—so positive about the possibilities!" (courtesy of Mark Walker)

Writing

1. Take the Teaching Styles Inventory in Appendix 2. Summarize your results, and then write a journal entry about an area of those results that surprised you. After that, choose the results in another area and write an essay describing how you could apply those results in an ESL writing class that you might teach.

2. Use the results of the Perceptual Learning Style Preference survey you took in the last chapter and the results of the Teaching Style Inventory (above). Write a brief essay that defines your teaching and learning styles in the light of

those results. As you write, be aware that you are developing your own theory of second language acquisition as you develop your philosophy of teaching ESL writing.

3. Examine several ESL writing textbooks. Using the Evaluation Procedure in Chapter 5, determine which one of the books you would use in an ESL writing class. Write a report describing the class you consider appropriate for that book; include the type of writing program, the program goals, and the student needs and objectives. Also describe the learning setting, including class size, student age, language proficiency, learning and teaching styles, and cultural backgrounds.

4. Design a lesson plan form that would be useful for you. Share your form with peers; after the discussion, revise your form to better meet your needs.

5. Make three sequential lesson plans for the class for which you would use the textbook you chose in question #3. Use the form you designed in question #4.

CHAPTER 6

Collaborative and Cross-Cultural Activities

From a new teacher's learning log: "I prepared and prepared for my first class, but I was so nervous. I know I talked too fast because when I finished my lecture and completed the lesson plan, I still had 30 minutes 'til the end of class—so embarrassing!"

Overheard in an ESL teachers' office area: "Gotta go teach class—anybody have something I can do?"

The goal of the ESL writing teacher is to provide information about and contexts for practicing clear, fluent, effective communication of written ideas. Successful teaching is the result of dynamic interactions among curriculum and syllabus design, teachers and students, methodology and instructional materials (Richards, 1990a; Ur, 1992). Although single, discrete activities provide the teacher with "something to do" and can help bring about learning by offering students motivation and/or fun, they should also be based on a coherent theory of teaching, support the objectives of the class, and be integrated into the lesson plan. That is, any activity should have a rationale: Why do it? What part will this activity play in the learning process? What is expected to occur as a result of the activity? (Hutchinson and Waters, 1987). The teacher must also consider the cross-cultural differences in the classroom: Does the activity require any physical or verbal actions that are taboo or inappropriate in the cultures of the student participants? (Shoemaker and Shoemaker, 1991).

One of the first steps toward fluent writing is learning how to approach writing. ESL students need to be taught repertoires of strategies to use as they generate ideas, draft pieces of writing, and encounter feedback from peers and teachers (Cohen and Cavacanti, 1990). In other words, there is much more to learning successful writing than simply learning the grammar and vocabulary of English. Students need to know that writing involves not only linguistic processes but also social and cognitive processes (Edelsky, 1989;

D. Johnson, 1989). They must learn when it is appropriate to write, what is appropriate to write for an identified audience in a specific situation (i.e., the interaction between writer, text, and reader), and how to organize ideas appropriately for that audience and purpose. To assist their students toward those goals, ESL writing teachers must research U.S. academic writing and the discourse communities that design, assign, and evaluate those assignments. They must gather that information, identify the rules of use of that discourse community, and provide opportunities for students to identify, understand, practice, and fulfill the expectations of the U.S. academic discourse communities they will enter.

Teachers must also consider the classroom atmosphere in which teaching and learning take place. David Nunan's research to identify the "good language learner" has showed that formal instruction is necessary and worthwhile—but insufficient—for second language acquisition. "Motivation, a preparedness to take risks and the determination to apply their developing language skills outside the classroom characterized most of the responses from these 'good' language learners. In terms of classroom learning, most [students] stressed the importance of communicative language tasks. Also significant were affective factors in the classroom" (1989a, p. 15). In other words, teachers must work to create a positive, supportive environment even though the culturally determined student expectations may impose limitations on the social climate of the classroom (Crookes and Chaudron, 1991). Implicit in this classroom climate is the concept of **community**, in which students help each other as much as possible (Hairston, 1986b); it is central to the communicative (or community) approach that learners exchange meanings and express opinions of their own (Brookes and Grundy, 1990). In ESL writing classes, collaborative and communicative activities raise student awareness concerning audience expectations and allow students to learn about the organizational patterns of written academic English.

Fundamental to any philosophy of teaching is the tenet that classroom time should be spent on activities that the students cannot do—or cannot do as well—outside the classroom; often, then, classes focus on what is difficult or problematic for the students. But differences in culture, age, background, education, and objectives present teachers with special challenges in deciding what, exactly, the focus of classroom time should be. After all, language learners show individual variation in their learning patterns, styles, and preferences, and students have individual needs and expectations. Moreover, each language community and each classroom is different, so teachers need to modify relevant techniques, approaches, and activities to suit those local contexts (Hudelson, 1991). And teachers need to examine their own attitudes toward teaching and learning since these attitudes can affect their students' success.

Selection and Design Criteria for Classroom Activities

Teachers and researchers (Breen, 1985; Dubin et al., 1986; K. Morrow, 1977; Oxford, 1990; Scarcella, 1990, 1992; Tikunoff, 1985) have suggested criteria for the analysis and selection of classroom activities:

1. **appropriacy of task:** the activity supports the objectives of the class;
2. **meaningful context:** the need to explain to students the purpose, the expectations, and the audience for each activity;
3. **authenticity:** texts or types of discourse, roles, and situations that students need and find relevant;
4. **facilitation:** clear communication of the instructions concerning the process and the outcome(s) of the activity, and adequate guidance in performing the tasks;
5. **feedback opportunities:** between student and student, student and teacher, student and self, student and group, students and teacher;
6. **accountability:** the evaluation of the activity by both the teacher and the students.

None of the suggestions that follow in this and in the next chapter is a complete lesson plan for an ESL writing class. The assumption is that a teacher comes to this chapter with (a) a syllabus that is based on an analysis of student needs, (b) lesson plans with specific objectives, and (c) a textbook that enables the goals of the course. The focus of this chapter is to provide teachers with underlined areas of activities, not with a random list of tasks to get them through a class. Each section is based on pedagogical theory and contains sample tasks, each of which might serve as a springboard for additional activities and can function as a supplement to textbooks and lesson plans in the ESL writing class. The activities in this chapter are organized around the idea of the classroom community, from start-up/warm-up activities (to build communal bonds) to cross-cultural activities that raise student awareness and allow students to understand the culturally derived attitudes and outlooks of others. Most of the tasks can be adapted for all levels of language proficiency, but complex tasks (or parts of the task that are more complex) are identified with a cross (✚). Activities that are especially appropriate for newer teachers are indicated by an arrowhead (➤). "*Caveats*" in relevant sections present potential problems identified by experienced teachers and offer possible solutions. Because of the integration of pedagogy and teaching philosophy, the categories and the learning tasks often overlap.

Start-Ups

Establishing a classroom atmosphere of mutual trust and respect begins the first day of class. Teachers should plan non-threatening activities that will allow students to get acquainted and initiate relationships. Using interactive and collaborative tasks such as the following can foster the creation of the classroom community.

The First Days: Introductions

►Interviews: One student interviews another, or two students interview one in groups of three. The teacher provides a question sheet with enough room for written answers. Sample questions:

1. What's your name? What country are you from? What city or town?
2. How many brothers / sisters do you have? What are their ages?
3. What was your biggest achievement? favorite secondary school class?
4. What is your favorite activity? hobby? sport? Why?
5. Where have you traveled? Describe a travel experience you have had.

Following the interviews, students can (a) introduce their interviewee to the class; (b) write a paragraph for homework about that interviewee; (c) create additional questions based on the original questions to ask their interviewee.

Unfinished Sentences: Students complete sentences such as the ones below in class or at home, then share and discuss their completed sentences in groups of four or five:

1. I feel happy when . . .
2. On Saturday, I like to . . .
3. The most important thing in my life is . . .
4. One thing that makes me angry is . . .
5. The most beautiful place I have ever been is . . .

During group discussion, students can (a) take notes on what they hear, (b) ask questions about what they hear, (c) and/or collectively choose one sentence for each student in the group as the most interesting, about which they'd like to hear more. Follow-up activities: students choose one of their own sentences and write more detail about it (either in class or at home) and then share their expanded work.

►Timeline: Each student makes a timeline, highlighting the most important events of his/her life, following the form below or another form. Then students post their timelines on a board or around the classroom. The other students view them silently, taking notes about the questions they wish to ask the writers. Or the students share the timelines in groups of three to five, in much the same way as the "unfinished sentences" activity above.

IMPORTANT EVENTS IN MY LIFE

1962	1968	1975	1980	1988	1991
born in X	began school	Argentina visit	Family moves to U.S.	Married	Son born

►Authority Lists: Ask students to spend five minutes writing lists of subjects that they know about. At first, students may feel that they are not authorities on any topic, but key questions may stimulate their memories: What do you do in your leisure time? What are your hobbies? What gives you pleasure? What do you do well? What could you teach a younger brother or sister? These lists can function as the basis for group discussion and/or for both immediate and later choice of writing topics. Students might add to the lists at various times during the course.

Simulation: The radio has just announced that a natural disaster (such as a typhoon, an earthquake, a tornado, a hurricane, a blizzard) is imminent. Everyone must find a safe place and take a few important things with them. Each student makes a list of ten things s/he would take. Students then share lists in pairs or small groups and, through discussion, prioritizing, defending choices, and reaching consensus, collectively list twenty things a survivor would need. ✚Each pair or group writes an authentic letter to the Department of Civil Defense (U. S. Office of Civil Defense, Training and Education, The Pentagon, Washington, D.C. 20310) to request information about actual materials to use in a natural disaster (Shoemaker and Shoemaker, 1991). Students might then revise their letters, write final drafts, and mail the letters.

Warm-Ups

Many students entering a classroom have completed their reading and writing assignments but have not really thought about the class itself. Introducing the class and "warming up" the students (getting them ready for class activities) can be time-consuming and frustrating for a teacher. Often, journal writing or a warm-up activity can shorten the introductory time; in addition, asking students to prepare for a discussion or classroom activity after they arrive in class will often result in better discussions and more successful activities because the short preparatory time allows students to collect their thoughts and focus on the class. Finally, planning regular warm-up activities signals the students that class begins on time; students who arrive late may have to complete the warm-up activities as homework.

Caveats

Writing students whose language proficiency is limited will need more guidance and more time to do warm-ups, as much as fifteen minutes to focus, plan, and write a spontaneous paragraph. Those students might warm up with a daily diary entry ("What I Did Yesterday") or by answering questions on a worksheet or on the board. Below are sample warm-ups.

►Focused Freewriting: For the first five minutes of class, have students write whatever comes to mind, without stopping, on a personal topic that is easily accessible. Some suggestions:

1. If you were in class in your home country today, what would you be doing?
2. Describe X as you remember X when you were a child; how is X different now? Examples: a relative, a place, a family member, a room in your house in your country.
3. Write four words that describe how you are feeling now. Choose one; explain why you are feeling that way.
4. Which would you choose, fame or money? Why?
5. Remember one incident from (yesterday, one week ago, one year ago) and describe it.

►Focused Journal Entries: Ask students to write in their journals for the first five minutes of class, to warm up for class. Journal activities can include

1. summarizing the main ideas from the last class
2. predicting what will occur in class
3. summarizing the reading they did for the day's class
4. writing about a problem they are having with the assigned writing
5. analyzing, in writing, what they are learning as they work on their current essay. (For more information about journals, see below.)

Group Projects (discussed in detail later in this chapter): Whether students are working on a student newsletter, on booklets about their countries, on an advice manual for incoming international students, or on recipe books, working on these projects in groups at the beginning of class will serve as a warm-up.

Collaborative Learning and Group Work

The use of collaborative and group activities in the ESL writing classroom has been the single most influential composition teaching strategy over the past decade (S. D. Reid, 1992b). Group and collaborative work in language classrooms provides non-threatening situations for developing communicative skills and fulfilling the linguistic need for interaction (Long and Porter, 1985; Peyton and Reed, 1991; Peyton and Staton, 1991; Pica et al., 1987). Collaborative activities unite and integrate all skills: conversation and discussion, comprehension of spoken and written text, and information for extended written compositions (Blanton, 1992; Brumfit, 1984). Learners use each other's resources and work toward common goals; the result is the strengthening of the positive classroom climate and community. As Lilia Savova and Richard Donato point out, "the feeling of positively contributing to the successful achievement of a task, typical for group work, increases students' motivation to learn, fosters learners' allegiance to each other, and stresses the value of every learner's contribution to the learning process . . . Their need to teach others causes them to seek assistance that results in peer-teaching and problem-solving strategies" (1991, p. 13). Although an effective class will not rely entirely on group work and collaboration, using these techniques for part of a class will enable students to use multiple learning styles in the learning process.

Research with both NES and ESL students has shown that students can and do teach each other in many successful ways (Bassano and Christison, 1988; Dansereau, 1988; Gaies, 1985; Scarcella and Oxford, 1992). The following list suggests small group discussions, collaborative writing, and other related activities for classroom strategies that may help learners to establish the mind-set for successful collaborative work.

Objectives	Activities
1. to lower inhibitions	interviewing classmates, sharing experiences, small group discussion of experiences, writing about experiences
2. to build self-confidence	listing strengths, complimenting each other, listing accomplishments, reporting accomplishments to the class
3. to develop motivation	explicit discussion and writing about the short-term and long-term rewards of learning to write English

4. to learn cooperatively	peer review groups and collaborative writing
5. to develop tolerance	writing about what students don't understand, about feelings of ambiguity (of being overwhelmed, frustrated); sharing and discussing in small groups
6. to take risks	writing about and discussing individual opinions; taking a stand in writing
	(adapted from H. D. Brown, 1989, pp. 5–6)

Collaboration and small group work can be especially successful in ESL writing classes. Writing is usually easier, better, and more successful when talking, drafting, revising, reading, and editing in groups are part of the writing process. Students exchange information in an open-ended, real-life context to fulfill personal goals (Blanton, 1992; Savova and Donato, 1991). In small groups, students can

- collaboratively gather information, generate and support opinions, and respond to ideas
- problem-solve, evaluate, and make decisions
- role-play or participate in simulation activities in the process of discovery
- collaborate in reader response activities: annotating, analyzing, evaluating articles and student essays.

The social communities of peer groups provide student writers with a real audience, and because student writers are often alienated from their audience and find it difficult to remember what the readers need to know (Gere, 1987), working in a small group of peers allows writers to explore the effectiveness of their ideas. They discover what they know and don't know, and what their readers understand and don't understand. They are able to articulate and test ideas before committing them to paper. (For more information on the use of peer review and peer response groups, see the Chapter 7.)

Caveats

Blindness and randomness can be disadvantageous corollaries of group and collaborative work. First, while almost any classroom lecture, discussion, or activity can be restructured into small group work, collaborative activities work best when they are part of an overall sequence that has some individual writing, reading, or thinking, some small group collaboration, and some synthesis with the class as a whole. As James Corder (1991) points out, no one model of teaching guarantees that students will learn; different occasions, audiences, subject matter, and opportunities demand different methods of teaching. Indeed, while collaborative learning may allow students to discover knowledge, and while it does place the burden of the responsibility for learning on the students, it may descend into pretentious "multivoiced monologues" (ibid, p. 2) (randomness). In contrast, the traditional lecture, which many international students find both worthwhile and comfortable, allows the teacher to share the burden and responsibility for learning with the students. Furthermore, it can provide students with a more direct conduit to knowledge.

Second, students may not react positively to group work. Some students do not learn efficiently in groups; in the diverse ESL writing classroom, differing student learning styles and strategies may impede group work (randomness). Some students may not know how to negotiate or may not choose to negotiate; in fact, an entire group may sit silent as a stone during the activity. These unprepared or uncooperative students can derail small group activities (blindness, randomness), and the teacher will experience as many feelings of failure as the students. Another problem occurs in peer review and peer response groups, when students give misleading, wrong, and even counterproductive feedback (because of the inherent blindness and randomness). The substantial breakdown of trust the teacher encounters in this situation is frustrating; the sense of community may be fractured as a result.

As a consequence of all these variables and constraints, teachers cannot simply assign students to a group and expect them to operate successfully. Students grouped into small units must be trained in the kinds of strategies to use (H. D. Brown, 1991; Fox, 1990; Oxford, 1990; Scarcella and Oxford, 1992). These students need discussion of, preparation for, and guidance in their peer collaboration. Small group work and collaboration should therefore be (a) modeled by the teacher, (b) structured and facilitated by the teacher, at least in the initial stages, and (c) based on learning strategies that the teacher describes for the students and allows them to investigate and practice (A. Cohen, 1990; O'Malley et al., 1985; Rubin, 1987; Scarcella and Oxford, 1992). And the newer the teacher or the students to group and collaborative work, the more planning and structuring is necessary.

Planning Group Work

Successful writing groups are often those that balance personalities, learning styles, and tasks to be accomplished. It is often helpful for each student to have a role in the group, a contribution to make: as a recorder, an "idea- person," a harmonizer, an organizer, and so on. Initially, teachers might form groups that consist of a talkative student, a quiet student, a more experienced writer, and a less experienced writer. Often ESL writing groups consist of three to five students: larger groups may work better when students are brainstorming at the beginning of a project or presenting results; smaller groups work best for organizing, reviewing, revising, or editing student drafts. A two-person (pair) group can be very successful, particularly in the review and revision processes, if the partners trust each other and have specific tasks. At the beginning of a class, groups can be organized randomly (students count off "1, 2, 3, 4," and then are grouped with like numbers) or by proximity (four desks near each other form a group). Sometimes groups are formed at the beginning of a term and are maintained throughout the class. In group reporting situations, the spokesperson from the group can report to the class, or the groups can be "fragmented" by having each group count off and then reassemble with like numbers. Each new **fragmented group** will consequently have a representative from the previous groups. Following are some general guidelines for group work.

- Select the groups so that each student can participate fully.

- Review the ground rules: Collaboration does not necessarily mean agreement, but minority opinions must be respected (and recorded and reported).

- Explain what the task is, why they'll be doing it, and how long they will have to complete it (as a rule, tell the students they have less time than you have actually planned); a statement of realistic purpose and clear roles for each member of the group is essential.

- Give the groups a limited task: Write instructions on the board or on a handout.

- Model the task: In a reader-response task for a textbook essay, the teacher might put another essay on a transparency and use an overhead projector and a marker pen to annotate the essay for the class, speaking aloud as s/he reacts to the essay ("I wonder why the author said this. . . . What does this word mean? . . . Oh, I don't agree with this at all. . . . Nice description here.").

- If you have the groups report to the class, have the class applaud (or give positive feedback in other ways) after each presentation (to ease the discomfort and to promote enthusiasm and a sense of community).

- At the end of the activity, have the students write in their journals, analyzing the success of the activity, or reporting the results, or describing the process of the activity.

Caveats

Group work can sometimes leave the teacher feeling "on the outside" and the students with the perception that the teacher isn't teaching. During group or collaborative work, the teacher should establish a pattern of facilitation, mediation, and mini-conferencing (2- to 3-minute individual student conferences). Students should realize that the teacher is a knowledge/experience resource. As the group work proceeds, the teacher can (a) circulate, answering questions and encouraging discussion, (b) intervene as necessary, (c) briefly join each group, or (d) mini-conference with students either in the groups or at the teacher's desk. Below are sample activities that use collaboration and group work.

➤Shared Notes: Students take notes about a lecture or mini-lecture on a topic (perhaps suggested by the students or by student needs) developed by the teacher. In small groups, they compare their notes with other notes taken by group members. In what ways do the notes differ? Analyze the possible reasons for those differences. Try to reach consensus on what the major idea(s) of the lecture were. ✦Construct a summary of the main points of the lecture. Discuss what makes note-taking difficult.

Group Summaries: In small groups, students read and individually summarize an essay, an article, a chapter, or another reading passage in about 250 words. Students compare their summaries with the other summaries in the group. In what ways do the summaries differ? ✦Students can analyze the possible reasons for those differences. What makes summarizing difficult? (For specific information concerning peer review and peer response groups, see Chapter 7.)

✦Newspaper Completion: Make copies of a newspaper feature article (not an editorial or a straight news story): cut off the last paragraph (or more). Ask students to read the article. Then, based on their discussion of the main points of the article, have them reach consensus on what the end of the article said. Have the group write that last part, then share the different last paragraphs with other groups.

Newspaper Headlines: Make copies of newspaper headlines (that require only general knowledge, not current events); each group might have a different headline. Ask the groups to brainstorm questions relating to the story behind the headline, then to answer those questions and write the story together.

Curiosity Lists: Students in a small group should brainstorm questions or issues they are curious about. Again, the teacher may, in modeling this activity, stimulate discussion by inventing questions:

"How do snow fences function? . . . Why do baby girls in the United States wear pink and baby boys wear blue? . . . Does exercise have a positive psychological effect? . . . How does El Niño affect the weather? . . . Why do starlings have wishbones? . . . What is the study of proxemics? . . . What is a Type A personality? . . . How do water towers work?" Follow-up activities: ✚Investigate the answers to questions through interviews with experts and library research; then write an investigative essay.

➤Sentence Combining: Using actual sentences from student essays, the teacher first explains the rationale and principles for sentence combining and then models sentence combining on the board or on an overhead projector transparency. Groups are given sentences to combine in a variety of ways and then share their sentences in "fragmented groups" (see above) or on the board.

Round Robin Brainstorming: Students are asked to brainstorm for an essay topic, either in pairs or in groups, either orally or in writing, with quantity rather than quality being the most important factor. Or they might brainstorm two sides of an argumentative topic, with each person in the group taking turns. The recorder in the group then reports to the class, or the teacher lists the ideas on the board, or each group shares with another group.

✚Group Problem-Solving: The teacher presents a problem (which s/he has perhaps solicited from or discussed with the class previously). The students set up criteria to evaluate potential solutions, then brainstorm solutions, prioritize solutions, and evaluate the implementation of those solutions. Each person in the group should serve as a recorder; at the end of the discussion, they share their notes and write a single document together. After they select a solution, they make the necessary adjustments to that solution and present it to the class. Sample problems:

- how to change the TOEFL to make it a better test
- what advice the group would give to new students about adjustments to U.S. academic classes
- what NES writing tutors in U.S. writing centers should know about ESL students, and how they can best help ESL students
- how the group would spend half a million dollars
- the best ways to settle an argument with a friend

Analysis of Advertisements: Students are given several advertisements from two very different magazines such as *Home Beautiful* and *Muscle*. Each group may have different advertisements, or all groups can have the same ads. The groups are instructed to describe the ads and to decide what kind of people might respond positively to each ad. ✦All students take notes as they formulate criteria for the analysis, and then they decide whether or not each ad is successful and why. Students can then share their analyses with the class and/or write paragraphs/essays about the targeted audience for each of the magazines.

✦Outrageous Claim: The teacher will have to begin this exercise by modeling some outrageous claims. Samples: high school athletes who want to play college sports should not have to go to class— instead, they should be paid university employees; subliminal advertising should be legalized; Arnold Schwarzenegger is the best U.S. actor. Have groups agree on a single claim that is clearly unsupportable (the more outrageous, the better); then have them create similarly outrageous support. All students should keep notes; at the end of the discussion, the claim and the support should be shared, polished, and then articulated on an overhead transparency (by the best scribe in the group). The spokesperson for the group should present the information on the overhead (often to the great amusement of the class).

Culturgrams: Sophia Shang (1991) suggests using Culturgrams (a series of bulletins developed by and available from the Brigham Young University's David M. Kennedy Center for International Studies in Provo, Utah) to further cross-cross-cross-cultural understanding in the ESL classroom. Students can read these brief introductions to the cultures of their peers, then interview those peers about the contents. The objective of such materials: "the better you understand and are prepared to deal with your own and other people's expectations, values, and desires, the more effective you can be in your interactions" (Tyler, 1985, p. 1). Follow-up activities: (a) summarizing the information in one Culturgram; (b) writing a paragraph or essay concerning the results of the interview with the peer from the country of the Culturgram; ✦(c) asking a student from the country of the Culturgram to read the bulletin, then analyze and write about it, adding to the information in the Culturgram.

The Journal (Daybook, Learning Log)

Journal writing, another innovation in writing classrooms, has probably been the most widely used and successful activity during the last decade. It has grown from an adjunct activity to a fully integrated part of the writing class. One reason for the popularity of journal writing is the flexibility it offers students and teachers. As Ken Autrey suggests, journals are a valid genre in themselves and should not be marginalized as simply diaries (1991). Journals can be used as opportunities for student-teacher dialogs; as places to record notes, gather materials, and plan writing; and for write-to-learn activities that stress metacognition (that is, writing to discover what the student has learned, and reflecting on the processes of learning to learn). Another reason for the popularity of journals is that they engage students in non-threatening exploration and development of ideas; they are "the most consistently effective tool for establishing fluency" (Kirby et al., 1988, p. 57).

Journal entries are an integral part of the writing process. Students can practice invention heuristics (that is, idea-gathering strategies) as they make notes about their plans, then write a preliminary "rehearsal draft" or "discovery draft" before writing sections of the paper and revising those drafts, all in their journals. They might write two introductions or two conclusions, then analyze which is more appropriate for their audiences and purposes. They can write entries that complement formal assignments (such as an analysis of the audience for a professional essay), or expand on formal assignments (for example, writing a "preface" to a finished paper, indicating what the student-writer perceives as the strengths and weaknesses of his/her paper, the purposes of and audience for the paper, and other relevant comments). They can experiment with different rhetorical forms and purposes as they become familiar with their writing processes. In these ways, students will learn to value the impact of their own voices as writers. The fundamentals of establishing successful journal writing in and out of class include the following points:

- begin the journal on a small scale
- initially, model writing journal entries for students
- explain journal assignments in detail
- use student examples (with permission), and analyze them, using the overhead projector, with questions such as

  How do you think the writer felt about this entry?
  Who is the audience?
  Which details are the most memorable?
  How did you feel when you read this entry?

- set aside some regular class time for journal writing (see Start-Ups and Collaborative Work, above)
- have students date and number entries in the margin (for ease of grading).

Journals are, of course, not meant to substitute for an entire writing program. After all, revision is not usually a part of journal entries, and accuracy is of limited importance. Journal writing is a written genre with limited features and functions; it includes few rhetorical forms, purposes, audiences, and styles (Jones, 1988). And because journal writing requires patience, persistence, and the development of expertise in both students and teacher, it takes time and energy to learn and to teach the skills. But journals can also serve students well in their search for coherence, unity, and inner voice that will give them fluency (Benitéz, 1990).

Caveats

Evaluation of student journals is widely thought to be their greatest drawback. Just reading student journals can be extremely time-consuming; assessing them can be frustrating as well. Many advocates of journal writing insist that journals should not be evaluated, just "credited." That is, students should date and number their journal entries in the margins, making counting (and giving credit) easier for the teacher. Other teachers and researchers, however, think that evaluating journals as pieces of writing encourages students to participate fully in the writing process (Parsons, 1989). Some teachers have maximum or, more often, minimum page or word limits for creditable journal entries. Students are then given credit for thoroughness and completeness rather than for quality of thought, organization and/or mechanics. The teacher can even ask students to choose one entry out of three for the teacher to read and respond to; the teacher records that other entries were made, but reads only the chosen ones (Walworth, 1990). Below are suggestions for three general kinds of journal activities; each category includes several sample activities.

Dialog Journals: These are interactive journals in which students write entries to and for the teacher, and the teacher responds with a journal entry of his/her own. The students can leave the back of each page empty for teacher response. In a dialog journal, students can

1. ask the teacher questions about class material;
2. discuss problems they may be having in the writing process;
3. write retrospective analyses of the class;
4. generate topics for discussion; and/or
5. express personal concerns (Peyton and Reed, 1990).

The teacher reads the entries without correcting, responding to what is written, not how it is written. Since the focus is on fluency and communication, the teacher responds to queries, gives information, encourages, comments on successes and accomplishments, discusses topics, and expresses concern. This exchange is real-world communication that involves a mutual search for meaning in a personally relevant context. Research on dialog journals demonstrates that teachers' responses are taken seriously by students, that individual attention is appreciated (Blanton, 1987; Dolly, 1990; Hayes et al., 1986; Peyton and Reed, 1991; Porat, 1988; Reyes, 1991), and that students feel "empowered having teachers respond to their lives and ideas authentically and respectfully" (Peyton, 1990, p. xii).

Dialog journals need not be only between teacher and students. Students can be paired with (or they can choose) student dialog partners in the class. Each pair can communicate perceptions of class work, react to class discussion, review each other's drafts, question ideas, and ask for feedback; the content of the journals can be as personal or impersonal as the dialog partners choose. Journal partners can also be established with students from two classes in the same writing program, either of similar or dissimilar fluency levels, if the teachers of those classes are willing. Moreover, with the advent and use of computers in ESL writing classes, dialog partners can live around the world. Students can write each other on electronic mail, discussing issues of mutual concern, asking cross-cultural questions, and responding to each other's ideas (Cummings, 1986; Mabrito, 1991; Naiman, 1988; Robb, 1991; Sayers, 1986). In these and in other dialog partner situations, partners learn to respond honestly and directly in a nonjudgmental way, offering options for future dialog. Students are reading as well as writing; they "have the opportunity to use writing to communicate and to express concepts that are important to them, to accomplish real purposes, to be read by an interested audience, and to receive a reply that is genuine and meaningful" (Peyton, 1990, p. 11).

Metacognitive Entries: "Metacognitive" means thinking about the ways you think, writing about the ways you write, and learning about the ways you learn. Metacognitive journal entries provide opportunities for an integration of all three areas of reflection: students write about the ways they think, write, and learn. By investigating their learning styles and strategies, and by analyzing their writing rituals, strengths, and weaknesses, students become more able to reflect upon their decision-making processes in writing. For example, the idea that writing demands multiple and nearly continuous decision-making is often a surprise for students (the perspiration-versus-inspiration argument). As they consider their thought and decision-making processes, they begin to understand themselves as writers, and as a result, they may begin to monitor their performance as members of the writing community (Marting, 1991). As the semester progresses, students can continue to examine their composing processes, their reader response skills, and the positive changes in their writing; most important, they become aware of two facts: (a) they are learning, and (b) learning is their responsibility. In addition, such journal entries provide the teacher with feedback: students' perspectives can prove invaluable in reviewing and revamping lesson plans. Below are some possible metacognitive journal assignments.

On the Writing Process

➤1. How did you decide to select (or discover) this topic?

➤2. Describe the process you went through to write this paper.

3. When you encountered a problem in writing this paper, how did you solve it? Be specific!

4. What was the easiest part of writing this paper? The most difficult? Why?

5. Identify three major revisions you made in this paper. Why did you make them and what effect did they create?

➤6. What do you like best about this paper? ✚Why?

7. What do you think is the weakest part of this paper? ✚Why?

8. If you had one more opportunity to revise this paper, what would you change? How? Why?

9. How would you like your readers to feel, think, and/or act when they have finished reading your paper?

After In-Class Writing

1. How did you feel when you first read the assignment?

2. What did you do first? Second? After that? Then what?

3. What kinds of decisions did you make?

✚4. If you had twice as much time, in what ways would your paper have been different?

On Collaborative and Group Work

1. In your opinion, what is the greatest advantage of peer groups for you? The greatest disadvantage? Why?

✚2. How would you describe yourself as a peer responder?

➤3. How did you help your peers during the peer review session in class today?

➤4. What did you learn during the peer workshop that you'll be able to use in your essay?

5. How did your peers help you? Be specific.

At the End of the Semester/Final Examination

➤1. What was easy about the class? Difficult?

➤2. What problems did you encounter during the course? How did you solve them?

➤3. What still troubles you about your writing? Why?

➤4. What did you learn?

<u>Learning Log Entries</u>: The write-to-learn movement has spread not only through English Departments but through other disciplines as well, as the Writing Across the Curriculum movement has changed the way some professors view writing. Students in biology, psychology, natural resources, and business classes go beyond note-taking to explore, react, make connections, and evaluate material in their learning logs or daybooks. Empirical research results have been mixed concerning the statistical gains made by writing in the disciplines, but advocates point out that, at the very least, writing about class material helps students master that material, demonstrate understanding of what they have learned, and develop higher-order thinking skills such as analysis and synthesis (Maimon, 1989; 1991a; McLeod, 1991b). Teachers indicate that both NES and ESL students discover ways to relate and integrate their background knowledge with class sources, and that they develop skills in writing for and responding to an audience (Janopoulos, 1992b; McLeod, 1991b; Porter et al., 1990; Walworth, 1990).

Learning log entries serve students in ESL writing classes in equally beneficial ways. Like NES, ESL students

- summarize the main ideas of the class;
- reflect on what they learned during a class;
- predict what test questions might be;
- interpret and synthesize material; and
- explore ideas in their journals (Fulwiler, 1987; Lucas, 1990).

Learning log entries expand on the concept of note-taking because they link old information with new as the student writes and thinks at the same time (Benítez, 1990). Some teachers stop a class discussion that has slowed or that has gotten too emotional and ask students to commit their thoughts to paper. In many TEFL/TESL graduate programs, teachers in training keep learning logs in which they summarize, synthesize, and reflect on their student teaching experiences (Ching and Ngooi, 1991; Fleckenstein, 1989; Jarvis, 1992; Pritchard, 1987; Richards and Lockhart, 1991–1992; Richards and Nunan, 1990).

Cross-Cultural Activities

Despite their preparation for entering U.S. culture, ESL students can be expected to react to the overload of the unknown in the new culture with curiosity, confusion, frustration, and/or anger. New classroom experiences such as collaborative work, participating in analytic discussions, and self-reflection and analysis in journals can affect ESL students profoundly. These encounters with what Carol

Archer calls "culture bumps" (1986) may hinder language learning. ESL writing classes can assist students in recognizing and expressing their feelings, examining their beliefs and native cultures, and observing and understanding aspects of the new culture. In addition, learning about U.S. academic expectations and writing formats can increase student awareness; the ESL writing classroom is a safe place in which to identify and practice appropriate behaviors and to make mistakes. Moreover, learning about the factors affecting rhetorical patterns in U.S. academic prose can help students manage the adjustment of their evolution into full participants in the new culture. The activities below have as objectives (a) the cross-cross-cross-cultural education of ESL students in a writing class, (b) the introduction of U.S. cultural concepts, and particularly of U.S. expectations concerning academic writing, and (c) opportunities for student identification and practice of those expectations.

Journal Entries: The assignments below offer students an informal opportunity to raise awareness of their own culture by closely observing small, discrete aspects of U.S. culture and then comparing the two. In a series of journal entries, perhaps two or three a week, students can compare some of the following practices in their own countries and (at least what they have so far observed) in the United States. As well as describing the similarities and differences, ✚students might try (a) interviewing U.S. students about these questions and/or (b) analyzing why the differences might occur. Note that the factual and clearly descriptive assignments are more appropriate for students with a lower level of English language proficiency, while the assignments that require supported opinion and ✚analysis are more successful for students with more advanced levels of language proficiency.

➤1. How do friends greet each other and say goodbye? Does age make a difference?

✚2. Discuss the use of the use of the pronoun "I" in conversation.

3. What persons are given the most respect? ✚Why?

➤4. What foods do you eat for breakfast? lunch? dinner? snacks?

➤5. What are the most popular games that are played outdoors (indoors) by children (adults)?

6. What are the conventional phrases used on the telephone?

7. What is fashionable dress for students your age?

8. Where do friends often meet for pleasure? What do they do?

➤9. How do most people travel short distances?

10. What careers have strong appeal for young people? ✚Why?

11. How are apologies offered? For what situations are apologies required?

12. How are compliments (or gratitude or directions) expressed? ✚Which situations demand compliments? ✚Why?

(adapted from Valdes, 1986)

Group Project: Divide students into groups of individuals from different cultural backgrounds. Ask each student to bring information (and perhaps artifacts) to the group concerning (a) a holiday, (b) a legend/myth, (c) a folktale, (d) a superstition, (e) a joke, (f) a tradition, and/or (g) a saying from their countries. Students should share their information, answering questions and taking notes. Follow-up activities can include

1. journal entries summarizing what the students learned;

2. writing about the holiday or superstition; writing an explanation of the saying or the tradition; and/or ✚translating the folktale or the myth (to be published in the student newsletter, a booklet for the program or a public school class);

3. adding U.S. students to the group to share their culture (and learn);

➤4. a formal writing assignment about the holiday, the myth, the tradition (including pre-writing, drafting, student workshopping, revision, and final drafting).

Essay Assignment: A U.S. student who is your friend is going to visit your country. S/he asks you to help prepare her/him for the visit:

➤1. If you were going to teach this U.S. student your native language, how would you begin? What would you teach first? second? after that? What specific problems might the U.S. friend have with your language? What errors would s/he be likely to make?

➤2. What might surprise the U.S. friend about your country?

➤3. In addition to the language, what might the friend find difficult to understand?

4. What cultural problems might the friend encounter? ✚What serious cultural errors might s/he make? How can s/he avoid these errors?

5. What suggestions would you give the friend that would enable her/him to have a successful and pleasant visit? ✚Explain your reasons for these suggestions.

Nonverbal Communication: The teacher gives a mini-lecture that defines and explains nonverbal communication—proxemics, eye contact, the concept of time, gestures, etc. (for background, see Barnes,

1990; P. Byrd, 1986; Samovar and R. Porter, 1991; Valdes, 1986)—and gives some examples, including examples of gestures. Teachers should be careful to <u>emphasize the following in describing effective cross-cultural communication</u>:

1. an openness to new ideas and behaviors;
2. the ability to be non-judgmental (no right or wrong answers);
3. an interest in understanding people of different cultures;
4. an awareness that diversity of cultures exists within all countries (that none of us is a "typical" example, and that age, status, and geography, among other factors, cause differences in culture);
5. a willingness to listen, really listen, to others.

(courtesy of Jean Griswold, Colorado State
University Office of International Students)

Students participating in this nonverbal communication activity take notes, then share those notes in small groups (groups may be formed of students from different countries or they may be from the same country). The groups then discuss this topic:

> Some nonverbal communication is not the same in all countries, and therefore they may no be understood by members of another culture. Think about gestures in your cultural that have a different meaning for people in the United States. Describe each gesture and its meanings.

Follow-up activities:

1. Students write a short essay that introduces the idea of gestures as communication and then describe the gestures they have discussed in their groups.
2. ✚Discussion and journal assignment: In some cultures, time is a precious gift that should be used wisely and not wasted. In other cultures, people believe that they should not be ruled by the clock; to them, fully enjoying what one is doing is more important than keeping an appointment or meeting a deadline. In an essay, discuss some of the consequences of these two philosophies; use specific examples.

✚<u>Essay Assignment</u>: The teacher gives a mini-lecture on the concept of social and economic status in the United States; class discussion follows. The writing assignment: discuss the status of the professions of doctor, waitress, and teacher in your country. Give specific examples to support your discussion. Students gather information from their home experience and interview or survey other students from their own country to obtain the necessary information. Peer review groups workshop with the rough drafts. The final draft is read by students in the class, who then write a journal entry or a series of summaries about what they learned about other cultures.

➤Proverbs: A class discussion about the definition and explanation of proverbs begins this activity; the teacher might put several U.S. proverbs on the board and discuss the meaning and the cultural overtones of each. Or the teacher might give students several North American proverbs and ask them to discuss or write about possible meanings. Examples:

Two heads are better than one.   All's well that ends well.
Experience is the best teacher.   Love is blind.

Then the teacher might put on the board translations of proverbs from other cultures and ask students to describe and then predict the meaning of each. Examples:

The rice has turned into porridge .(courtesy of Yusuf Vlanet, Indonesia)
Laugh and grow fat.   (courtesy of Kazuaki Goto, Japan)
An empty wagon makes noise.   (courtesy of Sue Leon Lim, Korea)
Better an open enemy than a false friend.
                    (courtesy of Nidal Slaibi, Saudi Arabia)

At the beginning of each succeeding class, one student should put a proverb from his/her country on the board and explain it to the rest of the class. ✚Follow-up activity: students compile the proverbs, along with the explanations, and publish them (Williamson, 1991–1992).

Essay Assignment: The object of this assignment is to raise the students' awareness of the gender differences in their cultures. Following the pre-writing and group discussions suggested here, students can write an essay about their discoveries. The assignment: imagine that you have two weeks to live as a person of the opposite sex. If you are female, imagine you have two weeks to be a male; if you are male, imagine that you are a female. Consider the resulting differences in social roles, everyday life, and feelings. As you prewrite in your journal, answer the questions below:

1. What about your life would be better? Try to list at least three things.
2. What about your life would be worse? Try to list at least three things.
3. What about your life would not be changed? Try to list at least three things.
4. What would you most enjoy being able to do in those two weeks that you can't do now? Describe one thing in detail.
5. What would you least enjoy having to do during those two

weeks that you would probably have to do? Describe one thing in detail (courtesy of Barbara Kroll, 1991).

Newspapers and Culture: Students can learn much about cultures by comparing newspapers from their own countries and from the United States (Chimombo, 1987). In a sequence of classes, students can examine

- the front page (types of stories, headlines, level of detail)
- the advice column (what bothers the seekers of advice in each country? why do they seek advice from a stranger?)
- classified advertisements (how do the classifications differ? what abbreviations are used? what is most frequently advertised for sale?)
- ✦the editorial page (what issues are commented on? how do the political cartoons reflect the culture? what do citizens write about in letters to the editor?)

Follow-up activities include journal entries analyzing differences; individual or collaborative writing of news articles, advice columns, letters to the editor, or classified advertisements; writing for the student newspaper/newsletter.

➤Vice-Virtue Words: The teacher puts on the board two headings, *Vices* and *Virtues*, and explains the meaning of each. To begin the discussion, s/he might write "laziness" as a U.S. vice and "efficiency" as a U.S. virtue. Then a pair of students from the same country is asked to indicate which vices and virtues are the least- and the most-respected characteristics in their cultures. ✦The students write their prioritized lists on the board and then discuss their choices in small groups of two to three pairs each. Follow-up assignment: write a journal entry or a brief essay (either individually or in pairs) about the most-valued characteristics in your culture. Give specific examples to support your decisions.

Group Projects

Country Booklets: The teacher sets up a liaison with an elementary school class in the local area. The ESL students are to prepare written materials about their native countries for the elementary school students. The project will take one day a week during the course; it can be done individually, in pairs (from the same country), or in small groups (from the same country). The ESL writing students visit the elementary class early in the term, and, following introductions and a short discussion of the project, briefly interview (on a 1 to 1 or 1 to 2 ratio) the elementary students about what the young students would like to know about the writing students' countries. The students prepare pieces of writing each week; they can use library encyclopedias for maps and facts, but they should also write unique pieces about their families, their hobbies, their leisure time activities, their schooling, and so on. The elementary students might make the covers for the booklets, or the ESL students can do this; when the booklets are complete, the ESL students deliver them to the elementary school students (and food might be provided to enhance the interaction). Possible alternatives: folktale booklets for a secondary school class; an international recipe book for a community group.

✦Student Newspaper/Newsletter: Students in one ESL writing class (high intermediate or advanced classes in an intensive program work best) can be responsible for the student newspaper. They will work on it as a special project during two to four classes at the beginning of the term and in one class a week during the rest of the course. Depending on the length of the course, one to four issues of the newspaper/newsletter might be completed. Students can self-select or be assigned to one of several groups responsible for various parts of the newspaper/newsletter, such as interviews, advice column, jokes and sayings, fashion, movie and restaurant reviews, photography, editorials, features, or sports. If the students have access to computers, they can even form a committee that will type and lay out the newspaper; otherwise, the teacher or program clerical support will do the actual publishing. Each group has a series of tasks to accomplish (e.g., gathering information, drafting and revising information, peer reviewing each other's writing, and submitting the final drafts for publication). Each group organizes itself, works out a time schedule, and regularly meets outside of class. The teacher will function as a facilitator and a resource. In addition, students in the class can solicit excellent short pieces of writing from other writing classes to publish in the newsletter/newspaper. When the newspaper/newsletter is ready, students distribute copies throughout the writing (or intensive language) program, and copies are sent to appropriate administrators and departments throughout the university or college.

➤New Student Manual: This one-day-a-week project will provide incoming ESL students (new to the U.S., to the school, to the town) with "survival" information that goes beyond the program brochures and university bulletins. The project begins with a student-designed survey of current (new and not-so-new) students in the program, asking what kinds of information they would have been glad to have when they arrived, what situations surprised them, etc. Following the analysis of the needs assessment, students (in groups) design and write sections of the manual (for example, housing concerns, finding special foods, supporting student organizations, activities to meet fellow students). Students share and peer review those sections before submitting them for publication; copies of the publication are delivered to program administrators, the international student office, or the graduate office.

Caveats

While group projects are excellent activities, they are often difficult for the new teacher to manage, especially if no direct support and resources are available (such as clerical assistance, personal or program liaison with professors, understanding about academic or community processes outside the writing program, knowledge of community people and resources, information about publicity outlets, or travel arrangements for students). A teacher new to the teaching situation may therefore spend much time coordinating a group project. In addition, establishing and maintaining the essential motivation and forward progress for students involved in a group project require the teacher's time and energy to plan sequential activities, meet with students outside of class, draw on the individual strengths of group members, provide adequate materials, etc. Finally, group projects succeed when the appearance of student responsibility and freedom is balanced by a carefully woven safety net constructed by the teacher. When, for example, a group member is absent or nonparticipatory, a resource is suddenly unavailable or inappropriate, or a problem arises within the group, the teacher must be ready to step in unobtrusively to restore the balance and encourage the students to move ahead— sometimes a difficult task even for an experienced teacher. Fortunately, the time spent planning and managing group projects decreases as teachers become more experienced, and students who participate in these projects remember them as the highlights of their writing classes.

Conclusion

Effective language teaching reflects the degree to which teachers are able successfully to communicate their intentions, maintain student engagement and interest in the class, and monitor student performance (Richards, 1990a). Teachers should assess the total context in which instructional plans are formulated and develop materials from which additional, sequential materials can be created. At the end of each class, teachers should review the activity—and the new concepts of the lesson—and ask students to immediately evaluate their understanding of the material. After class, teachers will assess the use of those materials and revise them for future use. In short, activities should be a means to an end, not simply a means: the ESL writing teacher must therefore (a) define instructional objectives that are theoretically sound and appropriate for the students; (b) set meaningful learning tasks and activities to attain objectives; (c) inform learners of what tasks they have to perform; (d) provide guidance in how to perform communicative, authentic tasks; (e) provide practice in performing the tasks; (f) give helpful feedback; (g) reflect on and evaluate such classes; and (h) then revise the lesson accordingly.

Discussion Questions

1. Individually or in a small group, design and prepare a set of interview questions for an ESL writing teacher. Then interview the teacher to determine the teacher's approach to teaching: to the teaching of writing, the classroom activities used by the teacher, and what the teacher considers the main problem(s) in the teaching of ESL writing. Discuss the results in small groups.

2. Discuss, in a small group or as a class, the cultural ideas that could be taught by studying a U.S. newspaper. Consider not only the types of articles used in the activity in this chapter but also such sections as the personal column, obituaries, and the sports section. What specific issues might be shocking to students from Middle Eastern and/or Asian cultures? How could you approach the freedom of speech vs. censored news issue through the editorial page?

3. Examine the cultural perceptions of personality characteristics below. Discuss your perceptions of these characteristics as they might apply to cultures with which you have come in contact. How might you approach such different characteristics in an ESL writing classroom?

reserved	vs.	friendly, outgoing
rushed, time conscious	vs.	relaxed, easy going
realistic, hard-headed	vs.	optimistic
team worker	vs.	independent
quality conscious	vs.	output oriented
unemotional	vs.	emotional
serious, businesslike	vs.	fun-loving, joking
self controlled	vs.	self-indulgent

4. Look at the general procedures for group work in this chapter. Using the blindness-randomness criteria from Chapter 5, articulate the potential for blindness or randomness in each group work procedure.

5. Reread the group work exercises in this chapter. Then discuss, in pairs or in small groups, what overall class objective(s) for each of these activities might be. How might each activity fit into a teaching sequence?

6. With a partner, choose three activities described in this chapter. Working together, modify each activity for a specific class that you describe (in terms of age, level of language proficiency, objectives, and needs). Indicate what problems are possible for each activity, and a solution for each.

Writing

1. As you have read the previous chapters, you have begun to formulate your own philosophy of teaching ESL writing. Brainstorm for ten minutes as you begin to formulate your comprehensive theory of the teaching of ESL writing.

2. Individually, or in a small group, choose three activities in the chapter. Indicate how, for each of the activities, a teacher might reinforce the objectives of the class and the activity at the end of the class.

3. Choose one of the cross-cultural activities in this chapter; write a four-class to six-class sequence involving that activity. Share your sequences with others in the class.

4. Write a brief essay describing what you learned about your teaching philosophy as you developed the class sequences in question #3.

5. Choose four of the activities in the cultural section of this chapter. In a series of paragraphs, discuss the possible philosophy of teaching behind each: is each a language-based, pattern-model–based, process-based, or a combination-based philosophy? How do you know?

CHAPTER 7

English for Academic Purposes (EAP) and Integrated Skills Activities

Although nothing is inherently wrong with spot drilling, grammar practice, comprehension questions, and individual skills tasks, a successful second language classroom is usually based on (a) a rationally planned, **sequenced** series of lesson plans that (b) integrates many of the complex skills that are essential to language learning and (c) provides students with authentic learning experiences that are (d) related to their lives, their learning styles and strategies, and their learning objectives. The ESL writing classroom is no exception; activities that integrate language skills and seem "real" to the students will produce positive feedback and substantial language learning. Most important is the reality of the classroom itself as a language-learning environment (Breen, 1985); the classroom generates its own authenticity, its own sense of community. Of course, authenticity alone does not enhance the quality of the learning experience and need not necessarily involve actual materials and roles from the contemporary world, although the more real those materials and roles, the greater their validity in the eyes of the students. Materials and learning sequences from the real world outside the classroom provide students with experiences they will recognize as useful for their long-term learning.

From the perspective of the teacher, the **authenticity** of a task must be directly related to learner purpose(s): interacting with a professor during a conference, writing an adequate paper for an academic class, understanding the expectations of the academic audience, and so forth. Recent articles on cognition and the theory of expertise (Brown, Collins, and Duguid, 1989; M. Carter, 1990) suggest that novice writers who attempt to perform in areas of knowledge (or "domains") in which they have little or no specific knowledge (or schemata) rely on "**global strategies** that are so general that they could be used in practically any domain, *strategies that are most likely culturally generated*" (M. Carter, 1990, p. 281, italics mine). For example, an inexperienced NES writer assigned a psychology research paper may resort to her/his prior knowledge (in this case, high school) and produce a five-paragraph theme in pseudo-academic prose that relies

177

heavily on a single library source. The less experienced the writer, the more that writer is dependent on and seeks "what the teacher wants," demanding that the teacher be more and more specific about form, content, and language that the student can imitate as he begins to develop "local," or more specified, writing strategies. In contrast, even slightly more experienced writers have more **local strategies**; they have some knowledge of and practice in such writing strategies as reading and analyzing academic assignments, generating ideas, getting started, overcoming writer's block, revising, determining audiences, writing for a purpose, and so forth. Yet these writers may be novices in local strategies of producing academic prose for discipline-specific discourse communities: an engineering technical report, an ethnographic sociology study, a political science term paper, a management task analysis.

If many NES writers are inexperienced with the local strategies of academic discourse communities, many ESL students are unaware of even the general strategies of English writing. Because not many cultures appear to teach rhetorical patterns directly (Leki, 1992), because there appear to be rhetorical rules or conventions that govern different categories of texts even within a particular language (Grabe and Kaplan, 1989; Sherman, 1992), and because the conventions of academic prose differ among cultures, students from different cultures often intuitively organize written material differently from NESs. That is, ESL writers "employ a rhetoric and sequence of thought which violate the expectations of the native reader" (Kaplan, 1966, p. 4). In U.S. academic classes, discipline-specific writing conventions differ in such diverse areas as "preferred length of sentences, choice of vocabulary, acceptability of using first person, extent of using passive voice, degree to which writers are permitted to interpret, [and] amount of metaphorical language accepted" (Leki, 1991, p. 124). Moreover, the ESL writer is likely to have "a different notion of what constitutes evidence, of the optimal order in which evidence ought to be presented, and of the number of evidentiary instances that need to be presented in order to induce conviction in the reader" (Kaplan, 1990, p. 10). As a result, students can face misunderstanding and even failure in their academic written work because they are often unaware of the content expectations and of the rhetorical (or formal) problems in their prose.

The approaches and activities described below represent the results of both research and experience currently implemented in many ESL academic writing classrooms that strive to engage students in rhetorical problem-solving in a context of meaningful communication (Mangelsdorf, 1989; Shriver, 1992). Included are (a) the value of sequencing authentic assignments, (b) the connection between writing and reading assignments, (c) integrated skills activities in the writing classroom, and (d) designing writing assignments.

Sequencing Assignments

Sequencing activities is essential to successful teaching; incremental assignment sequences, which often begin at a concrete level and then move to more complex and abstract concepts, help ESL writing students to develop critical thinking skills and experience success in learning (Knodt, 1991; Leki, 1991–1992). Although the sequencing of assignments begins during the first steps in syllabus development, students probably are not aware of the rationale behind disparate and possibly **spiraling** activities designed to review previous material. In order to give students responsibility for their own learning, teachers need to make the sequencing clear. Integrating several activities into a series of classes, and making certain that students can see both the reason for and the links among the activities, can provide coherence in a class. At the beginning of a course, when many students feel that the responsibility for the class is the teacher's, they may not understand the reasons for such explanations. But as the course progresses and students take more responsibility for their learning, they should expect—and even ask for—objectives.

The three approaches described below have been separated and detailed for the purpose of explanation and differentiation, but in practice these sequences often overlap.

1. The writing process approach. Although writing processes are not linear, as they write students will usually employ many of the same sequences: invention and prewriting during the early stages, shaping and organizing, and revising and editing. Classroom activities can, therefore, follow (or anticipate) such a progression. Examples: the teacher previews and then gives a writing assignment, explains the assignment, has students do some prewriting about possible topics in their journals, then has them work in small groups to discuss their topics.

2. The concept/application approach. Lessons that relate concepts developed through class work to the students' own writing form a time-honored learning sequence. For example, as students read and discuss professional or student essays, teachers can provide information concerning rhetorical techniques, language, and audience relationships in the essays (showing students how the author of the professional essay employed evidence, transitions, and so on), and then have students discuss, perhaps in small groups, how they could use those techniques in their own writing. Students might then apply what they have learned in class to their notes, drafts, or revisions.

3. <u>The individual/social approach</u>. Experienced ESL writing teachers alternate individual activities (such as reading essays, writing in journals, drafting) with social group activities (for example, annotation of texts, peer revision workshops, whole class discussion). Often, when individual work precedes group work and that individual work leads to class discussion, student resistance to group work is lowered and the group activity may be more successful. For example, a class may begin with an individual "warm-up" journal entry, followed by a teacher-centered presentation. Then the teacher may ask small groups to do an activity that follows from the lecture, and afterwards to report the results to the class. The individual-social-individual alternating pattern draws on the varied learning styles and coping strategies of the students.   (courtesy of Stephen Reid)

Sample Sequences

Below are two series of lesson plans for sequenced writing classes. Each begins with the end of a previous class (prior class); at the end of each class, homework assignments are given. The minutes listed beside activities indicate the time spent in class on each activity. In this chapter, as in Chapter 6, a cross (✚) indicates activities more appropriate for students with intermediate or advanced language proficiency; an arrowhead(➤) indicates activities especially appropriate for the less experienced teacher. Notice the ways in which skills and concepts that work toward the objective of the course are **spiraled** through several classes through the use of various activities and approaches (concepts are bold-faced).

SEQUENCE 1: READING-WRITING
LOW INTERMEDIATE TO ADVANCED LEVELS

Prior Class: studying **summary** writing; completing another sequence

ASSIGNMENT: students choose and purchase a non-news popular magazine in an area of personal interest (such as *Popular Mechanics*, *Seventeen*, or *Rolling Stone*).

Class 1: journal entry: why I chose this magazine (5 min.)
➤mini-lecture on concept of **audience** (students take notes) (10 min.)
small group: share notes; write a collaborative summary (15 min.)
share: why each magazine was chosen (5 min.)
individual worksheets: analysis of target **audience** from table of contents, **advertisements**, photographs (10 min.)

ASSIGNMENT: select one article; read and **summarize** (100 words) (5 min.)

Class 2: small group discussion: share **summaries** orally; answer questions about article from group members; indicate difficulties with writing summaries (20 min.)

►class discussion: **summary**—writing techniques, problems (10 min.)

►mini-lecture: **advertising** in the U.S. (students take notes) (10 min.)

►brief class discussion: describe **advertising** in their magazines: techniques, success/failure for target audience (5 min.)

ASSIGNMENT: notes in journal: create **criteria** for a successful advertisement (5 min.)

Class 3: small groups: share **criteria**; select and prioritize by consensus (15 min.)

groups' recorders put criteria on board; class discussion, decisions about class consensus concerning **criteria** (10 min.)

►individual work: apply criteria to three **ads** in chosen magazine; identify successful, unsuccessful advertisements (10 min.)

small groups: discuss selected **ads** from different magazines; feedback from group concerning applied **criteria** (10 min.)

ASSIGNMENT: first draft, written analysis of magazine's target **audience** (5 min.)

Class 4: teacher models, prepares, facilitates workshop for **analysis essay** about magazine's target audience (10 min.)

peer response groups: read drafts, give and get feedback

possible worksheet (teacher mini-conferences, answers questions) (25 min.)

journal entry: analysis of peer responses; plans for revision (10 min.)

ASSIGNMENT: second draft, written analysis (5 min.)

Class 5: peer review: read 2 **analysis essays** by peers; be prepared to comment on the one you preferred (and why) (15 min.)

list on board why student readers liked essays (10 min.)

review concept of **audience** (5 min.)

journal entry: what was easy and difficult about writing this essay? why? what problems did you encounter? how did you solve them? what did you learn about writing? (10 min.)

ASSIGNMENT: final draft, written analysis (5 min.)

SEQUENCE 2: ►LIBRARY/RESEARCH WORK
ADVANCED ESL AND FRESHMAN COMPOSITION

Prior Class: students complete teacher-designed survey of class **research** and **library** skills (collect) (20 min.)

ASSIGNMENT: ►**library** browse exercise: Go to the current periodical display area in the library. Walk through the aisles with the slanted shelves and look at EVERY periodical displayed. For **journals** not in your major field, spend two seconds reading the title, then move on.

For journals that you consider relevant to your major field, write the title of the journal and its call number (located on the bottom of each slanted shelf below the periodical). Also, write the titles of three really "odd" or surprising **journals** that you find. Then, on the back of the exercise sheet, write:

➤1. a paragraph describing the three "odd" journals

➤2. a sentence about the most surprising thing you discovered doing this exercise (15 min.)

Class 1: small groups share "odd" paragraphs, "surprise" sentences; share exercise about **major field journals** (15 min.)

➤teacher gives summary of **library** survey information (5 min.)

➤mini-lecture: selecting a **research topic** (10 min.)

➤class discussion: set criteria for selecting **research topic** (10 min.)

➤individuals: make notes in journal about possible topics (5 min.)

ASSIGNMENT: journal brainstorming to find a **research topic**; read chapter about **research** in textbook (5 min.)

Class 2: warm-up: summary of textbook reading about **research** (10 min.)

➤lecture: what IS **research** (rationale, processes, purpose, audience)? students take notes; class discussion (20 min.)

➤possible student **research topics** on board; class brain-storming about lecture (above); class questions to authors about **topic** (10 min.)

➤journals: how to improve **topic**, based on what they learned (5 min.)

ASSIGNMENT: read textbook chapter (**library research**); complete research worksheet (general information + what do I know about the topic? what don't I know?) (5 min.)

Class 3: warm-up: based on assigned reading, predict what is going to happen in class today (5 min.)

➤more student **topics** on the board; lecture based on those topics the use of **periodicals** in **research**: why to use, how to find, use of abstracting and indexing **journals**, which to use for which **topic**, etc. (30 min.)

➤journal: where I can find what I don't know; teacher mini-conferences (10 min.)

ASSIGNMENT: textbook reading (using **periodicals**); meet in library for next class to do **periodical research** (5 min.)

Class 4: class meets in library; **library exercise** based on student topics (students learn to use one of the Wilson indexing **journals**, locate three articles about the **research topic**, photocopy one article, complete exercise by listing call number, location of journal, etc.); teacher conferences, facilitates (50 min.)

ASSIGNMENT: paragraph in journal describing **library exercise** experience; complete library exercise

Class 5: small groups discuss **library exercise** (hand in) and experiences (15 min.)

➤class discussion: problems and solutions in **library research**
(10 min.)

➤lecture: using **secondary sources** in research; students take
notes (20 min.)

ASSIGNMENT: textbook reading: **writing references**; read photo-
copied article, summarize it, and write a **bibliographic
reference** for it (5 min.)

The Writing–Reading Connection

Writing and reading research points to the necessity of integrating
reading into the writing classroom (see Chapter 3 for a review of
reading-writing connection research). For ESL classes, however, some
serious implementation problems arise. Christina Haas and Linda
Flower (1988) explain, for example, that teaching even NESs to read
and write rhetorically is difficult. Teaching ESL writing students to step
outside themselves, imagine audience response, identify and
acknowledge the context for writing, and set purposeful goals may go
beyond their language and writing abilities. Similarly, teaching ESL
students to read rhetorically, to take into account "that the text is the
product of a writer's intention and is designed to produce an effect on
a specific audience" (ibid, p. 182), is a challenge. Finally, it is difficult
to find appropriately simple (but not simplistic) authentic reading
material for basic and intermediate level ESL students (Trimble, 1985);
while much "adapted" (that is, rewritten, reorganized, re-presented)
material is available, it usually alters the fundamental nature of
discourse in order to provide workable comprehension exercises. At
worst, the students learn reading techniques that simply do not work
with authentic material; at best, the skills they learn do not transfer
with ease to authentic material.

It is fortunate that the ESL writing classroom can provide many
opportunities for integrating authentic reading and writing material.
The four areas detailed below explain ways in which the complex
interaction of reading and writing can be integrated in the ESL writing
class.

Journal (Daybook, Learning Log) Writing and Reading

1. Informal, writer-based prose in journals allows students to respond
   to reading and evaluate those responses, individualizes instruction,
   and reinforces learning experiences (Fulwiler, 1987).

2. Writing in learning logs can help students make sense of writing
   assignments and tasks; early in the process, they can (a) describe

their audience and purpose(s), (b) summarize reading they are using as sources, (c) defend decisions they have made, (d) anticipate problems, and (e) analyze solutions.

3. "Pre-reading writing" about texts (that is, having students write about a topic before they read about it) serves to explore topics and ideas that can trigger associations and raise students' awareness of those associations; subsequent class discussion can identify an author's ideas and biases.

4. Analyzing supporting detail and relevant evidence in both professional and student texts will help writing students read—and write—to learn.

5. "The ESL writing class can incorporate lessons which assist students in preparing academic assignments, by using readings as a basis to practice such skills as summarizing, paraphrasing, interpreting, and synthesizing concepts" (Kroll, 1991, p. 254).

Reading (and Writing about) Peer and Self-Writing

Even at the lowest level of language proficiency, students can read (and reread) their own authentic writing and the writing of others in the class. Writing about that reading provides students with ways to respond to writing (their own or others') and eventually, to elaborate, clarify, and illustrate their responses by references to associations and prior knowledge (Bleich, 1986; Carson and Kuehn, 1992; Eisenberg, 1986). Asking students to reread their own writing enables them to invent, plan, draft, and troubleshoot (Grant-Davie, 1989, p. 4). Less experienced writers should be taught the strategies of rereading and given opportunities to reread their drafts so that they can reestablish contact with the purpose of the paper. In addition, students in ESL writing classes should have multiple opportunities to read the writing of peers and respond to that writing, sharing relevant feelings and attitudes, interpreting, questioning, and evaluating (for more information about peer response and review, see Chapter 8).

Because student writing is inherently interesting to student writers (particularly if the students choose their own topics and/or write collaboratively), students are providing their own reality, their own authenticity; the classroom has become not only a community but a real-world community. As students in ESL writing classes work with authentic text, reading and analyzing ideas, structure and style, and also analyzing purpose and audience, they develop an awareness of and respect for other authors and academic texts (Campbell, 1990; Subbiah, 1992).

Nonfiction Reading and Writing

Although the use of authentic materials introduces the problem of level of difficulty, students who encounter authentic, relatively short essays about topics they understand (that is, topics about which they have prior knowledge) are willing to work to comprehend the material (E. Bernhardt, 1991). Moreover, the teacher can intervene with various activities that will assist the students in their comprehension of the material. The beginning of one general sequence for reading and writing about nonfiction essays follows. Archeology is used as a sample content topic, but other topics (in a textbook essay, newspaper, or journal) can be substituted. Approximate times for each activity are indicated; complex tasks have a cross (✚), and activities especially appropriate for less experienced teachers are indicated by (➤).

NONFICTION READING AND WRITING SEQUENCE

Prior Class: discussion of and practice annotation of a text

Class 1: pre-reading writing (about the topic: a cross-cultural issue like proxemics or the U.S. dedication to household pets, the Olympics,- sibling rivalry, **archeology**, etc.) (10 min.)
➤vocabulary preparation: half a dozen words on a transparency, preferably in the context of a sentence from the reading so that students can guess the meaning (perhaps with help) (10 min.)
➤individual work (or teacher reads aloud): reading the title and the first and last sentences of each paragraph quickly (15 min.)
journal entry: students predict what the article will be about (5 min.)
ASSIGNMENT: read the article; annotate in the margins (5 min.)

Class 2: warm-up: use annotations to write 3 questions about the essay (5 min.)
small group or class discussion based on the questions (20 min.)
mini-lecture on some cultural or ✚rhetorical aspect of the essay (10 min.)
➤small group discussion about the mini-lecture (10 min.)

ASSIGNMENT: reread and summarize article (25–100 words); bring an **"artifac**t" from your country to class (5 min.)

Class 3: warm-up: discuss one idea in the article ✚or give an opinion supported by examples about one idea in the essay (10 min.)
small groups: share **"artifact"**; answer questions from group (what is it? what is it used for? who uses it? when? does it come in different sizes?) (20 min.)
➤essay assignment: write a description of your artifact that will be put in a time capsule and buried for 100 years. Think about your audience! (5 min.)
journal entry: notes about describing **artifact** for essay (10 min.)
ASSIGNMENT: prewrite and begin drafting paragraph/✚essay (5 min.)

Class 4: warm-up: problems (or successes) with the writing assignment
(5 min.)
➤mini-lecture: organizational form of description essay (10 min.)
small group writing workshop (structured, worksheet); teacher mini-
conferences (25 min.)
journal entry: revisions and notes based on workshop feedback
(10 min.)
ASSIGNMENT: rough draft, artifact essay (5 min.)

(courtesy of Shelley Reid)

Reading and Writing about Literature

Advocates of reading literature in the ESL writing classroom
indicate that literature provides content that heightens cultural
awareness and sensitivity (Gajdusek, 1988; Murdoch, 1992b), stimuli
for writing (McGroarty and Galvan, 1985; Spack, 1985), and the
opportunity for extended discussion and analysis of ideas and
linguistic structures (McKay, 1982). Jean McConochie states that
"Writing assignments that prompt rereading and reflection help
students to extend their understanding and thus their literary pleasure"
(1982, p. 125). Reading and then writing about literature offers
students situations not only to analyze but to appreciate aesthetic
quality and, more important, to relate to their own lives (Oster, 1989).
Some teachers (Hurley and Sherman, 1990; Stoller, 1990) like a
multimedia approach to the study of literature in the writing
classroom: reading a short story and then watching a film of the story.
The following sequence adapted from Jacqueline Costello (1990),
which gives the teacher a more traditional role, is widely used for
teaching and analyzing a short story, and it could be used to discuss
poetry, folktales, or—in a more expanded sequence—novels as well:

LITERATURE READING AND WRITING SEQUENCE

Class 1: near the end of class, teacher reads aloud the beginning of a short
story
➤individual journal entries: students write observations about what
they heard: what can they infer about the characters, place, place,
and style just from the beginning of the story? (15 min.)

ASSIGNMENT: Students read short story, write 4–5 questions about the
work (5 min.)

Class 2: class discussion based on student questions about story; students
participate in the discussion and take notes (25 min.)
➤mini-lecture: some cultural aspect of the story (10 min.)
small group discussion concerning mini-lecture information (10 min.)

ASSIGNMENT: reread short story; write for ten minutes (focused free-writing) about ideas gained during class discussion (5 min.)

Class 3: small groups: share ideas from focused freewriting (15 min.)
➤mini-lecture and class discussion: some grammatical items from the short story (20 min.)
➤writing assignment: a personal narrative stimulated by the short story for a specific audience (classmate, sister, roommate); for example, reflect upon the impact of a single incident from the past on your present life (10 min.)
ASSIGNMENT: brainstorm/pre-write for the writing assignment (5 min.)

Class 4: class discussion: topic ideas for writing assignment (15 min.)
small group writing workshop: feedback from peers concerning topic (questions, areas of interest, etc.); teacher circulates, mini--conferencing (20 min.)
journal entry: summarize best ideas received from group members; make notes about plan for writing the essay (10 min.)
ASSIGNMENT: rough draft, narrative essay (5 min.)

Integrated Skills Activities

Performance-based activities that integrate all language skills and that are learning-centered, student-centered, and meaning-centered can only enhance students' acquisition of skills (Dubin and Olshtain, 1986). Tasks that have unambiguous instructions and well-defined expectations, a clear and appropriate context, and a real-world focus that will allow students to transfer the skills to other situations lend authenticity to the writing class. Below are tasks that implement the characteristics of sequenced activities discussed above and integrate all language skills.

Surveys

Teaching students how to design, administer, and interpret surveys fulfills many of the goals of the ESL writing teacher: clear objectives, integrating language skills, sequential lesson plans, authenticity, ease of materials, student attention to processes, and a viable product. Furthermore, student-designed surveys integrate all language skills: discussion and analysis of topics and appropriate survey questions/statements; development of vocabulary and critical thinking skills while writing the questionnaire; social interaction and problem-solving with real-world participants in the administration of the survey; collaborative tabulation and interpretation of the results; a written report and/or recommendations based on those results; delivery and/or publication of the results; individual written metacognitive analyses of the processes.

Teachers who decide to use a survey for a sequence of classes must know something about formulating surveys and should communicate that information to their students.

- Survey questions should be simply stated and have only one point each.
- Valid survey questions are relatively free of value words and are written to elicit responses without biasing the respondents.
- Demographic information about respondents is necessary (age, gender, native country/language, level of education, etc.) both for interpretation and to establish a comfort-level.
- The surveys that are easiest to administer and tabulate ask respondents for a yes/no or a scaled response (strongly agree, agree, don't know/neutral, disagree, strongly disagree).
- A more complex essay task involves questions that function as an interview, in which the students take notes based on responses;
- Tabulation of survey results is time-consuming, and interpretation of the results requires an objective approach (and, in the cases of group work, negotiation).
- There should be an authentic, real-world product at the end of a survey sequence.

Following are suggestions for information-gathering surveys, with possibilities for authentic reporting and/or use:

- food, music, entertainment preferences of ESL students in program. Use the results to plan a program party.
- ways students spend money (food, hobbies, entertainment, books, sports, etc.). Post the results on the program bulletin board.
- student study habits (time, place, food, rewards, etc.) or writing rituals. Report results in the student newspaper/newsletter.
- amount and type of homework given in writing classes (or all intensive language program classes), including level of difficulty, time spent doing homework, and comments about the importance in the learning process to students doing the homework. Deliver results to program administrators.
- hobbies/leisure time activities of students. Report results on fliers given to student participants.
- the best eating places (or restaurants) in the local area. Print results in the student newspaper/newsletter.

Other, more controversial topics that may involve a yes/no response to one question followed by an interview concerning the answer include

- keeping dogs in urban areas
- banning bicyclists from roads
- smoking in public places
- parking problems at the university
- the ideal age for a driver's license

Following is a sample series of sequenced lesson plans for a survey module; included is an authentic survey developed by students with low intermediate language proficiency in a reading/writing class at the Intensive English Language Institute (IELI) at the State University of New York at Buffalo.

SURVEY SEQUENCE

Class 1: lecture on use and design of surveys (students take notes) (20 min.)
➤assignment (class discussion) + plus reporting plan: survey (10 min.)
small groups: discussion of potential topics, rationale (each group may have a different topic) for survey (15 min.)

ASSIGNMENT: focused freewriting for 10 minutes (what do we need to find out? + sample questions) (5 min.)

Class 2: class discussion of potential topics on the board (15 min.)
➤small groups: share freewriting, begin to formulate survey; teacher circulates, answers questions, intervenes (30 min.)

ASSIGNMENT: journal entry: analysis paragraph of group work, survey draft (5 min.)

Class 3: fragmented groups (representative from each original group in each new group); share surveys, get feedback (25 min.)
original groups: share feedback; revise surveys; teacher circulates, reviews surveys (20 min.)

ASSIGNMENT: final draft, survey (may have to meet outside of class) (5 min.)

Class 4: ➤warm-up: individual freewriting predicting survey results; teacher reviews final drafts of surveys (10 min.)
original groups: share predictions (10 min.)
class discussion: role playing for administering survey: how many respondents needed, where to find, etc. (25 min.)

ASSIGNMENT: administer survey (in pairs, or individually) (5 min.)

NOTE: Students should have several days to collect the information; a weekend and/or another class sequence may intervene here.

Class 5: small groups: share, tabulate survey results (25 min.)
➤initial group (or class) discussion about the report; teacher circulates, mediates, acts as resource (20 min.)

Assignment: journal entry: description and detailed analysis of experience in administering the survey (5 min.)

Class 6: original groups: workshop, report of results (25 min.) fragmented groups: share draft of report, get feedback (20 min.)

Assignment: meet outside of class, complete report results (ready for reporting) (5 min.)

Class 7: mini-lecture: publication process for reporting (may be different for different groups) (10 min.) small groups: implementation of publication of reports (20 min.) ➤class discussion: what was easy / difficult with this sequence? why? what problems did each group encounter? how did they solve those problems? (15 min.)

Assignment: short analytic essay: what I learned from this survey experience (5 min.)

SAMPLE SURVEY: ASSIGNMENT GIVEN TO STUDENTS

GOAL: To prepare an information booklet for IELI students.

Part 1: Take an opinion poll
In-class Activity: Discuss and construct survey
Discuss survey procedures

Homework: Each student must survey <u>five</u> (5) other IELI students; only <u>one</u> of these may be from this class.

Part 2: Interview students for more information
In-class Activity: Discuss and choose interview question

Homework: Each student must interview two (2) other students.
Both students must be from other levels in the IELI.
These interviews will be the Journal Assignments for this week—write the interviews in your journal.
Optional: Students may interview an IELI teacher.
Due date: Interviews and 2 free entries are due on FRIDAY.

Part 3: Humor: list of bad and good excuses for not doing homework
In-class Activity: Generate and choose excuses.
Ask other students for their best excuses (contest?)

Part 4: Read and summarize a short article on study skills
In-class Activity: Preread, read, and summarize an article as a class.

Part 5: Self-interview: "Letter to the Editor" about IELI homework
In-class Activity: Discuss purposes and audience, list possible topics.

Homework: Each student will write a short letter expressing an opinion about homework. DUE DATE: Wednesday.

Part 6: Letter to new students: most important facts and recommendations
In-class Activity: Review information, discuss audience, write letter.

STUDENT-GENERATED SURVEY QUESTIONS

1. When do you do homework? (Morning; Lunch; Afternoon; Night)
2. Where do you do homework? (Dorm room; Cafeteria; Other___)
3. Do you like homework? (Yes; No; Maybe/Sometimes)
4. Is the homework difficult for you? (Yes, always; Yes, some of it; No, not usually)
5. How long does it take to do homework? (1–2 hours; 3–4 hours; 5–6 hours; 7+ hours)
6. Do you always finish your homework? (Yes; No; Maybe/Sometimes)
7. Which subject has the most homework? (Reading-Writing; Grammar; Spoken; Listening)
8. Does someone help you with your homework? (Yes; No; Sometimes)
9. Do you get good grades on your homework? (Yes; No; Maybe/Sometimes)
10. Do you have homework every day? (Yes; No)

STUDENT-GENERATED INTERVIEW QUESTIONS

1. Is homework helpful to you?
2. Do you get good grades on homework?
3. Do you think the IELI teachers give too much homework?
4. How would you change the amount of homework?

(courtesy of Shelley Reid)

Games, Role-Play, and Writing

Games and role-play in ESL writing classes can have several objectives. The simplest is a step outside the intricate sequencing process of lesson planning. Games can function simply as a student attention-getter, as a pleasant way to spend the last ten minutes of an otherwise dense class, as a Friday afternoon community builder (Crookall and Oxford, 1990). Role-play can be a "hip pocket" activity for the teacher to use when things go wrong, or in the middle of a difficult chapter to relieve tension. In some cases, both types of activities can become integral parts of larger sequences of learning. Each of the activities below furthers language skills and prepares students for real world tasks; each uses all the language skills, and each can become part of a series of sequenced lesson plans.

➤Chain Stories: On a single piece of paper (or an overhead transparency), each student writes the first sentence of a folktale, murder mystery, spy novel, romantic novel, or superhero story, then passes it on to another student in class (or in a group). Each student adds a sentence to each story (or, in the case of a small group, each student has two chances to add sentences as the papers are passed around), striving for coherence and fun. Stories are shared (a) on the overhead projector, (b) read aloud by the teacher or by a class member, (c) passed from group to group for sharing.

➤Wheel of Fortune Vocabulary: Use vocabulary words from reading, from writing process terminology, from literature analysis, and so on. Divide class into teams (or have three students play the game each time). Put the number of spaces on the board that the word contains. Each group (or player) selects a letter in sequence; selections can continue until a letter is not part of the word. Students can guess what the word is before the letters are complete; following an incorrect guess, the next player has a turn. (courtesy of Shelley Reid)

➤Strip Stories: Helps students internalize the sequencing and the coherence devices used in U.S. academic writing. The teacher selects a paragraph that has clear cues (transitional phrases, chronology), then types the sentences, one to a line, and cuts the sentences apart. Each student receives one of the sentences. Students must share their sentences with others in order to put the paragraph back together.

➤Pair Process Descriptions: Pair students as they arrive for class. Ask each pair to write a paragraph describing a simple-sounding, relatively complex process. Then have two pairs of students, who wrote about different processes, share their processes; as one pair reads the process, the other pair.role-plays that process. Suggestions: placing a long-distance call, buying popcorn at the movies, putting on a coat, tying a shoelace, braiding hair, using chopsticks, dancing the salsa.

Situations and Writing

There are two kinds of situational writing. The first, often found in ESL writing textbooks, provides student writers with as much situational context as possible. Students then "enter" the completed situation, role-playing one of the characters in that situation and responding, usually in writing, to or about the situation. Particularly for students with lower levels of language proficiency, the more detail they are given, the more the writing exercise is "guided" by the vocabulary and sentence structures of the background information and the questions that follow. A variation of situational writing provides students with the skeleton of a situation and asks them to supply the necessary detail before they enter the situation and respond to it. This kind of situational writing activity allows student writers to develop description, either by gathering authentic information or by creating it, preferably in collaboration with others. Then the students enter or immerse themselves in that situation and respond to it in whatever role(s) they choose for themselves. The opportunity to be creative in the development of detail, and then to role-play in the response, can be both appealing and successful, especially for students with at least an intermediate level of language proficiency. The following exercises are the latter kind; each asks the students to work cooperatively to develop a writing situation and then to respond, as a particular kind of writer, for an articulated purpose, and for a specified audience.

➤Accident Reports: The students create the specifics for a two-car, non-fatal accident; salient facts are put on the board. Each small group is assigned a single personality who will write a (formal or informal) collaborative report: (a) a police officer writes for the Police Department; (b) Driver A, who was at fault, writes a report for his insurance company; (c) Driver B writes for his insurance company; (d) Driver A writes to his mother (friend, brother) (adapted from Hedge, 1988).

➤Persuasion: A student returning to school at the beginning of the semester stopped off in Las Vegas (or Atlantic City) and in the gambling casinos lost all his/her money for school tuition. Now the student must write a letter to persuade someone to give him/her the necessary tuition money. Divide the students into groups. Have each group write a persuasive letter to one of the following: the President of the United States, the director of the university Student Financial Aid Office, his/her grandmother, a best friend. It is important that the letter embroider the facts and not be strictly truthful.

  Writing a Commercial: The students work in pairs or small groups. The situation: you work for an advertising agency. Your task is to write a commercial that will appear in a newspaper (or in a magazine or on television). You must identify the target market: who is the audience for this commercial? Then you must design an advertisement that will successfully sell the product. Suggestions: an automobile (such as Honda, Cadillac, Mercedes-Benz), a food product (Ben and Jerry's Ice Cream, Skippy Peanut Butter, Pizza Hut Pizza). The groups might add art work, but they must write copy for the advertisement.

  Community Advocacy: Students in groups can identify a school or community issue and respond to it (a) with letters to the editor of the student/community newspaper, (b) by designing and reporting on a survey concerning the issues; and/or (c) by gathering and organizing materials to present at a student leadership meeting or a city council. Topics might include the renovation of student dormitories, building bike paths, the need for a new park.

✦News Articles: The teacher brings in two newspaper articles from two very different sources (for example, from a tabloid and *U.S. News and World Report*, or from the *New York Times* and *Rolling Stone* magazine) about a single feature story (such as a Grateful Dead concert, a football game, a strange human interest story). The stories should be of approximate length; make enough copies of each story to give to half the class. Also give each student a worksheet with questions about the story. Example: What sort of event was it? Where did it take place? When? Who was involved? What happened to each of the participants? What was the outcome? How did people feel? Each student will read his/her article, take notes, and complete the worksheet. Then students in pairs (one who read article A and one who read article B) compare notes, share extra details, and analyze the audience for each of the news articles. Class discussion follows, and then all students will write a journal entry analyzing which article was personally preferable (adapted from Hedge, 1988).

Situational Letters: The situations below allow students to write for a specific purpose and a specific audience; in some cases, the audience is familiar so that the writers and the readers will have shared experiences. In others, students will need to identify and analyze the audience, then learn to choose appropriate vocabulary and tone in achieving the proper voice for an unknown audience.

➤1. You are planning to take a vacation in the U.S. Choose a state and write the state tourism bureau for information concerning that state: a highway map, motels and hotels, historic and tourist areas, and so on. Sample addresses:

   North Carolina Travel Development Section, Raleigh, NC 27611
   New York Travel Bureau, 99 Washington Ave., Albany, NY 12245
   Oregon Travel Information Section, Rm. 105, State Highway
     Bldg., Salem, OR 97310
   Texas Travel and Information Division, Austin, TX 78701
   Utah Travel Dept., Council Hall, Capitol Hill, Salt Lake City, UT
     84114
   Vermont Information–Travel Development, 61 Elm St.,
     Montpelier, VT 05602
   Washington Travel Development Division, 101 General
     Administration Bldg., Olympia, WA 98504

2. You have a problem with your apartment, such as insufficient heat, noisy neighbors, or a leaky faucet. Write your landlord; without being offensive, briefly describe the problem and suggest a solution.

3. Choose someone who has helped you (the mail delivery person, your host family, a bus driver, your best friend) and write a letter of appreciation to them, telling them how much you value them and why.

4. The U.S. Consumer Information Service has hundreds of free brochures of information; write for the free Consumer Information Catalog, Pueblo, CO 81009.

5. You have bought a product at a local store (perhaps a television, a camera, or a washing machine), but the product is defective. Write a letter to the store manager, describing the problem and suggesting a remedy.

➕6. Choose an issue of importance such as gun control, civil rights, or funding for medical research. Research the issue. Write your opinion about the topic to the U.S. Congressman from your district; support your opinion with your research.

7. Your class chooses to invite a famous person to speak to the class. Write a letter of invitation to that person and a letter of thanks after s/he has spoken.

Designing Activities and Writing Assignments

Writing assignments can have a profound effect on students, so they should be as fair and as carefully designed as possible; therefore, designing writing tasks for an ESL writing class requires careful thought and preparation (Cumming, 1991b; Hayward, 1990). Successful writing tasks "bias for the best." That is, they offer the writers the best possible chance to demonstrate their strengths and to improve their writing. Effective writing assignments (sometimes called "**prompts**" because they prompt the student to write)

- interest both the writer and the reader;
- are accessible to all the writers;
- involve the writers in the topic;
- are comprehensible to the writers;
- are unbiased with regard to the cultures of the students;
- are not culture bound (that is, they do not require intimate knowledge of U.S. culture);
- allow students to learn as they write.

Research in cognitive psychology (Bereiter and Scardamalia, 1987a) and in reading and writing has shown that student writers perform most successfully when the writing topic taps into their background knowledge—that is, they write best about subjects they know (see Carrell, 1984c, 1992; Carrell and Eisterhold, 1983; Cheskey and Hiebert, 1987; McKay, 1989; Newell and MacAdam, 1987; Tedick, 1990). The production of successful prose is thus at least partially dependent on the student's prior knowledge, not only of the subject matter but also of the cultural context in which the assignment will be written. Teachers designing writing assignments should therefore consider the prior knowledge of their students as well as other topic variables: the wording, the mode of discourse, the rhetorical specifications, and the subject matter (Hamp-Lyons, 1992; Johns, 1990; Peyton et al., 1990; Tedick, 1990). In addition, teachers designing writing assignments or explaining writing activities should make certain that they state explicitly their expectations and their criteria for evaluation. Similarly, when students choose their own writing topics, they should consider what they know: they should write about what they know about (and read about what they don't know).

As teachers begin designing writing tasks, there are political considerations. As Ilona Leki (1992) and Robin Scarcella (1990) point out, the learning of language and culture almost certainly changes students. It may be presumptuous, for example, to require writing assignments that ask ESL students to practice self-exploration and discovery of self through writing because that imposes tasks that reflect our North American cultural fascination with self. Instead, many ESL students have a different objective: to use written English only in the most utilitarian and pragmatic ways that will enable them to function satisfactorily in an academic environment. Indeed, once they have completed their U.S. academic work, ESL students may have little, or perhaps no need to write English. With these issues in mind, the teacher can first evaluate the purpose and audience for each assigned task.

Researchers have begun to investigate the organizational structures and content presentations expected by the academic audience by (a) surveying academic faculty (Bridgeman and Carlson, 1984; Canesco and P. Byrd, 1989; Horowitz, 1986a; Kroll, 1979; Ostler, 1980; West and P. Byrd, 1982), and (b) examining various forms of academic discourse (Casanave and Hubbard, 1992; Grabe and Biber, 1988; Swales, 1990a). In order to better design authentic, academically oriented ESL writing classes, teachers are developing writing assignments that have as their objective real-world products. Daniel Horowitz (1992) suggested selecting content that is based on a body of knowledge to which all writers have had equal access, and then phrasing the prompt in an English for Academic Purposes (EAP) frame, such as the following:

- describe the functions of (Example: *letter grades*)
- what purpose does (Example: *technologies associated with horticulture*) serve?
- explain the purpose of (Example: *volunteerism*)

Other EAP frames might include

- identify and describe (Ex.: *the target market for a consumer product*)
- determine (Ex.: *the availability of handicap-accessible buildings on the campus*)
- evaluate (Ex.: *the environmental policy of an organization*)
- give an overview of (Ex.: *the use of illegal drugs in Europe*) (examples mine)

As teachers develop and assign writing tasks or class activities, they might use the following evaluation criteria: Is the task

- too broad or too narrow to be accomplished within the assignment parameters?
- too simple or too complex in terms of syntax or background knowledge?
- culture specific or culture bound?
- too abstract or philosophical?
- too unacademic or otherwise inappropriate?

Finally, students should have the opportunity to give feedback to the teacher concerning the success of assigned topics. A journal assignment that evaluates the topic (what did you like about this topic? what problems did you have? how would you modify this topic?) or a postscript at the end of the final draft of the paper (what was the most successful part of this paper? what did you know about the topic? what was interesting for you/your reader about this topic? what would you change if you had more time?) will allow the teacher to see the topic from the students' perspectives.

Duane Roen (1989) suggests that teachers constructing ESL writing assignments should focus on three objectives: (a) to guide students to address authentic audiences, purposes, and topics; (b) to use process approaches to help students define and solve the many rhetorical problems that writing entails; and (c) to make it possible for students to receive appropriate feedback or evaluation as they write. The writing tasks that follow attempt to fulfill those criteria.

Writing Self-Assessment: At the beginning of the course, either as an initial writing sample or as a series of freewriting journal assignments, each student should write for 10–20 minutes on his/her feelings about and experiences with writing both in his/her own language and in English. How do the students feel when they write? Have they ever written anything they are proud of? Have they had any writing disasters? What have they been taught about successful writing? What do they really believe makes successful writing?

The writing exercises can be followed with discussions in small groups answering questions: How much do you like writing in your own language? What are the features of a well-written text? Another follow-up exercise involves a full class discussion about the social nature of writing (that is, writing for a purpose for a specific audience) and the de-mythologizing of writing processes.

►Audience Analysis: For the first formal (reader-based) writing assignment, have students choose (or assign) one classmate, preferably not from their own country, as an audience. Ask the students to interview each other, first asking for basic demographic information and then concentrating on the interests and knowledge of the other about their chosen topics. What does this single-person audience know/not know about the topic? What questions would s/he like answered in the essay about the topic? What would interest her/him about the topic? How will learning more about the topic be important to her/him? Students will then write an audience analysis, characterizing their partner and linking that information to how the writer will present the topic in the upcoming essay.

✦Academic Assignment Analysis: The teacher collects authentic assignments given in academic classes and makes an overhead transparency or copies of each for the students. Teachers can first model the evaluation of an assignment in terms of audience expectations, annotating the transparency. Then students, individually, in pairs, or in small groups read each assignment and then discuss (a) the audience expectations, (b) the purpose(s) for each assignment, and (c) ways of fulfilling the assignment. Two authentic examples of undergraduate writing assignments follow. The boldfaced phrases indicate the problems encountered by students studying these assignments.

Adult Education Assignment: "Myself as a Life Long Learner"

Every member of the class, including the instructor, identifies something that he or she wants to learn about this semester. The assignment involves (1) writing up a plan by which you will learn this new thing; (2) keeping a diary as you go about the process of learning. (The diary should include insights you get about the **nature of learning** in general as well as specific thoughts regarding your own learning).Write a descriptive statement (**of whatever length**) that summarizes how you believe you learn best when you have something you want to learn about.

Comments: Students didn't understand the phrase "the nature of learning" (but agreed that presumably the instructor would make that clear in class), and they were unsure about instructor expectations concerning both quantity ("whatever length") and quality.

Political Science Research Term Paper

Each student will be required to write a 15–20 page paper and present it to the class. The topic must deal with some aspect of political economy. An illustrative list of possible subjects for research papers is attached. **The paper should be chosen in consultation with the instructor with a rough outline submitted by the tenth week of the course**. The paper should draw on the extensive literature on political economy noted in the appendices of your two textbooks. It should **focus on policy decisions** taken or under consideration in the U.S. or other governments for dealing with specific challenges to the international economic system, or debates underway on how to reform the international monetary or trading system. The paper should **describe the circumstances** confronting policy makers and analyze relevant policy options. If the paper deals with past policy decisions, it should explain why policy makers took the decision, what options were rejected, and whether another policy response   would have been more appropriate.

Comments: Students misunderstood the boldfaced sentence, thinking they should conference with the instructor <u>after</u> they had written an outline and during the tenth week of class; in addition, they did not understand that the instructor had essentially outlined two major areas to be covered in each paper, and that by following that outline and allowing an equal number of pages for each major area, they would be fulfilling reader expectations.

Expectancy Exercise: The objective of this exercise is (a) to observe the differences in student expectations and (b) to teach appropriate expectations for academic writing (Brodkey, 1983; Micek, 1992; J. Reid, forthcoming). The teacher puts several topic sentences on the board; each should be clear enough to elicit an appropriate second sentence from a native speaker of English. (It is helpful to have NESs actually write second sentences before the class.)

1. Milk is one of the most important sources of nutrition for humans.
2. The burial ceremony in Indonesia has three rituals.
3. My most embarrassing moment happened in an airport.
4. Cambodian New Year is the most exciting holiday in my country.
5. Acapulco is known as the best city in Mexico for vacations.
6. Swimming is my favorite sport.
7. In Saudi Arabia, parents have separate responsibilities for raising their children.
8. Spelling is one of the most frustrating skills to learn in English.

Then students in pairs write a complete <u>second sentence</u> for each of the three to four topic sentences on the board. Following this, the students divide into small groups and discuss their second sentences, coming to consensus on the best (1 or 2) second sentences. The group recorder then puts the second sentences on the board or on a transparency with the first sentence. Some of the second sentences will probably be inappropriate: simple restatements of the first sentence, sentences that diverge from the main idea, expansions of the original sentence that change the meaning of what will follow. Class discussion about the differences in second sentences should follow, with the teacher intervening with information about what NESs would expect.

This exercise can be modified by using authentic student sentences, some of which will not present the clear choices (for NESs) of the sentences above. Students might put their sentences on the board, write them on a transparency for the overhead projector, or share them with a group. Their peers should offer sample second sentences, then perhaps third sentences, and finally a collaborative paragraph. For an additional modification, students might present a topic sentence or a thesis statement to their peer review group; peers would strive to answer these questions: "What do I <u>expect</u> the rest of the paragraph/essay will be about? What questions do I <u>expect</u> will be answered? What other questions am I interested in having the writer answer?"

Reformulation Exercise: This is a two-stage process that begins with ESL students writing an essay or a paragraph on a given topic. Each piece of writing is given to a NES, who first corrects the syntactic and mechanical problems (or the teacher and ESL students can make these corrections before giving the papers to the NESs). Then the NESs rewrite (reformulate) the syntactically and mechanically correct papers, maintaining the ideas of the ESL student but recasting them into language and phrasing that a NES would use. The ESL students read the reformulations individually and then discuss them in groups (R. Allwright et al., 1988; A. Cohen, 1990; Gast, 1990). Alternative: the teacher can reproduce the originals and reformulations, and then, using the overhead projector, place each paper side by side with its reformulation, discussing with the class the rationale for the differences.

Four-Paper Paper: For a major paper in the course (or, on a smaller scale, any formal paper the students write), students will actually write one substantial paper and three shorter metacognitive papers that describe and analyze the processes involved in the production of the major paper. All four papers will be written for an audience; each will contain an introduction, a body, and a conclusion, and each will contain specific detail and evidence. The three shorter papers will be two pages each (500 words):

1. The first paper will be an introduction to the topic: why the student chose the topic, what s/he knows and doesn't know about the topic, and how/what/where the student will find out more about the topic. It can also include an analysis of audience and purpose. This paper can be turned in before the final draft of the major paper and/or can serve as a preface to the final draft of the major paper.

2. The next paper functions as a progress report: it describes an interview of an expert about the topic (that is, a description of the planning and implementation of the interview) and analyzes how useful the interview was. It also describes other work done on the paper (such as drafting two introductions and choosing one, finding a newspaper article about the topic, etc.). This paper can be turned in prior to the final draft of the major paper; it may also accompany the final draft.

3. The final short paper is a "post-mortem" of the major paper. It will describe what was easy and what was difficult about writing the major paper, what problems were encountered and how those problems were solved, what the student learned from writing the paper; what the best part of the paper is, and how the student would improve the paper if s/he had another chance to revise it.

Conclusion

In an English for Academic Purposes (EAP) writing class or program, teachers should seek to empower ESL students for their academic work. The primary objective of ESL writing classes should be to introduce students to authentic forms of academic writing and to give them opportunities to develop composing skills and gain control of the language and rhetorical skills they will need in their academic work. In that way, teachers will assist their students in the process of entering the academic discourse community (Johns, 1988). In addition, "The effective writing teacher is not one who has developed a 'method' for the teaching of writing, but one who can create an effective environment for learning, in which novice writers feel comfortable about writing and can explore the nature of writing—and in doing so discover their own strengths and weaknesses as writers" (Richards, 1990b, pp. 114–115).

Discussion Questions

1. Discuss the following question as a class or in small groups: Can writing be taught in a classroom through a range of tasks and activities? Why or why not?

2. Based on the activities presented in this chapter, discuss what kinds of writing should/should not be taught in ESL writing classes.

3. Read and consider the following authentic EAP writing prompts from upper division classes in different disciplines. Discuss, first in small groups and then in "fragmented" groups, the potential effectiveness and/or inappropriateness of the prompts. Using the criteria presented in this chapter, discuss the audience expectations and purpose(s) of each writing prompt. What problems might ESL students encounter in understanding each assignment, and how might you assist those students in fulfilling the assignment? How might each assignment be modified and improved?

A. <u>Fisheries and Wildlife</u>: Annotated Bibliography of Wildlife Diseases of the Central Rockies Region

> Prepare an annotated bibliography with a minimum of 10 references for one selected wild animal species (or group of species like bats) and for one disease (or group of diseases, like intestinal parasites) from the Central Rockies Region (Colorado, New Mexico, Arizona, Utah, Wyoming, Idaho, and Montana). The species and disease must be approved ahead of time to avoid duplication. The summary or abstract for each reference should be short (4–6 lines) and should include the disease and species studies, locations and dates, and should emphasize the sample size, results, and conclusion and not necessarily techniques. Provide a subject index for each reference with the common and scientific names of the species and disease, and location (see attached sample).

B. <u>Sociology</u>: Neighborhood Autobiography Assignment

> (a) In what type of community did you spend most of your early life? Urban, rural, suburban? Describe it. What type of a neighborhood would you say you lived in? Was it made up of families like yours or was it mixed in terms of social class, economic status, ethnic or minority families, etc.? Was it homogeneous or heterogeneous? Describe and explain.

> (b) What were the relationships between families, children? Did people socialize within the neighborhood or did they prefer to go outside?

> (c) At what age did you start playing with boys and girls in your neighborhood? What were the main activities of these groups? Did these playmates come from families that resembled yours?

> (d) How was your life and your family's life influenced by these various patterns of relationships? Do you and/or your family maintain contact with people of your "old neighborhood"?

C. Agricultural Economics: Critique of Unassigned Articles

Four general subject areas will be addressed during this semester. These areas are: (1) industrial organization, (2) product marketing, (3) international trade, and (4) marketing in developing economies. You are to critique 5 articles not previously assigned on the reading list. (Not more than 2 articles should be selected from one "subject area." Articles from "popular" publications are generally not acceptable.) The critique should be only one page, typed single-spaced. It should contain the author, title and source of the article, including library call number (if applicable of publication which contains the article). Give a brief summary of the content; critique the article by presenting your evaluation of the strength and weakness of the article.

4. Gather in small groups. Each group should choose one sequence of activities (from this chapter or another source). Analyze and discuss the sequence in terms of the following criteria: objective(s), focus, level of challenge, authenticity (or potential for transferability to real-world skills), interactiveness, and integration of skills.

5. From the Games and Role Play section of this chapter, choose two of the activities. In pairs, identify ways of sequencing each of these activities, and discuss what the overall objectives of a class might be in which the activity took place: language-based, pattern-model–based, process-based, etc.

6. Interview an instructor or professor in a content area (math, biology, engineering, etc.) in which your ESL students may take classes. Explain that you are collecting typical academic writing assignments from various departments and would like a sample of one writing assignment s/he gives. Ask the teacher to comment on particular problems her/his students have with the assignment. Later, gather in groups to discuss the interviews and share the assignments.

Writing

1. As a source of professional growth, begin keeping a journal of personal reflections about teaching. Observe and/or teach several ESL writing classes; then reflect in writing, recollecting as much detail as possible, the lessons taught, the events that took place, your reactions and interpretations to the teaching/learning situation, insights about the situation, and ideas for future teaching situations.

2. Using the criteria discussed in this chapter, develop three writing prompts; indicate the language proficiency of the students for each of the prompts as well as your criteria for evaluation. Share your prompts with peers in a small group, and analyze each prompt.

3. Choose one of the writing prompts designed in #2 (above). Respond to that prompt as though you were the student; that is, write the essay. When

you have completed the task, re-analyze the prompt in a brief essay. Consider the effectiveness and success of your essay, and so of the prompt, by using the following criteria:

    a. Were the instructions clear?

    b. Was the prompt easily accessible?

    c. Was it interesting enough to engage you as the writer?

    d. Was gathering information for the essay easy?

    e. Did you have problems with organization of supporting detail?

    f. Was the resulting essay interesting for the intended audience?

    g. How might you modify the prompt to make it more successful?

4. Choose a short story or a poem that you would like to teach in a reading-writing class. Write a four- to-six-class sequenced lesson plan for that piece of literature.

5. Begin formulating your teaching philosophy about teaching academic writing skills in an ESL class. Freewrite for ten minutes in your learning log; then re–read what you have written, choose one idea from that freewriting, and freewrite again, this time on the single idea.

CHAPTER 8

Responding to Student Writing

> I tell my students that writing is largely a matter of fixing things. And that the better they get at fixing things the better they will get at writing. Now, fixing things requires reading Students who do not learn to read their own papers with a discerning eye will not be able to fix things. (Katz, 1988, p. 111)

> My responses to students' writing are multiple, adapting to the changing contexts, shifting needs, and varied tempos of the writer's progress. I am coach, setting contexts, offering strategies, and engaging students in interactive practice. I am co-creator, teasing out students' incipient meanings. I am dialoguer, echoing, questioning, challenging.
>
> (Lauer, 1989, p. 21).

Responding to and evaluating student writing are often parts of the same process, but the terms "responding" and "evaluating" need to be carefully described and distinguished. First, although <u>evaluation</u> often includes response and some response contains judgment, not all <u>response</u> is evaluative or leads to a grade. Moreover, response to student writing can come from various readers, including classmates, other peers, teachers, and the student writer. Some response is primarily descriptive ("the main idea in this essay is X"); other responses are personal and reactive ("the part I liked best was Y"). In contrast, evaluation consists of those comments that explain or justify a judgment or value—most commonly, a grade (S. D. Reid, 1991). And because grading usually occurs on the final draft of a paper, the marginal comments and comments at the end of the student paper tend to be evaluative because they are written in the context of the grade that is assigned to the paper.

Responding to student writing is an ongoing process, not a single act. Response parallels the writing processes of idea generation and revision, and it begins immediately after students start working on their topics. Response activities during the writing process include:

- writers discussing their topics in small groups, and peers responding
- writers reading aloud from their drafts, and class members listening and responding
- students writing tentative thesis statements at the board, and students and the teacher responding
- teachers responding orally to students' questions in class and during peer workshops
- students interviewing each other about topic ideas, about their plans for an essay, or about their revision plans
- writers annotating their own drafts, describing or labeling key features (such as thesis statements, specific detail, transition devices, introduction techniques) of their own writing
- teachers conferencing with students both during class and outside of class, responding to writer's notes, plans, and drafts
- peer review groups responding to each other's writing, sometimes in a reader-response mode (descriptive), sometimes in a criteria-based mode (reactive).

In the same way that the processes of idea generation and revision are recursive and ongoing, responses—written and oral—to student writing by a variety of audiences are essential for successful writing (Jenkins, 1987; Leki, 1992; Semke, 1984). Students, teachers, and peers play important roles in the response process: student writers are continuously writing, reading, and revising their prose; peers offer the social context within which response occurs; teachers identify certain competencies on the part of the learners and intervene appropriately in the process.

Student Response

To achieve authenticity in writing, teachers can (a) arrange for student control of topics so that the students write about areas in which they are interested; (b) build toward students' academic writing goals; and (c) create situations in which students become colleagues or teachers in the writing process (D. Johnson, 1989). To give students opportunities to share their strategies and their work, teachers can establish non-teacher audiences for their students: class newspapers and magazines, pen pals, computer-networked interactions, electronic mail exchanges (Batson, 1989; Daiute and Dalton, 1989; Joram et al., 1992; Mabrito, 1991; Schwartz, 1989), and, particularly, **peer review groups** (also called peer response, peer critique, or peer editing workshops, depending on the focus of the groups). If students are to master writing as a communicative process, they must not only write regularly but also regularly try out their drafts and get feedback from a variety of readers. Texts do not evolve in a vacuum (Freedman, 1992; Lawson et al., 1990); peer review groups enable students to realize that social, political, and personal contexts influence writing.

Issues in Peer Review

By broadening the kind of feedback that students receive, peer review and peer discussion of texts help NES and ESL writers at all levels of writing proficiency understand their interactive relationship with their readers (Freedman and Sperling, 1985; Hillocks, 1982; Nystrand, 1990; Richard-Amato, 1988). "Their fellow students' questions, varied interpretations, and misunderstandings dramatize the necessity of the writers providing verbal signs that will enable readers to draw on their own resources to make the intended meaning. The writer can become aware of the responsibility for providing verbal means that will help readers gain required facts, share relevant sensations or attitudes, or make logical transitions" (Rosenblatt, 1988, p. 27). **Peer review workshops** reinforce a system of values central to the classroom community: respect for negotiation and cooperation, a spirit of mutual responsibility, and a setting for respect and trust (Freedman, 1992; Vataloro, 1990). Finally, students in peer review groups learn and practice a "language of response" that they can then use to articulate ideas about their own writing.

One of the greatest benefits of peer review groups is the immediate presence of real-world readers. Researchers of both NES and ESL writing have demonstrated that, with carefully designed and implemented peer review groups, the concept of audience provided by peer response allows writers to think not just about readers as readers but also to actually read the text through the eyes of potential readers, trying to judge the meaning these readers would make (Grimm, 1986; James, 1981; Mittan, 1989; Moore, 1986; Shriver, 1992). In fact, research with ESL writing students has shown that student feedback on peer writing can be more valuable than teacher feedback (Cumming, 1985; Zhang and G. Jacobs, 1989). Peer review shows student writers that not all readers construct the same meaning from a single text (Flower et al., 1990; Gere and Stevens, 1989), an important lesson for inexperienced writers. Students learn to identify their audience and analyze the social context in which their audience—their discourse community—will read their writing (Hare and Fitzsimmons, 1992; Kirsch, 1989; Smagorinsky, 1991a). As a result, student writers begin to adopt the perspectives of their audiences and to assess their writing in terms of how their readers may react to or comprehend their text (Beach and Liebman-Kleine, 1986; Durrant and Duke, 1990).

Small **peer response groups** can also provide a context for a variety of thinking, writing, talking, learning, and role-play situations that form a "powerful educative force of peer influence" (Bruffee, 1984). Students learn, for example, that they are responsible for their own writing and for communicating with an audience; they learn critical thinking skills such as analytical reasoning and problem-solving (Kroonenberg, 1992a). Ronald Barron suggests that student response to writing should involve neither evaluation nor error hunting: "Instead, members of effective response groups treat the papers they are examining as 'works in progress' and recognize that their goal is to serve as a sympathetic reader suggesting methods for writers to use in improving their papers. Ideally, a dialogue should be created between the writer and other members of the group which clarifies the intent of the writer's essay and sharpens the way it is achieved" (1991, p. 24). With the help of their "respondents," student writers form and test hypotheses about their writing and their audiences; they discover that their peers are having similar difficulties, which diminishes the isolation and apprehension they may feel about their own writing problems, and they learn to provide "cues" that help readers identify the rhetorical situation and the direction of the text (Tyler and Bro, 1992). Ideally, as the students make choices, express intentions, and read and reread their own and others' writing, they become increasingly able to identify lack of substance, organizational weaknesses, unclear writing, and illogical ideas (Allaei and Connor, 1990, p. 19). With continued experience in peer collaboration and peer review, they become more able to identify strengths and weaknesses in their own writing, to ask for specific feedback from their peers, to develop expertise in the common tasks they must perform, and to discover the specific demands of the target academic culture (Braine, 1989; Keh, 1990).

Caveats: Group Work

Establishing viable peer response/review groups can be challenging in an ESL writing class. Learning to write honestly and frequently in a second language, to share work and to respond to another's work, to accept criticism, and to work on revisions are often new behaviors for ESL students that may be difficult to achieve (Ballard and Clanchy, 1992; Basham and Kwachka, 1992). It is also difficult for students to enter into the processes of writing if they lack fluency, experience, and knowledge of academic reader expectations; it is equally difficult to perform successfully and to respond appropriately in unknown situations. Fortunately, although students are not by nature good evaluators of their own writing, they <u>can</u> learn to describe the mental processes they went through as they wrote, what they experienced, and what they wanted their readers to experience (M. Smith, 1991). However, students must be <u>taught</u> to give productive response; unplanned or informal collaboration and response are usually neither efficient nor effective (Dassin, 1991; Hafernik, 1984; Hansson, 1992; Krest, 1988). Teachers must therefore introduce and then nurture new attitudes and behaviors.

First, because a high level of comfort is crucial for collaboration and group work, teachers should discuss the possible areas of discomfort with their students. As Sara Allaei and Ulla Connor (1990) reported, some ESL students (and some NESs as well) feel uncomfortable making negative statements about peer writing; others are reluctant to share writing or feel constrained by weak language skills. Still others are not immediately willing to accept the processes of peer response; they do not trust the feedback of their peers, and they are unwilling to share their thoughts with classmates. They may actually feel that peer review groups are merely a time-filler or a change of pace in the classroom, a game not to be taken seriously. Moreover, part of the preparation for peer response groups is learning to tolerate and respect others in the group, and learning that the group dialogs will result in alternatives, not ultimatums (Barron, 1991; Smagorinsky, 1991a). To instill and encourage a level of comfort, and to persuade students to commit to the process, teachers should explain to their students the benefits of collaborative or group work. Such collaboration

- strengthens the community of the class and offers writers an authentic audience (Dansereau, 1988; McGroarty, 1989a)
- diversifies the pace of the class and breaks the monotony of the lecture format (Oxford, 1990), and
- offers students with different learning styles and strategies additional opportunities for learning (Peck, 1991; Scarcella and Oxford, 1992; Wenden and Rubin, 1987).

In addition, the students need to understand that the goal of peer response/review workshops is not so much to judge (as the teacher's role is often viewed) as to cooperate in a communicative process, helping others in the classroom community to balance individual purposes with the expectations of the readers.

Finally, peer response workshops need to be carefully structured, at least at the beginning of the course. Otherwise, student participation in peer review will be at best vague, overly flattering, and superficial ("I think the paper is, ummm, really interesting") and at worst mechanized, detached, and as a result, ineffective. Students should have precise instructions and clear directions about the roles they will play in the group and the tasks they are expected to accomplish. Teachers should model peer response roles by showing "safe" essays (such as a published essay, the teacher's work-in-progress, or student essays from previous courses) on the overhead projector. They can teach students the "language of response" by annotating the text orally and in writing, writing marginal comments, asking questions about the text, and modeling appropriate behaviors as well as appropriate language (Gast, 1990).

Peer Review Worksheets

Students learn about their own writing processes by writing about them.* A classic exercise in writing-to-learn is a note from student to teacher, stating what s/he was trying to do in a paper, what seemed to work, what didn't, how the paper changed, what decisions were made during the composing stages, and what s/he learned from the assignment. In peer review workshops, planning and reflecting on learning and writing processes are equally as valuable for readers and writers. Asking students to write their analyses will deepen their understanding of the draft, focus their attention on the text, and provide the writer with a record of suggestions for revision. "Peer revision tends to be especially productive after students have spent a half hour or so doing this kind of thoughtful, written analysis, in or out of class" (C. Cooper, 1991, p. 8). Robert Mittan (1989) suggests a four-task exercise for peer review pairs or groups; as the course progresses, the teacher can add to the baseline instructions with more essay-specific tasks. The student should

1. offer a positive response to the writing ("What I liked best was . . . . ").
2. identify the purpose of the writing ("The main idea is . . .").
3. ask questions directed to the writer ("What do you mean here about . . . ?").
4. offer suggestions to the writer (an opportunity for open-ended, expressive writing).

Mittan also suggests that teachers consider collecting the peer review sheets and treating them as writing assignments, either at the time of the response groups or as part of the writer's final draft of the writing. Reading and responding to student critiques benefit the students who have given thoughtful, helpful responses, and grading them shows the students the value of participation. Moreover, teachers can give feedback on a reviewer's inadequate performance that may enhance his/her next peer response. In more advanced classes, teachers can also have students evaluate (perhaps for the teacher's eyes only) the peer reviews of classmates: what was helpful (perhaps a grudging admission) and what was not (a much needed opportunity for the student to reject some of the responses as invalid). In these ways,

*See a discussion of metacognitive activities in Chapter 6.

teachers prepare their students for the kind of active, adaptive, productive reading, reviewing and rereading of their own and other texts.

Below are several structured worksheets that teachers can give students for peer review. Many of the questions/exercises should contain more space after each question or statement so that students can respond on the sheet. The questions/exercises can be shortened, modified, mixed and matched to better suit each classroom situation. Most of the worksheets can function with most levels of language proficiency. The more complex questions or worksheets are identified with a cross (✚). One suggestion: at the end of each workshop, leave ten minutes for students to (a) evaluate the impact of the workshop in their journals, and (b) actually work on the revisions suggested by the workshop.

WORKSHEET: READER-WRITER RESPONSE

1. Writer: What one question would you like your reader to answer, or what one problem did you need a second opinion about?
2. Reader: Answer the question. Be specific. Then complete the following statements:
   - a. The best part of this paper was _____
   - b. When I finished the essay I thought/felt _____
   - ✚c. One place I disagreed was where you said _____
   - d. One experience or idea I had that was similar to this was _____
   - e. When you said _____ , I thought about _____
   - ✚f. One suggestion I want to make to improve the paper is _____

WORKSHEET: GROUP RESPONSE

Instructions: The writer provides draft copies for the readers.

1. Readers: Ask the writer: "How can we help you?"
2. Writer (who comes to class with notes that anticipate the question): Indicate specific areas in which you need help.
3. Readers: Listen and take notes, then offer verbal and written feedback and suggestions.
4. Writer: Listens and takes notes. (S/he retains full authority to evaluate the advice and make the final decisions.)

WORKSHEET: DESCRIPTIVE RESPONSE

1. The subject/topic of this paper is _____
2. The intended audience for this paper is _____

3. The main ideas of this paper, in order, are _____

4. This essay has _____ paragraphs (sentences).

✦5. This piece of writing is written from the point of view of a person who is _____. (Describe the writer/narrator—this may be a persona, not the student herself.)

WORKSHOP: IDENTIFICATION EXERCISE

1. Write "Lead-in" in the margin next to the writer's lead.

2. Put an asterisk (*) in the margin next to the sentence(s) that contain the writer's main idea or thesis.

3. Write "hook" next to paragraph hooks and transitions used at the beginning of the body paragraphs.

4. Label one example of each of the following uses of the senses: sight, sound, touch.

5. Write "passive" next to one passive voice sentence.

WORKSHOP: READER RESPONSE AND REVISION

1. Reader: Read through the draft twice. Then, without looking back at the essay,
   a. write one sentence that states what you think is the dominant idea.
   b. explain what you liked best.
   c. describe where you were confused.
   d. what specific detail do you remember most clearly?

✦2. Reader: Show where the writer could use more details, images, facts, or description. Suggest a revision.

3. Writer: Complete these sentences:
   a. Having someone else read my essay was _____ because _____

   b. The most helpful comment I received from the group was _____

   c. The least helpful comment was _____ because _____

(S. D. Reid, 1992b)

WORKSHEET: AUDIENCE ANALYSIS

1. What occasion or questions do you think influenced the writer to write this essay (paragraph)? (Why do you think the writer chose this topic?)*

2. Who is the audience the writer is trying to change or influence?

*In this exercise, questions in parentheses restate the original question in simpler language.

3. What attitudes, knowledge, and assumptions would such an audience have that the writer will have to consider? (What does the audience know? Not know?)

4. What questions would the audience have in mind that they would expect the writer to respond to?

5. What do you think the writer's purpose is in writing this paper?

6. In your opinion, what change or action does the writer hope to cause? (How does the writer want the audience to think, to feel, or to act when they finish reading the essay/paragraph?)

+7. What means does the writer use to influence the readers?

+8. Does the essay work? Does it respond adequately to the situation or problem that caused it to be written? Does it answer the questions that its readers will need? Will the readers be likely to act or to change their opinions after reading it?

(adapted from Hairston, 1986)

WORKSHOP: WRITTEN RESPONSE

1. What do you like most about your partner's writing? Choose the most interesting idea and write a paragraph explaining WHY it captured your attention.

2. In your own words, write what you think your partner's focus is.

+3. On the back of this page, write a short letter to your partner explaining how her/his writing can be improved. BE VERY SPECIFIC and explain WHY you think these changes will be helpful to the reader.

(adapted from Mittan, 1989)

Caveats: Peer Review

Peer review is not a panacea, nor should it be the primary focus of an ESL writing class, particularly at the beginning of a course. Group work, peer review workshops, and peer response groups can be difficult to facilitate effectively. Less experienced teachers should introduce such work slowly, using group work only sparingly as they teach students to appreciate and value the results of collaboration. In addition, group work with students whose language proficiency is especially limited can be even more challenging for the teacher; raising the comfort level of the students and instilling the self-confidence necessary to perform in groups may take much time and energy. At the same time, the students may not have the coping strategies to benefit from group work, especially early in the course; inappropriate use of peer review strategies can nullify any benefit the group work might offer and can actually irritate the students. Moreover, even when response groups are functioning successfully, the teacher can feel isolated from the students and feel unable to evaluate the effectiveness of group work. Teachers should therefore view group work as one of a variety of classroom approaches to the teaching of ESL writing; experimenting with group work, then evaluating (and having the students evaluate) the success of that work is essential.

Alternative Audiences

While peer response groups offer the most efficient and easily organized additional audience for student writers, other possibilities exist for readers of student writing-in-progress. Using **multiple audiences** for feedback and learning offers three advantages: (a) students spend more time working with their writing; (b) students learn that different readers have differing reactions to their writing (that is, there is no one single "right" way to communicate successfully); and (c) students work on their oral skills as well as their writing skills (Blanton, 1992; Hvitfeldt, 1992). There are, of course, some disadvantages of seeking multiple audience feedback for ESL writing students. First, any additional time spent outside of class may be difficult and time-consuming to arrange, schedule, and monitor. Second, most NES participants in such programs are relatively naive and need preparation and training before successful audience intervention activities can take place. Finally, not all ESL student writers will respond positively to alternative audience experiences; they too need preparation. The alternatives offered below are not inclusive, nor are they equally viable at all post-secondary institutions.

Among the possibilities for multiple audience response is the college or university **writing center**, which is usually available to all students who desire assistance with their academic writing. This center is staffed by writing professionals whose job it is to advise and encourage inexperienced writers. In addition, the professional staff is often supplemented with student tutors who receive credit for their service. Writing center personnel do not function as writers <u>for</u> students, however, and they do not edit student papers for errors. ESL students therefore need preparation for their visits to the writing center. In the same way students must practice the negotiation and oral skills necessary for small group work and peer review, they must form their objectives and then take responsibility for writing center visits. Similarly, writing center personnel, who may be trained teachers of NES composition, or student tutors with limited training (Kroll, forthcoming), may need preparation and training (provided, perhaps, by the ESL writing teacher) for their encounter with ESL students (J. Reid, 1993). At present, writing center literature usually instructs personnel to

- be collaborative and Socratic (ask the student questions to guide him/her to independent decision-making)
- have students read their papers aloud in order to "hear" errors
- avoid "appropriating" student text
- encourage students to "discover" the form for their material.

NES composition teachers and writing center personnel who encounter ESL student writers often need to revise these objectives and approaches. First, most ESL students seldom need to be encouraged to think independently; they are often motivated and intelligent writers. Second, an international student reading his/her writing aloud is not a successful technique for editing, since the focus of that reading is often on the difficulty of oral production, and, for the most part, the students do not "hear" their errors. In addition, ESL students' knowledge and experience with the formats of academic prose are limited. In many cases, they cannot "discover" form because they have had no previous experience with it. For ESL students, then, the writing center becomes a place to learn about organization and presentation of material, an objective that restricts the collaboration of the meeting and increases the intervention and the range of suggestions given by the writing center personnel (Powers, forthcoming; J. Reid and Powers, forthcoming).

Writing tutorials offer another audience possibility for ESL writing students. The writing class is divided into small groups that meet weekly with a writing tutor, outside of and in addition to class time, perhaps in the writing center. For tutorials to function effectively, the same group should meet together for the length of the course and be required to attend. Otherwise, the sense of community within the group will suffer, and the tutorials will become fragmented and less helpful. Writing tutors are usually paid writing faculty, graduate teaching assistants, or graduate students in a class who receive credit for the tutoring. Each tutorial meeting is planned and executed by the group, with the tutor functioning as the mediator and facilitator; topics of tutorials include idea generation for writing, discussion of individual student papers, revision plans, and so on. The objectives of the small group will resemble the types of interaction and sharing among the students during in-class small group work. Note: The tutorial facilitators may need preparation and training which ESL writing teachers can provide.

Native-speaker **peer editors** are yet another source of readers for ESL student writing. Usually, peer editors participate in a volunteer program, although sometimes the peer editors are assigned their role as part of another class, earning credit for their participation. Peer editors do not teach; therefore, they need not be experts in English or in writing. Rather, they function as NES readers who respond as native speakers to the writing of their ESL partners. Peer editors are paired with ESL student writers; the partners meet weekly or biweekly on an informal basis. Although the ESL student is responsible for arranging and planning the meeting, usually the partners read through the ESL paper together, with the peer editor indicating places in the prose that "don't sound right" or are difficult to understand (Jenkins, 1987). The pair discuss possible solutions to each problem. Peer editors need training (usually a single meeting with the ESL teacher), but not in grammar or in teaching composition skills; rather, they should receive some cross-cultural education about ways to offer advice without doing the actual writing. And NES peer tutors need to understand the benefits of the peer partnership, among them the information about linguistic differences and the opportunity to learn about cultural differences.

The use of multiple audiences in the ESL writing class changes the roles of the teacher and the students, both in and outside the classroom. Teachers should work with the ESL student writers (a) to prepare them for the input they will receive about their writing, (b) to model and then have students practice appropriate oral and behavioral skills for the encounters, and (c) to prepare students to listen, to share, and to articulate their ideas. As the course progresses, the teacher will find that students who often sought daily interaction with the teacher begin to find the alternative audiences just as satisfactory. Eventually, the hours given over to "office hours," during which students may walk in and talk with the teacher, diminish dramatically (J. Reid, 1990). In fact, the teacher may feel isolated from her/his students; the process of "letting go" is analogous to the latter stages of parenting. ESL writing students who participate in these opportunities for multiple audiences evaluate them positively. Below are sections from two student responses that are typical.

> As for the Writing Tutorials, I found that the sessions were beneficial to me. I had the chance to discuss my essay topic with another person before writing any drafts. In addition, I had the chance to revise the whole written essay before final submission. All in all the writing tutorial sessions were regarded as additional coachings in writing (as time was limited in normal class lecture to write much, not counting the few in-class writings we had). Specifically, talking of the revision part, my writing tutor really helped me to synthesize the essays I had written—she helped me in correcting grammatic mistakes, without unnecessary "junks" and on top of these, shaping up an essay that had a skeleton and the "flesh" to cover up.
>
> Weoi-Choo Ong (Malaysia)

> The Peer Editor programme was done by native Americans, who checked out rough drafts, looked for any simple mistakes and pointed

those out to us so that we could correct something which never seemed wrong to us. Maybe it didn't work for every student, but it worked very well in my case. My Peer Editor helped me mostly by point out where a synonym word sounds better than the word I had used. Like he point out where "would" would be more appropriate than "should." He also showed me where to use more specific words instead of a generalized one. For example, at one place in my research paper, he said that "bad" can be used to represent a lot of things, so it is better to use "slanderous" or "offensive" instead of that. So the Peer Editing programme has helped me in improving my English.

Azmat Rahman (Bangladesh)

Teacher Response

Writing is essentially social; it takes place in a specific context for a reader, and the situation for writing influences its purpose. In terms of the social activity of writing, however, school-writing can be excessively artificial (M. Cohen and Riel, 1989). The normal relationships of writers to readers are <u>expert to novice</u> or <u>colleague to colleague</u>, and the purposes for writing include informing, persuading, and/or entertaining that audience. In normal reader-writer relationships, people choose to write to friends about their feelings and experiences, to publish journal articles about their research, to advise others about processes (such as directions to a party or instructions for waxing skis), to inform and persuade (for example, textbooks, memos to working colleagues, newspaper articles and editorials).

School-writing, however, differs in both the writer-reader relationship and in purpose. Because the teacher usually <u>initiates</u>, <u>designs</u>, <u>assigns</u>, and <u>evaluates</u> the writing of the students, the teacher is the expert, and the writer is explaining material about which the teacher is often more informed than the student. Moreover, the purposes for school-writing are unusual: often the teacher expects students not to inform or persuade, but rather to demonstrate knowledge learned as part of a class. The student understands this "hidden agenda" and realizes that her/his purpose is not to inform or entertain, but rather to demonstrate knowledge for the purpose of achieving a satisfactory grade.

In addition to the anomalies of audience and purpose in school writing, ESL writing teachers face unusual social interactions during their various responses to student writing. First, the teacher plays several different roles, among them coach, judge, facilitator, evaluator, interested reader, and copy editor (Freedman and Sperling, 1985; H. Johnson, 1992; Moxley, 1989). Teachers inevitably offer writers more response and more intervention than an ordinary reader (Radecki and Swales, 1988). Second, because the students know that the teacher is the ultimate authority, at least in terms of their grades, the student-teacher relationship is unbalanced: each response from the teacher, even those that are intended to be purely descriptive, is seen by the student as evaluative. While students can, with practice, listen to peer responses to their writing and analyze the comments, selecting those they find relevant and helpful, teacher response often results in what researchers have labeled the "good girl syndrome": the student who immediately surrenders authority over her text and abdicates responsibility for her writing, assuming that the teacher's comment is absolute (Freedman and Sperling, 1985).

Still, teacher response to student writing is an essential part of the teaching process because writing instruction must be individualized, and because, as María de la Luz Reyes states, "mere exposure to standard writing conventions [does] not improve student use of them" (1991, p. 291). Response, or "**feedback**," can be defined as any input from reader to writer that provides information for revision (Keh, 1990). But for response to be effective, three results must be avoided:

- the student doesn't comprehend the response;
- the student understands the response but does not know how to implement it;
- the student understands the response and implements it, but the writing is not improved (Burnham, 1986).

The key question in offering feedback therefore is: how can the teacher provide response that is genuine, effective and long-lasting? Successful teacher response can be either **formative** (immediate intervention in discrete parts of an essay) or **summative** (a response that is an overview of more general considerations in an essay). However, it must help students to improve their writing by communicating feedback detailed enough to allow students to act, to commit to change in their writing. Student writers "need to learn to distinguish when they are performing well from when they are not, and they need to know how to take corrective action when they are not" (Freedman, 1987, p. x). Teacher response depends on the type and purpose of the assignment, and it can be transmitted in a variety of ways: in dialog journals, mini-conferences during class workshops, written comments on student drafts, and student-teacher conferences. As teachers consider how to respond to student writing, they face the following questions:

1. Exactly when—and how frequently—during the writing process should I respond?
2. How can I respond to the student's writing so that the student can process the comments and apply the specifics of my response?
3. What form(s) of response (written, oral, individual, group, class, formal, informal) would be most successful for the students?

4. When should my response be global or summative (focusing mainly on the major strengths or weaknesses) or discrete (focusing on single items within the essay)?

5. What are my objectives for this writing task (for example, improvement in topic sentences, organization, details)? What do I want the student to learn?

Whether teachers respond verbally or in writing, they must select their role as respondent and they must consider the perceptions of the student: What does the student consider her/his problems to be? What does the student perceive as strengths in the piece of writing? How can the teacher's feedback lead to revision and then to the cognitive change that will allow the student to really <u>re-vise</u>, see differently, and therefore be capable of transferring the change to other pieces of writing? <u>Different ways for the teacher to intervene include:</u>

1. becoming the <u>audience</u> in order to ask questions about the purpose of the essay. For example, "I have a question about X here." "I wasn't persuaded by this evidence—do you have more statistics?" "Is this always true?" "Does this contradict what you said above?"

2. becoming a <u>reader</u> responding to the ideas and content : "When I read this paragraph, I **felt** . . ." "I thought about X when I read this essay." "When I read the first paragraph, I thought the essay was going to be about Y, but when I finished I realized it was probably about Z."

3. acting as a <u>writing consultant</u> by sending the student back to the writing process: "This paragraph needs more detail; try a pre-writing strategy to collect more information." "Write another introduction—then show both to your peer review group in class tomorrow."

4. becoming a <u>describer</u> of the main rhetorical features: "The last paragraph of your essay focuses on your third point; now you need to write a concluding paragraph." "Your thesis statement indicates that you will discuss X, but in the second paragraph you talk about Y—why?" "You have five short sentences in a row here. Try combining several of the sentences in this paragraph."

One way of discovering student perceptions is to have students annotate their own drafts with comments or queries to the teacher about perceived problems before they hand in the text or attend a conference. The teacher then responds, in writing or verbally, giving direct and appropriate feedback on the points raised by each student. This kind of response facilitates the teacher's understanding of the writer's problems and intentions, and allows students more control over the feedback they receive (Freedman, 1989). More important, it makes students responsible for locating and analyzing the sources of dissatisfaction in the text. For the teacher, responding to student-generated queries is less frustrating, more satisfying, and less time-consuming than simply responding without student input (Charles, 1990; Jenkins, 1987).

Conferencing

The writing conference is a face-to-face conversation between the teacher and the student, usually outside the boundaries of the classroom. It is a negotiated teaching event, a chance for both parties to address the student's individual needs through dialog. Conferences can take place for several reasons: a getting-to-know-you meeting at the beginning of the semester, a brief discussion concerning topic selection and/or a progress report on a major paper, or a discussion of a revision plan. But most teacher-student conferences focus on an essay in progress. The meeting calls for careful and detailed response by the teacher in order to help the student test and apply suggestions and comments before the final draft and the graded evaluation. Susan Florio-Ruane and Sandra Dunn (1985) have summarized the advantages of individual conferencing: by listening to the student and reading the work in progress, the teacher can come to know the writer's intentions, resources, growth, and needs. In a similar way, students should prepare for conferences by bringing a set of questions they have prepared beforehand. For the student, talking with a teacher about her work and responding to thoughtful questions is a way to expand and clarify thinking about audience and purpose as well as an opportunity to receive technical assistance and advice.

Writing conferences have recognizable parts:

- Openings: "How are you?" "How is your writing going?"
- Student-initiated comments and questions: "My main question is about content. I don't know how much detail I need here."
- Teacher-initiated comments and questions: "How did you choose this topic?" "What is this paper about?" "Who is your intended audience?" "What are you going to do next?" "If you were to add information here, how would you do it?" "How do you feel about the paper so far?" "What do you like best about the paper?"
- Reading of the paper: the student or the teacher might read the paper aloud, or both might read it silently, together.
- Closings: often, a conference can be usefully concluded by giving the student a minute or two to write out her/his plans for revision. "What are the two most important changes you intend to make?"

The tone of the writing conference is usually positive: the teacher encourages the student to think about writing as something that can be organized and improved and gives her/him an opportunity to talk about writing and reflect on individual processes. The actual conference usually contains a balance between asking questions and instructing; teachers should intervene, but should not take over the job. When the student's responses to questions suggest that s/he wants or needs help, the teacher should try to get <u>her/him</u> to do the actual writing and revision. For example, the teacher can model ways of solving problems and discussing alternatives, then ask the student to do the same; allowing the student to see a teacher struggle to solve a problem can be illuminating. By the end of the conference, <u>the student should have formulated a plan of action</u>; s/he should understand what the immediate writing tasks will be following the conference.

Conferences can be especially valuable for ESL student writers because they allow students to control the interaction, actively participate, learn to negotiate meaning, and clarify the teacher's responses. But ESL students, even more than NESs, are inexperienced in the behavior and even the language of the student-teacher conference, particularly because the "manners" of the conference differ substantially from teacher-student interaction in the classroom. ESL students come to conferences with rules of speaking that may conflict with the interaction teachers might like to see operate in conferences: initiating conversation, asking questions for clarification, negotiating meaning, and so on. It is therefore incumbent on the teacher to prepare ESL students for conferences: to explain the purposes of conferences, to teach the differences in language expectations between the U.S. classroom and the conference, to discuss the format and the rules of speaking expected by the teacher during the conference, and to use role-play in class to practice the behaviors of the student participants, particularly in contributing input and negotiating revisions (Goldstein and Conrad, 1990).

The initial responsibility of writing teachers is to structure the conference (a) by giving students responsibility for preparing to take an active role in the conference and (b) by preparing for the conference themselves. Because ESL student writers have probably had little or no experience with conferencing or with the responsibility of planning a conference, it is necessary to provide them with planning materials. Below are suggested worksheets for student-teacher conferencing; space for writing on the planning sheet is essential, and students should be required to bring the planning worksheet to the conference. It is then advisable for the teacher to begin a conference with and be guided by the worksheet that describes the writer's sense of purpose, audience, and form. During the conference, the teacher can estimate how successfully the writer has achieved his/her purpose for the particular audience, and can encourage the student to establish and use evaluation criteria as s/he revises the writing.

CONFERENCE-PLANNING WORKSHEETS

Initial Conference (about a topic)

1. Topic for my essay: _____
2. Intended purpose of my essay: _____
3. Intended audience for my essay: _____
4. Pre-writing about my topic: _____

_____

Essay Draft Conference

Statements 1–3 (above) plus

4. In that group work, my peers asked the following questions about my topic:_____
5. In the group work we did in class, my peers made the following suggestions:_____
6. The problem(s) I'm having with this draft are: _____

Guided Conference Preparation

1. Explain your topic or purpose for this paper.
2. Describe a difficulty you are having as you write this paper.
3. List three questions you need to discuss during the conference.

(courtesy of Shelley Reid)

Revision Planning Conference

1. I thought the best part of my essay was _____
2. I thought the weakest part of my essay was _____
3. According to your [i.e., the instructor's] comments, the strengths and problems in the essay draft are as follows:

STRENGTHS	PROBLEMS
a. _____	a. _____
b. _____	b. _____
c. _____	c. _____

4. Based on the feedback, here is my plan for revising this essay (list specific steps you intend to take and specific paragraphs you intend to revise):
   a. _____

b. _____

c. _____

5. Three questions I want to ask you [i.e., the instructor] are:

a. _____

b. _____

c. _____

(S.D. Reid, 1991)

Metacognitive Questions

Instructions: Answer 3 (or 4 or 5) of the following questions that are most appropriate for your own essay.

1. How I think I would improve on this paper if I had time for one more draft.
2. What I hope most readers will not notice.
3. A serious problem I had writing this draft, and how I tried to solve the problem.
4. A risk I took as I wrote this paper.
5. How the audience I chose most influenced me.
6. What most intimidated me while I wrote this paper.
7. When an idea from the textbook inspired me or influenced me.
8. Where my idea generation notes helped me.
9. What I learned about choosing a topic.
10. What I learned from reading other students' drafts.
11. Writing strategies that I rejected, and why.
12. How I experimented with vocabulary or syntax.
13. Help I experienced in gathering material for paper.
14. Where my native language, family, religion, or gender helped or interfered.
15. What I really want the teacher to look for is _____

(adapted from C. Cooper, 1991)

Mini-conferencing

Informal, spontaneous student-teacher conferencing often takes place in class, particularly during small group work. In a mini-conference, the teacher sits beside one student in the group, or individual students talk with the teacher outside the group, about the writing in progress. The teacher gives support, makes suggestions about the organization of ideas, assists with the language, and/or extends the students' thinking about the topic (Hedge, 1988) in a brief but timely response (2–4 minutes) that is often crucial to keeping a student's writing on track. Mini-conferencing has some distinct advantages: (a) it occurs during the regular flow of classroom learning; (b) the student-teacher relationship does not have to change dramatically; (c) the immediate intervention is efficient, a natural part of the writing process; and (d) it is not a separate activity but rather is integrated into the student's immediate needs. Students can raise their hands while working individually on their writing or working in a group activity, or they can sign up on the board and take turns speaking with the teacher as they seek clarification about their writing, mediation concerning the advice they are receiving from peers, or specific questions about a writing task. Or the teacher can simply circulate as students work, checking progress, asking questions, and offering suggestions in a mini-conference format.

Caveats

While student-teacher conferences have become an important instructional technique for many NES and ESL composition teachers, and while some teachers have found that teaching by conference is even more valuable than classroom experiences (Carcinelli, 1980; Garrison, 1974; M. Harris, 1986), not all teachers find conferencing successful. Among the possible problems with student-teacher conferencing:

1. Particularly for new teachers, structuring and implementing conferences may take excessive amounts of time, and the actual conferences may not be as effective as other teaching techniques, classroom work, and/or written comments on student drafts.

2. Teachers may find that their teaching styles and/or some of their students' learning styles may make some students more open to advice-seeking and conference intervention than others.

3. Teachers may differ greatly from each other in how they interact with individual students in student-teacher conferences (or even in mini-conferences), so some teachers are more comfortable and more successful with conferencing than others (Freedman and Sperling, 1985; Katz, 1988).

4. There is tremendous variation across students in the way they interact with the teacher in a conference. "[W]hile a student *may* contribute input, *may* set the agenda, and *may* negotiate meaning, these are not guaranteed—even in conferences with the same teacher"(Goldstein and Conrad, 1990, p. 455).

5. ESL conferences do not necessarily result in revision, and when revision does occur after a conference, it is not always successful.

6. Students who need help most with their writing are often the

least successful at getting help from the teacher during the conference because they are unable to take charge and to negotiate meaning.

Since long-term improvement and cognitive change are the objectives of any teacher intervention, it is necessary for ESL writing teachers to carefully evaluate the effectiveness of conferences for their students and to then use conferencing to its fullest, to use it sparingly, or not to use it at all.

Conclusion

The roles the teacher adopts when reading student texts, and the kinds of response teachers—and others—give to student texts have been the subjects of much research and discussion during the past decade. Because student papers create a rhetorical situation unlike that produced by any other text, special conditions are imposed upon all three elements of the interaction: the writer, the text, and the reader. In the past, teachers focused on evaluating their students' products. Today, teacher-response roles show "a movement away from the traditional (and ego-satisfying) representation of teacher as authority and power-broker to an acceptance of the teacher as *cointerpreter* of student writing and *facilitator* of the revision process" (Lawson et al., 1990, p. 87).

ESL student writers need and deserve responses to their writing during the process, both to the form and to the content of that writing. Feedback should begin early in the process, with discussion of initial nonwritten plans and ideas for writing and then comments (written or oral, individual or group, teacher or peers) on student writing that will enable the writer to communicate more effectively. Such feedback should be informative and detailed enough to help the student writers return to the task of writing but not so overwhelming that they cannot form a revision plan. As they write, receive response, and revise, students should be able to feel good about what they have done well and realize that they can improve on what they have not done effectively (M. Smith, 1991).

Much remains to be known about the design and implementation of response to ESL student writing. Research results about the effect of response on student writing have been "inconclusive, sometimes contradictory, and, in second language writing, sparse. More research is needed, especially in second language writing, to look not only at teachers' written responses but at combinations of classroom settings, course goals, and grading procedures in order to discover what forms our responses can most profitably take" (Leki, 1990, p. 66).

Discussion Questions

1. What kinds of group/collaborative work have you experienced in academic classes? Choose one memorable experience. In a small group, share your prior experience with others. Then, as a group, discuss the following questions about each person's experience:

    A. How was the group organized?

    B. How effective did you think the group work was at the time? Has your opinion changed as you now view the work from a greater distance? Why or why not?

    C. How would you modify that group work experience to improve its effectiveness? Be specific.

2. Read the student essays written on the topic for the Test of Written English (TWE) in the Discussion section at the end of the next chapter (question #6). Then, in a small group, plan a writing conference for each of the student-writers. Decide the questions you might ask, and the advice you might give in each conference.

3. In small groups, discuss the approaches available to teachers in student-teacher writing conferences. Which do you think you might use? Why? Which would you feel less comfortable using? Why?

4. Read the following passage. Then discuss the concept of discourse communities based on Bartholomae's description. Indicate what advice you might give students to better prepare them for the variety of discourse communities they will encounter.

> David Bartholomae (1991) has described the responses of a cross-curricular faculty committee judging a campuswide writing contest as a "conflict of discourse communities." For example, the five non-English Department members judged an English major's paper as wonderful, while Bartholomae felt it was overwritten, vague, flowery, wordy, and generalized. The Sociology paper was deemed fine by all committee members except the sociologist, who called it "the worst excesses of ethnographic pedantry." The Chemistry laboratory report was labeled excellent by all members except the chemist, who called it formulaic, mechanical and incomplete. In the end, the awards were given, but none was unanimous.

5. "Texts reflect life and the multitude of tastes and standards in real life" (Belanoff, 1991, p. 62). How might this statement relate to teacher response of student texts?

6. Which of the alternative audiences discussed in this chapter would you find the easiest to implement? Which might be most beneficial for students with low levels of language proficiency? Why?

7. Divide into small groups of six each. In pairs within the group, plan a student-teacher writing conference, with one partner playing each role. As two group members role-play the student-teacher conference, the other members of the group take notes. At the end of each simulated conference, the group should discuss the strengths and weaknesses of each and offer suggestions for improvement.

Writing

1. In your own experience as a writer in a first or second language, what kind of teacher intervention did you experience? Which kinds of intervention did you find most (or least) beneficial? Write a brief essay analyzing the value of teacher intervention in your own writing.

2. Choose one of the peer review workshop sheets from this chapter and modify it for an ESL class that you specify in terms of age, objectives, and language proficiency. Share your modified worksheet with others in the class.

3. Write an entry in your learning log, describing and analyzing your attitudes toward student-teacher conferencing. Would you choose to use conferencing with your ESL writing students? Why?

4. Write a paragraph explaining the kinds of cross-cultural information you might use in training a group of NES undergraduates who had volunteered to become writing tutors for your ESL writing students. Share this information with others in the class.

5. Using the worksheets in this chapter as models, design:
   a. a worksheet that combines several types;
   b. a conference planning worksheet for conferences with your students.

6. Write a brief analysis of the simulated student-teacher conferences (see Discussion Question 7, above). What did you learn that you might be able to apply to actual student-teacher conferences?

7. Reflect on the issue of response to student writing. Then write a brief essay describing your attitudes toward response that will be useful to you as you develop your philosophy of teaching ESL writing.

8. Read the brief drafts of the student essays below. Write formative comments in the margins (that is, comments about discrete strengths and weaknesses that will send the student back into the writing process to re-form the paragraph). Then write a summative comment in your learning log (that is, a comment that sums up your overall impression of the essay). Both kinds of comments should conform to your philosophy of response. Then write a paragraph describing what you hope the student writers will do in response to your comments.

Task: Describe a successful piece of writing you did recently. Show the reader why it was successful.

When I wrote an article about potassium contamination, I was referring to a problem in a small town in Taiwan. My father was a surgeon there. He did 6–10 operations in one day once a week. That was how I started to notice the problem. I was at the hospital for a few weeks, and after getting some information from my father and from research findings in the hospital's library I began writing. the article. I hope to make people aware of this problem so that some steps could be taken to improve the situation.

In my article I first listed the cases that occurred in the town. Then I stated my suggestion. To support my arguement I used the reports from other authoritative researches and combined with my experience at the hospital. Then I tried to capture the empathy of the audience. To convince them the problem needed to be solved soon. Then in the conclusion I gave the solution that I thought could help the people in some instances.

I feel my article made a good point because since then this problem has been faced.   Sue-Lan Kao (PRC)

Task: Using the results of the [learning styles, personality, left-right brained, writing rituals] surveys, select one or more results that describe your learning processes. Write a 500–word essay that will interest your buddy.

When I study i have to do it in a particular way to learn effectively, and I also need special environment. These things I gess is cause lot of my personality, which is showen by my different procedures and habits I have, both when I study and in my leisure time.

When it concerns my learning style, the most efficient way for me is to see the material I have to learn. I have to read it in my own tempo, so I have time to think. I am also very individualistic when I study. I do not like to work in groups, because then I cannot take breaks when I want it and one often talk about other things than the asignment, and that is just wasting of time.

When I study, I also think that the environment is important. First, I have to study at an informal place. My favorite place to study is in my one bed. Second I need to have it totally quit around me if I am going to concentrate. However, I cans stand a little noice because I use to put earplugs in my ears when I am studying. Finally I want to have a tidy room when I study, so I always tidy it before I begin studying.

As a person I always think I am under time pressure. I hate to use too long time on things. I like to do things spontaniously, but if I am going to get time enough for everything, I have to plan. For example, when I am going out for dinner with somebody it has to be planned. I also talk very fast (when I speek Norwegian of course), and I interrupt people when they talk. That is because I am unpasiont and whant to get to the point as fast as possible. These attitudes I have when I am studying and I have in my leisure time shows that I am an unpassiant, individualistic and structuriced person.

Anne Waaden (Norway)

CHAPTER 9

Evaluating Student Writing

H. DOUGLAS BROWN states that testing occurs any time we "try" something: cooking a special meal, going roller-blading, writing an essay. As we "perform," we are also evaluating that performance and responding to that evaluation. We also respond to and evaluate others: "Nice shirt." "That was a terrible movie!" "What an exciting game!" In each case, we form a judgment; testing, then, is "a method of measuring a person's ability or knowledge [or clothes, ideas, opinions, etc.] in a given area" (1987, p. 219). The methods of measurement can be formal—the final score in a soccer competition, a TOEFL examination score—or as informal as a compliment or a quizzical facial expression. The methods may measure broadly—winning the presidency or the Miss America contest, a single grade for a course—or as narrowly as the success or failure of buying an ice cream cone or a detailed analysis of the prepositions used in an essay.

As ESL writing teachers evaluate the writing of their students, the primary objectives should be **long-term improvement** and **cognitive change** (Leki, 1992) as evidenced through revision of students' texts. Because evaluation is often interwoven with more objective, less judgmental teacher response, revision is often linked with evaluation; that is, evaluation is also a form of intervention and response, and the result of the evaluative intervention should be some change in student writing. It is inevitable that teachers evaluating school writing must eventually assign a grade to the writing; that grade will be based on (a) criteria developed and articulated by the teacher and (b) revisions made in various drafts by the student as a result of response and advice from other students, the teacher, and the student writer. This chapter addresses the apparent dichotomy between accuracy and fluency, the link between evaluation and student revision of texts, and the place of evaluation in response.

Accuracy and Fluency

The dichotomy between fluency and accuracy has existed in language teaching for decades: on which should the language teacher concentrate? Traditionally, accuracy has been defined as the focus on discrete elements of the rules of language, while fluency has been defined as the focus on the communication of ideas without consideration of discrete language elements (Lennon, 1991b). During the audio-lingual period of ESL teaching, accuracy was considered the more important; currently, with the focus on communicative strategies, fluency seems more important. This is probably a false dichotomy: a focus on fluency does not necessarily exclude consideration of the systematic properties of language. After all, it is not possible to communicate successfully without some knowledge and monitoring of the language of the message. A focus on accuracy demands concentration on discrete points of language, but does not necessarily curb creativity and self-expression, ignore cognitive processes, or overlook personality traits of the learner. Fraida Dubin and Elite Olshtain (1986) suggest that attention to form is more beneficial when it is used in controlled situations, usually in the early stages of the language learning process; it is less useful at more advanced levels (some research calls it debilitating) to focus exclusively on accuracy and form in situations where the production of language forms should be peripheral and automatic (McLaughlin, Rossman, and McLeod, 1983).

At the basis of the accuracy-fluency controversy is the question of **error**. Once thought to be deviant behavior, error is now seen as a natural phenomenon in learning of all kinds: learning to ice skate, to type, to analyze literature, to speak a first or second language. Of course, errors in written language can be due to inattention, memory lapse, or indifference (Michaelides, 1990; Sloan, 1990), and in an in-class writing situation, NES as well as ESL students will make hasty "performance errors." But in general, ESL errors are neither random, sporadic nor deviant; instead, they are systematic, regular, and rule-governed, the result of intelligence, not stupidity (Kroll, 1991; Raimes, 1991; Scovel, 1988).

Errors, the result of conscious or unconscious attempts by students to use what they have learned, are influenced by three factors: **native language transfer**, **overgeneralization**, and **difficulty level**. For example, when second language students encounter a language form, they often infer rules from knowledge of their native language; they "transfer" that knowledge into a hypothesis about the second language. For that reason, students from the same native language background may well make similar types of second language errors, though their hypotheses (and therefore the resulting language) may not be exactly the same. Such first language transfer occurs not only with grammatical structures but also with first language writing skills and strategies. Researchers have found that ESL writers transferred both good and weak writing skills from their first language into English (Carson and Kuehn, 1992; Jones and Tetroe, 1987), and that many ESL students who have not developed good strategies for writing in their first language will not have appropriate strategies to transfer to their second language (Mohan and Lo, 1985). In a similar way, ESL students may hypothesize about a language form by extending the use of a rule they have learned in the second language. For example, if the rule says that third-person singular verbs must take an "s" ("he runs"), second language students may "overgeneralize" and apply the rule to second-person singular verbs ("you runs"). The hypothesis is incorrect, but it is a systematic application of a rule. Finally, if a language rule is particularly complex or difficult, students may make errors as they attempt to construct the language form, or they may avoid the form altogether (Dagut and Laufer, 1985; Schachter, 1974). In each of these cases, students who can identify or "monitor for" language errors can learn to formulate new hypotheses and adopt new learning strategies to correct the errors. But the process takes time, motivation, and teacher intervention.

Barbara Kroll (1990a) analyzes the accuracy vs. fluency debate by demonstrating that ESL writing proficiency can be broadly divided into "plus-syntax and minus-syntax," and "plus-rhetoric and minus-rhetoric." Kroll defines <u>syntax</u> as the facility to use the grammatical system of standard edited English in such categories as sentence structure, word form, word order, verb tense, etc. In contrast, a piece of writing with <u>rhetorical</u> competence

1. limits and focuses on the topic in a manner appropriate to its overall approach and length,
2. remains focused on the topic throughout,
3. creates and uses paragraphs effectively,
4. maintains a consistent point of view,
5. sequences ideas in a logical manner, and
6. uses coherence and cohesion devices appropriately and as necessary (1990a, p. 43).

<u>ESL writing often has a split between accuracy of language use and fluency</u> of ideas. According to Kroll, "one paper can provide insightful commentary on a substantive topic while replete with problems in spelling and punctuation [+ rhetoric and – syntax]. Another paper can exhibit a wide range of sentence structures, flawless syntax, adherence to mechanics, yet lack development and support of its central thesis [– rhetoric and + syntax]" (p. 40). Still another paper may be hard to read because it contains both second language errors and a lack of coherence [– rhetoric and – syntax].

Kroll's work describes what is often, though not always, an essential difference between international students who study in the United States and non-native speakers of English who are permanent residents in the U.S. Students who have studied English as a foreign language (EFL), and who have entered post-secondary institutions in the U.S. following several years of EFL study in their native countries, have, for the most part, acquired English visually; they have learned about the structures of the language, but their practice in producing English has been limited to the classroom. In terms of writing, while cultures evolve writing styles appropriate to their own histories and the needs of their societies, not many cultures appear to teach rhetorical patterns directly in the school setting; there are virtually no courses on writing in most countries outside the U.S. (Leki, 1992). Therefore, most international students will have different assumptions about the expectations of their discourse community. Their writing will demonstrate grammatical understanding, but their limited fluency and coherence, and particularly their limited knowledge of academic forms and audience expectations, may result in writing that typifies Kroll's – rhetoric category. In contrast, U.S. residents (immigrants and refugees) who have lived and attended elementary and/or secondary schools in the U.S. have acquired much of their English through their ears (aurally); although they may have had ESL classes alongside their regular public school work, their English was learned mainly through immersion in the language. As a result, their spoken language may be fluent and comprehensible and their writing may appear fluent. However, because they have limited knowledge of the structure of the language, their writing, in Kroll's categories, often is – syntax.*

Teachers of heterogeneous ESL writing classes need to incorporate both fluency- and accuracy-oriented work that leads to better academic language proficiency. The integration of these two areas of learning and evaluating will enable student writers to develop the communication strategies and academic language skills needed for successful academic work (Dubin and Olshtain, 1986). And because error is an integral part of the learning process, teachers should not only tolerate but encourage student risk-taking in language use. Error can be approached in the classroom as normal, natural, and necessary, an interesting, intellectually engaging issue. Marking student errors in the interest of discussion and remediation is seen by most students as an important source of teacher feedback (Willig, 1988). As Leki points out, students both want and expect correction (1991). When teachers

*Because this book focuses primarily on international ESL students who come to the U.S. to study, a full discussion of the needs of U.S. resident students for whom English is a second (or third) language is not possible. For detailed discussion and information, see *Understanding ESL Writers: A Guide for Teachers* by Ilona Leki (St. Martin's Press, 1992), *Teaching Language Minority Students in the Multicultural Classroom* by Robin Scarcella (Prentice Hall Regents, 1990), and J. Reid's "Teaching ESL Students" in Lynn Troyka's *Annotated Instructors' Edition of The Simon and Schuster Handbook for Writers* (3rd ed.) (Prentice Hall, 1993) focus on both accuracy and fluency in their classroom, their long-term goal should be to assist their students to strive for stylistic flexibility and what sociolinguists call language versatility: the ability to shift language style as NESs do to achieve communicative impact (Hare and Fitzsimmons, 1992; Scovel, 1988).

Revision

Response to and evaluation of student writing have as their goal revising (literally, "seeing again"), a goal that is much easier said than met. Teachers and learners (whether NES or ESL students) do not necessarily share common information, skills, and values concerning revision (Fitzgerald, 1987; Goldstein and Conrad, 1990; Sperling and Freedman, 1987). ESL students seem particularly limited in their repertoire of strategies for revising their writing, even when they understand the teacher's feedback (A. Cohen, 1987). Moreover, research on the revising strategies of NES and ESL students has indicated that less experienced writers tend to revise at the word level and often get "writer's block" when the exact vocabulary is not immediately available, thereby circumventing real revision. Inexperienced writers also tend to edit, to "clean up" their papers, rather than to revise them. That is, they correct surface structures, concentrating on accuracy (changing misspelled words, monitoring for agreement and verb tense problems). In the end, these students abandon their writing when the discrete elements seem correct. These inexperienced writers need a more complete set of strategies to help them identify higher order changes: reordering lines of reasoning or answering questions about their purposes and readers (Oxford, 1990; Scarcella and Oxford, 1992).

The focus of inexperienced writers on accuracy rather than on fluent communication differs from the revision strategies of NES experienced writers, who employ the word-level strategies only at the end of the writing process as they proofread their final drafts. Before that, they revise at the sentence level, primarily by adding and/or deleting elements (Sommers, 1980, 1982, 1992). They read and reread their writing, searching for answers to questions: What does my essay as a whole need for successful communication? What needs to be supported for my audience? How can my purpose be better emphasized? And these writers strive for overall communication and fluency: as they change sentence elements in one part of the essay, they recognize the potential for changes in other parts of the essay.

Effective revision, then, is not a series of discrete stages applied hurriedly to small pieces of text just before turning in the final draft. Rather it is a recursive shaping of thought, a sequence of changes in a piece of writing. Teachers must therefore prepare their students for revision not only by intervening in their writing but also by modeling successful revision processes, by demonstrating that revision is necessary for all writing, and by using class time to teach students to revise (Hairston, 1986; Shriver, 1992). For example, teachers must demonstrate for their students the skill of seeing their writing through the eyes of their readers, for without the perspective of the reader, student writers will be unable to make global revisions (Kroll, forthcoming). Only as students become more proficient readers will they begin to recognize the multiple cognitive cues that can stimulate revision: they may remember something they want to add, observe something they want to change, modify ideas as their perspective changes, and develop thoughts as they discover what they want to say. In an article aptly titled "Writing Teaches Writing," Donald Murray explains his processes as he reads his own writing: "I sit back to read this stranger text, asking what it needs. If I read well it will tell me: more evidence here, please; make this line of reasoning stronger; rub that out; build up my case in this section" (1990, p. 79). Finally, as part of the revision process, students should be encouraged to become not only critical and questioning about their writing but appreciative and self-encouraging about their writing as well.

As Chapter 8 described, peer response offers an opportunity for different insights, and so different cues, for revision; arranging for students to help each other, and training those peer reviewers in the skills and strategies of critical reading, will help students learn the processes and the importance of revision. Teacher evaluation, as well as more descriptive responses and interventions, can provide student writers with the necessary information and motivation for successful revision, particularly if the comments are made on the premises that (a) revision will occur, (b) the intervention will result in cognitive change, and (c) the students, as a result of learning about and practicing revising, will be able to transfer their new skills to other writing tasks.

Caveats

Effective revision strategies develop slowly, sometimes at glacial speed. At first, students will not be confident enough to rework their writing and may be capable only of smaller, surface-level corrections. Then, as they become more effective revisers and begin to revise more globally, their writing often deteriorates (Belanoff, 1991), to the despair of both students and teachers. It is possible that risk-taking (in this case, innovative revision) and immediate improvement cannot occur at the same time (Leki, 1990); as a result, teachers must learn to tolerate drops in writing proficiency and effectiveness, much the way they tolerate developmental error, as students learn about revision. The

processes of change that students undergo as they learn to revise will take time, teacher support and resources, and patience for both students and teachers. But with training, practice, and encouragement, students will begin to recognize the value of revision and to discover their individual revising processes (Chenoweth, 1987; Kirby et al., 1988).

Grading Scales

In general, there are two basic types of grading: **analytic** and **holistic**. Both can be useful tools for evaluating student writing, but each has different purposes. Analytic scoring separates various factors and skills and so can be used by teachers and students to diagnose writing strengths and weaknesses. Holistic scoring assesses the overall competence of a piece of writing, but it neither diagnoses problems nor prescribes remedies for the writing.

Analytic Scoring

Analytic scoring evaluates the various components of a piece of writing separately. For example:

1. Begin with 100 points and subtract points for each deficiency:
appropriate register (formality or informality)	–10 points
language conventions	–10 points
accuracy and range of vocabulary	–5 points
TOTAL	–25 points from 100 = 75 points

2. Give a percentage of the overall grade for each component:
introduction	10%
topic sentences	20%
sentence structure	20%
use of transitions	10%
grammar	20%
vocabulary	10%
conclusion	10%

3. Assign split grades for each component:
organization	A
content	C
mechanics	B

One of the most widely used analytical scales for ESL writing is the Composition Profile in *Testing ESL Writing: A Practical Approach* (H. Jacobs et al., 1981). The profile offers an analytic method of assessing the writing of ESL students that can also be used to provide learners with feedback about their writing. The Composition Profile has five weighted components, with content the first and most heavily weighted; the others are organization, vocabulary, language use, and mechanics. Below are the Composition Profile and another analytic scale.

ESL COMPOSITION PROFILE

Holly Jacobs, Stephen Zingraf, Deanna Wormuth, V. Faye Hartfiel, and Jane Hughey*

Student			Date	Topic
Score	**Level**	**Criteria**		**Comments**
C O N T E N T	30–27	EXCELLENT TO VERY GOOD: knowledgeable • substantive development of thesis • relevant to assigned topic		
	26–22	GOOD TO AVERAGE: sure knowledge of subject • adequate range • limited development of thesis • mostly relevant to topic but lacks detail		
	21–17	FAIR TO POOR: limited knowledge of subject • little substance • inadequate development of topic		
	16–13	VERY POOR: does not show knowledge of subject • non-substantive • not pertinent • OR not enough to evaluate		
O R G A N I Z A T I O N	20-18	EXCELLENT TO VERY GOOD: fluent expression • ideas clearly stated/supported • succinct • well-organized • logical sequencing • cohesive		
	17-14	GOOD TO AVERAGE: somewhat choppy • loosely organized but main ideas stand out • limited support • logical but incomplete sequencing		
	13-10	FAIR TO POOR: non-fluent • ideas confused or disconnected- • lacks logical sequencing and development		
	9-7	VERY POOR: does not communicate • no organization • OR not enough to evaluate		
V O C A B U L A R Y	20-18	EXCELLENT TO VERY GOOD: sophisticated range • effective word/idiom choice and usage • word form mastery • appropriate register		
	17-14	GOOD TO AVERAGE: adequate range • occasional errors of word/idiom form, choice, usage *but meaning not obscured*		
	13-10	FAIR TO POOR: limited range • frequent errors of work/ idiom form, choice, usage • *meaning confused or obscured*		
	9-7	VERY POOR: essentially translation • little knowledge of English vocabulary, idioms, word form • OR not enough to evaluate		
L A N G U A G E	25-22	EXCELLENT TO VERY GOOD: effective, complex constructions • few errors of agreement, tense, number, word order/function, articles, pronouns, prepositions		
	21-18	GOOD TO AVERAGE: effective but simple constructions • minor problems in complex constructions • several errors of agreement, tense, number, word order/function, articles, pronouns, prepositions, *but meaning seldom obscured*		

| U | 17-11 | FAIR TO POOR: major problems in simple/complex construc-
| S | | tions • frequent errors of negation, agreement, tense,
| E | | number, word order/function, articles, pronouns, preposi-
| | | tions and/or fragments, run-ons, deletions • *meaning confused or obscured*
| | 10-5 | VERY POOR: virtually no mastery of sentence construction rules • dominated by errors • does not communicate • OR not enough to evaluate |

| M | 5 | EXCELLENT TO VERY GOOD: demonstrates mastery of con-
| E | | ventions • few errors of spelling, punctuation, capitalization,
| C | | paragraphing
| H | 4 | GOOD TO AVERAGE: occasional errors of spelling, punctua-
| A | | tion, capitalization, paragraphing, but *meaning not obscured*
| N | 3 | FAIR TO POOR: frequent errors of spelling, punctuation,
| I | | capitalization, paragraphing • poor handwriting • *meaning confused or obscured*
| C | |
| S | 2 | VERY POOR: no mastery of conventions • dominated by errors of spelling, punctuation, capitalization, paragraphing • handwriting illegible • OR not enough to evaluate |

TOTAL SCORE   **READER**   **COMMENTS***

SAMPLE ANALYTIC SCALE

Rate each feature for its overall merit by circling the appropriate number. Total the points in each category and write the total at the bottom.

Introduction

Informative title and lead-in	1	2	3	4	5
Clear thesis statement	1	2	3	4	5

TOTAL _____ (out of 10)

Support

Specific examples and details	4	8	12	16	20
Connections between ideas	2	4	6	8	10

TOTAL _____ (out of 30)

Organization

Transitions	2	4	6	8	10
Paragraph unity and coherence	2	4	6	8	10

TOTAL _____ (out of 20)

Style

Sentence structure	1	2	3	4	5
Vocabulary	1	2	3	4	5
Grammar	1	2	3	4	5
Mechanics and spelling	1	2	3	4	5

Rhetorical Stance

Purpose clear throughout	2	4	6	8	10
Audience expectations met	2	4	6	8	10

TOTAL _____ (out of 20)

Grades: A = 90–100   B = 80–90   C = 70–80   D = 60–70   F = below 60

Holistic Scoring

In holistic scoring, the evaluator reads each paper without marking anything, then rates the paper as a whole (holistically), assigning a single score within a given range (on scales of, for example, 1–4, 1–6, 1–9). The point of holistic scoring is that it "employs a reader's full impression of a text without trying to reduce her judgment to a set of recognizable skills" (Huot, 1990, p. 201). The greatest advantage of holistic scoring is its efficiency: in large-scale readings, with appropriate training, raters can score substantial numbers of papers reliably in a relatively short period of time.

Before reading and scoring papers, the raters at large-scale essay readings are "trained" to a set of standards, either **implicit** or **explicit**. At its most implicit, holistic scoring is "a guided procedure for sorting or ranking written pieces. The rater takes a piece of writing and either (1) matches it with another piece or pieces in a graded series or (2) scores it for the prominence of certain features important to that kind of writing or (3) assigns it a letter grade or number. The placing, scoring, or grading occurs quickly, impressionistically, after the rater has practiced the procedure with other raters" (C. Cooper and O'Dell, 1977, p. 3). Training raters for holistic scoring involves the selection of benchmark (or rangefinder) papers by those responsible for training (room leaders and/or table leaders for large-scale readings, program supervisors, etc.). The selected papers represent typical, easily identified low range papers (for example, on a 1–6 scale, scores of 1 or 2), middle range papers (scores of 3 or 4), and upper range papers (scores of 5 or 6). Raters are then trained to the implicit standards of those benchmark papers through a process of reading, scoring, discussing scores, discussing discourse community standards, and reaching consensus or near-consensus on the scores (Bridgeman and Carlson, 1984). **Discrepant scores** (those given by two raters that differ by more than one number) are resolved through training. Raters are then expected to inculcate the standards and to apply them to other papers during the reading. Because implicit standards are based on each group of papers, the process of holistic scoring is usually **norm-referenced:** each paper in the group is compared with other papers in that group alone, and not with papers from other groups.

In more explicit holistic scoring situations, a written scoring guide describes the characteristics of each holistic rating (for example, the characteristics of a "2" paper). The trainers select benchmark papers that closely parallel the criteria described in the scoring guide that has been developed as a result of discussions between readers and testmakers. Raters are then trained to the standards—the criteria—of the scoring guide with benchmark papers. With the assistance of a scoring guide that supplies general criteria for consideration, with training of the readers by experienced raters, and with benchmark papers, a high rate of consensus or near-consensus between two readers can be achieved. Unlike implicit scoring standards, explicit scoring guides with scoring criteria can function across groups of papers; that is, the same scoring guide can be used with many different sets of student writing. The scoring guide establishes the standards for **criterion-referenced** evaluation.

At present, the most widely known ESL holistic scoring procedure occurs with the Test of Written English (TWE), a section of the TOEFL examination that asks students to write spontaneously for 30 minutes on a single assigned topic. A typical TWE holistic scoring session for a worldwide administration of the TWE (possibly 120,000 papers) involves more than a hundred trained raters who score papers for three days. Each paper receives two independent scores, and any discrepancies are resolved by a third reading. Raters are trained to the TWE scoring guide.

TEST OF WRITTEN ENGLISH (TWE) SCORING GUIDE
Revised 2/90*

Readers will assign scores based on the following scoring guide. Though examinees are asked to write on a specific topic, parts of the topic may be treated by implication. Readers focus on what the examinee does well.

Scores

6 **Demonstrates clear competence in writing on both the rhetorical and syntactic levels, though it may have occasional errors.**

A paper in this category
- effectively addresses the writing task
- is well organized and well developed
- uses clearly appropriate details to support a thesis or illustrate ideas
- displays consistent facility in the use of language
- demonstrates syntactic variety and appropriate word choice

5 **Demonstrates competence in writing on both the rhetorical and syntactic levels, though it will probably have occasional errors.**

A paper in this category
- may address some parts of the task more effectively than others
- is generally well organized and developed
- uses details to support a thesis or illustrate an idea
- displays facility in the use of language
- demonstrates some syntactic variety and range of vocabulary

4   Demonstrates minimal competence in writing on both the rhetorical and syntactic levels.

A paper in this category

- addresses the writing topic adequately but may slight parts of the task
- is adequately organized and developed
- uses some details to support a thesis or illustrate an idea
- demonstrates adequate but possibly inconsistent facility with syntax and usage
- may contain some errors that occasionally obscure meaning

3   Demonstrates some developing competence in writing, but it remains flawed on either the rhetorical or syntactic level, or both.

A paper in this category may reveal one or more of the following weaknesses:

- inadequate organization or development
- inappropriate or insufficient details to support or illustrate generalizations
- a noticeably inappropriate choice of words or word forms
- an accumulation of errors in sentence structure and/or usage

2   Suggests incompetence in writing.

A paper in this category is seriously flawed by one or more of the following weaknesses:

- serious disorganization or underdevelopment
- little or no detail, or irrelevant specifics
- serious and frequent errors in sentence structure or usage
- serious problems with focus

1   Demonstrates incompetence in writing.

A paper in this category

- may be incoherent
- may be underdeveloped
- may contain severe and persistent writing errors

Papers that reject the assignment or fail to address the question must be given to the Table Leader.

Papers that exhibit absolutely no response at all must also be given to the Table Leader.

Holistic scoring procedures have uses beyond large-scale testing. The TWE scoring guide is also widely used to evaluate intensive language program placement tests as well as pre- and post-tests in writing classes. In addition, holistic scoring can be used by teacher-trainers or writing program supervisors to train ESL writing teachers to the community (or program) standards for effective writing. For ESL writing classes, the teacher can use holistic scoring to grade in-class writing quickly; giving the students the holistic scoring guide can provide them with another perspective on their writing and with descriptive criteria for reference as they write and/or revise. Furthermore, advanced ESL writing students are easily trained to a scoring guide, particularly the TWE scoring guide; having them score student papers (which are usually anonymous and often from another class) raises their consciousness about scoring procedures and audience expectations. A classroom holistic scoring session can demonstrate to students that the teacher's evaluation of their papers is not a subjective, personal process but rather a logically executed measurement that uses certain criteria. And the criteria on the scoring guide used for in-class holistic training can serve as a springboard for discussion and even for setting up grading criteria for future writing assignments.

Holistic scoring remains somewhat controversial (see reviews by Huot, 1990; Raimes, 1990), principally because the complexity of writing is difficult to evaluate reliably, particularly in large-scale scoring situations. Liz Hamp-Lyons, for example, calls holistic training a "coercive process" unless the training combines clear goals, standards, and expectations with subtle management and conscious work to establish a collegial, participatory reading community. "The context in which reader training occurs, the type of training given, the extent to which training is monitored, and the feedback given to readers all play an important part in maintaining both the reliability and the validity of the scoring of essays" (1990, p. 88). Certainly holistic scoring is a limited form of evaluation: it does not offer students diagnosis, feedback, and assistance for improving writing. It is not therefore a particularly useful tool for much of the response and evaluation processes in the ESL writing classroom, but it is one of the evaluation schemes available to the writing teacher.

Teacher Evaluation

"Think about it. Have you even noticed that you can find lots of articles on assessment and evaluation, but how many articles have you seen published on grading—on the actual giving of grades? Not very many. Most of us would just rather not talk about it at all; it's the dirty thing we have to do in our own offices "(Belanoff, 1991, p. 61). Pat Belanoff speaks of the "myth of assessment": teachers regularly respond, evaluate, mark, and grade student papers, but, contrary to myth, they "don't always agree on which characteristics of a good piece of writing are most significant" (p. 58). According to Belanoff, the inability of teachers to agree on grading systems and standards is not something to be ashamed of; rather, she states, it is "a sign of strength, of the life and vitality of words and the exchange of words [because] texts reflect life and the multitude of tastes and standards in real life" (p. 62). If absolute standards could be established, computers could grade student papers, but the variety and richness of teaching and learning writing would be lost. Instead, evaluating student writing is the result of who teachers are: what they have read, what their values are, what their philosophy of teaching writing is, who their colleagues are, and what their education and prior experience have been.

That is not to say that evaluation is essentially arbitrary and unfathomable. It does mean that each teacher must work to develop her/his philosophy of evaluation and to communicate that philosophy to ESL writers in her/his classes. In addition, teachers should develop the criteria by which they will evaluate student writing and articulate those criteria—those standards—by which the classroom community of writers will be judged. Evaluation of writing should not be mysterious; students should not think, even in jest, that the final drafts of their papers are tossed down a flight of stairs, with the "A" papers landing on the highest step, and the "F" papers on the lowest. Rather, teachers should make clear to their students that they use their prior knowledge and specific criteria to judge whole discourses, using a complex set of variables that they can explain. Students must understand that each teacher has her/his standards; each reads a text and has the ability, upon reflection, to articulate those standards for herself/himself and for the students.

Forming a Philosophy of Evaluation

The responsibility of the teacher in the evaluation process begins well before the final student drafts are turned in, even before the writing is assigned, with writing tasks that are thoughtfully developed, clearly defined, and precisely expressed for the students. Assignments define the emphases and the structure of a writing course; they reflect some of the values held by the teacher (Larson, 1986). In developing a writing assignment, the teacher must be clear about the purpose of the assignment and how it fits into the objectives of the class syllabus, the sequence of lessons, and the overall program curriculum. In defining her/his expectations about the response to a new writing assignment, the teacher would be wise to write the the essay for the assignment herself/himself, in essence becoming a student. (See Chapter 8 for a discussion of writing assignment development.)

As teachers begin to formulate their philosophies of responding to, evaluating, and grading student writing, they should also consider that research with ESL writing and revision has shown that

1. academic-content-area professors find many categories of errors much less disturbing than limitations in content or rhetorical

style (T. Kobayashi, 1992; Santos, 1988); the issue of error gravity—that is, which errors do and do not interfere with communication—is therefore one that teachers should become familiar with;

2. in contrast to NES writers, ESL students want and appreciate teacher correction of errors (A. Cohen and Cavacanti, 1990; Leki, 1986; Willig, 1988); however, despite teacher correction, errors in ESL writing will persist (Semke, 1984; Zamel, 1985);

3. some improvement of grammatical accuracy will occur if the errors are located for the students and if encouragement is balanced with correction (Cardelle and Corno, 1981; Robb et al., 1986).

In a recent well-designed research project, Ann Fathman and Elizabeth Whalley found that students showed significant improvement in grammatical accuracy if the errors were underlined, and that comments on both grammar and content can be given at the same time without overburdening the students. In addition, they found that "general comments giving encouragement and suggesting revisions helped improve the content of composition rewrites; however, simply having students rewrite their work also showed some improvement in content" (1990, p. 186).

Correction of error is effective when the feedback concerning the error is clear; that is, the response must adequately describe the problem and suggest methods of correction. Moreover, students should be ready to learn, to commit to the change, and have the appropriate background knowledge to be able to revise their writing. In addition, the students must have the strategies to deal with the feedback and to correct the error, the time to digest and then to practice corrections, and the opportunity to verify the use of the correction (Cardelle and Corno, 1981; A. Cohen, 1990). Finally, students should have ample opportunity to write about their revision processes. Metacognitive entries in a learning log, for example, allow students to "write to learn," to remember, and to transfer their learning into other writing situations. In short, research in the change process and in student revision indicates that feedback without follow-up (in the forms of discussion, practice, graded revisions, and metacognitive journal entries) will be less effective, and perhaps not effective at all (Bishop, 1990; J. Reid, 1991b).

Forming an approach to error in student writing is only a part of an evaluation philosophy. Teachers planning their evaluation procedures will choose from among a variety of response forms that depend on many variables:

- the expectations of students from previous learning experiences
- the gravity of certain errors in obstructing communication

- the personalities of the students (who needs confidence-building? who needs to be encouraged to be more careful? who needs directness?)
- the teacher's grading load
- the age(s), background, and objectives of the students
- the criteria set for a particular piece of writing (Hedge, 1988).

In addition to carefully crafted writing assignments and knowledge of student needs, another essential part of the evaluation process that takes place before evaluation of student writing begins if the formulation of **grading criteria**. Writing teachers and students need to have clear agreement as to what will be commented on and how such comments might lead to revision. As early as the first week of class, the teacher has a responsibility to inform students about grading policies and grading criteria. It is vital to the classroom community that teachers share their objectives and expectations with their students and ask students about their objectives and expectations (Yorio, 1989). The more teachers engage in talk with students (and colleagues) about their reactions to texts, the more they will be able to construct evaluations that are firmly embedded in the classroom and in the broader academic community. Moreover, because writing tasks are a form of testing (that is, students are asked to demonstrate knowledge of writing skills), evaluation of those tasks should provide students with (a) a diagnosis of the task's strengths and weaknesses, (b) the motivation to revise and improve their writing, and (c) a reward for hard work (J.D. Brown, 1992).

Among the decisions the teacher will make before evaluating the first set of student papers (which s/he will communicate to the class) are

- whether all written work will be turned in for grading:
  early drafts reviewed by peers but not graded by the teacher?
  later draft reviewed by teacher and marked but not graded?
  only three out of every ten journal entries (selected by the student) graded?

- whether written work will be graded in a variety of ways:
  some revision without feedback
  in-class writing scored holistically?
  small assignments given a+ or a-?
  some writing without teacher intervention?
  larger assignments graded with A, B, C?

- how the final grade for the course will be determined (see policy sheets in Chapter 6 for samples)

- how the final draft of each major paper will be evaluated (the grading criteria).

As the course progresses, teachers will establish baseline criteria for specific assignments beforehand (below are sample evaluation guides). Advanced writing students can be given the opportunity for input into the grading criteria for individual assignments; however, the students will probably not be able to establish the criteria alone. Teachers will also make decisions about **marking** student papers. Some options include

- writing corrections above each error
- writing correct language forms for errors not yet taught
- indicating an error and identifying it with a symbol (e.g., VT = incorrect **v**erb **t**ense, WO = incorrect **w**ord **o**rder)
- underlining errors, and asking students to identify and correct
- indicating an error on a line by making a check-mark in the margin; student finds the error and corrects it

Teachers in the process of formulating a philosophy of evaluation might consider Elaine Lees taxonomy of evaluation (1988). She divides the activity of evaluating student writing into seven areas, some of which are **teacher-responsible** and others **writer-responsible.** The first three areas—**correcting**, **emoting**, and **describing**—are teacher-responsible activities in which the teacher marks, articulates feelings and thoughts, and describes what s/he finds. The second three—**suggesting**, **questioning**, and **reminding**—are attempts by the teacher to make direct contact with the student. They also shift the burden of revision to the student, who will use the comments to begin to form her/his revision plan. The final area, **assigning**, is a way to see whether or not the student has accepted responsibility; the teacher asks for specific revisions, feedback, and/or rewriting in which the student will demonstrate changes in her/his writing.

Evaluation Criteria

Many factors can be evaluated in writing, among them content, purpose and audience, rhetorical matters (organization, cohesion, unity), and mechanics (sentence structure, grammar, vocabulary, and so forth). Writing assessment works best and is most fair to learners when it takes into account who the learner is, the parameters of the situation in which the learner produces writing, and the overall context in which educational success is to be achieved for the student writer (Hamp-Lyons, 1990). Ideally, teachers should approach every evaluation as if they were readers encountering the work for the first time; they should give the students the best possible reading of their work. Evaluation of student writing usually begins with response: written comments on a draft, student-teacher conferencing, brief teacher interventions in class. <u>The major objective of such evaluative responses is to focus on how to help the writer solve problems by giving specific advice that is honest but never cruel or sarcastic.</u>

Below are examples of grading criteria, presented in a variety of ways (by percentages, by questions, by statements). Teachers might consider the language that seeks to quantify the evaluating process in each, then modify and construct language of their own, and share the results with their students.

SAMPLE GRADING CRITERIA

Attendance and satisfactory participation at scheduled conference	10%
Attendance and satisfactory participation in peer review groups	10%
Adequate pre-writing and drafting, turned in with final draft	10%

Final draft:

clear purpose; addresses identified audience	10%
clear overall organization	10%
clear inner paragraph organization	10%
sufficient development in each paragraph	10%
coherence and cohesion techniques	10%
correct grammar	10%
well-structured sentences	10%
TOTAL	100%

SAMPLE QUESTIONS FOR USE IN JUDGING A PIECE OF WRITING

1. Does the writing carry out the specific directions of the assignment?
2. Is the writer's purpose in the paper clear?
3. Does the writer make clear how all parts of the paper relate to her/his purpose?
4. Is the overall plan for the whole paper evident, and can the reader follow the writer's plan?
6. Are the data (examples, detail, facts, experiences) used in the paper relevant and adequate to the writer's purpose and for the audience?
7. Does the writer's conclusion build on the body of the paper?
8. Is the style reasonably clear, free of distracting errors?

(adapted from Larson, 1986, pp. 111–112)

CRITERIA FOR GOOD WRITING

Content
- The paper is focused on a particular subject.
- The purpose of the paper is clear to its readers.
- The thesis is well supported.

Organization
- The introduction gets the reader's attention and prepares the reader for what is coming.
- The organization is easy to follow.
- There is clear transition from one idea to the next.
- Individual paragraphs are coherent.
- All details develop the purpose of the paper.
- The conclusion draws the paper to a close, summarizes main points, and reemphasizes the paper's purpose.

Style
- Sentences reflect a variety of syntactic structures.
- Vocabulary reflects a concern for the audience and purpose of the paper.

Correctness
- Mechanics are correct: accurate punctuation, capitalization, spelling, and grammar.
- Words are used accurately and appropriately.
- Sentences are complete and correct.

(adapted from M. Smith, 1991, pp. 158–159)

Cover Sheets

In addition to grading criteria, teachers can develop cover sheets as a first page for each student paper. A cover sheet allows the teacher to respond to the student writing, either in lieu of or in addition to marginal comments, and to adhere to the criteria established on the sheet and given to students as they draft their papers. After the paper has been evaluated, the cover sheet functions as a map for student revision and a resource for revision conference.

SAMPLE COVER SHEET

Name_____Date_____
Essay

	Strengths	Problem Areas
Purpose and audience		
Focus		
Development		
Organization		
Grammar and Sentence Structure		

Suggestions for revision:

Writer's plans for revision:

Cover sheets can change over a course term in several ways, as the number of criteria grows. Students help design criteria, either individually or as a class, and these criteria can be incorporated into cover sheets. Finally, as assignment objectives change and/or as the students accumulate more skills, evaluation categories can be added: "effective transitions (or coherence)," "good lead-in," or "successful use of outside research sources."

Evaluating Evaluation

While teachers mark and grade a piece of writing, they should consider these questions:

About marks in the margin or in the text:

1. Are my marks/comments correct?

2. Are the meanings of my marks/comments clear to the student? Can the students read my handwriting?

3. Have I put the mark/comment close enough to the error so that the student can identify it?

4. Have I identified errors in ways that will enable the student to study them and learn to avoid them in the future?

5. **Am I labeling** ("awkward," "bad," "poor," etc.) **rather than teaching**? Will the student know how to improve a sentence if s/he didn't think it was "awkward" in the first place?

6. Have I pointed out strengths as well as weaknesses, given encouragement as well as criticism?

7. Have I made some specific suggestions to show the student how to improve as well as telling why?

In the general comment at the end of the paper:

1. Does the comment reflect what I have said in the margins and the text?

2. Is the order of my points effective and logical? Do I discuss larger, more important issues (such as organization, development, thought) before the less important areas (mechanics)? Do I complete one comment before going on to another?

3. Are my comments vague or too abstract? If I said "Work on coherence," will the student know where and how to apply this advice? Have I clearly identified the coherence problem (or whatever) in the text?

4. Have I made specific suggestions to get the student started on revision ("Work on development by asking yourself, 'What

evidence can I use here?' "). Have I directed the student to the text itself when/if I thought it might be helpful?

5. Are my comments expressed in a way that makes the student feel s/he can improve? Have I avoided being curt, sarcastic, personally critical? Have I remembered a time when I was learning a new skill?

6. If I question the student's logic, am I sure it's more than a simple difference of opinion?

7. Can I honestly say something good about this piece of writing? Did I?

8. Do my comments offer suggestions and open avenues for improvement for the student to consider, or do they rewrite the assignment in my own preferred style?

(S. D. Reid, 1992b)

Portfolio Assessment

In much the same way that artists, photographers, and models have portfolios of their best work at the end of a course, student writers can present to the teacher a portfolio of their writing, a collection of texts produced over a defined period of time to the specifications of a particular context (or to several different contexts) (Bridwell-Bowles, 1990; Lucas, 1992; Smit et al., 1991). Christopher Burnham defines the curricular process of a portfolio writing class: "at specific points during the semester, students submit 'finished drafts' of papers developed in class workshops. Instructors respond to these drafts not to provide an evaluation with a grade but to provide suggestions for revision as well as some general commentary about the individual's development as a writer" (1986, p. 126). Student-teacher conferences during the course encourage interaction and negotiation beneficial for revision (M. Smith, 1991), and metacognitive learning log entries describe why students are choosing portfolio papers and how they are revising them. At the end of the course, teachers grade the portfolios which represent the results of what the students have learned and the best work they have produced during the class (Condon and Hamp-Lyons, 1991; Gold, 1992). Portfolio evaluation has several advantages.

- It reinforces commitment to writing processes and multiple drafts.

- It establishes the course as developmental and sequential.

- It establishes a classroom writing environment as the basis for effective writing.

- It encourages students to assume responsibility for their own writing.
- It allows a more complex look at the complex activity of writing.

Portfolio grading has disadvantages as well. First, teachers may not be able to prepare their students for final grades, and the resulting "surprises" for students who receive grades only at the end of a course may cause frustration and anger. Moreover, if students improve and improve their consecutive drafts, without grades, all students may expect the final grade of "A" for their best, portfolio work. Second, if the cumulative drafts of students are carefully commented on but not graded, students may learn to practice "irresponsible revision." That is, they may revise only what the teacher marks, either just "getting by" or relying absolutely on teacher comments and becoming teacher-dependent. And as such students do less and less work on successive drafts, the teacher may find himself doing more and more. The most dramatic result of this imbalance of responsibility occurs when the teacher is the sole or most authoritative responder to student writing. Then a final portfolio may be more a reflection of teacher-writing than of student work. That is, constant teacher intervention can result in the appropriation of student text.

One solution that retains the advantages of the portfolio approach is the modified portfolio approach. Students write 7 or 8 papers during the class; each "final" product is preceded by group work, peer workshops, drafting, and revising draft. Each is turned in, evaluated, and graded. The students then revise several "final" drafts—correcting errors, adding detail, considering larger issues. During the last two weeks of the course, students select two of the revised essays, and the teacher chooses one, for additional revision and rewriting. Students apply the knowledge of writing they have accumulated during the course and the cognitive changes they have made as they revise these three papers for an additional (and presumably better) grade.

Plagiarism

North American academic culture has what appears to many international students to be a peculiar attitude about what is called plagiarism: the use of words and ideas of others without giving appropriate credit. Perhaps because of the focus on the individual in this culture, a person's written words and ideas are owned by that person. Even though the words and ideas in an article have been used before ("there is nothing new under the sun"), the specific combination of words or ideas is owned by the original author.

Therefore, when a student writer (or, for that matter, any writer) uses the words or ideas of another, the writer must reference the "original" author. If the writer uses the words exactly, s/he must use quotation marks as well.

In many other cultures, the use of the words and ideas of another honors that person. The ESL writing teacher should not, therefore, react viscerally when student writers commit the (North American) sin of plagiarism. Instead, the teacher must explain the cultural norms surrounding the use of secondary materials before the opportunity to commit plagiarism arises. It is the responsibility of teachers to give their students frequent, carefully monitored opportunities to practice the skills of paraphrase, summary, quotation, and citation (Campbell, 1990; McCormick, 1989, 1991). Initial assignments might include open-ended writing tasks that require students to read and incorporate information from reading texts into their writing (Johns, 1985) and to work with secondary sources in research (Spatt, 1987). In these exercises, "students develop an awareness of and respect for other authors and academic texts which enables them to use information from background text appropriately in their own writing" (Campbell, 1990, p. 227).

Conclusion

The foundation for effective evaluation of ESL student writing rests on careful, thoughtful preparation by the teacher; planning and evaluating are complementary and continuous processes. That preparation begins with the formulation of a philosophy of evaluation and the development of approaches to evaluation. It continues with the articulation of clearly designed criteria to the students, and the application of those criteria in the early stages of student writing by teacher intervention and peer response workshops. The actual evaluation of a student draft should show respect for each student's paper and work from the perspective of the student-writer. It should identify strong as well as weak points and comment constructively so that the student will be able to form a clear revision plan.

Students, too, have responsibilities in the response and evaluation processes. First, they must commit to the principle that revision is an integral and ongoing part of the writing process. They must be able and willing to learn to read and reread their papers from the perspective of their audience, and to "listen" for cues that will stimulate revision. They should be open to the responses of others and able to evaluate those responses; in workshops, "group interaction reinforces the notion that writing is not just what you end up with but the activities you undertake in creating it" (Spear, 1988, p. 4).

Discussion Questions

1. A 1991 article by Luke Prodromou used the following list to discuss the problems with ESL testing. Examine the list. Do you agree or disagree with the points? Why?

Testing emphasizes:	Teaching emphasizes:
failure	success
correctness	appropriateness
impersonality	personalization
anxiety	pleasure
marks	results
boring content	interesting content
judgment	support
extrinsic motivation	intrinsic motivation
competition	cooperation
teacher control	student control
solemnity	humor
fragmentation	integration
crime and punishment	give and take
stick and carrot	ripeness is all
product	process

2. In small groups, discuss examples of informal tests that teacher can administer in a classroom to determine student competency in ESL writing.

3. Think about your own use of language. As a child, did you learn any usage error that persists in your adult language (for example, misuse of *lay* and *lie,* or the pronunciation of a word)? How do you cope with this single language problem? By monitoring closely? By avoiding it?

4. Language errors that have been learned and habituated are said to be "fossilized." To correct them, the learner must essentially "unlearn" and relearn. How does "fossilization" present difficult problems for the ESL learner and teacher?

5. Discuss the following statement: the study of the writing of second language learners is the study of errors of those learners. Do you agree or disagree? Why?

6. In a small group, study the following list of criteria for evaluating writing components (adapted from Hedge, 1988) and prioritize them as Very Important (VI), Important (I), and Less Important (LI). If you identify other grading criteria, add and prioritize them.

_____ correct grammar		_____ originality of ideas	
_____ length		_____ neat handwriting	
_____ spelling		_____ wide vocabulary use	
_____ punctuation		_____ introductory techniques	
_____ paragraph development		_____ appropriacy of title	

| _____ conclusion techniques | _____ successful cohesion |
| _____ clear purpose | _____ well-structured sentences |

7. Using the Test of Written English (TWE) scoring guide in this chapter, read the 30-minute student essays below and score them holistically (1 to 6). When you finish, discuss the scores you assigned each paper and come to consensus or near-consensus on the scores with a small group or the rest of the class.

Essay Task: Many people enjoy active physical recreation like sports and other forms of exercise. Other people prefer intellectual activities like reading or listening to music. In a brief essay, discuss one or two benefits of physical activities and of intellectual activities. Explain which kind of recreation you think is more valuable to someone your age (Carlson,Bridgeman,Camp, and Waanders, 1985).

SAMPLE #1

Recreational activities are of two types—1) physical and 2) intellectual or mental. Physical activities include walking, running, or playing some games. The advantages of physical activities are that they help you keep your body in shape and they increase your stamina and concentration which is of use in our day-to-day life. A person who is physically fit has lesser chances of having any major illness.

Some people enjoy intellectual activities like reading or listening to music. Reading broadens your view of the world as one can learn a lot of things by reading different kinds of books which do not necessarily have to be from your field of activities. Listening to music after a long tiring day helps you to freshen up and it is good for relaxing your nerves after a tiring and nerve racking experince. Studies have shown that even plants can respond to music.

There is no such thing as a recreational activity for a particular age group. Old people have been known to play to keep themselves fit. Many young people have an obsession with reading to the point that they are oblivious to their surrounding.

Choice of recreation is a personal aspect. Physical activities are said to be for the young but the old can also enjoy it. The best recreational activity for my age group would be playing some game 4 days a week and reading or listening to music the remaining two or three days.

Perlini Dandekar (India)

SAMPLE #2

Today, we all know how physical activities affect our life style, for example live longer, feel better, look better. In books, magazines, T.V. the public will inforce any types of activities. This new era is more physical than sedentary. We will give many thanks to who did those researcher. I considerate physical activities or exercise the best thing that man kind explore. Without going in depth, one of the benefits that I personally get out from is to feel more energetic, without doing some exercise I feel depress sleepy not motivate. Whereas, intellecutal activities are more for relaxation, my opinion of course, after a hard day at work I cheerish a good story. They are also benefits from this activities; more prone to public news, or be able to appreande quickly any material that you would read. Also the ability to express yourself in writing, verbaly or any occasion that is presented t you. As you see, both have benefits for me. one it keeps me going, the autre teaches me about what are the world. Both, in my opinion, are good fitness, one is physically, the authre is mentally.

Anna Lewan (Italy)

SAMPLE #3

Many people are enjoying activities daily. The physical activities I enjoying the most is baseball. It gives me several physical advantages. The most important and the most intersted to me is group-spirit. Next, is the fun and healthy spot. Finally it has the philosphical value to my life. On the other hand, the intellectual activities is my another hobby; it calms me down like music. It is harmony to the environment.

Camping is the kind of recreation to my age of people. It is a sport that fits all age I think.

Hong Yi Jong (Taiwan)

Writing

1. Write a journal entry, brainstorming ideas about correction of student papers. In your opinion, what are the purposes of correction? What makes correction effective or ineffective?

2. Brainstorm for ten minutes in your learning log on your feelings about plagiarism. Then share your ideas with others in class.

3. Begin articulating your standards for good writing. First, look at the analytic and holistic scoring guides in this chapter. Then, formulate a list of criteria that you might use (and share) with your ESL writing students.

4. Using the sample criteria lists for evaluation in this chapter as a foundation, construct a handout for students in an ESL writing course (and specify the language proficiency and objectives of that class) that reflects your philosophy of evaluation.

5. Write a spontaneous, 30-minute essay using the TWE topic above. Then score your own paper holistically, using the TWE guide.

6. Read the brief student essays-in-progress below. Using the ideas about standards for good writing that you wrote about in #3 (above), respond to these drafts in three ways: (a) on accuracy/mechanics; (b) in marginal comments concerning content; and (c) in summative end comments that will send the student back to the writing and revising process. Then share your written responses with others in a small group, and come to some consensus about the most valuable comments for each student writer.

SAMPLE #1, BASIC LEVEL

My Teacher

My teacher is a man. He is an intelligente teacher, He is try to develope my English Writing. My teacher is a very sociable person, He always says good morning to me and my classmates when he comes to class every day. Sometimes my teacher comes to class before us, and he always puts his books on the desk near the blackboard. My teacher doesn't wear a coat in this summer. He often wears trousers and a shiart. My teacher abhors to come to class late, so he always tells the students to get early to class, and he askes the students to talk in English but if anyone takes with anthor in any language insted of English, he askes them to stop talking.

When the class is ready to begin, My teachers always explains what we are going to do during the class particularly. Then he usually teachs a lesson at the blackboard, and often gives us an activity to do if during the class, Sometimes he digests us to catgories to do activity during the class. When we finish he collects our books and assignment in it, and he always answers our questions while we are working in class.

The class which we are study is hard because its need to alot of vocabulary, but the teacher trys to make it easy by providing us with guide papers and all the students pay attention to the teacher when he explains the lessone.

In conclusion I am very happy that I am a student in this teacher's class, Because he is a serious person, and a friendly person also.

Saud Bin M. Al-Battal (Saudi Arabia)

SAMPLE #2, INTERMEDIATE LEVEL

A Market Day

Actually "a market day" in my country means more than that. Some years ago, a market day in my country was each Sunday, where farmers went to the main plaza in town in order to sell or exchange theirs products. Each one set up his own table, arranging his fruits, vegetables or flowers in a baskets, so they could get people attention. It was some bargain, too. If someone wanted to buy something he or she would ask for a lower price and get it. Also, if someone didn't want to buy but also exchange he or she would ask for exchange and do it. Nowadays, a market day is the first sunday of eache month, when farmers, artisons and anybody who wants to see goods goes to the city's central park and do it. It is as colorful as olden times, everybody sets up his or her table, and they arrange their product in baskets trying to imitate past days. There are not bargains anymore; they set up the prices, and that's it. Also, sellers don't exchange goods any more. Besides, these market transactions the actual market day has amusing spectacles for example, a band of musicians from the main university in town joing to the market, and they play folklore music. Meanwhile, groups of dancers dance to the rhythm of the songs. Even more, if someone wants to eat, there are a lot of different kinds of food. Some people prepared their best recipe and sell it. I really enjoy the actual market day because we preserve our cultural traditions and we have fun too.

Gloria Arango (Colombia)

7. Using the criteria suggested by Kroll's article on +/– rhetoric and +/– syntax, analyze the papers above. Then, in your learning log, design one lesson sequence for one of the student writers above.

8. Reread Elaine Lees's taxonomy of tasks for evaluating student revision in this chapter. Then, using one of the TWE student essays above, implement each of those tasks and label each accordingly.

9. In your learning log, spend 15 minutes revising the ideas and writing from #3 (above). What changes will you make? Why?

CHAPTER 10

Teaching ESL Writing: Becoming a Professional

> Knowledge emerges only through invention and re–invention,
> through restless, impatient, continuing, hopeful inquiry.
>
> (Friere, 1970, p. 58)

Teaching, like learning, requires "a willingness to examine and often risk one's beliefs and patterns of actions and thoughts" (Larsen-Freeman, 1986, p. 267). Furthermore, teaching is lifelong learning, a constant interplay between knowing and experimenting, reflection and change. As Vivian Zamel indicates, research aimed at finding the best method has been "based on the faulty assumptions that there was a best method and one just had to find it, that teaching writing was a matter of prescribing a logically ordered set of written tasks and exercises, and that good writing conformed to a predetermined and ideal model" (1987, p. 697). This book does not provide teachers with prescribed curricula, syllabi, and classroom methods (such as the Silent Way, Total Physical Response, and Suggestopedia).* Instead, its objective is to assist in the development of the teacher as a decision-maker and problem-solver who is able "to live with complexity and to appreciate ambiguity" (Clarke and Silberstein, 1988, p. 697)—to become, in short, a professional.

Results of a survey of ESL methods courses at fifty-five U.S. institutions showed that while current methodology classes cover traditional and innovative methods, theories of language learning, skills approaches, and to a lesser extent curriculum design, they are often deficient in three areas: culture and cross-cultural communication skills; using technology in teaching ESL; and, most surprising, professionalism and professional development (Grosse, 1991). As members of the profession, ESL teachers have a responsibility for the development and betterment of the field as well as for their own professional development. Unfortunately, bettering the field is a political and practical necessity. Many working ESL teachers are marginalized in their jobs. Often ESL programs and classes are even

---

*For a discussion of these and other prescribed methodologies, see Blair (1991).

257

located off-campus, and many are considered remedial programs in which part-time, temporary teachers are underpaid and overworked. There is little time for "developing" in this downward spiral. As a result, the field remains largely invisible and unrewarded.

Charlotte Grosse (1991) suggested that one way to further professionalize the field is to encourage ESL teachers, new and experienced, to raise their own and others' awareness of the value of their work. As Mary Ann Christison put it, "We will have trouble valuing our teaching if we do not value the field" (Brittner-Mahyera et al., 1992). Teachers, no matter how busy or beleaguered, must work to empower the profession. By being proactive, not only in their classes but also in their institutions and communities, they can demonstrate the expertise they have to offer and so broaden understanding of the field. Telephone calls from institutional colleagues, even those complaining about their ESL students, are opportunities for education and heightening awareness. Involvement in community organizations and activities likewise can open doors to demonstrations of the validity and viability of the profession.

Individual Professional Development

In addition to raising the awareness of those outside the profession, teachers forming their educational philosophies must also situate themselves within the field of teaching ESL (TESL). They should reach out to others in the field, seeking and offering support, sharing and gleaning ideas. Becoming a professional includes keeping abreast of current theory, analyzing and applying theory to the classroom, and participating fully in the opportunities for development offered by others in the field.

Continuing education and professional development for ESL writing teachers includes reading major journals, enrolling in relevant courses, participating in (and offering) workshops, and becoming involved with professional organizations. In other words, teachers must "learn from and join with the community of scholars in rhetoric and composition working to identify the questions that must be addressed and the methods for addressing those questions . . . about the nature of the composing process, about transforming thought into words, and about shaping prose to meet the needs of audience and purpose" (Kroll, 1989, p. 6).

Attending and participating in local, regional, and international professional conferences are valuable opportunities for professional teachers. The flagship organization for ESL professionals is International **TESOL** (Teachers of English to Speakers of Other Languages). More than twenty thousand teachers, teachers-in-training, administrators and researchers world-wide benefit from their membership in TESOL through the annual convention, the many TESOL publications, and the TESOL Summer Institute. Part of the mission of TESOL is to encourage access to and standards for English language instruction, profession preparation, and employment. TESOL has more than a dozen "special interest" sections for its members, including the Higher Education, Applied Linguistics, C.A.L.L., Teacher Education, and Teaching English Internationally Interest Sections. In addition, nearly fifty TESOL Affiliates, which are independent organizations, serve ESL professionals in states and regions in the U.S. and abroad. Each affiliate hosts conferences and publishes a newsletter. Each contains the name of TESOL plus a reference to the locale: CATESOL (California TESOL), NYSTESOL (New York State TESOL), I-TESOL (Intermountain TESOL), Illinois TESOL/BE (Bilingual Education), etc.

The National Association for Foreign Student Affairs: Association of International Educators (**NAFSA: AIE**) focuses on the entire experience of international students in the U.S. as well as American students who go abroad to study. The five sections of NAFSA are the Community Section (for community volunteers who work with ESL students); the Admissions Section (personnel who work with international admissions and visa requirements); the Foreign Student Advisors Section (for those who work directly with and counsel international students); and the Administrators and Teachers of English as a Second Language (ATESL) Section. National and regional NAFSA conferences in the U.S. cover the entire range of international education; grant and travel awards allow members to pursue professional development; and publications from this organization inform on that broad scope.

Annual or semi-annual conferences planned by these organizations provide professional opportunities for networking and education. Just as important, they offer members a chance to serve the profession. Giving presentations, working on conference planning and arrangements, and becoming active in the governance of a professional organization are excellent avenues for professional development. Moreover, the stability, the visibility, and even the viability of the field is dependent on professionals who work together to better the status of the field.

Theory: The Foundation of the Profession

By definition, members of any profession continue to read analytically throughout their careers, both in the field and beyond—especially in the professions of education, psychology, and communication. For ESL writing teachers, continued professional development is essential because the field is relatively new and still subject to substantial growth and change. J. T. Zebroski states how theory benefits the teacher: it "has helped me to excavate and to uncover my own assumptions about writing. It has aided me in crafting a more coherent and unified course structure. It has encouraged me to try out some new methods of teaching writing. It has helped me to relinquish control and to emphasize classroom community" (1986, p. 58).

Because there is no single comprehensive pedagogical theory for teaching ESL writing, teachers need to examine and form their own "coherent perspectives, principles, models—tools for thinking about second language writing in general and ESL composition in particular, and for analyzing and evaluating competing views" (Silva, 1990, p. 11). Identification of appropriate theory in relevant disciplines and study of historical developments and research are the responsibility of the ESL writing teacher. Reflection on and discussion of that information are necessary elements in the formation of a teaching philosophy. The ESL writing teacher must therefore research the field, investigating, integrating, and interpreting existing literature in both NES and ESL writing.* Tony Silva (1990) lists the following criteria essential for coherent pedagogy:

- It is adequately informed by appropriate and valid theory.
- It regards writing as an interactive task.
- It reflects understanding of historical developments.
- It is informed by current work in relevant disciplines.
- It is sensitive to the cultural, linguistic, and experiential differences of individuals and societies.
- It is supported by viable empirical and classroom-based research.

Ann Johns (1990) suggests that there are currently four theoretical approaches to the teaching of NES writing. Although the approaches overlap, they are appropriate in a summary discussion of ESL pedagogical theories.

1. **The expressivist approach**: Writing is perceived as an art, with the focus on the individual discovery of the true self. Teachers in expressivist (or process) classrooms are non-directive; they facilitate classroom activities designed to promote writing fluency and empower the students. This approach leads quite naturally to a process classroom.

2. **The cognitivist approach**: Writing is seen as a thinking and problem-solving process. Classes using this approach are most often

*The annotated bibliography for this chapter at the end of the book identifies some of the journals in the field valuable for ESL writing teachers.

English for Academic Purposes (EAP) and English for Specific Purposes (ESP) classrooms. Planning by student writers is extensive: defining the rhetorical problem, exploring its parts, generating alternative solutions, arriving at well-supported conclusions, and translating those ideas into words. Students in cognitivist classrooms develop a large repertoire of general and local strategies to draw upon to direct their creative processes (Flower, 1989a, b). They often focus on pattern-model tasks, on what Linda Flower and John Hays, call "a pocket of stored plans for creating appropriate formats" (1980, p. 30). Strategy training is fundamental to this approach; students learn to develop their image of the reader, the situation, and their own goals.

3. **The interactive approach**: The focus of the class is on the writer who is involved in dialog with an audience. In these classrooms, both the writer and the reader take responsibility for coherent communication, and the writing-reading connection is primary. The critical ingredient in the interpretive process is the transaction between writer and reader, with the writer's sense of the reader's expectations and the reader's sense of the writer's intentions (Shriver, 1992; Zamel, 1992). That is, for appropriate communication, writers organize their discourse in a manner that is familiar to the reader who is striving for cohesion and the direct explanation of informa-tion. Many intensive English writing programs combine or integrate their writing and reading classes, and undergraduate and graduate writing courses that stress the writing-reading connection use an interactive approach.

4. **The social constructionist approach**: Writing is seen as essentially a social act in a specific context (Coe, 1987) Learning to write is part of becoming socialized into the academic community, and purpose in writing is constrained by the assumptions of one's culture. In such classrooms, language, focus, and form stem from the discourse community to which the writing is directed. Students learn a pragmatic view of composing: that the shared goals and expecta-tions of different discourse communities must shape their writing. EAP and ESP writing classes that ask students to focus on the academic discourse communities for whom they will be writing in future work use the social constructionist approach (Faigley, 1986).

From Theory to Practice: Reflective Teaching

While examination of theoretical issues can provide teachers with an ongoing theoretical foundation, only when theory is applied in the classroom—and evaluated—can a teaching philosophy be formed. "Critical reflection refers to an activity or process in which an experience is recalled, considered, and evaluated, usually in relation to a broader purpose. It involves examination of past experience as a basis for evaluation and decision-making and as a source for planning and action" (Richards, 1990c, p. 9).

Reflection is part of teaching; teachers assess activities as they occur, then analyze their effectiveness later. David Nunan has written extensively about the investigations that teachers can make into their teaching practices and the opportunities for critical reflection to improve their teaching (1988, 1989b and c, 1990). His work includes various checklists and self-analysis sheets that allow teachers to "observe" their teaching in retrospect and make improvements. For example, after each class, a teacher might review the lesson plan and ask the following questions:

1. Does the lesson plan
   A. accurately reflect what went on in class?
   B. only marginally describe what went on?
   C. not reflect at all what went on?
2. What changes did I make in the lesson plan during the class? Why?
3. Was the lesson plan generally successful? Why or why not?
4. What changes might make the class more successful next time?
5. Were there clear relationships between parts of the lesson plan?
6. What did I learn about teaching today? about my students?

Some of the answers to these questions can also be gathered from students through short three- to four-minute "postscript" journal entries assigned at the end of each week or each class module. These student entries will enable the teacher to view each class from the students' eyes.

Teachers forming their teaching philosophies might begin by considering the following questions:

- What should happen in an ESL writing classroom? What should not happen?
- What should the learners be doing in an ESL writing class? What should they learn? Why?
- What forms of interaction (teacher–students, student–students, student–student, teacher–student) are successful in the ESL writing class?
- What do I know about myself as a teacher now? What would I like to learn about myself as a teacher? (Nunan, 1989a).

And as each teacher investigates approaches and teaching methods, s/he must consider the long-term effects of the class s/he teaches: **"What will the students do after I wave goodbye?"**

Self-observation (perhaps through the use of a videotape) and peer-observation are credited by many teacher trainers as excellent ways to analyze and understand how successful a learning opportunity is (Allwright, 1986, 1988; Gaies and Bowen, 1990; Kumaradivelu,

1990). Peer review (or, more positively, **peer exchange**) can be beneficial; observing colleagues teach provides insights into teaching approaches and activities, and the comments of peer observers offer opportunities for change as well as exchange. But peer exchange, like self-observation, should have a focus; preparation for either is necessary (Richards and Lockhart, 1991–1992). The questions below, which are concerned with specific areas of classroom management and lesson plan implementation, can be used by the classroom teacher or by a peer visiting the class (Richards, 1990a; Richards and Nunan, 1990).*

1. Were there any cultural misunderstandings during class?
2. Did everyone in class understand the directions for activities?
3. Was every student involved directly in the activities sometime during the class?
4. Were student groupings appropriate? effective?
5. Was the pacing of activities appropriate? Was too much or too little time spent on one activity?

Reflection on and analysis of a series of lesson plans can occur briefly during a class (an illumination of sorts); at the end of each class, in a scribbled note on the bottom of a lesson plan; at the end of a sequence of lessons in a teacher's journal; and after the course has ended, upon re-reading the journal entry. Barbara Kroll, an Applied Linguistics professor and ESL teacher for a quarter century, offers a description of an in-class epiphany:

> One clear mistake that I made [early in my teaching career] was to assume that I knew what was best for [my students] and that what they had to say was of little or no value in shaping the course that I would provide for them. I have since learned that we not only must ask students to tell us about their difficulties in achieving writing proficiency, but we must also *listen* to what they don't yet know how to say but so much want to tell us. For example, in one class where most of the students seemed to be having trouble writing an essay that seemed to adhere to the basic principles of organization and coherence, I . . . selected three papers from the class to duplicate and distribute to the class. . . . I asked the class to look over the papers and to pick one as the "best" of the three and then to provide reasons. Several students picked the five-paragraph essay, which I felt I had stacked the deck with, pointing to all its handbook virtues. But a few holdouts argued vociferously that the paper was poorly presented and did not have the attributes of good writing.
>
> Had I stopped the discussion there and attempted to convince the "holdouts" that the paper *did* exhibit typical academic prose, I would have lost out on hearing the reasons they attributed to its lack of

*See Appendix 3 for sample teacher-observation sheets.

success. In fact, what they went on to explain was that they hated the paper for precisely the reasons which I was telling them were its strengths. They claimed it was too direct, it left nothing to the reader's imagination, it announced what it was going to do in the first paragraph, leaving little reason to go on and read the rest, it gave too many details for each of the points it raised, and it wasn't easy to read. What followed from what at first seemed a disastrous lesson plan was a term-long discussion on attributes of English prose which prove valuable in the academic world, and a tremendous amount of learning for both the students and myself. (1989)

Below is another example of reflection, this one from a teacher who, in his first ESL teaching experience, worked in a low-intermediate writing class. For nearly two weeks, his class participated in an original detective story unit that he designed. The sequence was successful: students assumed characters in the story, read what their characters had reported to the police, discussed clues, and finally discovered the murderer. A year later, when asked to reflect on the classes, he responded (below). Note that the differences he discusses involve (a) more student input and responsibility, (b) more student interaction and activities, (c) more writing, (d) more reading, and (e) less teacher control, all benchmarks of a more experienced, more comfortable teacher:

> I think I'd do it a little differently now. (Actually, I hope I am doing a lot of things differently now.) Anyway, I think I might give them the basic story first and have them think up questions they have (who, what, etc.) instead of inventing the questions for them. We could then list those questions. Then the information gap part of this would start with different people or groups being given different stories. Groups 1, 2, and 3 would meet, make sure they understand the information, then break to other people to find more information. People could then write paragraphs with whatever opinion they have (not one that is given to them). If possible, a debate would round out the exercise. Emphasis would be put on supporting any ideas and putting them down in a coherent form. I would also spend a little more time prepping the students . . . perhaps a logic section or some sort plus reading/writing on crime.
>
> (courtesy of Mark Dorr, Warsaw, Poland)

Reflective teaching involves assessing the origins, purposes, and consequences of a teacher's intentions and actions in the classroom (Bartlett, 1990). Teachers step outside themselves and see their actions in light of their historical, social, and cultural context. One activity teachers (and researchers) have found valuable for introspection is journal writing (Dass, 1992). In much the same way that students benefit from metacognitive entries in their daybooks, teachers can reflect on their teaching practices in writing, analyze classroom behaviors, and return to earlier entries to gain insights into their progress. Keeping a reflective teaching journal enables the self-examination and introspection that allows teachers to challenge their beliefs and the causes and effects of those beliefs (Bailey, 1990; Bishop, 1991; Jarvis, 1992; P. Porter et al., 1990).

Action Research

The logical result of reflective teaching is classroom teachers who are also researchers. Teacher-researchers, in James Berlin's view, rightfully reclaim their classrooms and empower their philosophies of teaching: "Each and every teacher is . . . responsible for researching her students, and doing so in order to improve the quality of student learning" (1990a, p. 5). Although teachers may not officially call their activities "research" and may never officially share the results of their investigations with others, they regularly perform the processes of research and use the results to better their teaching. **Action research**, or classroom-based research, is defined as trying out ideas in practice as a means of improvement and increased knowledge (Kemmis and McTaggert, 1982). It is a constant cycle of observing, analyzing, and modifying classroom practice in classroom situations. In order to do action research, teachers need to

- conceptualize their practice in theoretical terms
- be aware of issues amenable to research
- have skills in data collection and interpretation (Nunan, 1989c, p. 62).

The term "action research" describes the immediacy of the act. A theorist "has the leisure to examine other relevant research, consider alternatives, restructure or redesign the problem, and retest it. A teacher, on the other hand, must perceive problems in action and exercise . . . reflective action" (Hillocks, 1990, p. 16). In this way, too, action research builds on what teachers do; it focuses and articulates the investigation and interpretation of data that are already part of the classroom teacher's world. Teachers regularly interpret data such as test scores and student papers, lesson plans and student evaluations, to determine class success and student progress. They modify their behavior based on observational data such as classroom interactions and student feedback, and they will implement the results of this and other research as they plan curriculum, write sequenced lesson plans, and design activities for their classes. In other words, teachers are constantly doing research: they are investigating, integrating, and interpreting data. Richards suggests the following overview questions for teacher research:

Structure of the Class

- How clearly are the goals of activities communicated to students?
- Is there a clear relationship between different activities within a lesson?
- Is there any sense of development within a lesson, or it is merely a succession of unrelated activities, the logic for which is not apparent?
- What kind of opening and closing does the lesson have?

Activities Analysis

- What kinds of tasks or activities are employed during a lesson?
- What kinds of demands do these tasks create
- Is the pacing of tasks adequate? Is too little time spent on some tasks and too much on others?
- For how much of the lesson are students actively engaged in learning tasks?
- Are the tasks interesting and challenging to the students?
- How does the teacher give feedback on task performance?
- How effective is the teacher's feedback? (adapted from Richards, 1990c, pp. 126-127)

Caveat

It is important that classroom research build on what is currently happening rather than eliminating existing classroom activities, approaches, and procedures. Teacher-researchers tend to be unduly self-critical and therefore risk throwing the proverbial baby out with the bath water. Instead, action research must be carefully interpreted and implemented with deliberation. Change, after all, takes time, patience, and resources.

Conclusion

Writing involves a complex group of skills, and the teaching of writing is a complex process. This book has sought to ground the readers in the theoretical background and issues of the complex field of teaching composition to ESL students so that teachers can begin to form their philosophies of teaching. "Begin" is the operative word. Members of the profession of teaching "locate themselves in a set of beliefs about teaching and learning, find a teaching style that they are comfortable with, acquire confidence in their ability to teach, and remain sufficiently dissatisfied with their own progress to continue to look for ways to improve" (Pytlik, 1991, p. 49). The details of second language writing instruction reflect assumptions about the nature and philosophy of teaching and learning. Among the questions that teachers must address as they formulate, implement, reflect upon, and modify their teaching philosophies are the following.

Classroom Management
- What rules govern classroom behavior?
- How are expectations for positive and negative classroom behavior communicated and reinforced?
- How are problem students dealt with?
- How is attention to instructional tasks maintained?

Teacher–Student Interaction
- How much teacher-to-student communication occurs in a lesson?
- How much student-to-teacher interaction is there?
- To what extent does the lesson engage the learners?
- How is student attention and interest maintained?
- What turn-taking patterns are observed?

Grouping
- What grouping arrangements are employed?
- Is there a clear relationship between grouping patterns and instructional goals?
- Are grouping arrangements effective?
- How are groups established? Do students always work with the same partners or in the same groups?

Teaching resources
- What teaching aids are used?
- How effective is the teacher's use of aids, such as overhead projector, blackboard, or audiocassette or videocassette player?
(Richards, 1990b, pp. 126–127)

John Fanselow has argued that the value of teaching is in "learning ways of looking as a means to expand our repertoire of teaching practices; discovering something about our beliefs and teaching practices that we have not seen before; being freed to try teaching practices that others, or even ourselves, have judged inadequate; becoming more aware of our beliefs and the ways they can control the range of our teaching practices; using evaluations of teaching practices to explore our beliefs rather than judge them, and to free us to try alternatives rather than to prescribe" (1992, p. 2). As teachers examine the issues discussed in this book, they will almost certainly conclude that teaching is both an art and a science. "To the extent that it remains an art, it permits individual teachers to exercise such personal gifts as they may be endowed with. To the extent that is can be related to a science or sciences and thus itself become an applied science, it can have developed in a coherent way, be given continuity, and be taught" (Prator, 1991, p. 12).

Discussion Questions

1. Ann Johns (1990) posits four different approaches that illustrate the current theory and research in NES composition. Discuss each of the four approaches summarized in this chapter. Which do you find most compatible with your own teaching? Why?

2. How does the concept of <u>audience</u> differ among the following approaches: expressivist, cognitivist, interactivist, and social constructionist? How might teachers espousing each of these approaches design activities for their students?

3. In small groups, discuss the criteria Silva (1990) presents in this chapter for a coherent theory of teaching ESL writing. How might each of the approaches discussed by Johns fit Silva's criteria?

4. Below are four quotations from early articles concerning theories of composing. Read each one, then discuss the meaning of each with a small group of peers. How relevant is each to current composing theories? What is the relevance of each for teachers of ESL writing? Which best describes the ways you think about composing? Why?

> a. "Writers of formal written discourse have two goals . . . stylistic control and a completely autonomous text . . . a text that does not need context, gestures, or audible effects to convey its meaning."
> (Flower, 1979, p. 29)

> b. "If the writing of the discourse and the reading of it are successful, both participants will meet not on the page, but in the deep structure of meaning, the underlying form of discourse."
> (Augustine, 1981, p. 225)

> c. Basic writers are "typically less skilled at planning and overwhelmed by the multitude of decisions they need to make. [They] use overly generalized, inadequately qualified thesis statements, and . . . sometimes end up writing trivial subjects without significant implications."
> (Coe, 1981, p. 264)

> d. "Those who realize that writing can be a recursive process have an easier time with waiting, looking, and discovery. Those who subscribe to the linear model find themselves easily frustrated when what they write does not immediately correspond to what they planned."
> (Perl, 1980, p. 368)

5. What is your attitude toward the teacher-as-researcher? Are you aware of the reasons for that attitude?

6. Observe an ESL writing class as an action researcher. Before you enter the classroom, select one of the topics below. Read some current literature on the subject, and then formulate two questions about the topic. Collect data about your research topic (by taking notes, making an audio tape, or another collection method).

> A. seating arrangement(s) during the class
> B. amount of student time on-task
> C. percentages of teacher-talk and student-talk during the class

D. sequencing of tasks in the class

E. question-asking by the teacher in the class

F. types of feedback given during an ESL writing class

7. Choose a partner or join a small group to do some collaborative research. Choose one of the topics below (or come to consensus about another topic). Decide on a plan for collaboration and a research hypothesis (that is, what do you think will happen?). Read some current literature on the topic.

   A. Teacher–student interaction in an ESL classroom

   B. NES cultural classroom cues

   C. Characteristics of successful ESL teaching

   D. Feedback given by students during group work

8. Below are some descriptions from experienced teachers of classes that did not go as expected. Read about each situation. Then discuss, in pairs or in groups, alternative solutions to each of the problem classes.

A. Students were supposed to bring a rough draft to class of their first essay. I'd been preparing them for collaborative work, individual responsibility, etc. I'd prepared a handout to facilitate the group work, so I thought the peer review would be good. Wrong. Five students had NO DRAFT or only a bit of pre-writing; half the class had only half a draft or less. So I put the students who had drafts in groups and got them to work. Then I had the other students work on their drafts individually, and I also assigned them to do the peer review worksheet with a fellow no-draft person outside of class and before the next class.

B. I thought I had a dynamite class planned, but nothing seemed to work. The students admitted they'd been up most of the night finishing the essays that were due. That, coupled with the 8 a.m. class hour, did us in. They didn't want to do anything in class except to turn in their papers and go back to bed. Next time an essay is due, I'm going to have them do some kind of activity that calls for talking with each other collaboratively, or I'll have them do some in-class writing, so I don't have to struggle to get them through the class.

C. I handed back the final drafts of persuasion essays, all marked up, and the usual silence settled over the class. Usually I do this at the end of class, telling students to go home and really look at their papers, then come to see me if they still want to talk. But today I experimented. I carefully paired students up, based on needs and possibilities for sharing their papers. At this point in the semester, we've established a lot of trust and a real sense of community, so I thought it might work. I asked the students to look at each other's paper and give advice on revision. At the end of the class, I asked them to evaluate the experience. It didn't work for most of them. They couldn't get past MY marks, and some were embarrassed. I won't do it again, but I guess it was worth trying.

D. I dread discovering that I suddenly have ten minutes left in a class, so I usually take three times the material I need. Sometimes the first activity takes the whole period because the students get excited. Other times I have to keep intervening just to move the class along.

          (courtesy of Zsuzsa Rónay, University of Szeged, Hungary)

Writing

1. J. T. Zebroski states: "The primary objective of a writing course is to encourage students, through a variety of experiences and by means of writing assignments that require reflection upon these experiences, to arrive at a more explicit and conscious 'theory' of writing that can guide them and help them to better understand and control their own behavior" (1986, pp. 58–59). Write a single statement of your opinion of your primary objective in teaching ESL writing.

2. Using a pre-writing technique, begin to consolidate your thoughts concerning a theory of teaching ESL writing.

3. Among the areas and issues you might consider as you focus on your ESL teaching philosophy are the following:

Composing and Revising Processes	Cross-Cultural Training
The Writing-Reading Connection	The Change Process
Collaborative Learning	Teaching and Assessing Writing
Contrastive/Error Analysis	Cohesion and Coherence
The Process Classroom	Computer-Assisted Language Learning
Learning Styles and Strategies	Curriculum and Syllabus Design
Contrastive Rhetoric	Schema Theory
Accuracy vs. Fluency	Responding to Student Writing
Peer Review	Revision
Conferencing	Classroom Community
Writing Across the Curriculum	Peer Review

Select three to five of these (or other) areas/issues that seem most relevant to your theories of teaching and learning writing, and summarize your thoughts on each.

4. This book has focused on both the theoretical aspects of teaching ESL writing and the practical application of those theories. Using this text, and at least seven additional sources, write an eight- to ten-page paper that formulates your philosophy of teaching ESL writing.

5. Using the data you collected in #6 (above), write a four- to six- page report of your research. Include a brief literature review, a description of the project, the data and results, pedagogical implications of the results, and recommendations for future research.

6. With your collaborative research peer/group, write a six- to eight- page report of your data-gathering research (#7, above). Decide how to collaborate on the writing, then meet regularly to read each other's sections, negotiate meaning, and integrate the information.

7. In your reflective journal, write a "post-script" about one of the research reports (above). What was easy? Difficult? What problems did you encounter? How did you solve them? What did you learn?

APPENDICES

Appendix 1: Personality Surveys

Type A / Type B Personality Inventory

<u>Directions:</u> Answer the questions below. Then discuss the Type A and Type B personality. Which are you?

1. When you brush your teeth, do you always put the cap back on the toothpaste? Do you squeeze the tube in the middle or do you fold it up from the bottom?

2. You are going to the airport to catch a plane. Do you leave your house early enough to arrive at least half an hour before boarding or would you rather arrive just as the boarding of the plane begins?

3. Do you prefer to plan your free time or do you prefer spontaneity?

4. When you leave your car or apartment, do you double check to make sure the windows are closed and the doors are locked?

5. How do your bureau drawers look? Are socks all matched and stored symmetrically, or does it resemble the aftermath of a tornado?

6. When you go to the grocery store, do you take a list? Do you follow the list?

7. Do you talk fast? Do you interrupt people when they are talking?

8. When you go to the library to do an assignment, do you proceed with a series of planned steps or do you take the time to look for other interesting material?

9. Are you usually on time? Do people who are late irritate you? Is is hard for you to "find time" to do things (e.g., get a haircut, exercise regularly)?

10. Do you usually do more than one thing at a time?

Environmental Writing Inventory

Directions: As you prepare to write an assignment, which of the following environmental aspects do you prefer? Which are important for you? Answer the survey below. Circle "not important" if you so consider that aspect. Then discuss your preferences with your classmates.

Place: Formal (desk, straight-backed chair, library)

                                                                    not important

   Informal (bed, floor, soft chair)

Surroundings   clean   messy   not important

Time: early morning   late morning   early afternoon

                                                                    not important

   late afternoon   evening   late evening

   Other: _____

Tools: pencil   computer   yellow pad

                                                                    not important

   pen   spiral notebook   highlighter

   Special: _____

Clothing: formal   informal

                                                                    not important

   Special: _____

Light: bright   soft   dark   not important

Temperature: warm   cool   not important

Sound: quiet   noisy   music   not important

          radio   television   Special: _____

Sustenance: food   Specify _____

                                                                    not important

          drink   Specify _____

Rewards: Do you promise yourself rewards for getting started? If so, what?
          Do you promise yourself rewards for finishing? If so, what?

Other: What other "rituals" do you have that make your writing more comfortable and/or effective?

Appendix 2: Learning and Teaching Style Surveys

Perceptual Learning Style Preference Questionnaire

<u>Directions:</u> This survey will show you how you prefer to learn English. Read each of the statements below. Then mark the appropriate box for each statement: that you Strongly Agree (SA), Agree (A), are Undecided (U), Disagree (D), or Strongly Disagree (SD). Mark only one box for each statement, the box that most accurately identifies your feelings about each statement as it concerns learning English. When you finish, use the scoring guide at the end of the survey to discover your learning style preferences.

Statements	SA	A	U	D	SD
1. When the teacher tells me the instructions I understand better.					
2. I prefer to learn by doing something in class.					
3. I get more work done when I work with others.					
4. I learn more when I study with a group.					
5. In class, I learn best when I work with others.					
6. I learn better by reading what the teacher writes on the chalkboard.					
7. When someone tells me how to do something in class, I learn it better.					
8. When I do things in class, I learn better.					
9. I remember things I have heard in class better than things I have read.					
10. When I read instructions, I remember them better.					
11. I learn more when I can make a model of something					
12. I understand better when I read instructions.					

Statements	SA	A	U	D	SD
13. When I study alone, I remember things better.					
14. I learn more when I make something for a class project.					
15. I enjoy learning in class by doing experiments.					
16. I learn better when I make drawings as I study.					
17. I learn better in class when the teacher gives a lecture.					
18. When I work alone, I learn better.					
19. I understand things better when I participate in role-playing.					
20. I learn better in class when I listen to someone.					
21. I enjoy working on an assignment with two or three classmates.					
22. When I build something, I remember what I have learned better.					
23. I prefer to study with others.					
24. I learn better by reading than by listening to someone.					
25. I enjoy making something for a class project.					
26. I learn best in class when I can participate in related activities.					
27. In class, I work better when I work alone.					
28. I prefer working on projects by myself.					
29. I learn more by reading textbooks than by listening to lectures.					
30. I prefer to work by myself.					

Learning Style Preferences Self-Scoring Sheet

Directions: There are 5 questions for each learning style category in this survey. The questions are grouped below according to each learning style. Assign each question you answered a numerical value as follows:

SA = 5   A = 4   U = 3   D = 2   SD = 1

Fill in the blanks below with the numerical value of each answer. For example, if you answered Strongly Agree (SA) for question 6 (a visual preference question), write a 5 (SA) on the blank next to question 6 below.

Example: Visual

6 – _5_

When you have completed all the numerical values for Visual, add the numbers. Multiply the answer by 2 and put the total in the appropriate blank.

Follow this process for each of the learning style categories. When you are finished, the score at the bottom of the page will help you determine your major learning style preference(s), your minor learning style preference(s), and those learning styles that are negligible. See the next page for information about each learning style preference.

If you need help, ask your teacher.

Visual			**Tactile**		
6 -	_____		11 -	_____	
10 -	_____		14 -	_____	
12 -	_____		16 -	_____	
24 -	_____		22 -	_____	
29 -	_____		25 -	_____	
TOTAL	_____ x 2	_____ (Score)	TOTAL _____	x 2	_____ (Score)

Auditory			**Group**		
1 -	_____		3 -	_____	
7 -	_____		4 -	_____	
9 -	_____		5 -	_____	
17 -	_____		21 -	_____	

20 - _____		23 - _____
TOTAL _____ x 2 _____ (Score)		TOTAL _____ x 2 _____ (Score)

Kinesthetic

2 - _____

8 - _____

15 - _____

19 - _____

26 - _____

TOTAL _____ x 2 _____
(Score)

Individual

13 - _____

18 - _____

27 - _____

28 - _____

30 - _____

TOTAL _____ x 2 _____
(Score)

Major Learning Style Preference Scores: 38–50 _____

Minor Learning Style Preference Scores: 25–37 _____

Negligible: 0–24 _____

Explanation of Learning Style Preferences*

Students learn in many different ways. The questionnaire you completed and scored showed which ways you prefer to learn English. In many cases, students' learning style preferences show how well students learn material in different situations.

The explanations of major learning style preferences below describe the characteristics of those learners. The descriptions will give you some information about ways in which you learn best.

Visual Major Learning Style Preference

You learn well from seeing words in books, on the chalkboard, and in workbooks. You remember and understand information and instructions better if you read them. You don't need as much oral explanation as an auditory learner, and you can often learn alone, with a book. you should take notes of lectures and oral directions if you want to remember this information.

*Adapted from the C.I.T.E. Learning Styles Instrument, Murdoch Teacher Center, Wichita, Kansas. Used with permission.

Auditory Major Learning Style Preference

You learn from hearing words spoken and from oral explanations. You may remember information by reading aloud or moving your lips as you read, especially when you are learning new material. You benefit from hearing audio tapes, lectures, and class discussion. You benefit from making tapes to listen to, by teaching other students, and by conversing with your teacher.

Kinesthetic Major Learning Style Preference

You learn best by experience, by being involved physically in classroom experiences. You remember information well when you actively participate in activities, field trips, and role-playing in the classroom. A combination of stimuli—for example, an audio tape combined with an activity—will help you understand more material.

Tactile Major Learning Style Preference

You learn best when you have the opportunity to do "hands on" experiences with materials. That is, working on experiments in a laboratory, handling and building models, and touching and working with materials provide you with the most successful learning situations. Writing notes or instructions can help you remember information, and physical involvement in class related activities may help you understand new information.

Group Major Learning Style Preference

You learn more easily when you study with at least one other student, and you will be more successful completing work well when you work with others. You value group interaction and class work with other students, and you remember information better when you work with two or three classmates. The stimulation you receive from group work helps you learn and understand new information.

Individual Major Learning Style Preference

You learn best when you work alone. You think better when you study alone, and you remember information you learn by yourself. You understand new material best when you learn it alone, and you make better progress in learning when you work by yourself.

Minor Learning Styles

In most cases, minor learning styles indicate areas when you can function well as a learner. Usually a very successful learner can learn in several different ways.

Negligible Learning Styles

Often a negligible score indicates that you may have difficulty learning in that way. One solution may be to direct your learning to your stronger learning styles. Another solution might be to try to work on some of the skills to strengthen your learning style in that "negligible" area.

The TLC Teaching Style Inventory
A self-diagnostic tool to identify one's preferred teaching style
Developed by Harvey F. Silver and J. Robert Hanson
(Revised, 1989)

Purpose:

The Teaching Style Inventory (TSI) is a simple self-description test based on Carl Gustav Jung's Theory of Psychological Types (1921). The instrument is designed to help you identify your own teaching profile based on your preferences for particular behaviors. The behaviors fall into the following ten categories: classroom atmosphere, teaching techniques, planning, what one values in students, teach-student interactions, classroom management, student behaviors, teaching behaviors, evaluation and goals.

Directions:

Based upon your conscious preferences and pertinent to the way you teach, rank in order the behavior descriptions in each category by assigning 5 to the behavior which best characterizes your teaching style, a 3 to the behavior which next best characterizes your teaching style, a 1 to the next most characteristic behavior, and a 0 to the behavior which least characterizes you as a teacher.

As you read through the list of behaviors in each category, you may find it difficult to choose the behavior that best characterizes your teaching style. This is understandable since every teacher operates in a variety of ways in different situations, yet each of us does have preferences for some behaviors over others. Keep in mind that there are no right or wrong answers. All the choices are equally acceptable. The aim of the inventory is to describe how you teach, not to evaluate your teaching ability.

CHOOSING TEACHING PREFERENCES

In each of the following ten sets of behaviors, rank the four responses in order of:

First preference	5 points
Second preference	3 points
Third preference	1 point
Fourth preference	No points

Be sure to assign a different weighted number (5, 3, 1, or 0) to each of the four descriptions in the set. Do not make ties.

I. Classroom Atmosphere

The classroom atmosphere I feel best about emphasizes the following:

_____ 1. A warm, friendly supportive atmosphere in which students are encouraged to work collaboratively, and to share their personal thoughts, feelings, and experiences; to interact with one another.

_____ 2. An organized, systematic, activity-oriented, teacher-directed atmosphere in which students are actively engaged in purposeful work.

_____ 3. An intellectually stimulating atmosphere in which students are provided with a variety of resources and activities designed to develop their critical thinking skills, and to stretch their limits of performance.

_____ 4. A flexible, innovative atmosphere with a minimum of restrictions in which students are encouraged to create their own activities for learning. A classroom with many resources chosen or designed to stimulate curiosity.

II. Teaching Techniques

My teaching techniques often provide for activities:

_____ 5. which usually have right or wrong answers and require students to draw upon recall, memory and comprehension. My instructional strategies may include drill, lecture, programmed instruction, seatwork, homework, question and answer sessions, practice, worksheets, workbooks, hands on activities, demonstrations, field trips and competitive games.

_____ 6. in which students are personally and emotionally involved in their learning, and in which they work collaboratively and cooperatively with others. My instructional strategies may include small group discussion, sharing personal feelings and experiences, social problem-solving, role plays, simulations, peer tutoring, small and large group projects, team games, sensitivity training, team-building and consensus decision-making.

_____ 7. in which students can explore their creative abilities, find ways for self-expression, gain inspiration and explore personal values. My instructional strategies may include open-ended discussions, discussing moral dilemmas, values clarification, creative and artistic activities, personal contracts, creative writing, divergent expression, synectics, guided fantasy, inventing, imagining, writing poetry, using analogies, and exploring alternative belief systems.

_____ 8. in which students are challenged to think critically, to deduce consequences, to compare and contrast, to analyze, synthesize and evaluate alternatives. My instructional strategies may include independent research, reading assignments, written essays, debating issues, brainstorming, problem-solving, divergent thinking, the Socratic method of questioning, lecture, systems analysis, theorizing, and research methods.

III. Planning

I am most comfortable and do my best teaching when my plans:

_____ 9. account for the students' personal, social, and survival skills, rather than following a curriculum guide or textbook. I tend to respond to the "here and now" class needs in order to capitalize on spontaneous events for instruction. My plans may be well developed but not followed.

_____ 10. follow prescribed curriculum guides or text chapters, which are translated into specific weekly or daily plans. Any variation in activity is thought out in detail, and schedule changes are rarely made.

_____ 11. are based on the interests and curiosities of the students. Curriculum guides, texts, and materials are used as resources for a constantly changing program rather than as the program itself.

_____ 12. follow a broad outline in which the main concepts or themes are identified and looked at from several directions and disciplines; focus on conceptual objectives rather than measured results. Units are organized around key open-ended questions or themes, with details left to emerge during instruction.

IV. Preferred Qualities of Students

I especially like young persons who:

_____ 13. are honest with their feelings, are sensitive to the rights and feelings of others, and place a high value on relationships with significant adults, friends, and getting along with people.

_____ 14. are clear about what they like and don't like, have well defined goals, are task oriented, organized, neat, complete their work on time, are respectful and well prepared in class.

_____ 15. have insights and original ideas, who are concerned with larger issues, sometimes question the way things are done, and may have artistic interests and abilities.

_____ 16. are relatively mature and knowledgeable, are excited by ideas, able to articulate their thoughts and can work well independently.

V. Teacher-Student Interaction

I am at my best when teaching students who:

_____ 17. are interested in ideas and theories behind the facts, like to work independently, display patience and persistence in completing difficult tasks and strive for perfection.

_____ 18. have strong personal interests, look beyond facts and details to see broader perspectives; are open to the unusual; are not confined by convention; are interested in solving problems with particular reference to human welfare.

_____ 19. are comfortable sharing their personal thoughts and feelings; like to work cooperatively with another student or in small groups; are interested in other people and act on their behalf; relate to me positively and cooperatively.

_____ 20. like to take action on their ideas, who learn best from direct experience and step by step procedures, have a high energy level for completing tasks, and want to have clear answers/products which tell them then-and-there how well they are doing.

VI. Classroom Management

I *manage* my class by:

_____ 21. establishing well-defined rules and procedures, and covering content in an orderly, prescribed manner, by sticking to a good lesson plan.

_____ 22. responding to and being sensitive to my students' needs; by allowing students to work cooperatively in an informal setting.

_____ 23. providing a flexible structure which allows students to choose learning activities from a variety of alternatives. The work environment may include projects or questions which are offered more for the stimulation of ideas and for the richness of the experience than for attaining and measuring specific outcomes.

_____ 24. constructing learning situations where students are challenged to think for themselves, to discover and apply new knowledge and concepts, and to work through and find solutions to problems.

VII. Appropriate Behaviors

In working with students to achieve appropriate behavior, I prefer to:

_____ 25. assist students to think/feel through the consequences and the significance of their behavior in order to enable them to acquire an internal sense of discipline and morality.

_____ 26. establish clear standards and expectations for correct behavior, preferably in a written form, such as policy. Punitive consequences for infractions of rules is consistent and predictable— "Firm but Fair."

_____ 27. arrange a person to person conference, enlist the help of a small group of students, or even to bring up the issue with the whole class in order to help the student to behave in a socially acceptable manner.

_____ 28. examine the basis and justification for the rules, in order to make sense to students and to me. At times, I am a bit annoyed when students don't use self discipline to behave in an obviously sensible and prudent way.

VIII. Teaching Behavior

As I teacher I tend to be:

_____ 29. insightful, chaotic, creative. I try to inspire my students to explore possibilities and to find ways of self-expression.

_____ 30. intellectual and knowledge oriented. I try to serve as a resource person to my students and assist them in their inquiries. I try to stimulate my students' intellectual development, asking "why" questions which require independent thought.

_____ 31. pragmatic, work- and efficiency-oriented. I tend to be the primary source of information and tasks and spend the majority of my time communicating information and directing students as to what to do and how to do it.

_____ 32. warm, friendly, and empathetic. My main focus is to stimulate students to work cooperatively, to feel good about themselves, to participate in open-ended discussions, and to share their personal thoughts and feelings.

IX. Evaluation

In considering the evaluation of student work (assignments, grades, etc), I am inclined to emphasize the following factors:

_____ 33. what is observable, measurable, and quantifiable. The focus is on what the students know and can demonstrate.

_____ 34. the student's abilities to reason, to conceptualize, to understand, and the ability to apply what has been learned to new situations.

_____ 35. each student's achievement in light of his efforts, individual abilities, and personal problems or needs.

_____ 36. opportunities for students to evaluate their own work, and to establish their own aesthetic and performance criteria.

X. Educational Goals

In summary, my educational goals generally center around:

_____ 37. providing support for the development of a positive self concept, the acquisition of survival skills, and teaching skills which enable one to communicate and interact better with students.

_____ 38. the mastery of specific content and skills by being able to read, doing basic arithmetic, finding and collecting information, presenting data, and organizing facts.

_____ 39. understanding of concepts, interpreting ideas, hypothesizing, research methods and critical thinking.

_____ 40. the development of a student's personal potential and competence, creative abilities, and the clarity of personal beliefs in relation to themselves and the human community.

CATEGORIZING BEHAVIORS

In each of the ten categories, the behaviors correspond to four different teaching styles. The teaching styles are based on the different ways people prefer to use their perception (sensing and intuition) and their judgment (thinking and feeling). The preference for either type of perception function is independent of the preference for either type of judgment function. As a result, four distinct combinations occur:

1. Sensing/Thinking   (ST)
2. Sensing/Feeling   (SF)
3. Intuitive/Thinking (IT)
4. Intuitive Feeling   (IF)

SCORING

Before scoring your Teaching Style Inventory, please rank order the styles based upon your own immediate perceptions of your teaching preferences. Please carefully read the style descriptions which follow and then determine which description is most characteristic, next most characteristic, third most, and least characteristic. Remember that everyone operates in all four styles, but that we tend to choose one particular style more often than the others.

Teaching Domains

Sensing/Thinking Teachers: are primarily outcomes-oriented (skills learned, projects completed). They maintain highly structured, well-organized classroom environments. Work is purposeful, emphasizing the acquisition of skills and information. Plans are clear and concise.

Discipline is firm but fair. Teachers serve as the primary information source and give detailed directions for student learning.
(Preference _____)

Sensing/Feeling Teachers: are empathetic and people-oriented. Emphasis is placed on the students' feelings of positive self-worth. The teacher shares personal dealings and experiences with students and attempts to become personally involved in students' learning. The teacher believes that school should be fun and introduces much learning through games and activities that involve the students actively and physically. Plans change frequently to meet the mood of the class..
(Preference _____)

Intuitive/Thinking Teachers: are intellectually oriented. The teacher places primary importance on students' intellectual development. The teacher provides the time and the intellectual challenges to encourage students to develop skills in critical thinking, problem solving, logic, research techniques and independent study. Curriculum planning is developed around concepts frequently centering around a series of questions or themes. Evaluation is often based on open-ended questions, debates, essays or position papers.
(Preference _____)

Intuitive/Feeling Teachers: are innovatively oriented. The teacher encourages students to explore their creative abilities. Insights and innovative ideas highly valued. Discussions revolve around generating possibilities and new relationships. The classroom environment is often full of creative clutter. The teacher encourages students to develop their own unique styles. Curriculum emphases focus on creative thinking, moral development, values, and flexible, imaginative approaches to learning. Curiosity, insight, and artistic self expression are welcomed.
(Preference _____)

Teaching Styles Self Profile

1. Most characteristic _____

2. Next most characteristic _____

3. Third most characteristic _____

4. Least characteristic _____

Now that your teaching styles have been entered based on your personal judgments, turn to the directions for computing your Teaching Style Inventory scores; then complete the Teaching Styles Profile. You are now in a position to compare the subjective or personal analysis of your teaching style preference with the identification of style from the Teaching Style Inventory.

SCORING TEACHING PREFERENCES

To complete your teaching preference score for each of the four teaching styles, transfer your rank numbers from the answer sheets to the scoring sheet below for each of the behaviors. Compute your score by adding the rank numbers for each column.

		Column 1 (SF)	Column 2 (ST)	Column 3 (NT)	Column 4 (NF)
I.	Classroom Atmosphere	1. _____	2. _____	3. _____	4. _____
II.	Teaching Techniques	6. _____	5. _____	8. _____	7. _____
III.	Planning	9. _____	10. _____	12. _____	11. _____
IV.	Preferred Qualities of Students	13. _____	14. _____	16. _____	15. _____
V.	Teacher/Student Interaction	10. _____	20. _____	17. _____	18. _____
VI.	Classroom Management	22. _____	21. _____	24. _____	23. _____
VII.	Appropriate Behaviors	27. _____	26. _____	28. _____	25. _____
VIII.	Teacher Behavior	32. _____	31. _____	30. _____	29. _____
IX.	Evaluation	35. _____	33. _____	34. _____	36. _____
X.	Goals	37. _____	38. _____	39. _____	40. _____
	TOTALS	_____	_____	_____	_____

Appendix 3: Teacher Observation Sheets

Peer Exchange and Self-Observation Sheets*

Lesson Plan Analysis (Self-Reflection)

1. What are the specific objectives for the class session?
2. How can I set the scene for the lesson?
3. What is the general pacing strategy, that is, about how much time will the students spend on each major objective?
3. What learning activities and tasks will the students participate in to accomplish those objectives?
4. How will the learning be assessed, and how will students receive feedback?
5. What alternative scenarios are available in case one of the planned activities does not work?

Peer Exchange Descriptive Observation

TEACHER _____ OBSERVER _____

CLASS _____ Attendance _____ Date _____

LESSON OUTLINE

_____ minutes _____

_____ minutes _____

_____ minutes _____

_____ minutes _____

_____ minutes _____

ASSIGNMENT: _____

*Each of these observation sheets should be laid out on a single full page with adequate space for detail and comments.

Peer Exchange Descriptive Observation

1. Brief description of the class: objectives and activities

2. Methods of instruction used

3. Interaction Ratios

    A. teacher-talk to student-talk: _____

    B. teacher–students (lecture) : _____

    C. students–students: _____

    D. teacher–student: _____

    E. student–students: _____

Descriptive Self-Observation of Writing Assignment

1. Objectives for the writing assignment:

2. Purpose for writing:

3. Sequence of activities:

    A. students prepared for writing assignment

    B. motivation for writing

    C. group / pair / individual work

    D. response and feedback opportunities

        (1) by peers

        (2) by teacher

4. Assessment of written assignment:

Self-Observation / Peer Exchange: Checking Learning

1. Learning was checked by asking students to

    A. perform a task: _____

    B. do an exercise: _____

    C. answer questions: _____

    D. other: _____

2. Did students check themselves or others? How? How might they have been part of the checking?

2. What other ways might have been used?

3. How was class work organized to permit the check on individual learning?

4. What form(s) did the feedback take?

    A. teacher

        (1) written: _____

        (2) oral: _____

        (3) other (e.g., nonverbal cues): _____

    B. student(s):   individual: _____ groups: _____

        (1) written: _____

        (2) oral: _____

        (3) other: _____

5. How successful was the feedback?

6. How did students respond to the feedback?

7. What evidence of learning was collected?

    A. written: _____

    B. oral: _____

    C. other: _____

(adapted from Pak, 1986, pp. 45-47)

Teacher Feedback/Teacher Interaction Questions

1. What is the ratio of "teacher-talk" to "student-talk"? That is, am I using primarily the lecture format, am I dominating discussions, or am I allowing students to participate fully during the class?

2. What sort of questions do I ask? Do the questions require a simple yes/no answer to affirm my statements, or do I give students opportunities to analyze, form opinions, and discuss those ideas? And how long do I wait for answers? How do I prepare students to answer questions?

3. What are my patterns of feedback in the classroom? That is, how do I answer questions, give praise, or give clarification and correction?

4. What are the typical patterns of interaction in my classroom: teacher/students, students/students, small group work, pair work? What are the ratios of each? Which patterns seem most successful for learning? Why?

5. How much time does the class spend on learning activities? That is, what is the time-on-task during which the students are actively engaged in instructional tasks?

6. What events in the classroom cause me to deviate from my planned lessons? How often does that happen? Is the result usually positive or usually negative?

7. How do I use the classroom space? What are the possibilities for different seating arrangements? And when different seating arrangements are used, what is the effectiveness of those changes?

(adapted from McGroarty, 1989b; Nunan, 1989c; Richards, 1990b; Richards and Lockhart, 1991–1992; Underhill, 1992)

GLOSSARY

Action Research Also called classroom-based research, action research comprises questions concerned with bettering teaching are investigated by, reflected upon, and answered—though not necessarily published—by teachers.

Basic Writers Students who Shaughnessy (1977) described as "severely underprepared" student writers; ESL students are often included in this category.

CAI Computer-Assisted Instruction.

CALL Computer-Assisted Language Learning.

Case Study Research Studies that involve careful and detailed observations of a single "case" over a period of time and/or a small group of writers during a single situation; often associated with "think-aloud protocols."

Cognitivist Approach Pedagogy that sees writing as a thinking and problem-solving process in which defining rhetorical expectations, generating solutions to writing problems, and developing writing strategies are the foci of the class.

Coherence The underlying organizational structure that makes the words and sentences in discourse unified and meaningful for the reader.

Cohesion Specific words and phrases (e.g., transitions, pronouns, repetition of key words and phrase) that tie prose together and direct the reader.

Collaboration Student writers grouped to work together in order to (a) strengthen the community of the class, (b) negotiate meaning with the authentic peer audience, (c) diversify the pace and activities of the class, and (d) offer students with differing learning styles and strategies additional opportunities for learning.

Collaborative Learning Pedagogy that uses thoughtfully organized group activities as a means of enhancing academic achievement and affective variables.

Communicative Competence An approach to language teaching that holds that (a) teaching materials should be authentic and contextualized, (b) activities real and purposeful, (c) the individual learner needs are paramount, and (d) language is learned for the purpose of communicating effectively.

Contrastive Analysis Studies that examined features of a native language and contrasted them with features of a foreign language; more recently extended to include error analysis, which examines actual language performance of learners in order to determine the sources of error.

Contrastive Rhetoric Investigation of the different ways writers from different cultures organize and present written material that reflect the preferences of each particular culture; writers from one culture who write for readers in another culture often have problems with fulfilling audience expectations.

Controlled Writing Activity in which students are asked to copy pieces of discourse, making discrete changes or filling in the blanks in the discourse.

Culture The overall system of perceptions and beliefs, values, and patterns of thought that direct and constrain a social group.

Curriculum A general statement of the goals of the course that articulates the intended and attainable outcomes of the writing class or writing program.

Discourse Written or spoken chunks of language; expression that contains more than one sentence that also has meaning.

Discourse Community A group of people who share values, aims, aspirations, and expectations concerning the way ideas are presented in writing; also called "interpretive communities." Examples: the Engineering Department discourse community, the English Department community.

ESE Edited Standard English: that is, correct written English discourse.

EAP English for Academic Purposes: that is, studying English in order to study at an English speaking institution.

EFL English as a Foreign Language: often limited to students studying English in their native countries.

Empirical Research Studies in which data about writing are gathered and statistically analyzed (e.g., through a survey, through text analysis).

Error Analysis An extension of the research of contrastive analysis that examines the actual language performance of ESL/EFL learners in order to determine whether the source of errors is first language interference or developmental.

Error Gravity Research Studies that investigate the "irritation" or "acceptance" levels of native speakers of English (usually university professors) to specific second language errors.

ESL English as a Second Language: often limited to students studying English in an English speaking country.

Ethnographic Research Studies in which observers enter a specific setting (such as an elementary school classroom) to collect data and to analyze writing processes.

Expressive Writing Pedagogy focused on sincerity, spontaneity, originality, and individual discovery.

FTA Foreign Teaching Assistant; also called an ITA (International Teaching Assistant).

Formative Response Feedback given by students or teachers that allows students to act, to revise their writing.

Freewriting A pre-writing activity that requires writers to put all their ideas on paper quickly, without revisions to words and sentence structure that could "interrupt" thought; also called brainstorming and quickwriting.

Holistic Scoring Evaluation of a piece of writing in which the rater reads the paper without marking on it, then rates the paper as a whole (holistically) and assigns the paper a single "whole" score within a given range (on scales of, for example, 1-4, 1-6, 1-9).

Invention Heuristics Organized lists of questions that help writers generate, develop, and arrange ideas.

LEP Limited English Proficiency: often limited to immigrant and refugee students in the United States.

Metacognition The processes of thinking about thinking, learning about learning, and thinking about how one learns.

NES Native English Speaker.

NNS Non-native speaker of English.

NS Native speaker of English.

Paradigm A common body of beliefs and assumptions held by most practitioners in the field.

Peer Review Groups Student writers grouped collaboratively who develop an interactive relationship with their readers by writing, talking, reading, and learning about their own and others' writing; also called peer response, peer evaluation, peer critique, or peer editing workshops.

Prewriting Initial stages of writing; can involve freewriting, listing, looping, outlining, and so on.

Reader-Based Prose A research term suggested by Linda Flower (1979) that describes writing in which the writer expresses thoughts for an audience instead of just for her/himself.

Revision A sequence of changes, often recursive, in a piece of writing, changes that occur continuously through the writing of a piece of discourse.

Rhetoric Any use of formal language that seeks to persuade, explain, or describe.

Schemata Conventional knowledge structures that are activated as we collect and interpret experience; analogous to computer files into which data is constantly being placed.

Schema Theory Research Studies of the impact of background knowledge on learning; in ESL writing, three kinds of schema form the basis for investigation: content schemata, linguistic schemata, and formal (or rhetorical) schemata.

Sheltered Writing Classes Classes organized for and populated by non-native speakers of English.

Strategies What people do in order to learn and how they manage those efforts.

Syllabus The specific descriptions of the intended outcomes of a course, including the plan for the course, and the criteria to be met by those who teach and/or take the course.

TEFL Teaching English as a Foreign Language.

TESL Teaching English as a Second Language.

Think-Aloud Protocols Case study research in which writers speak their thoughts as they compose, or plan, or revise their writing.

Writer-Based Prose Writing in which the writer expresses thoughts for her/himself, in contrast to Reader-Based Prose, in which the writer expresses thoughts for an audience.

Writer's Workbench A series of computer text-analysis programs developed by Bell Laboratories.

WAC Writing Across the Curriculum, a curriculum that focuses on writing in all academic disciplines.

ANNOTATED BIBLIOGRAPHY

Chapter 1: Overview of Native English Speaker (NES) Composition

Bartholomae, D. and Petrosky, A. (1986). *Facts, Artifacts, and Counterfacts.* Upper Montclair, NJ: Boynton/Cook.
A teacher's book for Basic Writing that does not pander to the myth of intellectual deficiency, but rather offers students academic discourse to interpret that allows them to become more familiar with the language and discourse of the university.

Connor, R. and Glenn, C. 1992. *The St. Martin's Press Guide to Teaching Writing.* New York: St. Martin's Press.
This teacher-training book is based on three hypotheses: writing is teachable, students learn to write from trial-and-error rather than lecture-oriented classes, and theory and teaching methods must "work" in order to be valid for teachers. Clearly written, it is a valuable addition to current teacher-training programs.

Elbow, P. (1973). *Writing Without Teachers.* London: Macmillan Education.
A popular presentation of Elbow's theories and practice of freewriting that will assist writers to free themselves from constraints that impinge on successful writing.

Irmscher, W. F. (1979). *Teaching Expository Writing.* New York: Holt, Rinehart, and Winston.
The first widely used standard text for composition teacher-training in the early '80s; the clear, detailed writing contains excellent explanations and sound advice concerning classroom strategies and all relevant aspects of teaching writing.

Lindemann, E. (1987). *A Rhetoric for Writing Teachers* (2nd Ed.). New York: Oxford University Press.
An academic approach for the composition teacher-training class; it summarizes much research on the theories of rhetoric, then intersperses information about theory and practice with the major issues in the teaching of writing, with substantial information on classroom management and materials.

Murray, D. (1985). *A Writing Teacher Teaches Writing* (2nd Ed.) Boston: Houghton Mifflin.
A personal, highly readable account of Murray's philosophy of teaching that contains valuable suggestions for collaborative learning and teacher-response classrooms.

North, S. M. (1990). *The Making of Knowledge in Composition: Portrait of an Emerging Field.* Upper Montclair, NJ: Boynton/Cook.
The author wrote this book for the methodological community of composition teachers in the 90s. Beginning with a historical overview of the emerging field of composition, he then devotes sections of the book to answering such questions as what do we do (Practitioners), what does it mean (Scholars), and what happens (Researchers).

Reid, S. D. (1992). *The Prentice-Hall Guide for College Writers* (2nd Ed.). Englewood Cliffs, NJ: Prentice Hall.
   A freshman composition textbook based on Kinneavian "aims" (Observing, Remembering, Investigating, etc.) that uses both experienced writers' and student writers' essays to provide content and strategies for effective academic writing.

Shaughnessy, M. (1977). *Errors and Expectations: A Guide for Teachers of Basic Writing.* New York: Oxford University Press.
   An important exploration of Basic Writers' essays that focuses on error analysis and the teaching of coping strategies that allow Basic Writers to write effective academic prose.

Tate, G. and Corbett , E. P. J. (Eds.). (1988). *The Writing Teacher's Sourcebook* (2nd Ed.). New York: Oxford University Press.
   A collection of seminal articles in the research and teaching of composition that provides an overview of the development of the field.

Weiner, H. S. (1981). *The Writing Room.* New York: Oxford University Press.
   A practical book for new Basic Writing teachers that offers general advice, curricular suggestions (especially the ideas of focusing on rhetoric, not grammar, and of practicing writing) and materials.

Chapter 2: Overview of ESL Composition

Celce-Murcia, M. (Ed.). (1991). *Teaching English as a Second or Foreign Language* (2nd Ed.). New York: Newbury House.
   This updated edition is widely used in introductory ESL methods courses. The articles, written by well-known experts in the field, range from a review of second language acquisition research to the teaching of grammar to issues in ESL writing.

Connor, U. and Johns, A. M. (1990). *Coherence in Writing.* Alexandria, Va.: Teachers of English to Speakers of Other Languages (TESOL).
   Written by a group of international authors, the papers in this collection focus on the following areas: a theoretical overview of coherence that attempts to define coherence; coherence models—that is, how coherence actually functions, studies of student writing, and pedagogical approaches.

Douglas, D. (Ed.). (1990). *English Language Testing in U.S. Colleges and Universities.* Washington, DC: National Association for Foreign Student Affairs (NAFSA).
   A book "intended for those working with international students on U.S. college and university campuses" (p. v). It includes articles explaining and evaluating large-scale discrete point tests as well as direct tests of writing. In addition, it provides information for teachers and administrators concerning the interpretation of test scores.

Krashen, S. (1983). *Principles and Practices in Second Language Acquisition.* New York: Pergamon Press.
   A readable explanation of second language acquisition that describes the "natural approach," the "monitor model," the "affective filter," and other curricular approaches to teaching ESL. While the research is thin, the application of the theories has proved workable, particularly in the beginning or basic levels of the second language classroom.

Kroll, B. (Ed.). (1990). *Second Language Writing: Research Insights for the Classroom.* New York: Cambridge University Press.

This seminal collection of articles is addressed to the teacher-in-training as well as to experienced teachers in the field of ESL. It is divided into two sections: the first presents "the current state of thinking on what the teaching of writing to nonnative speakers entails" (p. 3); the second section presents a "variety of specific studies, each focused on a different aspect of writing and/or the writing classroom" (pp. 3–4).

Larsen-Freeman, D. (1986). *Techniques and Principles in Language Teaching.* New York: Oxford University Press.

A clear, basic, brief overview of widely used ESL teaching methods such as grammar-translation, audio-lingual, the Silent Way, Community Language Learning, etc. The book is arranged in chapters that give the general organization and atmosphere of each classroom methodology as well as the techniques, approaches, and principles used in ESL classrooms that implement each method.

Long, M. L. and Richards, J. C. (Eds.). (1987). *Methodology in TESOL: A Book of Readings.* New York: Harper and Row (Newbury House).

A collection of informative, representative articles on general issues of ESL teaching methodology, and, more important, key articles in the skill areas of grammar, reading, writing, listening, speaking, and vocabulary. The authors, teachers of ESL, EFL, adults, and children in a variety of settings, provide an equally various set of viewpoints to help the reader become aware of both issues and answers in teaching ESL.

Raimes, A. (1983). *Techniques in Teaching Writing.* New York: Oxford University Press.

A brief language-based methodology textbook for use by ESL writing teachers; it contains many ideas for classroom activities.

Chapter 3: Pedagogical Issues in ESL Writing

Althen, G. (Ed.). (1981). *Learning Across Cultures: Intercultural Communication and International Educational Exchange.* Washington, DC: National Association of Foreign Student Affairs (NAFSA).

An introduction to the field of cross-cultural communication, this collection of articles contains chapters on the dynamics of cross-cultural adjustment, cross-cultural counseling, English language teaching, communication and problem-solving across cultures, and learning styles.

Byrd, P. (Ed.). (1986). *Teaching Across Cultures in the University ESL Program.* Washington, DC: NAFSA.

An excellent collection of papers that provide background discussions of relevant issues in cross-cultural communication, useful descriptions of cultural programs developed at several institutions, and explanations of materials and methods developed by individual teachers for use in cross-cultural classrooms.

Connor, U., and Kaplan, R. B. (Eds.). (1987). *Writing Across Languages: Analysis of L2 Text.* Reading, MA: Addison-Wesley.

A collection of articles that describe the concept of contrastive rhetoric, discuss empirical research in the contrastive rhetoric of many languages with English, and suggest applications of such research in the teaching of ESL writing. The book is an excellent sourcebook for contrastive rhetoric.

Devine, J., Carrell, P., and Eskey, D. (Eds.). (1987). *Research in Reading as a Second Language.* Washington, DC: TESOL.

A series of papers presented at the Third Annual Colloquium on Research in Reading as a Second Language at the 1985 TESOL Convention. Papers focus on ESL reading as interaction with a text, in which reading is an active process that involves reader, text, and writer. Each article is followed by a respondent's short discussion of issues.

Kaplan, R. B. (Ed.) (1983). *Annual Review of Applied Linguistics: 1982.* Rowley, MA: Newbury House Publishers.

This third volume of the series is directed toward studies related to written text, more specifically to contrastive rhetoric articles that study the rhetorical differences between English and such languages as German, Hindi, Korean, Mandarin, and Marathi. Kaplan introduces the collection and provides an integrative essay in conclusion.

Leki, I, and Carson, J. (Eds.). (Forthcoming). *Second Language Perspectives on Reading in the Second Language Classroom.* New York: Newbury House / Heinle and Heinle.

This collection of articles on the ESL reading-writing connection is the first to examine the importance and potential impact of reading on writing. The articles range from an overview of the history of reading in the ESL writing classroom, through theoretical chapters on both the cognitive and social perspectives of literacy development, to practical chapters on how the reading-writing relationship informs classroom practices.

Purves, A. (Ed.). (1988). *Writing Across Languages and Cultures: Issues in Contrastive Rhetoric.* Newbury Park, CA: Sage Publications.

The collection of research articles from scholars of several countries addresses the issue of cultural expectations in the assessment of writing by non-native speakers of a language. How these writers deviate from the norms of the foreign culture in the kinds of material they choose, the style, and the organization of their prose is examined by the researchers.

Pusch, M. (Ed.) (1979). *Multicultural Education: A Cross-Cultural Training Approach.* La Grange Park, IL: Intercultural Network.

Originally designed for faculty in teacher education programs, this collection of papers includes discussions of the theories of intercultural communication, definitions of cultures, teaching strategies, evaluation procedures, and suggestions for in-service training for ESL faculty.

Samovar, L. A., and Porter, R. E. (Eds.). (1991). *Intercultural Communication: A Reader* (6th Ed.). Belmont, CA: Wadsworth.

This book contains interesting and informative articles by a large number of international educators in the field of cross-cultural communication. Each chapter examines current issues in the field, ranging from the sociocultural necessity of effective communication to cultural-specific essays, from the impact of Confucianism in East Asia to Arabic concepts of effective persuasion, to the cultural patterns of the Masai.

Tannen, D. (Ed.). 1982. *Spoken and Written Language: Exploring Orality and Literacy.* Norwood, NJ: Ablex.

An interdisciplinary inquiry into the broad questions of orality and literacy and a close comparative analysis of spoken and written texts. A diverse group of authors presents empirical and ethnographic research from such fields as anthropology, sociology, education, and linguistics that analyze and contrast oral and written text.

Valdes, J. M. (Ed.). (1986). *Culture Bound: Bridging the Cultural Gap in Language Teaching.* 1986. Cambridge, MA: Cambridge University Press.
> This collection of articles brings together representative theoretical and practical material in the field of cross-cultural communication. Part I contains articles focusing on language, thought, and culture as they affect language learning. Part II presents cultural information about particular groups in order to assist teachers.

Wenden, A., and Rubin, J. (Eds.). (1987). *Learner Strategies in Language Learning.* Englewood Cliffs, NJ: Prentice-Hall.
> This text presents learner strategies as the key to learner autonomy and a source of insight into the difficulties of unsuccessful language learners. The authors offer suggestions for how teachers can take an active role in diagnosing student learning styles and doing strategy training.

Chapter 4: Curriculum and Syllabus Design

Bowen, J. D., Madsen, H. and Hilferty, A. (1985). *TESOL Techniques and Procedures.* Cambridge: Newbury House (Harper and Row).
> A basic ESL methodology text that includes historical perspectives and overviews of movements in ESL teaching. Oral and written communication techniques are provided, as well as planning and evaluation techniques for course design.

Brinton, D. M., Snow, M. A., and Wesche, M. B. (1989). *Content-Based Second Language Instruction.* New York: Newbury House.
> After a discussion of the rationale and context for content-based teaching, this book uses content-based ESL programs at universities in the U.S. and Canada to explore the most appropriate situations for content-based approaches: theme-based, sheltered, or adjunct instruction. Guidelines for the development of content-based programs and materials, as well as sample assignments and evaluation procedures, are included.

Dubin, F. and Olshtain, E. (1986). *Course Design: Developing Programs and Materials for Language Learning.* New York: Cambridge University Press.
> An introductory book for course designers that ranges from general curriculum planning to practical applications of syllabi in, particularly, the oral skills and reading classrooms. The authors offer an international scope, focusing on student needs and the communicative approach to language teaching.

Nunan, D. (1989b). *Syllabus Design.* Oxford: Oxford University Press.
> One of the texts in the Language Teaching Series (edited by C. N. Candlin and H. G. Widdowson). This book focuses on central issues referring to the selection and assessment of input in language syllabus design. The concepts and procedures discussed include needs analysis, goal- and objective-setting, selection and grading of content, and selection and grading of learning tasks.

Richards, J. C. (1990c). *The Language Teaching Matrix.* Cambridge: Cambridge University Press.

   A carefully researched, well-written book that focuses on teaching as a dynamic process. Discussions of such issues as the application of appropriate theories in the classroom, the development of instructional designs and strategies, and the study of what actually happens in the classroom give both new and experienced teachers valuable insights and opportunities for change.

Chapter 5: Blind Random: The First Weeks

Brown, H. D. (1987). *Principles for Language Learning and Teaching* (2nd Ed.). Englewood Cliffs, NJ: Prentice-Hall.

   A textbook for a graduate-level class in linguistics or ESL, this book lays the theoretical foundation for current understanding of the formation and use of cognitive strategies in second language learning. Its primary purpose, however, is to focus on interdisciplinary perspectives from linguistics, psychology, and education in order to give a "comprehensive, integrated understanding of the teacher-learning process" (xii).

Kirby, D., Liner, T., with Vinz, R. (1988). *Inside Out : Development Strategies for Teaching Writing* (2nd Ed.). Portsmouth, NH: Boynton/Cook Publishers, Heinemann.

   Although this book is intended for use in courses that train secondary school English teachers for NESs, many of the chapters are relevant to the teaching of ESL writing. Specifically, the discussions of classroom environment, journal writing, responding to student writing, and the sense of audience are clear and helpful.

McCarthy, B. (1987). *The 4MAT System: Teaching to Learning Styles with Right/Left Mode Techniques.* Barrington, IL: EXCEL, Inc.

   The author details a complete explanation of the 4MAT teaching model, with the goal of a simple and efficient way to improve the odds for students in all content areas. The model is based on research findings in learning styles, right- and left- brain dominance, creativity, effective management, art, and movement/dance.

Nunan, David. (1989c) *Understanding Language Classrooms: A Guide for Teacher-Initiated Action.* New York: Prentice-Hall International.

   Nunan believes that understanding language classrooms is itself a research process and that teachers are inevitably researchers. This book introduces teachers to classroom observation and provides them with the knowledge, the skills, and the tools to become reflective "action researchers." Such information will help them connect theory to practice.

Richards, J. C. and Nunan, D. (1990). *Second Language Teacher Education.* Cambridge: Cambridge University Press.

   A collection of 19 articles examining "major issues and practices in second language teacher education" (p. xi). Designed for use in ESL teacher-training courses, the book contains valuable information , in particular in the areas of self-evaluation and peer evaluation of teaching, descriptions of learning strategies of students, and suggested forms and procedures for classroom research.

Scarcella, R. (1990). *Teaching Language Minority Students in the Multicultural Classroom.* Englewood Cliffs, NJ: Prentice Hall Regents.

The author states that "In recognition of the need to provide teachers with information concerning language minority students of diverse cultural backgrounds, [this book] discusses strategies for culturally responsive education" (p. iv). Chapters provide insights into second language acquisition, suggestions for effective classroom interaction with (primarily public school) students, and culturally responsive activities.

Scarcella, R. and Oxford, R. (1992). *The Tapestry of Language Learning: The Individual in the Communicative Classroom.* Boston: Heinle and Heinle.

    The authors present their approach to teaching, which is analogous to the weaving of many strands into a tapestry. The foundation of this approach defines the role of the teacher as information-gatherer, decision-maker, motivator, facilitator of group dynamics, provider of language input, counselor and friend, provider of feedback, and promoter of a multicultural perspective. The book offers the theoretical bases for the approach and sequenced activities for the language classroom.

Skehan, P. (1989). *Individual Differences in Second Language Learning.* London: Edward Arnold/Hodder and Stoughton.

    A research-based and somewhat sophisticated book that surveys research on individual differences in second language learning. It covers studies of language aptitude, motivation, learner strategies, and personality variables; it also discusses research in interaction between learner type and methodology.

Chapter 6: Collaborative and Cross-Cultural Activities

Brown, H. D. (1991). *Breaking the Language Barrier.* Yarmouth, Maine: Intercultural Press.

    A book written for language learners that describes first and second language acquisition research in readable language that encourages students to risk, to identify their learning strengths and weaknesses, and to develop language learning strategies. In addition to the "user friendly" introduction to language acquisition research, ESL writing teachers will appreciate the appendices in this book, which contain various self-response surveys.

Oller, J. W. Jr. and Richard-Amato, P. A. (Eds.). (1983). *Methods that Work: A Smorgasbord of Ideas for Language Teachers.* New York: Harper and Row (Newbury House).

    A collection of articles by teachers about teaching that the authors call "success stories" to "inform and interest language teachers" (p. x). The book is arranged in sections ranging from "Pragmatic Orientations" to "Roles and Drama" to "Fun and Games." It is directed more, though not exclusively, toward younger language learners.

Oxford, R. L. (1990). *Language Learning Strategies: What Every Teacher Should Know.* New York: Newbury House.

    This book provides an eight-step model for strategy training, with appropriate training exercises; it also provides activities that students can use to practice those strategies. Based on language learning research, it includes surveys for assessing students' learning strategies, concrete examples of language learning strategies, and what the author calls "a networking chapter with real-life illustrations of learning strategies in action around the world" (p. xi).

Peyton, J. K. (Ed.) (1990). *Students and Teachers Working Together: Perspectives on Journal Writing.* Alexandria, VA: TESOL.

> A collection of essays that focuses on the problems in teaching ESL writing that can be solved in part by the use of journal writing: engaging students, developing fluency and confidence in writing, and providing opportunities for authentic communication. In particular, the articles by Laura Vannett and Donna Jurich, and by Tamara Lucas, offer ESL writing teachers a variety of successful, integrated journal activities.

Richard-Amato, P. A. (1988). *Making It Happen: Interaction in the Second Language Classroom.* New York: Longman.

> The author favors a "low-anxiety, interactional" classroom in which "communication is emphasized rather than syntactic form" (p. xiii). She begins her book with chapters on the theory of second language acquisition, and she includes several articles by well-known authors in the "Related Readings" at the end of the book. In between, she presents a methodology book that also contains multiple activities for the interactive classroom.

Richard-Amato, P. A. and Snow, M. A. (Eds.) (1992). *The Multicultural Classroom: Readings for Content-Area Teachers.* New York: Longman.

> An edited collection of 26 previously published articles that focuses on public school classrooms. The articles comprise the theoretical foundation for successful teaching in a multicultural classroom, specific cultural considerations, pedagogical strategies and activities, and management issues as they apply to content-specific areas.

Shoemaker, C. L. and Shoemaker, F. F. (1991). *Interactive Techniques for the ESL Classroom.* New York: Newbury House / Harper Collins Publishers.

> Based on theoretical principles of adult learning, this is an integrated language "resource book of exercises grouped according to types: warmups and mixers, puzzlers, competitive games, critical incidents, role plays, and simulations" (p. vii) that enrich, supplement, review, and reinforce curricular materials. Each activity is classified according to affective purposes, linguistic purposes, levels, group size, materials, and procedures.

Chapter 7: English for Academic Purposes (EAP) and Integrated Skills Activities

Carrell, P. L., Devine, J., and Eskey, D. E. (Eds.) (1989). *Interactive Approaches to Second Language Reading.* Cambridge: Cambridge University Press.

> This collection of articles presents current research in schema theory and its applications to the ESL reading classroom; in addition, it offers models of interactive reading curricula and applications of schema theory and interactive reading activities in the ESL reading classroom.

Hedge, T. (1988). *Writing.* Oxford: Oxford University Press.

> One of the *Resource Books for Teachers* series (edited by Alan Maley), this book offers "suggestions for helping students to overcome the difficulties they experience in developing clear, effective writing" (p. 6). It includes practical activities for EFL/ESL writers that are based on process writing, with information for each activity on level, topic, functions, form, focus, context, preparation, and in-class procedures.

Johnson, D. M. and Roen, D. H. (Eds.). (1989). *Richness in Writing: Empowering ESL Students.* New York: Longman.

This collection of articles focuses on the second language writer in the classroom and is based on two assumptions: (a) that "composing processes used by effective writers are powerful means by which students . . . can develop intellectually as they use language to discover and then express meaning," and (b) "students who have had authentic experiences with the communicative potential of their writing can then be invited to develop proficiency in the conventions of writing for a range of particular purposes and in different discourse communities" (Introduction by Stephen Gaies, pp. xi—xii). The articles offer teachers of ESL students of all ages activities and advice for producing successful academic writing.

Powell, D. (1981). *What Can I Write About? 7000 Topics for High School Students.* Urbana, IL: National Council of Teachers of English (NCTE).
　　Categorized by modes (such as description, comparison / contrast, process) and by function (for example, argumentation, research, creative writing, writing about literature), this book provides topics that include a comprehensive range of interests, knowledge, experience, feelings, and thoughts. While not all the topics are appropriate for ESL students, this resource book gives teachers countless ideas for generating writing assignments.

Chapter 8: Responding to ESL Writing

Beebe, L. M. (Ed.). (1988). *Issues in Second Language Acquisition.* New York: Newbury / Harper and Row.
　　A collection of articles by respected linguists who approach second language acquisition from multiple interdisciplinary perspectives: psycholinguistic, sociolinguistic, and neurolinguistic. These authors provide an integrated and worthwhile overview of theories of second language learning. Tom Scovel's article on classroom implementation of second language acquisition theory is especially readable and valuable for ESL writing teachers.

Freedman, S. W. (Ed.). (1985). *The Acquisition of Written Language: Revision and Response.* Norwood, NJ: Ablex.
　　This collection of articles covers a range from elementary school to university student writers. It is divided into sections on the varieties of response (student and teacher, in-class and out-of-class), revising and computing, and theories of revision. Directed primarily toward teachers of NESs, it contains valuable theory and practice in the areas of responding to student writing and teaching students to revise their writing.

Lawson, B., Ryan, S. S., and Winterowd, W. R. (Eds.). (1989). *Encountering Student Texts: Interpretive Issues in Reading Student Writing.* Urbana, IL: NCTE.
　　The chapters in this book, written by and for NES teachers of writing, address the teachers' "rigorous, personal descriptions of and reflections on how they *read* student writing" (p. 235). Contributing authors raise provocative questions concerning the assumptions they bring to student writing, the reading-writing connection as it applies to teachers reading student writing, and the complexities associated with that reading.

Leki, I. (1992). *Understanding ESL Writers: A Guide for Teachers.* New York: St. Martin's Press.
　　This book was written particularly for NES teachers of NES freshman

English classes in which there are non-native speakers of English. The focus is on immigrant students (U. S. residents) rather than international students: students who may have had limited study of the English language, either in their native country or in the U.S., but whose oral (and listening) skills may be highly developed from immersion in U.S. schools and culture. Their problems with reading and writing, and the problems faced by their teachers, are discussed in clear and cogent detail, with practical suggestions that are based on second language acquisition research and composition theory.

Smith, M. (1991). *The Macmillan Guide for Teachers of Writing.* New York: Macmillan.

Written for new teachers of NES freshman English, this book presents the teaching of writing as a complex process that "can be systematically learned, can always be changed and improved, and can be truly rewarding" (p. 1). The chapters on creating assignments and responding to writing are particularly relevant for ESL writing teachers.

Swales, J. (1990). *Genre Analysis: English in Academic and Research Settings.* New York: Cambridge University Press.

Although densely written, this book can be illuminating in its analysis of the specific genres of writing required by various discourse communities. Especially interesting for ESL writing teachers are the author's descriptions and analyses of text types frequently required in post-secondary education settings: the abstract, the research paper, and grant proposals.

Chapter 9: Evaluating ESL Writing

Cooper, C. (1991). *A Guide for Evaluating Student Writing.* New York: St. Martin's Press.

Written to accompany *The St. Martin's Guide,* (Axelrod and Cooper, 1991), a NES freshman composition textbook, this small Teacher's Manual focuses on the less experienced writing teacher. It includes sections on evaluation strategies for teachers and for students, evaluation advice for specific writing assignments (such as a remembering essay and evaluating essays), and methods for responding to portfolio grading. The last part of the text reprints "important journal articles on evaluation" (vi).

Hamp-Lyons, L. (1992). *Assessing ESL Writing in Academic Contexts.* Norwood, NJ: Ablex.

This collection of articles written by the growing number of researchers in ESL testing focuses on the testing of ESL writing. It begins with a clear, carefully written explanation of the issues in this research area. The following articles discuss assessment issues that range from validity questions concerning commercial writing tests to practical questions concerning classroom testing. Other issues include cross-cultural assessment, academic literacy, criteria and scoring models, needs assessment, and models of feedback.

Jacobs, H., Zingraf, S., Wormuth, D., Hartfiel, F., and Hughey, J. (1981). *Testing ESL Writing.* Rowley, MA: Newbury House.

This book, which gives a sound overview of ESL testing procedures for writing, focuses on the communicative aspects of written discourse as it provides guidelines for a composition testing program and training in the use of the Composition Profile. Both the book and the Composition Profile are out of print, but both are well worth owning. The text and Composition Profile sheets are available from Jane Hughey, 2516 Warwick, Oklahoma City, OK 73216.

Ruth, L. and Murphy, S. 1988. *Designing Writing Tasks for the Assessment of Writing*. Norwood, NJ: Ablex.

This book, for teachers, evaluators, and researchers, focuses on "the nature of the writing task and its interpretation" (p. xv). The first half is especially useful: it offers a thorough but readable literature review of NES writing assessment, followed by a series of recommendations concerning the selection of subjects, the wording of writing prompts, the writing of clear instructions, and the evaluation of student writing.

Spandal, V. and Stiggins, R. (1990). *Creating Writers: Linking Assessment and Writing Instruction*. New York: Longman.

Aimed at elementary and secondary teachers of NESs, this book offers practical strategies for integrating writing instruction in informal classroom-based assessment. The authors offer clear descriptions of holistic and analytic scoring procedures, with many examples of scoring guides and sample papers, as well as appropriate strategies for evaluating students' progress and problems.

Test of Written English Guide. (1990). Princeton, NJ: Educational Testing Service.

Upon request, ETS provides ESL teachers with the TOEFL *Test of Written English Guide*. This useful publication, updated regularly, provides information about the current status of the TWE and test dates, summaries of results of current ETS research on the TWE, sample TWE topics, an explanation of the scoring guide, and sample student papers that have been scored according to the guide. Write for a free copy: ETS, TOEFL Program, P.O. Box 6155, Princeton, NJ 08541.

Chapter 10: Teaching ESL Writing: Becoming a Professional

College Composition and Communication. Published monthly by the National Council of Teachers of English (NCTE), *CCC* "publishes articles dealing with the theory, practice, history, and politics of composition and its teaching at all college levels; research into the processes and teaching of writing; the preparation of writing teachers, and the relationship of literature, language studies, rhetoric, communications theory, and other fields to composition and to teaching" (editorial policy of the journal).

College English. Also published monthly by the National Council of Teachers of English (NCTE), this journal "provides a forum in which scholars working within any of the various subspecialties of the discipline can address a broad cross-section of the profession" (editorial policy of the journal). Articles are fairly sophisticated and are concerned with philosophies of teaching writing and literature.

College ESL. Subtitled "A Journal of Theory and Practice in the teaching of English as a Second Language," this journal is published twice a year by the Instructional Resource Center, The City of New York; the focus is "specifically urban immigrant and refugee adults in college and pre-college settings" (editorial policy of the journal).

Computers and Composition. Co-published three times a year by Michigan Technological University and Colorado State University, this journal publishes articles that explore the effects of computers on writing and on teachers and their classrooms at the college level, writing processes, and the effects of writing on an audience.

English Teaching Forum: Published four times a year by the United States Information Agency for the teacher of English outside the United States, it contains short practical articles by ESL teachers around the world on all aspects of teaching English as a Foreign Language (EFL), as well as audio-visual aids such as maps and records.

ESP (English for Specific Purposes) Journal. Published by Pergamon Press, the articles in *ESP Journal* concern the varieties of English found in different disciplines or discourse communities, in particular in professional and academic areas, and focus on the variety of texts produced and received by those communities.

Journal of Basic Writing. Published twice a year by the Instructional Resource Center at the City University of New York, *JBW* contains articles that focus on such matters as "the social, psychological, and cultural implications of literacy; rhetoric; discourse theory; cognitive theory; grammar; linguistics, including text analysis, error descriptions, and cohesion studies; **English as a second language;** and assessment and evaluation" (editorial policy of the journal) (emphasis mine).

Journal of Second Language Writing. Published quarterly by Ablex Publishing Company, this journal contains articles on topics related to the study and teaching of writing in a second language, including "theoretically grounded reports of research and discussions of central issues in second and foreign language writing and writing instruction at all levels of proficiency" (editorial policy of the journal).

TESOL Journal. Published quarterly by the Teachers of English to Speakers of Other Languages organization (TESOL), the *TJ* is a journal of teaching and classroom research with articles and special sections on ESL/EFL methodology and techniques, materials/curriculum design and development, teacher education, program administration, and classroom observation and research (editorial policy of the journal).

TESOL Quarterly. Also published four times a year by TESOL, the *TQ* contains articles that bridge theory and practice with research in such areas as psycholinguistics, first and second language acquisition, sociolinguistics, applied and theoretical linguistics, including reading and writing theory (adapted from the editorial policy of the journal).

Other journals of interest:

Applied Linguistics	*Reading Research Quarterly*
Japan Association of Language Teachers (JALT) Journal	*RELC Journal*
	Research in the Teaching of English
Journal of Advanced Composition	*Rhetoric Review*
Journal of Applied Linguistics	*Teaching English in the Two-Year College*
Journal of Teaching Writing	
Journal of Technical Writing and Communication	*TESL Canada Journal*
	TESL Reporter
Language Learning	*The Writing Instructor*
Modern Language Journal	*Written Communication*
Reader	

WORKS CITED

Abraham, R. (1985). Field dependence/independence in the teaching of grammar. *TESOL Quarterly, 19*(4), 680–702.

Abunowara, A. M. (1983). Contrastive analysis of Arabic and English passive structures. Unpublished master's thesis, Colorado State University.

Alderson, J. C., Kranhke, K., and Stansfield, C. (1987). *Reviews of English Language Proficiency Tests.* Washington, DC: TESOL.

Allaei, S. K. and Connor, U. M. (1990). Exploring the dynamics of cross-cultural collaboration in writing classrooms. *The Writing Instructor, 10*(1), 19–28.

Allen, W. P. (1981). A controlling frame for paragraph development. *ESL Reporter, 14*, 55–66.

Allwright, R. (1986). Making sense of instruction: What's the problem? *Papers in Applied Linguistics, 1*(1), 11.

Allwright, R. (1988). *Observation in the Language Classroom.* Harlow: Longman.

Allwright, R. L.,Woodley, M. P., and Allwright, J. M. (1988). Investigating reformulation as a practical strategy for the teaching of academic writing. *Applied Linguistics, 9*, 126–255.

Alptekin, C. (1988). Chinese formal schemata in ESL composition. *British Journal of Language Teaching, 26*(2), 112–116.

Althen, G. (1981). *Learning Across Cultures: Intercultural Communication and International Educational Exchange.* Washington,DC: NAFSA.

Anandam, K. (1983). Computer-based feedback on writing. *Computers, Reading, and Language Arts, 1*(2), 30–34.

Anderson, J. W. (1991). A comparison of Arab and American conceptions of effective persuasion. In L. A. Samovar and R. E. Porter (Eds.), *Intercultural Communication: A Reader* (pp. 96–106). Belmont, CA.: Wadsworth.

Arapoff, N. (1968). Controlled rhetoric frames. *ELT Journal, 32*(1), 27–36.

Arapoff, N. (1969). Discover and transform: A method of teaching writing to foreign students. *TESOL Quarterly, 3*(4), 297–304.

Archer, C. M. (1986). Culture bump and beyond. In J. Valdez (Ed.), *Culture Bound: Bridging the Cultural Gap in Language Teaching* (pp. 170–178). Cambridge: Cambridge University Press.

Arnaudet, M. and Barrett, M. E. (1984). *Approaches to Academic Reading and Writing.* Englewood Cliffs, NJ: Prentice-Hall.

Auerbach, B. and Snyder, B. (1983). *Paragraph Patterns.* New York: Harcourt, Brace, Jovanovich.

Augustine, D. (1981). Geometries and words: Linguistics and philosophy: A model of the composing process. *College English, 43*(3), 221–232.

Autrey, K. (1991). Toward a rhetoric of journal writing. *Rhetoric Review, 10*(1), 74–90.

Axelrod, R. B. and Cooper, C. R. (1987). *Reading Critically, Writing Well: A Reader and Guide.* Boston: St. Martin's Press.

Axelrod, R. B. and Cooper, C. R. (1991). *Reading Critically, Writing Well* (2nd ed.). New York: St. Martin's Press.

Bacig, T. D.,Evans, R. A., and Larmouth, D. W. (1991). Computer-assisted instruction in critical thinking and writing: A process/model approach. *Research in the Teaching of English, 25*(3), 365–382.

Badrawi, N. (1992) The reading dilemma: Meeting individual needs. *English Teaching Forum, 30*(3), 16–19, 31, 35.

Bailey, K. (1990). The use of diary studies in teacher education programs. In J. C. Richards and D. Nunan (Eds.), *Second Language Teacher Education* (pp. 215–226). New York: Cambridge University Press.

Ballard, B. and Clanchy, J. (1992). Assessment by misconception: Cultural influences and intellectual traditions. In L. Hamp-Lyons (Ed.), *Assessing Second Language Writing in Academic Contexts* (pp. 19–35). Norwood, NJ: Ablex.

Bander, R. (1983). *American English Rhetoric* (3rd ed.). New York: Holt, Rinehart and Winston.

Barnes, G. A. (1981). *Crisscross: Structured Writing in Context.* Englewood Cliffs, NJ: Prentice Hall.

Barnes, L. (1990). Intercultural communication stumbling blocks. In R. Spack, *Guidelines: A Cross-Cultural Reading/Writing Text* (pp. 78–87). New York: St. Martin's Press.

Barron, R. (1991). What I wish I had known about peer response groups but didn't. *English Journal, 80*(5), 24–34.

Bartholomae, D. (1985). Inventing the university. In M. Rose (Ed.), *When a Writer Can't Write: Studies in Writer's Block and Other Composing Process Problems* (pp. 134–65). New York and London: Guilford Press.

Bartholomae, D. (1991) Working with tests: Student representations of tradition, power, and authority. Paper presented at the Wyoming Conference on English (June), Laramie, WY.

Bartholomae, D. and Petrosky, A. R. (1986). *Facts, Artifacts, and Counterfacts.* Upper Montclair, NJ: Boynton/Cook.

Bartlett, L. (1990). Teacher development through reflective teaching. In J. Richards and D. Nunan (Eds.), *Second Language Teacher Education* (pp. 202–214). New York: Cambridge University Press.

Basham, C. and Kwachka, P. (1992). Reading the world differently: A cross-cultural approach to writing assessment. In L. Hamp-Lyons (Ed.), *Assessing Second Language Writing in Academic Contexts* (pp. 37–49). Norwood, NJ: Ablex.

Baskoff, F. (1971). *American English: Guided Composition.* Chicago: Rand McNally and Company.

Bassano, S. (1986). Helping learners adapt to unfamiliar methods. *ELT Journal, 40*, 13–19.

Bassano, S. and Christison, M. A. (1988). Cooperative learning in the ESL classroom. *TESOL Newsletter, 22*(2), 1, 8–9.

Bastürkmen, H. (1990). Literature and the intermediate language learner: A sample lesson with Hemingway's "Cat in the Rain." *English Teaching Forum, 28*(3), 18–21.

Batson, T. (1989). Teaching in networked classrooms. In C. Selfe, D. Rodrigues, and W. Oates (Eds.), *Computers in English and the Language Arts* (pp. 247–255). Urbana, IL: National Council of Teachers of English (NCTE).

Beach, R. and Liebman-Kleine, J. (1986). The writing/reading relationship: Becoming one's own best reader. In B. T. Peterson (Ed.), *Convergences: Transactions in Reading and Writing* (pp. 64–81). Urbana, IL: NCTE.

Beaman, K. (1984). Coordination and subordination revisited: Syntactic complexity in spoken and written narrative discourse. In D. Tannen (Ed.), *Coherence in Spoken and Written Discourse* (pp. 45–80). Norwood, NJ: Ablex.

Beebe, L. M. (Ed.). (1988). *Issues in Second Language Acquisition*. New York: Newbury/Harper and Row.

Belanger, J. (1987). Theory and research into reading and writing connections: A critical review. *Reading-Canada-Lecture, 5,* 10–18.Belanoff, P. (1991). The myth of assessment. *Journal of Basic Writing, 10*(1), 54–66.

Belanoff, P. (1991). The myth of assessment. *Journal of Basic Writing, 10*(1), 54–66.

Belanoff, P. and Dickson, M. (Eds.). *Portfolios: Process and Product.* Portsmouth, NH: Heinemann.

Benitéz, R. (1990). Using a learning log in an EFL writing class. *English Teaching Forum, 28(*3), 40–41.

Bennett, C. I. (1979). Teaching students as they would be taught: The importance of cultural perspective. *Educational Leadership, 36*(4), 259–268.

Bennett, C. I. (1986). *Comprehensive Multicultural Education: Theory and Practice.* Boston: Allyn Bacon.

Bennett, J. M. (1988). Student development and experimental learning theory. In J. Reid (Ed.), *Building the Professional Dimension of Educational Exchange* (pp. 105–119). Yarmouth, Maine: Intercultural Press.

Bennett, M. J. (1988). Intercultural communication. In J. Reid (Ed.), *Building the Professional Dimension of Educational Exchange* (pp. 121–136). Yarmouth, Maine: Intercultural Press.

Bensch, S. (Ed.). (1988). *Ending Remediation: Linking ESL and Content in Higher Education.* Washington, DC: TESOL.

Benson, B., Dening, M., Denzer, D., and Valeri-Gold, M. (1992). A combined basic writer/English as a second language class: Melting pot or mish-mash? *Journal of Basic Writing, 11*(1), 58–74.

Bentley, R.H. (1991). *And gladly count: Examining the error-reduction component of a writing program.* ERIC Document Reproduction Service No. ED 331 078.

Bereiter, C. and Scardamalia, M. (1984a). Knowledge telling and knowledge transforming in written composition. In S. Rosenberg (Ed.), *Advances in Applied Linguistics* (pp. 142–175). New York: Cambridge University Press.

Bereiter, C. and Scardamalia, M. (1984b). Learning about writing from reading. *Written Communication, 1,* 163–88.

Bereiter, C. and Scardamalia, M. (1987). *The Psychology of Written Composition.* Hillsdale, NJ: Laurence Erlbaum Associates, Publishers.

Berlin, J. (1990a). The teacher as researcher: Democracy, dialogue, and power. In D. Daiker and M. Morenberg (Eds.), *The Writing Teacher as Researcher: Essays in the Theory and Practice of Class-Based Research* (pp. 3–14). Portsmouth, NH: Boynton/Cook Heinemann.

Berlin, J. (1990b). Writing instruction in school and college English 1890–1985. In J. J. Murphy (Ed.), *History of Writing Instruction from Ancient Greece to Twentieth-Century America* (pp. 183–200). Davis, CA: Hermagoras Press.

Bernhardt, E. B. (1991). *Reading Development in a Second Language.* Norwood, NJ: Ablex.

Bernhardt, S. A., Edwards, P., and Wojalin, P. (1989). Teaching college composition with computers: A program evaluation study. *Written Communication, 6,* 108–133.

Berthoff, A. (1985). How we construe is how we construct. In P. L. Stock (Ed.), *Fforum: Essays on Theory and Practice in the Teaching of Writing* (pp. 166–170). Upper Montclair, NJ: Boynton/Cook.

Bialystok, E. (1985). The compatibility of teaching and learning strategies. *Applied Linguistics, 6,* 255–262.

Bialystok, E. (1990). *Communication Strategies: A Psychological Analysis of Second-Language Use.* Cambridge, MA: Basil Blackwell, Inc.

Biber, D. (1988). *Variations Across Speech and Writing.* New York: Cambridge University Press.

Bickes, G. and Scott, A. (1989). On the computer as a medium for language teaching. *CALICO Journal, 6*(3), 21–32.

Bickner, R. and Peyasantiwong, P. (1988). Cultural variation in reflective writing. In A. Purves (Ed.), *Writing Across Languages and Cultures: Issues in Contrastive Rhetoric* (pp. 160–174). Newbury Park, CA.: Sage Publishers.

Bishop, W. (1990). *Something Old, Something New: College Writing and Classroom Change.* Carbondale: Southern Illinois University Press.

Bishop, W. (1991). Teachers as learners: Negotiable roles in writing teachers' learning logs. *Journal of Teaching Writing, 10*(2), 217-240.

Bizzell, P. (1982). Cognition, convention, and certainty: What we need to know about writing. *PRE/TEXT, 3,* 213–43.

Bizzell, P. and Herzberg, B. (1987). *The Bedford Bibliography for Teachers.* Boston: St. Martin's Press.

Black, K. (1989). Audience analysis and persuasive writing at the college level. *Research in the Teaching of English, 23*(3), 231–253.

Black, M.C. and Kiehnhoff, D.M. (1992). Content-based classes as a bridge from the EFL to the university classroom. *TESOL Journal, 1*(4), 27–28.

Blair, R. W. (1991). Innovative approaches. In M. Celce-Murcia (Ed.), *Teaching English as a Second or Foreign Language* (2nd ed.) (pp. 23–45). New York: Newbury/Harper Collins.

Blanton, L. (1979). *Elementary Composition Practice: Book 1.* Rowley, MA: Newbury House Publishers, Inc.

Blanton, L. (1987). Reshaping ESL students' perception of writing. *ELT Journal, 41*(2), 112–118.

Blanton, L. L. (1992a). Text and context: Changing roles of reading for writers. Paper presented at the International TESOL Convention, Vancouver, B.C. (March).

Blanton, L.L. (1992b). Reading, Writing, and Authority: Issues in Developmental ESL. *College ESL, 2*(1), 11–19.

Blanton, L.L. (1992c). Talking students into writing: Using oral fluency to develop literacy. *TESOL Journal, 1*(4), 23–26.

Bleich, D. (1986). Cognitive stereoscopy and the study of language and literature. In B. T. Petersen (Ed.), *Convergences: Transactions in Reading and Writing* (pp. 99–114). Urbana, IL: NCTE.

Bliss, P. T., Burgmeier, A., Fulleright, P., Gilbert, W., Neufeld, J. K., and Richman, K. (1985). *Interface: Academic English in Context.* New York: Holt, Rinehart, and Winston.

Block, E. (1992). See how they read: Comprehension monitoring of L1 and L2 readers. *TESOL Quarterly, 26*(2), 319–343.

Blum, R. E. (1984). *Effective Schooling Practices: A Research Synthesis.* Portland, OR: Northwest Regional Educational Laboratory.

Bochner, S. (Ed.). (1982). *Cultures in Contact: Studies in Cross-Cultural Interaction.* Oxford: Pergamon Press.

Booth, W. (1963). The rhetorical stance. *College Composition and Communication, 14,* 139–145.

Bowen, J. D. and Madsen, H. (1985). *TESOL Techniques and Procedures.* Rowley, MA: Newbury House.

Braine, G. (1989). Writing in science and technology: An analysis of assignments for ten undergraduate courses. *English for Specific Purposes, 8*(1), 3–15.

Brannon, L. (1985). Toward a theory of composition. In B. McClelland and T. Donovan (Eds.), *Perspectives on Research and Scholarship in Composition* (pp. 6–25). New York: Modern Language Association.

Breen, M. (1985). Authenticity in the language classroom. *Applied Linguistics, 6,* 35–44.

Brennan, M. and Naerssen, M. V. (1989). Language and content in ESP. *ELT Journal, 43*(1), 196–205.

Brent, D. (1991). Computer-assisted commenting and theories of written response. *The Writing Instructor, 11*(1), 103–110.

Bridgeman, B. and Carlson, S. (1984). Survey of academic writing tasks. *Written Communication, 1,* 247–280.

Bridwell, L., Sirc, G., and Brooke, R. (1984). Revising and composing: Case studies of student writers. In S. W. Freedman (Ed.), *Acquisition of Writing Language: Response and Revision.* Norwood, NJ: Ablex.

Bridwell-Bowles, L. (1990). Responsibility vs. reliability: Diversity in assessing writing portfolios. Paper presented at the College Composition and Communication Conference, Chicago (March).

Brinton, D.M., Snow, M.A., and Wesche, M.B. (1989). *Content-Based Second Language Instruction.* New York: Newbury House Publishers.

Brittner-Mahyera, R.,Carkin, S.,Christison, M. A., and Huber, D. (1992). Valuing teaching. Paper presented at Intermountain TESOL (ITESOL), Provo, Utah (April).

Britton, J. (1985). Language and learning across the curriculum. In P. L. Stock (Ed.), *Fforum: Essays on Theory and Practice in the Teaching* of *Writing* (pp. 221–224). Upper Montclair, NJ: Boynton/Cook.

Britton, J., Burgess, T., Martin, N., McLeod, A., and Rosen, H. (1975). *The Development of Writing Abilities.* London: Macmillan.

Brock, M. (1990). The case for localized literature in the ESL classroom. *English Teaching Forum, 28*(3), 22–25.

Brodkey, D. (1983). An expectancy exercise in cohesion. *TESL Reporter, 16*, 43–45.

Brookes, A. and Grundy, P. (1990). *Writing for Study Purposes: A Teacher's Guide to Developing Individual Writing Skills.* Cambridge: Cambridge University Press.

Brossell, G. C. (1982). Rhetorical specifications in essay examination topics. *College English, 44*, 165–173.

Brown, G. (1990). Cultural values: The interpretation of discourse. *ELT Journal, 44*(6), 11–17.

Brown, H. D. (1986). Learning a second culture. In J. Valdes (Ed.), *Culture Bound: Bridging the Cultural Gap in Language Teaching* (pp. 33–48). Cambridge: Cambridge University Press.

Brown, H. D. (1987). *Principles of Language Learning and Teaching* (2nd ed.). Englewood Cliffs, NJ: Prentice-Hall.

Brown, H. D. (1989). Beyond communicative competence: Teaching learners how to learn. *The Language Teacher, XIII*(12), 2–6.

Brown, H. D. (1991). *Breaking the Language Barrier.* Yarmouth, Maine: Intercultural Press.

Brown, H. D. (1992). Sociocultural factors in teaching language minority students. In P. A. Richard-Amato and M. A. Snow (Eds.), *The Multicultural Classroom: Readings for Content-Area Teachers* (pp. 73–101). New York: Longman.

Brown, J. D. (1990). Where do tests fit into language programs? *JALT Journal, 12*(1), 121–140.

Brown, J.D. (1992). Classroom-centered language testing. *TESOL Journal, 1*(4), 12–15.

Brown, J. S., Collins, A., and Duguid, P. (1989). Situated cognition and the culture of learning. *Educational Researcher, 18*, 32–42.

Brownfield, S. (1984). Computer assisted ESL research. *CALICO Journal, 2*(1), 20–23.

Bruffee, K. (1986). Social construction, language, and the authority of knowledge: A bibliographic essay. *College English, 48*(8), 773–790.

Bruffee, K. A. (1984). Collaborative learning and the conversation of mankind. *College English, 46*(7), 635–652.

Brumfit, C. (1984). *Communicative Methodology in Language Teaching.* Cambridge: Cambridge University Press.

Buckingham, T. (1979). The goals of advanced composition instruction. *TESOL Quarterly, 13*(2), 241–254.

Buckingham, T. and Peck, W. (1976). An experience approach to teaching composition. *TESOL Quarterly, 10*(1), 55–65.

Budd, R. (1989). Simulating academic research: One approach to a study-skills course. *ELT Journal, 43*(1), 30–37.

Burke, K. (1945). *A Grammar of Motives.* Englewood Cliffs, NJ: Prentice-Hall.

Burnham, C. C. (1986). Portfolio evaluation: Room to breathe and grow. In C. Bridges (Ed.), *Training the New Teacher of College Composition* (pp. 125–138). Urbana, IL: NCTE.

Byrd, D. R. H. and Gallingame, G. (1990). *Write Away.* New York: Newbury House/Harper and Row.

Byrd, P. (Ed.). (1986). *Teaching Across Cultures in the University ESL Program.* Washington, DC: NAFSA.

Byrd, P. (1988). Cross-cultural half-way houses: Orientation within intensive English programs. In J. A. Mestenhauser, G. Marta, and I. Steglitz (Eds.), *Culture, Learning, and the Disciplines: A Theory and Practice in Cross-Cultural Orientation* (pp. 45–49). Washington, DC: NAFSA.

Byrd, P., Constantinides, J., and Pennington, M. (1989). *The Foreign Teaching Assistant's Manual.* New York: Macmillan.

Campbell, C. (1990). Writing with others' words: Using background reading text in academic compositions. In B. Kroll (Ed.), *Second Language Writing: Research Issues for the Classroom* (pp. 211–230). New York: Cambridge University Press.

Canale, M. and Swain, M. (1980). Theoretical bases of communication approaches to second language teaching and testing. *Applied Linguistics, 1*, 1–47.

Canesco, G. and Byrd, P. (1989). Writing required in graduate courses in business administration. *TESOL Quarterly, 23*(2), 305–316.

Caprio, M. (1990). The changing roles of the teacher and student in the second language classroom. *The Language Teacher, 14*(3), 17–20.

Carcinelli, T. A. (1980). The writing conference: A one-to-one conversation. In T. R. Donovan and B. W. McClelland (Eds.), *Eight Approaches to Teaching Composition* (pp. 101–131). Urbana, IL: NCTE.

Cardelle, M. and Corno, L. (1981). Effects on second language learning of variations in written feedback on homework assignments. *TESOL Quarterly, 15*, 251–261.

Carlson, S. (1988). Cultural differences in writing and reading skills. In A. Purves (Ed.), *Writing Across Languages and Cultures: Issues in Contrastive Rhetoric* (pp. 227–260). Newbury Park, CA: Sage Publishers.

Carlson, S., Bridgeman, B., Camp, R., and Waanders, J. (1985). *Relationship of Admission Test Scores to Writing Performance of Native and Non-Native Speakers of English* (TOEFL Research Report No. No. 19). Princeton, NJ: Educational Testing Service.

Carpenter, C. and Hunter, J. (1981). Functional exercises: Improving overall coherence in ESL writing. *TESOL Quarterly, 15*(4), 425–435.

Carrell, P. (1992). Awareness of text structure: Effects on recall. *Language Learning, 14*(2), 1–20.

Carrell, P. L. (1982). Cohesion is not coherence. *TESOL Quarterly, 16,(3)* 479–488.

Carrell, P. L. (1984a). The effects of rhetorical organization on ESL readers. *TESOL Quarterly, 18*(3), 441–469.

Carrell, P. L. (1984b). Facilitating reading comprehension by teaching text structure: What the research shows. Paper presented at the International TESOL Convention, Houston (March).

Carrell, P. L. (1984c). Inferencing in ESL: Presupposition and implications of factive and implicative predicates. *Language Learning, 34*(1), 1–22.

Carrell, P. L. (1987a). Readability in ESL: A schema-theoretic perspective. Paper presented at the International TESOL Convention, Miami (April).

Carrell, P. L. (1987b). Text as interaction: Some implications of text analysis and reading research for ESL composition. In U. Connor and R. B. Kaplan (Eds.), *Writing Across Languages: Analysis of L2 Text* (pp. 47–56). Reading, MA: Addison-Wesley.

Carrell, P. L. (1990). Reading in a foreign language: Research and pedagogy. *JALT Journal, 12*(1), 53–74.

Carrell, P. L., Devine, J., and Eskey, D. (Eds.). (1988). *Interactive Approaches to Second Language Reading*. Cambridge: Cambridge University Press.

Carrell, P. L. and Eisterhold, J. C. (1983). Schema theory and ESL reading pedagogy. *TESOL Quarterly, 17*(4), 553–574.

Carrell, P. L., Pharis, B. G., and Liberto, J. C. (1989). Metacognitive strategy training for ESL reading. Paper presented at the International TESOL Convention, San Antonio (March).

Carson, J.E. (and Kuehn, P.A. (1992). Evidence of transfer and loss in developing second language writers. *Language Learning, 42*(2), 157–182.

Carter, M. (1990). The idea of expertise: An exploration of cognitive and social dimensions of writing. *College Composition and Communication, 41*(3), 265–286.

Carter, R. and Long, M. N. (1987). *Literature in the Language Classroom*. Cambridge: Cambridge University Press.

Casanave, C.P. and Hubbard, P. (1992). The writing assignments and writing problems of doctoral students: Faculty perceptions, pedagogical issues, and needed research. *English for Specific Purposes, 11*(1), 33–49.

Celce-Murcia, M. (Ed.). (1991). *Teaching English as a Second or Foreign Language*. New York: Newbury/HarperCollins.

Chafe, W. (1982). Integration and involvement in speaking, writing, and oral literature. In D. Tannen (Ed.), *Spoken and Written Language: Exploring Orality and Literacy* (pp. 35–53). Norwood, NJ: Ablex.

Chafe, W. and Danielewicz, J. (1987). Properties of spoken and written language. In R. Horowitz and F. J. Samuels (Eds.), *Comprehending Oral and Written Language* (pp. 1–27). New York: Academic Press.

Chamot, A. U. and O'Malley, J. M. (1992). The cognitive academic language learning approach: A bridge to the mainstream. In P. A. Richard-Amato and M. A. Snow (Eds.), *The Multicultural Classroom: Readings for Content-Area Teachers* (pp. 39–57). New York: Longman.

Chapelle, C. and Green, P. (1992). Field independence/dependence in second language acquisition. *Language Learning, 14*(2), 47–83.

Chapelle, C. and Jamieson, J. (1986). Computer-assisted language learning as a predictor of success in acquiring English as a second language. *TESOL Quarterly, 20*(1), 27–46.

Chapelle, C. and Mizuno, S. (1989). Student strategies with learner-controlled CALL. *CALICO, 7*(2), 25–47.

Chappell, V. (1982). How ESL writers talk about their errors. Paper presented at the College Composition and Communication Conference, San Francisco (March).

Charles, M. (1990). Responding to problems in written English using a student self-monitoring technique. *ELT Journal, 44*(4), 298–303.

Chaudron, C. (1988). *Second Language Classrooms.* Cambridge: Cambridge University Press.

Chen-yu, F. (1981). Teaching advanced English composition to Chinese college students. Unpublished master's thesis, California State University, Fresno.

Cheng, P. (1985). An analysis of contrastive rhetoric: English and Chinese expository prose, pedagogical implications, and strategies for the ESL teacher in a ninth grade curriculum. Unpublished doctoral dissertation, Pennsylvania State University.

Chenoweth, N. A. (1987). The need to teach rewriting. *ELT Journal, 41,* 25–29.

Cheskey, J. A. and Hiebert, E. H. (1987). The effects of prior knowledge and audience on high school students' writing. *Journal of Educational Research, 80,* 304–313.

Chimombo, M. (1987). Towards reality in the writing class. *ELT Journal, 41*(3), 204–210.

Ching, L. P. and Ngooi, A. C. (1991). How journal writing improved our classes. *English Teaching Forum, 29*(3), 43–44.

Christensen, F. (1967). *Notes Toward a New Rhetoric: Six Essays for Teachers.* New York: Harper and Row.

Christison, M. A. (1990). Cooperative learning in the ESL classroom. *English Teaching Forum, 28*(4), 6–9.

Clark, J. L. (1987). *Curriculum Renewal in School Foreign Language Learning.* Oxford: Oxford University Press.

Clarke, D. F. (1989). *Talk About Literature.* London: Edward Arnold.

Clarke, M. A. and Silberstein, S. (1988). Problems, prescriptions, and paradoxes in second language teaching. *TESOL Quarterly (Forum), 22*(4), 685–700.

Clifford, J. (Ed.). (1991). *The Experience of Reading: Louise Rosenblatt and Reader-Response Theory.* Portsmouth, NH: Boynton/Cook.

Clutterbuck, M. (1988). Computers in modern languages. *BABEL, 23*(2), 29–30.

Coe, R. M. (1987). An apology for form: Or, who took the form out of process? *College English, 49,* 13–28.

Coe, R. M. and Gutierrez, K. (1981). Using problem-solving procedures and process analysis to help students with writing problems. *College Composition and Communication, 32,* 262–271.

Coffey, B. (1984). ESP: English for specific purposes. *Language Teaching, 17*(1), 2–16.

Cohen, A. (1987). Student processing of feedback on their composition. In A. Wenden and J. Rubin (Eds.), *Learner Strategies in Language Learning* (pp. 57–69). Englewood Cliffs, NJ: Prentice-Hall International.

Cohen, A. (1990). *Second Language Learning: Insights for Teachers, Learners, and Researchers.* New York: Newbury House/Harper and Row.

Cohen, A. and Cavacanti, M. C. (1990). Feedback on compositions: Teacher and student verbal reports. In B. Kroll (Ed.), *Second Language Writing: Research Insights for the Classroom* (pp. 155–177). New York: Cambridge University Press.

Cohen, M. and Riel, M. (1989). The effect of distant audiences on students' writing. *American Educational Research Journal, 26,* 143–159.

Coles, W. E. J. (1974). *Composing Writing as a Self Creating Process.* Rochelle Park: Hayden.

Coles, W. E. J. (1978). *The Plural I: The Teaching of Writing.* New York: Holt, Rinehart, and Winston.

Collie, J. and Slater, S. (1987). *Literature in the Language Classroom: A Resource Book of Ideas.* New York: Cambridge University Press.

Collier, R. M. (1983). The word processor and revision strategies. *College Composition and Communication, 35,* 149–155.

Comprone, J. J. (1986). Integrating the acts of reading and writing about literature: A sequence of assessments based on James Joyce's "Counterparts." In B. T. Petersen (Ed.), *Convergences: Transactions in Reading and Writing* (pp. 215–230). Urbana, IL: NCTE.

Condon, W. and Hamp-Lyons, L. (1991). Introducing a portfolio-based writing assessment: Progress through problems. In P. Belanoff and M. Dickson (Eds.), *Portfolios: Process and Product* (pp. 231–247). Portsmouth, NH: Heinemann.

Connor, R. and Glenn, C. (1992). *The St. Martin's Guide to Teaching Writing* (2nd ed.). New York: St. Martin's Press.

Connor, U. (1983). Cross-cultural differences and perceived quality in written paraphrases of English expository prose. *Applied Linguistics, 4*(3), 259–268.

Connor, U. (1984). A study of cohesion and coherence in English as a second language students' writing. *Papers in Linguistics: International Journal of Communication, 17,* 301–316.

Connor, U. and Farmer, M. (1990). The teaching of topical structure analysis as a revision strategy for ESL writers. In B. Kroll (Ed.), *Second Language Writing: Research Insights for the Classroom* (pp. 126–139). New York: Cambridge University Press.

Connor, U. and Johns, A. M. (1990). *Coherence in Writing.* Alexandria, VA: TESOL.

Connor, U. and Kaplan, R. B. (Eds.). (1987). *Writing Across Languages: Analysis of L2 Text.* Reading, MA.: Addison-Wesley.

Connor, U. and Lauer, J. (1985). Understanding persuasive essay writing: Linguistic/rhetorical approach. *Text, 5*(4), 309–326.

Constantinides, J. and Hall, C. (1981). Advanced composition: Beginning at the top. In M. Hines and W. Rutherford (Eds.), *On TESOL '81* (pp. 79–87). Washington, D.C: TESOL.

Cook, V. J. (1988). Designing CALL programs for common teaching. *ELT Journal, 42*(4), 262–271.

Cooper, C. and Odell, L. (1977). *Evaluating Writing: Describing, Measuring, Judging.* Urbana, IL: NCTE.

Cooper, C. and Odell, L. (Eds.). (1978). *Research in Composing: Points of Departure.* Urbana, IL: NCTE.

Cooper, C. R. (1991). *A Guide for Evaluating Writing.* New York: St. Martin's Press.

Cooper, G. and Hamp-Lyons (1988). Looking in on essay readers. Unpublished manuscript, Ann Arbor: University of Michigan English Composition Board.

Corbett, E. P. J. (1987). Teaching composition: Where we've been and where we're going. *College Composition and Communication, 38*(4), 444–452.

Corder, J. (1989). Asking for a text and trying to learn it. In B. Lawson, S. Ryan, and W. R. Winterowd (Eds.), *Encountering Student Texts: Interpretive Issues in Reading Student Writing* (pp. 89–97). Urbana, IL: NCTE.

Corder, J.(1991). Traditional lectures still have a place in the classroom. *The Chronicle of Higher Education, XXXVII*(39), B2.

Corder, S. P. (1981). *Error Analysis and Interlanguage.* Oxford: Oxford University Press.

Costello, J. (1990). Promoting literacy through literature: Reading and writing in ESL composition. *Journal of Basic Writing, 9*(1), 20–30.

Crandall, J. (1981). A sociolinguistic investigation of the literacy demands of clerical workers. Unpublished doctoral dissertation, Georgetown University, Washington, DC.

Crookall, D. and Oxford, R. (1990). *Simulation, Gaming, and Language Learning.*New York: Newbury House/HarperCollins.

Crookes, G. and Chaudron, C. (1991). Guidelines for classroom language teaching. In M. Celce-Murcia (Ed.), *Teaching English as a Second or Foreign Language* (pp. 46–47). New York: Newbury House/Harper Collins.

Cross, D. (1991). *A Practical Handbook of Language Teaching.* London: Cassell.

Crowhurst, M. (1991). Interrelationships between reading and writing persuasive discourse. *Research in the Teaching of English, 25*(3), 314–338.

Cumming, A. (1985). Responding to the writing of ESL students. In M. Maguire and A. Pare (Eds.), *Patterns of Development* (pp. 58–75). Ottawa: Canadian Council of Teachers of English.

Cumming, A. (1986). Intentional learning as a principle for ESL writing instruction. *TESL Canada Journal, 1*, 69–83.

Cumming, A. (1989). Writing expertise and second language proficiency. *Language Learning, 39*(1), 81–135.

Cumming, A. (1991a). Teachers' curriculum planning for ESL instruction. Paper presented at the 24th Annual British Columbia Teachers of English as an Additional Language, Vancouver (March).

Cumming, A. (1991b). Writing expertise in ESL composition instruction. Paper presented at the 24th Annual British Columbia Teachers of English as an Additional Language, Vancouver (March).

Cumming, A. (1992). Instructional routines in ESL composition teaching: A case study of three teachers. *Journal of Second Language Writing, 1*(1), 1–35.

Cummings, J. (1986). Cultures in contact: Using classroom microcomputers for cultural interchange and reinforcement. *TESL Canada Journal, 3*(2), 13–31.

Cunningham, D. (1987). Computer assisted language learning: Theoretical and practical indications. *BABEL, 22*(3), 7–8.

Curry, L. (1990). *Learning styles in secondary schools: A review of instruments and implications for their use* (U.S. Department of Education and Office of Educational Research and Improvement No. Grant No. G0-008690007-90). National Center on Effective Secondary Schools.

Dagut, M. and Laufer, B. (1985). Avoidance of phrasal verbs—A case for contrastive analysis. *Studies in Second Language Acquisition, 7*, 73–80.

Daiute, C. (1985). *Writing and Concepts*. Reading, MA: Addison-Wesley.

Daiute, C. (1986). Physical and cognitive factors in revising: Insights from studies in computers. *Research in the Teaching of English, 20,* 141–159.

Daiute, C. and Dalton, B. (1989). Peer response groups in the writing classroom: Theoretic foundations and new directions. *Review of Education Research, 58,* 119–149.

Dalgish, G. (1984). Computer-assisted ESL research. *CALICO Journal, 2*(2), 32–37.

Dalgish, G. (1985). Computer-assisted ESL: Research and courseware development. *Computers and Composition, 2*(4), 45–62.

D'Angelo, F. (1975). *A Conceptual Theory of Rhetoric*. Cambridge, MA: Winthrop.

D'Angelo, F. (1980). *Process and Thought in Composition* (2nd ed.). Cambridge, MA: Winthrop.

D'Angelo, F. (1986). The topic sentence revisited. *College Composition and Communication, 37*(4), 431–441.

Dansereau, D. F. (1988). Cooperative learning strategies. In C. W. Weinstein, E. T. Goetz, and P. A. Alexander (Eds.), *Learning and Study Strategies: Issues in Assessment, Instruction, and Evaluation* (pp. 103–120). New York: Academic Press.

Dasenbrock, R.W. (1991). Do we read the text we read? *College English, 53*(1), 7–18.

Dass, L. (1992). Developing student teachers' skills—the AR way. *English Teaching Forum, 30*(2), 10–13.

Dassin, M. M. (1991). Getting beyond the typo: Effective peer critiquing. *Composition Chronicle, 4*(4), 4–5.

Datesman, M. (1990). The interaction between extensive reading and writing. Paper presented at the International TESOL Convention, San Francisco (March).

Davies, N. F. and Omberg, M. (1987). *Academic Writing: Process and Product.* Englewood Cliffs, NJ: Prentice-Hall.

Davis, S. (1984). The ragged interface: Computers and the teaching of writing. In F. Bogal and K. K. Gottschalk (Eds.), *Teaching Prose: A Guide for Writing Instructors* (pp. 337–392). New York: W.W. Norton and Company.

De Beaugrande, R. (1979). The process of invention: Association and recombination. *College Composition and Communication, 30,* 260–267.

Dean, T. (1989). Multicultural classroom, monocultural teachers. *College Composition and Communication, 40*(1), 23–27.

Degenhart, R.,Takala, E., and Takala, S.(1988). Developing a rating method for stylistic preference: A cross-cultural pilot study. In A. Purves (Ed.), *Writing Across Languages and Cultures: Issues in Contrastive Rhetoric* (pp. 79–106). Newbury, CA: Sage Press.

Devenny, R. (1989). How ESL teachers and peers evaluate and respond to student writing. *RELC Journal, 20*(1), 77–90.

Devine, J. (1987). General language competence and adult second language reading. In J. Devine, P.L. Carrell, and D.E. Eskey (Eds.), *Research in Reading English as a Second language* (pp. 73–85). Washington, DC: TESOL.

Devine, J., Carrell, P. L., and Eskey, D. E. (Eds.). (1987). *Research in Reading as a Second Language.* Washington, DC: TESOL.

Diaz, S., Moll, L. C., and Mehan, H. (1989). Sociocultural resources in instruction: A content-specific approach . In *Beyond Language: Social and Cultural Factors in Schooling Language Minority Students* (pp. 187–230). Los Angeles, CA: Bilingual Education Office: Evaluation, Dissemination and Assessment Center, California State University.

Dobrian, D.N. (1990). A limitation on the use of computers in composition. In D. Holdstein and C. Selfe (Eds.), *Computers in Writing: Theory, Research and Practice* (pp. 40–57). New York: Newbury House/HarperCollins.

Dolly, M. (1990). Adult ESL students' management of dialogue journal conversation. *TESOL Quarterly, 24*(2), 317–320.

Dorazio, P. (1992). Writing Lab's network encourages peer review and refinement. *Technological Horizons in Education (T.H.E.) Journal, 19*(9), 73–75.

Douglas, D. (1990). *English Language Testing in U.S. Colleges and Universities.* Washington, DC: NAFSA.

Dubin, F. and Bycina, D. (1991). Academic reading and the ESL/EFL teacher. In M. Celce-Murcia (Ed.), *Teaching English as a Second or Foreign Language* (2nd ed.) (pp. 195–215). New York: Newbury House/Harper Collins.

Dubin, F., Eskey, D., and Grabe, W. (Eds.). (1986). *Teaching Second Language Reading for Academic Purposes.* Reading, MA: Addison-Wesley.

Dubin, F. and Olshtain, E. (1986). *Course Design: Developing Programs and Materials for Language Learning.* Cambridge: Cambridge University Press.

Dunkel, P. (Ed.). (1991). *Computer-Assisted Language Learning and Testing: Research Issues and Practice.* New York: Newbury House/Harper Collins.

Dunn, R. and Dunn, K. (1978). *Teaching Students Through Their Individual Learning Styles: A Practical Approach.* Englewood Cliffs, NJ.: Prentice-Hall.

Dunn, R., Dunn, K., and Price, G. (1989). *Learning Styles Inventory (LSI): An Inventory for the Identification of How Individuals in grades 3 Through 12 Prefer to Learn*. Lawrence, KS.: Price Systems.

Dunn, R. and Griggs, S. A. (1988). *Learning Styles: Quiet Revolution in American Secondary Schools*. Reston, VA: National Association of Secondary School Principals.

Dunn, R. and Griggs, S. A. (Forthcoming). A cross-cultural comparative analysis of the learning styles of selected racial and ethnic groups of students. *Kansas Association for Supervision and Curriculum Development Record*.

Dunnett, S., Dubin, F., and Lezburg, A. (1986). English language teaching from an intercultural perspective. In J. Valdes (Ed.), *Culture Bound: Bridging the Cultural Gap in Language Teaching* (pp. 123–129). Cambridge: Cambridge University Press.

Durrant, K. R. and Duke, C. R. (1990). Developing sensitivity to audience: Connecting theory and practice. *Teaching English in the Two-Year College, 16*(3), 165–173.

Dykstra, G. (1977). Toward interactive modes in guided composition. *TESL Reporter, 10*(3), 1–4.

Edelsky, C. (1989). Bilingual children's writing: Fact and fiction. In D. Johnson and D. Roen (Eds.), *Richness in Writing: Empowering ESL Students* (pp. 165–176). New York: Longman.

Eisenberg, A. (1986). Combined reading-writing instruction using technical and scientific texts. In B. Peterson (Ed.), *Convergences, Transactions in Reading and Writing* (pp. 204–214). Urbana, IL: NCTE.

Elbow, P. (1973). *Writing Without Teachers*. London: Macmillan Education.

Elbow, P. (1989). Toward a phenomenology of freewriting. *Journal of Basic Writing*, 8(2), 42–71.

Elbow, P. (1991a). Reflections on academic discourse: How it relates to freshmen and colleagues. *College English, 53*(2), 135–155.

Elbow, P. (1991b). Some thoughts on Expressive Discourse: A review essay. *Journal of Advanced Composition, 11*(1), 83–93.

Eliason, P. (1989). Perceptual learning style preferences of second language students: acquisition: A study of second language learners. *System, 17*(1), 249–262.

Emig, J. (1977). Writing as a mode of learning. *College Composition and Communication, 28*, 122–128.

English Language Institute. (1989). *MELAB Information Bulletin*. Ann Arbor: English Language Institute, University of Michigan.

Esling, J. (1991). Researching the effects of networking: Evaluating the spoken and written discourse generated by working with CALL. In P. Dunkel (Ed.), *Computer-Assisted Language Learning and Testing: Research Issues and Practice* (pp. 111–131). New York: Newbury House/Harper Collins.

Fagan, E. R. and Cheong, P. (1987). Contrastive rhetoric: Pedagogical implications for the ESL teacher in Singapore. *RELC Journal, 18*(1), 19–30.

Faigley, L. L. (1985). Non-academic writing: The social perspective. In L. Odell and D. Goswami (Eds.), *Writing in a Non-Academic Settings* (pp. 231–248). New York and London: Guilford Press.

Faigley, L. L. (1986). Competing theories of process: A critique and a proposal. *College Composition and Communication, 48,* 527–542.

Faigley, L. L. and Witte, S. (1981). Analyzing revision. *College Composition and Communication, 32,* 400–414.

Fanselow, J. (1992). *Contrasting Conversations: Activities for Exploring Our Beliefs and Teaching Practices.* New York: Longman.

Fathman, A. K. and Whalley, E. (1990). Teacher response to student writing: Focus on form versus content. In B. Kroll (Ed.), *Second Language Writing: Research Insights for the Classroom* (pp. 178–190). New York: Cambridge University Press.

Fazio, G., Pearce, J., Lear, P., and Rowley, G. (1990). *Practicing Paragraphs.* Fort Worth: Holt, Rinehart, and Winston.

Fish, S. (1980). *Is There a Text in This Class? The Authority of Interpretive Communities.* Cambridge, MA: Harvard University Press.

Fish, S. (1990). The common touch or one size fits all or just say yes. Paper presented at the Wyoming Conference on English, Laramie, WY (July).

Fitzgerald, J. (1987). Research on revisions in writing. *Review of Educational Research, 59,* 126–132.

Fleckenstein, K. S. (1989). Progress logs: Teaching writing process awareness. *Teaching English in the Two-Year College, 16,* 106–112.

Fleckenstein, K. S. (1992). An appetite for coherence: Arousing and fulfilling desires. *College Composition and Communication, 43*(1), 23–31.

Florio, S. and Clark, C. M. (1982). The function of writing in an elementary classroom. *Research in the Teaching of English, 16,* 115–130.

Florio-Ruane, S. and Dunn, S. (1985) Teaching writing: Some perennial questions and some possible answers. *Occasional Paper No. 85,* Lansing MI: Michigan State University.

Flower, L. (1979). Writer-based prose: A cognitive basis for problems in writing. *College English, 41*(1), 19–38.

Flower, L. (1989a). Cognition, context and theory building. *College Composition and Communication, 40*(3), 282–311.

Flower, L. (1989b). *Problem-Solving Strategies for Writing* (3rd ed.). San Diego: Harcourt Brace Jovanovich.

Flower, L. and Hayes, J. (1980). A cognitive process theory of writing. *College Composition and Communication, 31*(4), 365–387.

Flower, L., Hayes, J., Carey, L., Schriver, K., and Stratman, J. (1986). Detection, diagnosis, and the strategies of revision. *College Composition and Communication, 37*(1), 16–55.

Flower, L., Stein, V., Ackerman, J., Kantz, M. J., McCormick, K., and Peck, W. (1990). *Reading-to-Write: Exploring a Cognitive and Social Process.* New York: Oxford University Press.

Folman, S. (1988). Towards an EFL reading-writing model of academic learning. Paper presented at the International TESOL Convention, Chicago (March).

Fox, T. (1990). Gender interests in reading and writing. In T. Fox (Ed.), *In the Social Uses of Writing: Politics and Pedagogy* (pp. 51–70). Norwood, NJ: Ablex.

Frank, M. (1983). *Writing from Experience*. Englewood Cliffs, NJ: Prentice-Hall.

Frankenburg-Garcia, A. (1990). Do the similarities between L1 and L2 writing processes conceal important differences? *Edinburgh Working Papers in Applied Linguistics, 1*, 91–102.

Freedman, S. (1987). *Response to Student Writing*. Urbana, IL: NCTE.

Freedman, S. (Ed.). (1989). *The Acquisition of Written Language: Response and Revision*. Norwood, NJ: Ablex.

Freedman, S. (1992). Outside-in and inside-out: Peer response groups in two ninth-grade classes. *Research in the Teaching of English, 26*(1), 71–107.

Freedman, S. and Sperling, M. (1985). Teacher-student interaction in the writing conference: Response and teaching. In S. Freedman (Ed.), *The Acquisition of Written Language: Response and Revision* (pp. 106–130). Norwood, NJ: Ablex.

Freeman, D. (1989). Teacher training, development, and decision-making: A model of teaching and related strategies for language teacher education. *TESOL Quarterly, 23*(1), 27–45.

Friedlander, A. (1990). Composing in English: Effects of a first language on writing in English as a second language. In B. Kroll (Ed.), *Second Language Writing: Research Insights for the Classroom* (pp. 109–125). New York: Cambridge University Press.

Friere, P. (1970). *Pedagogy of the Oppressed*. New York: Seabury.

Fromkin, V. and Rodman, R. (1988). *An Introduction to Language* (4th ed.). Fort Worth: Holt, Rinehart, Winston.

Fulwiler, T. (1987). *The Journal Book*. Portsmouth, NH: Boynton/Cook.

Fulwiler, T. (1988). How does writing across the curriculum work? In G. Tate and E. P. J. Corbett (Eds.), *The Writing Teacher's Sourcebook* (2nd ed.) (pp. 248–260). Oxford: Oxford University Press.

Furey, P. (1986). A framework for cross-cultural analysis of teaching methods. In P. Byrd (Ed.), *Teaching Across Cultures in the University ESL Program* (pp. 15–28). Washington, DC: NAFSA.

Gaies, S. (1985). *Peer Involvement in Language Learning*. New York: Harcourt Brace Jovanovich.

Gaies, S. and Bowen, D. (1990). Clinical supervision of language teaching: The supervisor as trainer and educator. In J. Richards and D. Nunan (Eds.), *Second Language Teacher Education* (pp. 167–181). New York: Cambridge University Press.

Gajdusek, L. (1988). Toward wider use of literature in ESL: Why and how. *TESOL Quarterly, 22*(2), 227–257.

Gardiner, E.F. (1991). Ideologies, technologies, and teaching. *Journal of Teaching Writing, 10*(2), 241–253.

Garrett-Petts, W. F. (1988). Exploring an interpretive community: Reader response to Canadian prairie literature. *College English, 50*(8), 920–936.

Garrison, R. (1974). One-to-one tutorial instruction in freshman composition. *New Directions for Community Colleges, 2*, 55–84.

Garrott, C. L. (1984). *Cognitive style and impressions of student achievement in secondary French classes*. ERIC No. ED 242203, Research Report 143.

Gaskill, W. (1986). Revising in Spanish and English as a second language: A process-oriented study of composition. Unpublished doctoral dissertation, University of California, Los Angeles.

Gast, G. (1990). Using "non-existent student" essays as away of encouraging revisions. *TESL Reporter*, *23*(1), 5–8.

Geertz, C. (1973). *The Interpretation of Cultures*. New York: Basic Books.

Gere, A. and Stevens, R. (1989). The language of writing groups: How oral response shapes revision. In S. Freedman (Ed.), *The Acquisition of Written Language: Response and Revision* (pp. 85–105). Norwood, NJ: Ablex.

Gere, A. R. (1987). *Writing Groups*. Carbondale: Southern Illinois University Press.

Glenn, E. S., Withmeyer, D., and Stevenson, K. A. (1977). Cultural styles of persuasion. *International Journal of Intercultural Relations*, *3*, 132–148.

Gold, S. E. (1992). Increasing student autonomy through portfolios. In K. B. Yancey (Ed.), *Portfolios in the Writing Classroom: An Introduction* (pp. 20–30). Urbana, IL: NCTE.

Goldstein, L. (1992). Teaching teachers about learner variability. Paper presented at the International TESOL Convention, Vancouver, B.C. (March).

Goldstein, L. M. and Conrad, S. M. (1990). Student input and negotiation of meaning in ESL writing conferences. *TESOL Quarterly*, *24*(3), 441–460.

Grabe, W. and Biber, D. (1988) Who are they writing for: A linguistic comparison of freshmen argumentative essays and published English genres. Unpublished manuscript, Northern Arizona University.

Grabe, W. and Kaplan, R. B. (1989). Writing in a second language: Contrastive rhetoric. In D. M. Johnson and D. H. Roen (Eds.), *Richness in Writing: Empowering ESL Students* (pp. 263–283). New York: Longman.

Gradman, H. (1991). Second language students and extensive reading. *Modern Language Journal*, *71*(1), 39–51.

Grant-Davie, K. (1989). Rereading in the writing process. *Reader*, *21*, 2–21.

Greenberg, K. (1981). *The Effects of Variations in Essay Questions on the Writing Performance of CUNY Freshman*. New York: New York Instructional Center.

Greenberg, K. (1986). The development and validation of the TOEFL writing test: A discussion of TOEFL Research Reports 15 and 19. *TESOL Quarterly*, *20*(3), 531–544.

Gregg, J. (1986). Comments on Bernard Mohen and Winnie Au-Yeung Lo's "Academic writing and Chinese students: Transfer and developmental factors." *TESOL Quarterly*, *20*(2), 354–358.

Grellet, F. (1981). *Developing Reading Skills*. Cambridge: Cambridge University Press.

Griggs, S. A. and Dunn, R. (1989). The learning styles of multicultural groups and counseling implications. *Journal of Multicultural Counseling and Development*, *17*(4), 146–155.

Grimm, N. (1986). Improving students' responses to their peers' essays. *College Composition and Communication*, *37*, 91–94.

Grosse, C. (1991). The TESOL methods course. *TESOL Quarterly*, *25*(1), 29–49.

Gueye, M. (1989). Computers for EFL in developing countries: Problems and solutions. *CALICO*, *7*(1), 77–85.

Guild, P. and Garger, S. (1985). *Marching to Different Drummers*. Alexandria, VA: Association for Supervision and Curriculum Development.

Gumperz, J. J., Kaltman, H., and O'Connor, M. C. (1984). Ethnic style and the transition to literacy. In D. Tannen (Ed.), *Cohesion in Spoken and Written Discourse* (pp. 3–19). Norwood NJ: Ablex.

Gwin, T. (1990). Language skills through literature. *English Teaching Forum*, *28*(3), 10–13.

Haas, C. (1989). How writing medium shapes the writing process: Effect of word processing on planning. *Research in the Teaching of English*, *23*(2), 181–207.

Haas, C. and Flower, L. (1988). Rhetorical reading strategies and the construction of meaning. *College Composition and Communication*, *39*, 167–183.

Hafernik, J. J. (1984). The hows and why of peer editing in the ESL writing class. *CATESOL Occasional Papers*, *4*, 48–55.

Hagaman, J. (1980). Encouraging thoughtful revision in a Kinneavy-framed advanced composition course. *Journal of Advanced Composition*, *1*, 79–85.

Hainer, E. (1987). Cognitive and learning styles of limited English proficient and English proficient high school students. Unpublished doctoral dissertation, George Washington University.

Hairston, M. (1982). The winds of change: Thomas Kuhn and the revolution in the teaching of writing. *College Composition and Communication*, *33*, 76–88.

Hairston, M. (1986). On not being a composition slave. In C. W. Bridges (Ed.), *Training the New Teacher of College Composition* (pp. 117–124). Urbana, IL: NCTE.

Hall, C. (1987). Two types of student correction procedures in ESL composition. *Journal of Intensive English Studies*, *1*(1), 41–46.

Hall, C. (1990). Managing the complexity of revising across languages. *TESOL Quarterly*, *24*(1), 43–60.

Hall, E. (1991). Variations in composing behaviors of academic ESL writers in test and non-test situations. *TESL Canada*, *8*(2), 9–33.

Halliday, M. A. K. and Hasan, R. (1976). *Cohesion in English*. London: Longman.

Hamp-Lyons, L. (1986). No new lamps for old yet, please. *TESOL Quarterly*, *20*(4), 790–796.

Hamp-Lyons, L. (1987). Raters respond to rhetoric in writing. *TECFORS*, *10*(3 and 4), 16–27.

Hamp-Lyons, L. (1990). Second language writing: Assessment issues. In B. Kroll (Ed.), *Second Language Writing: Research Insights for the Classroom* (pp. 69–87). New York: Cambridge University Press.

Hamp-Lyons, L. (Ed.). (1991). *Assessing ESL Writing in Academic Contexts*. Norwood, NJ: Ablex.

Hansen, J. and Stansfield, C. (1982). Relationships of field dependent-independent cognitive styles to foreign language achievement. *Language Learning*, *31*, 349–367.

Hansen, L. (1984). Field dependence/independence and language testing: Evidence from six Pacific Island cultures. *TESOL Quarterly, 18*(6), 311–324.

Hanson-Smith, E. (1990). Word-processed composition. *TESOL Newsletter*, (3), 23.

Hansson, G. (1992). Readers responding—and then? *Research in the Teaching of English, 26*(2), 241–253.

Hare, V.C. and Fitzsimmons, D.A. (1991). The influence of interpretive communities on use of content and procedural knowledge in a writing task. *Written Communication, 8*, 348–378.

Harris, J. (1989). The idea of community in the study of writing. *College Composition and Communication, 40*(1), 11–22.

Harris, M. (1986). *Teaching One-to-One: The Writing Conference*. Urbana, IL: NCTE.

Harris, P. R. and Moran, R. T. (1979). *Managing Cultural Differences* (The International Management Productivity Series). Houston, TX: Gulf Publishing Company.

Harrison, T. M. (1987). Framework for the study of writing in organizational contexts. *Written Communication, 4*(1), 3–23.

Hatch, E. (1992). *Discourse and Language Education*. New York: Cambridge University Press.

Hayes, C. W., Bahruth, R., and Kessler, C. (1986). The dialogue journal and migrant education. *Dialogue, 3*(3), 3–5.

Hayward, M. (1990). Choosing an essay question: It's more than you know. *Teaching English in the Two-Year College, 16*(3), 174–178.

Heath, S. B. (1983). *Ways With Words: Language, Life and Work in Communities and Classrooms*. Cambridge: Cambridge University Press.

Heath, S. B. (1989). Sociocultural contexts of language development. In *Social and Cultural Factors in Schooling Language Minority Students* (pp. 143–186). Los Angeles, CA: Bilingual Education Office, Evaluation, Dissemination and Assessment Center, California State University.

Heath, S. B. (1992). Sociocultural contexts of language development: Implications for the classroom. In P. A. Richard-Amato and M. A. Snow (Eds.), *The Multicultural Classroom: Readings for Content-Area Teachers* (pp. 102–125). New York: Longman.

Hedge, T. (1988). *Writing*. Oxford: Oxford University Press.

Higgins, J. (1988). Response to Hirvela's article "Marshall McLuhan and the case against CAI." *System, 16*(3), 313–317.

Higgins, J. and Johns, T. (1984). *Computers in Language Learning*. Reading, MA: Addison-Wesley.

Hilbert, B.S. (1992). It was a dark and nasty night . . . It was a hard beginning. *College Composition and Communication, 43*(1), 75–80.

Hillocks, G. (1982). The interaction of instruction, teacher comment, and revision in teaching the composing process. *Research in the Teaching of English, 16*, 261–278.

Hillocks, G. J. (1990). Teaching, reflecting, researching. In D. Daiker and M. Morenberg (Eds.), *The Writing Teacher as Researcher: Essays in the Theory and Practice of Class-Based Research* (pp. 15–29). Portsmouth, NH: Boynton/Cook Heinemann.

Hinds, J. (1987). Reader vs. writing responsibility: A new typology. In U. Connor and R. B. Kaplan (Eds.), *Writing Across Languages: Analysis of L2 Text* (pp. 141–152). Reading, MA: Addison-Wesley.

Hinds, J. (1990). Inductive, deductive, quasi-inductive: Writing in Japanese, Korean, Chinese, and Thai. In U. Connor and A. Johns (Eds.), *Coherence in Writing* (pp. 87–110). Alexandria, VA: TESOL.

Hirokawa, K. and Swales, J. M. (1986). The effects of modifying the formality level of ESL composition questions. *TESOL Quarterly, 20,* 343–345.

Hirvela, A. (1988). Marshall McLuhan and the case against CAI. *System, 16*(3), 233–311.

Hoetker, J. and Brossell, G. (1989). The effects of systematic variations in essay topics of the writing performance of college freshmen. *College Composition and Communication, 40*(4), 414–421.

Hord, S. M., Rutherford, W. A., Huling-Austin, L., and Hall, G. (1987). *Taking Charge of Change.* Alexandria, VA: Association for Supervision and Curriculum Development.

Horowitz, D. (1986a). Essay examination prompts and the teaching of academic writing. *English for Specific Purposes Journal, 5*(2), 107–120.

Horowitz, D. (1986b). Process not product: Less than meets the eye. *TESOL Quarterly, 20*(1), 141–144.

Horowitz, D. (1986c). What professors actually require: Academic tasks for the ESL classroom. *TESOL Quarterly, 20*(3), 445–462.

Horowitz, D. (1988). To see our text as others see it: Toward a social sense of coherence. *JALT Journal, 10*(2), 91–100.

Horowitz, D. (1990). Fiction and non-fiction in the ESL/EFL classroom: Does the difference make a difference? *English for Specific Purposes, 9*(2), 161–168.

Horowitz, D. (1992). ESL writing assessments: Contradictions and resolutions. In L. Hamp-Lyons (Ed.), *Assessing ESL Writing in Academic Contexts* (pp. 71–85). Norwood, NJ: Ablex.

Horowitz, D. and McKee, M. (1984). Methods for teaching academic writing. *English for Specific Purposes, 7*(2), 5–11.

Hourigan, M. (1991). Poststructural theory and writing assessment: "Heady, esoteric theory" revisited. *Teaching English in the Two-Year College, 18*(3), 191–195.

Huckin, T. and Flower, L. (1990). Reading for points and purposes. *Journal of Advanced Composition, 11*(2), 347–362.

Hudelson, S. (1991). EFL teaching and children: A topic-based approach. *English Teaching Forum, 29*(4), 2–5.

Hugher, J. (1990). ESL composition testing. In D. Douglas (Ed.), *English Language Testing in U.S. Colleges and Universities* (pp. 51–67). Washington, DC : NAFSA.

Hull, G. (1987). Computer detection of errors in natural language texts. Some research on pattern matching. *Computers and the Humanities, 21,* 103–111.

Hull, G. and Rose, M. (1989). Rethinking remediation: Toward a social-cognitive understanding of problematic reading and writing. *Written Communication, 6*(2), 139–154.

Hull, G., Rose, M., Fraser, K. L., and Castellano, M. (1991). Remediation as social construct: Perspectives from an analysis of classroom discourse. *College Composition and Communication, 42*(3), 299–329.

Huot, B. (1990). Reliability, validity, and holistic scoring: What we know and what we need to know. *College Composition and Communication, 41*(2), 201–213.

Hurley, E. and Sherman, B. (1990). Bringing Hollywood to the ESL curriculum. *TESOL Newsletter, 24*(4), 7, 22.

Hutchinson, T. and Waters, A. (1987). *English for Specific Purposes: A Learning Centered Approach.* Cambridge: Cambridge University Press.

Hvitfeldt, C. (1992).Oral orientations in ESL academic writing. *College ESL, 2*(1), 29–39.

Hyland, K. (1992). Genre analysis: Just another fad? *English Teaching Forum, 32*(2), 14–17, 27.

Hyltenstam, K. and Pienemann, M. (Eds.). (1985). *Modeling and Assessing Second Language Acquisition.* San Diego: College-Hill Press.

Ibsen, E. (1990). The double role of fiction in foreign language learning: Towards a creative methodology. *English Teaching Forum,* 28(3), 2–9.

Indrasuta, C. (1988). Narrative styles of writing of Thai and American students. In A. Purves (Ed.), *Writing Across Languages and Cultures: Issues in Contrastive Rhetoric* (pp. 206–226). Newbury Park, CA: Sage Publishers.

Irmscher, W. F. (1979). *Teaching Expository Writing.* New York: Holt, Rinehart, and Winston.

Jacobs, G. (1988). Cooperative goal structure: A way to improve group activities. *ELT Journal, 42*(2), 97–101.

Jacobs, G. (1989). Miscorrection in peer feedback in writing class. *RELC Journal, 20*(1), 68–76.

Jacobs, H. L., Zingraf, S. A., Wormuth, D. R., Hartfiel, V. F., and Hughey, J. B. (1981). *Testing ESL Composition: A Practical Approach.* Rowley, MA: Newbury House Publishers.

James, D. R. (1981). Peer teaching in the writing classroom. *English Journal, 70*(7), 48–50.

Jamieson, J. and Chapelle, C. (1987). Working styles on computers as evidence of second language learning strategies. *Language Learning, 37*(4), 523–544.

Jamieson, J. and Chapelle, C. (1988). Using CALL effectively: What do we need to know about students? *System, 16*(2), 151–162.

Janopoulos, M. (1986). The relationship of pleasure reading and second language writing proficiency. *TESOL Quarterly, 20* (2), 247–265.

Janopoulos, M. (1992a). University faculty tolerance of NS and NNS writing errors. *Journal of Second Language Writing, 1*(2).

Janopoulos, M. (1992b). Writing across the curriculum and the NNS student. Paper presented at the International TESOL Convention, Vancouver, B.C. (March).

Jansen, C. J. M., Steehouder, M. F., Pilot, A., Schrauwen, R., and Looijmanis, P. J. M. (1987). ALEXIS: Computer assisted feedback on written assignments. *Computers in Composition, 4*(1), 32–45.

Jarvis, J. (1992). Using diaries for teacher reflection on in-service courses. *ELT Journal, 46*(2), 133–143.

Jenkins, R. (1987). Responding to student writing: Written dialogs on writing and revision. *The Writing Instructor, 6,* 82–86.

Johns, A. (1980). Cohesion in written business discourse: Some contrasts. *The ESP Journal, 1*(1), 35–43.

Johns, A. (1985). Academic writing standards: A questionnaire. *TECFORS, 8,* 11–14.

Johns, A. (1986). Coherence and academic writing: Some definitions and suggestions for teaching. *TESOL Quarterly, 20*(2), 247–266.

Johns, A. (1988). The discourse communities dilemma: Identifying transferable skills for the academic milieu. *ESP Journal, 7,* 55–60.

Johns, A. (1990). L1 composition theories: Implications for developing theories of L2 composition. In B. Kroll (Ed.), *Second Language Writing: Research for Insights for the Classroom* (pp. 24–36). New York: Cambridge University Press.

Johns, A. (1991). Interpreting an English essay competency examination. *Written Communication, 8*(3), 379–401.

Johnson, C. (1985). The composing processes of six ESL students. Unpublished doctoral dissertation, Illinois State University.

Johnson, D. (1985). Error gravity: Communicative effect of language errors in academic writing. *BAAL Newsletter, 24,* 46–47.

Johnson, D. (1989). Enriching task contexts for second language writing: Power through interpersonal roles. In D. Johnson and D. Roen (Eds.), *Richness in Writing: Empowering ESL Students* (pp. 39–54). New York: Longman.

Johnson, D. and Roen, D. (Eds.). (1989). *Richness in Writing: Empowering ESL Students.* New York: Longman.

Johnson, H. (1992). Fossilizing. *ELT Journal, 46*(2), 180–189.

Johnson, K. (1992). Cognitive strategies and second language writers: A re-evaluation of sentence combining. *Journal of Second Language Writing, 1*(1), 61–75.

Johnson, K. and Morrow, K. (Eds.). (1981). *Communication in the Classroom.* London: Longman.

Johnson, P. 1981. Effects on reading comprehension of building backgrounds knowledge. *TESOL Quarterly 15*(2), 169181.

Johnson, P. (1986). Acquisition of schema for comprehension and communication: A study of the reading-writing relationships in ESL. *RELC Journal, 17*(1), 1–13.

Johnson, R. K. (1981). On syllabuses and on being communicative. *The English Bulletin, 7*(4), 52–61.

Jones, C. S. and Tetroe, J. (1987). Composing in a second language. In A. Matsuhashi (Ed.), *Writing in Real Time* (pp. 34–57). Norwood, NJ: Ablex.

Jones, D. (1988). Knowing opportunities: Some possible benefits and limitations of dialogue journals in adult second language learning. Unpublished master's thesis, School for International Training (Brattleboro, VT).

Joram, E., Woodruff, E., Bryson, M., and Lindsay, P. (1992). The effects of revising with a word processor on written composition. *Research in the Teaching of English, 26*(2), 167–193.

Jordon, R. R. (1989). English for academic purposes (EAP). *Language Teaching: The International Abstracting Journal for Language Teachers and Applied Linguistics 22* (3), 150–164.

Kachru, B. (1982a). Models of English for the Third World: White man's linguistic burden or language pragmatics? *TESOL Quarterly, 10*(2), 221–232.

Kachru, B. (1982b). *The Other Tongue: English Across Cultures.* Urbana, IL: University of Illinois Press.

Kachru, B. (1985). Institutionalized second language varieties. In S. Greenbaum (Ed.), *The English Language Today* (pp. 207–210). London: Oxford University Press.

Kagan, S. (1989). Cooperative learning and sociocultural factors in schooling. In *Beyond Language: Social and Cultural Factors in Schooling Language Minority Students* (pp. 231–298). Los Angeles, CA: Bilingual Education Office, Evaluation, Dissemination and Assessment Center, California State University.

Kameen, P. (1978). A mechanical, meaningful and communicative framework for ESL sentence combining exercises. *TESOL Quarterly, 12*(4), 395–401

Kantor, K. J. (1984). Classroom contexts and the development of writing intuitions: An ethnographic study. In R. Beach and L. Bridwell (Eds.), *New Directions in Composition Research* (pp. 72–94). New York: Guilford Press.

Kaplan, R. B. (1966). Cultural thought patterns in intercultural education. *Language Learning, 16*, 1–20.

Kaplan, R. B. (1982). Contrastive rhetoric: Some implications for the writing process. *English Teaching and Learning, 6*, 3–4, 24–38,16–28.

Kaplan, R. B. (Ed.). (1983). *Annual Review of Applied Linguistics.* Rowley, MA: Newbury House Publishers.

Kaplan, R. B. (1988a). Contrastive rhetoric and second language learning: Notes towards a theory of contrastive rhetoric. In A. Purves (Ed.), *Writing Across Languages and Cultures: Issues in Contrastive Rhetoric* (pp. 275–304). Newbury Park, CA: Sage Publishers.

Kaplan, R. B. (1988b). Contrastive rhetoric: The Chinese connection. Paper presented at the TESOL Summer Institute Meeting, Flagstaff, AZ.

Kaplan, R. B. (1990). Writing in a multilingual/multicultural context: What's contrastive rhetoric all about? *Writing Instructor, 10*(1), 7–17.

Kasden, L. N. and Hoeber, D. R. (Eds.). (1980). *Basic Writing: Essays for Teachers, Researchers, and Administrators.* Urbana IL: NCTE.

Katz, A. (1988). Responding to student writers: The writing conferences of second language learners. Unpublished doctoral dissertation, Stanford University.

Kaufman, D. (1987). Word processors for enhancing writing and reading processes. Paper presented at the International TESOL Convention, Miami (April).

Keefe, J. W. (1979). Learning style: An overview. In J. W. Keefe (Ed.), *Student Learning Styles: Diagnosing and Prescribing Programs* (pp. 1–17). Reston, VA: National Association of Secondary School Principals.

Keefe, J. W. (1987). *Learning Styles: Theory and Practice.* Reston,VA.: National Association of Secondary School Principals.

Keefe, J. W. (Ed.). (1988). *Profiling and Utilizing Learning Style.* Reston, VA: National Association of Secondary School Principals.

Keefe, J. W. (1989). *Learning Style Profile.* Reston, VA: National Association of Secondary School Principals.

Keh, C. (1990). Feedback in the writing process: A model and methods for implementation. *ELT Journal, 44*(4), 294–298.

Kemmis, S. and McTaggert, R. (1982). *The Action Research Planner.* Victoria, Australia: Deakin University Press.

Kiefer, K. and Smith, C. (1984). Improving students' revising and editing: The Writer's Workbench system. In W. Wresch (Ed.), *The Computer* in *Composition Instruction: A Writer's Tool* (pp. 65–82). Urbana IL: NCTE.

Kinneavy, J. (1969). The basic aims of discourse. *College Composition and Communication, 21,* 297–304.

Kinneavy, J., McCleary, W., and Nakadate, N. (1985). *Writing in the Liberal Arts Tradition: A Rhetoric With Readings.* New York: Harper and Row.

Kirby, D., Liner, T., and Vinz, R. (1988). *Inside Out: Development Strategies for Teaching Writing.* Portsmouth, NH: Boynton/Cook Heinemann.

Kirsch, G. (1989). Authority in reading-writing relationships. *Reader, 21,* 56–67.

Kirsch, G. (1991). Writing up and down the social ladder: A study of experienced writers composing for contrasting audiences. *Research in the Teaching of English, 25*(1), 33–53.

Kleifgen, J. A. (1988). Learning from student teachers' cross-cultural communication failures. *Anthropology and Education Quarterly, 19*(3), 213–234.

Kleinmann, H. and Selekman, H. (1980). The dicto-comp revisited. *Foreign Language Annals, 13*(5), 379–383.

Knodt, E. A. (1991). "I can do that!" Building basic writers' confidence and skill. *Teaching English in the Two-Year College, 18*(1), 29–33.

Kobayashi, H. (1984) Rhetorical patterns in English and Japanese. Unpublished doctoral thesis, Columbia University Teachers College.

Kobayashi, H. and Rinnert, C. (1992). Effects of first language on second language writing: Translation versus direct composition. *Language Learning, 42*(2), 183–215.

Kobayashi, T. (1992). Native and nonnative reactions to ESL compositions. *TESOL Quarterly, 26*(1), 81–112.

Koch, B. J. (1983). Presentation as proof: The language of Arabic rhetoric. *Anthropological Linguistics, 25*, 46–60.

Kohn, A. (1987). It's hard to get out of a pair—Profile: David and Roger Johnson. *Psychology Today, 21*, 53–57.

Kraemer, A. J. (1973). *Development of a Cultural Self-Awareness Approach to Instruction in Multicultural Education.* Alexandria, VA: Human Resource Research Organization.

Krapels, A. R. (1990). An overview of second language writing process research. In B. Kroll (Ed.), *Second Language Writing: Research* Insights *for the Classroom* (pp. 37–56). New York: Cambridge University Press.

Krashen, S. (1988). Do we learn by reading? The relationship between free reading and reading ability. In D. Tannen (Ed.), *Linguistics in Context: Connection Observation and Understanding* (pp. 269–298). Norwood, NJ: Ablex.

Krashen, S. D. (1981). *Second Language Acquisition and Second Language Learning.* Oxford: Pergamon Press.

Krashen, S. D. (1982). *Principles and Practice in Second Language Acquisition.* Oxford: Pergamon Press.

Krashen, S. D. (1984a). Do we learn to read by reading? The relationship between free reading and reading ability. In D. Tannen (Ed.), *Linguistics in Context: Connecting Observation and Understanding* (pp. 269–298). Norwood, NJ: Ablex.

Krashen, S. D. (1984b). *Writing: Research, Theory, and Applications.* Oxford: Pergamon Institute of English.

Krest, M. (1988). Monitoring student writing: How not to avoid the draft. *Journal of Teaching Writing, 7*(1), 27–39.

Kroll, B. (1979). A survey of writing needs of foreign and American college freshman. *ELT Journal, 33*, 219–227.

Kroll, B. (1989). On becoming an ESL writing teacher. Speech presented at the Georgia State University Conference on Culture, Writing, and Related Issues, Atlanta (December).

Kroll, B. (1990a). The rhetoric-syntax split: Designing a curriculum for ESL students. *Journal of Basic Writing, 9*(1), 40–55.

Kroll, B. (1990b). Understanding TOEFL's Test of Written English. *RELC Journal, 22*(1), 20–33.

Kroll, B. (1991). Teaching writing in the ESL context. In M. Celce-Murcia (Ed.), *Teaching English as a Second or Foreign Language* (2nd ed.), (pp. 245–263). New York: Newbury House/Harper Collins.

Kroll, B. (Forthcoming). Teaching writing is teaching reading: Training the new teacher of ESL composition. In I. Leki and J. Carson (Eds.), *Reading in the Composition Classroom: Second Language Perspectives.* Boston: Heinle and Heinle.

Kroonenberg, N. (1990). *Learning styles and language learning: With a focus on cultural and linguistic background.* Unpublished manuscript, Teachers College, Columbia University.

Kroonenberg, N. (1992a). Developing critical thinking skills in the foreign language class. *Northeast Conference on Teaching of Foreign Languages Newsletter, 31*, 23–24.

Kroonenberg, N. (1992b). Learning styles and language learning. Pre-conference symposium at the International TESOL Convention, Vancouver, B.C. (March).

Kumaradivelu, B. (1990). Classroom observation: A neglected situation. *TESOL Newsletter, 24*(6), 5,32,34.

Lakoff, R. (1981). Persuasive discourse and ordinary conversation. Analyzing discourse: Text and talk. In D. Tannen (Ed.), *Proceedings of the Georgetown University Round Table on Languages and Linguistics* (pp. 25–42). Washington, DC: Georgetown University Press.

Larsen-Freeman, D. (1986). *Techniques and Principles in Language Teaching.* New York: Oxford University Press.

Larsen-Freeman, D. (1990) Working with the challenge. Workshop presented at the CoTESOL Spring Meeting, Fort Collins, CO (April).

Larson, R. L. (1986). Making assignments, judging writing, and annotating papers: Some suggestions. In C. W. Bridges (Ed.), *Training the New Teacher of College Composition* (pp. 109–116). Urbana, IL: NCTE.

Lauer, J. (1989). Interpreting student writing. In B. Lawson, S. S. Ryan, and W. R. Winterowd (Eds.), *Encountering Student Texts: Interpretive Issues in Reading Student Writing* (pp. 121–128). Urbana, IL: NCTE.

Lawrence, M. (1973). Enquiry method and problem solving in the ESL classroom. *TESL Reporter, 6*(1), 1–2,12.

Lawrence, M. (1975). *Reading, Thinking,Writing.* Ann Arbor: The University of Michigan Press.

Lawson, B., Ryan, S. S., and Winterowd, W. R. (Eds.). (1990). *Encountering Student Texts: Interpretive Issues in Reading Student Writing.* Urbana, IL: NCTE.

LeBauer, R. (1992). Reader-response literary theory: Its relevance for ESL. Paper presented at the International TESOL Convention, Vancouver, B.C. (March).

Lee, M.-S. (1976–77). Some common grammatical errors made in written English by Chinese students. *CATESOL Occasional Papers, 3*, 115–120.

Lees, E. O. (1988). Evaluating student writing. In G. Tate and E. P. J. Corbett (Eds.), *The Writing Teacher's Source Book* (2nd ed.) (pp. 263–267). New York: Oxford University Press.

Leithwood, K. A. (Ed.). (1986). *Planned Educational Change: A Manual of Curriculum Review, Development, and Implementation (CRDI) Concepts and Procedures.* Ontario: Ontario Institute for Studies in Education (OISE).

Leki, I. (1986). ESL student preferences in written error correction. Paper presented at the Southeast Regional TESOL Conference, Atlanta (October).

Leki, I. (1989). *Academic Writing: Techniques and Tasks.* New York: St. Martin's Press.

Leki, I. (1990). Coaching from the margins: Issues in written response. In B. Kroll (Ed.), *Second Language Writing: Research Insights for the Classroom* (pp. 57–68). New York: Cambridge University Press.

Leki, I. (1991a). The preferences of ESL students for error correction in college-level writing classes. *Foreign Language Annals, 24*(3), 203–218.

Leki, I. (1991b). Twenty-five years of contrastive rhetoric: Text analysis and writing pedagogies. *TESOL Quarterly, 25*(1), 123–143.

Leki, I. (1991–1992). Building experience through sequenced writing assignments. *TESOL Journal, 1*(2), 19–23.

Leki, I. (1992). *Understanding ESL Writers: A Guide for Teachers.* New York: St. Martin's Press.

Leki, I. and Carson, J. (Eds.). (forthcoming). *Reading in the Composition Classroom..* New York: Newbury House/Heinle and Heinle.

Lennon, P. (1991). Error: Some problems of definition, identification, and distinction. *Applied LInguistics, 12*(2), 180–196.

Li, C. M. and Thompson, S. A. (1982). The gift between spoken and written language: A case study in Chinese. In D. Tannen (Ed.), *Spoken and Written Language: Exploring Orality and Literacy* (pp. 104–111). Norwood, NJ: Ablex.

Liebman-Kleine, J. A. (1986). In defense of teaching process in ESL composition. *TESOL Quarterly, 20*(4), 783–788.

Liebman-Kleine, J. A. (1987). Teaching and researching invention: Using ethnography in ESL writing classes. *ELT Journal, 41*(2), 104–111.

Lindemann, E. (1987). *A Rhetoric for Writing Teachers* (2nd ed.). New York: Oxford University Press.

Liou, H.-C. (1991). Development of an English grammar checker: A progress report. *CALICO Journal, 9*(1), 27–55.

Long, M. and Richards, J. C. (Eds.). (1987). *Methodology in TESOL: A Book of Readings.* New York: Harper and Row.

Long, M. H. and Porter, P. A. (1985). Group work, interlanguage talk, and second language acquisition. *TESOL Quarterly, 19*(2), 207–228.

Lope, D. (1991). From reading to writing strategies. *English Teaching Forum, 29*(4), 42–44.

Lowenburg, P. H. (1982). Singapore-Malaysian English: Aspects of a non-native variety. *The American Language Journal, 1*(1).

Lucas, C. (1992). Introduction: Writing portfolios-changes and challenges. In K. B. Yancey (Ed.), *Portfolios in the Writing Classroom: An Introduction* (pp. 1–11). Urbana, IL: NCTE.

Lucas, T. (1990). Personal journal writing as a classroom genre. In J. K. Peyton (Ed.), *Students and Teachers Writing Together* (pp. 99–124).

Lundquist, T. (1990). Empowering ourselves as we empower our students. *TESOL Teacher Education Newsletter, 6*(1), 1, 4.

Lunsford, A. (1990). Composing ourselves: Politics, commitment, and the teaching of writing. *College Composition and Communication, 41*(1), 71–82.

Mabrito, M. (1991). Electronic mail as a vehicle for peer response. *Written Communication, 8,* 519–532.

Macrorie, K. (1970). *Telling Writing.* Rochelle Park, NJ: Hayden.

Macrorie, K. (1976). *Writing to Be Read* (2nd ed.). Rochelle Park, NJ: Hayden.

Maimon, E. (1989). *Thinking, Reasoning, and Writing.* White Plains, NY: Longman.

Mangelsdorf, K. (1989). Parallels between speaking and writing in second language acquisition. In D. Johnson and D. Roen (Eds.), *Richness in Writing: Empowering ESL Students* (pp. 134–145). New York: Longman.

Marney, S. (1990). Seven panic points for non-fluent ESL writers. *TESOL ESL in Higher Education Newsletter, 9*(2), 3–4.

Marshall, S. (1985). Computer assisted feedback on written reports. *Computers and Education, 9*(4), 213–219.

Marting, J. (1991). Writers on writing: Self-assessment strategies for student essays. *Teaching English in the Two-Year College, 18*(2), 128–132.

Matalene, C. (1985). Contrastive rhetoric: An American teacher in China. *College English, 47*(8), 354–357.

Maurice, K. (Ed.). (1986). Cultural styles of thinking and speaking in the classroom. In P. Byrd (Ed.), *Teaching Across Cultures in the* University *ESL Program* (pp. 39–50). Washington, DC: NAFSA.

McCarthy, B. (1987). *The 4Mat System: Teaching to Learning Styles with Right/Left Mode Techniques.* Barrington, IL: EXCEL.

McConochie, J. (1982). All this fiddle: Enhancing language awareness through poetry. In M. Hines (Ed.), *On TESOL '81* (pp. 231–240). Washington,, DC: TESOL.

McConochie, J. and Sage, H. (1989). Since feeling is first: Thoughts on sharing poetry in the ESOL classroom. In A. Newton (Ed.), *A Forum Anthology (Vol. IV)* (pp. 236–239). Washington, DC: USIA.

McCormick, F. (1989). The Plagiario and the professor in our peculiar institution. *Journal of Teaching Writing, 8,* 133–145.

McCormick, F. (1991). Quizzing the suspected plagiarist. *Composition Chronicle, 4*(3), 45.

McGroarty, M. (1989a). The benefits of cooperative learning arrangements in second language acquisition. *NABE Journal, 13,* 127–143.

McGroarty, M. (1989b). Educators' responses to sociocultural diversity: Implications for practice. In *Beyond Language: Social and Cultural Factors in Schooling Language Minority Students* (pp. 299–343). Los Angeles, CA: Bilingual Education Office, Evaluation Dissemination and Assessment Center, California State University.

McGroarty, M. (1991). English instruction for language minority groups: Different structures, different styles. In M. Celce-Murcia (Ed.), *Teaching English as a Second or Foreign Language* (2nd ed.) (pp. 372–385). New York: Newbury/Harper Collins.

McGroarty, M. and Galvan, J. L. (1985). Culture as an issue in second-language teaching. In M. Celce-Murcia (Ed.), *Beyond Basics: Issues and Research in TESOL* (pp. 81–95). Rowley, MA: Newbury House.

McKay, S. (1979a). Communicative writing. *TESOL Quarterly, 13*(1), 73–80.

McKay, S. (1979b). Situation writing. *Cross Currents, 6*(2), 47–53.

McKay, S. (1980). *Writing for a Specific Purpose.* Englewood Cliffs, NJ: Prentice-Hall.

McKay, S. (1981). Prewriting activities. *TECFORS, 4*(3), 1–2.

McKay, S. (1982). Literature in the ESL classroom. *TESOL Quarterly, 16*(4), 529–536.

McKay, S. (1983). *Fundamentals of Writing for a Specific Purpose*. Englewood Cliffs, NJ: Prentice-Hall.

McKay, S. (1984). *Composing in a Second Language*. Rowley, MA: Newbury House.

McKay, S. (1989). Topic development and written discourse accent. In D. Johnson and D. Roen (Eds.), *Richness in Writing: Empowering ESL Students* (pp. 253–262). New York: Longman.

McKee, M. (1983). Academic writing vs. composition. *TECFORS, 6*(5), 7–11.

McKendy, T. (1992). Locally developed writing texts and the validity of holistic scoring. *Research in the Teaching of English, 26*(2), 149–166.

McLaughlin, B., Rossman, B., and McLeod, B. (1983). Second language learning: An information processing perspective. *Language Learning, 33,* 135–158.

McLeod, S. (Ed.). (1986). *Strengthening Programs for Writing Across the Curriculum*. San Francisco: Jossey.

McLeod, S. (1989). Writing across the curriculum: The second stage and beyond. *College Composition and Communication, 40,* 337–343.

McLeod, S. (1991a). Setting up writing around the curriculum programs: Problems and practicalities. Paper presented at the Wyoming Conference on English, Laramie, WY (June).

McLeod, S. (1991b). Writing as a mode of learning. *Composition Chronicle, 4*(2), 7–8.

Meloni, C. (1990). Adjustment of Arab students to university life in the United States. *TESL Reporter, 23*(1), 11–19.

Mestenhauser, J. A. (1988). Making a world of difference through professionalism. In J. Reid (Ed.), *Building the Professional Dimension of Educational Exchange* (pp. 1–8). Yarmouth, Maine: Intercultural Press.

Meyer, B. J. F. (1982). Reading research and the composition teacher. *College Composition and Communication, 33,* 37–39.

Meyer, B. J. F. and Rice, G. E. (1982). The interaction of reader strategies and the organization of text. *Text, 2*(1–3), 155–192.

Micek, T. (1992). Integrating reading and writing: Using prediction to teach development. Paper presented at *Illinois TESOL/BE*. Chicago (April).

Michaelides, N. N. (1990). Error analysis: An aid to teaching. *English Teaching Forum, 28*(4), 28–30.

Miller, J. T. and Gold, R. (1988). Change: Getting them to meet you half way. *Management Solutions, 33,* 37–42.

Mitchell, R. and Brumfit, C. (1989). Research in applied linguistics relevant to language teaching: 1988. *Language Teaching: The International Abstracting Journal for Language Teachers and Applied Linguists, 22*(3), 145–149.

Mittan, R. (1989). The peer review process: Harnessing students' communicative power. In D. Johnson and D. Roen (Eds.), *Richness in Writing: Empowering ESL Students* (pp. 207–219). New York: Longman.

Moffett, J. (1968). *Teaching the Universe of Discourse*. Boston: Houghton Mifflin..

Mohan, B. and Lo., W. (1985). Academic writing and Chinese students: Transfer of development factors. *TESOL Quarterly, 19*(2), 229–258.

Montaño-Harmon, M. (1988). Discourse features in the compositions of Mexican English as a second language, Mexican-American Chicano, and Anglo high school students: Considerations for the formulation of educational policy. Unpublished doctoral dissertation, University of Southern California.

Moore, L. K. (1986). Teaching students how to evaluate writing. *TESOL Newsletter, 20*(5), 23–24.

Morain, G. G. (1986). Kinesics and cross-cultural understanding. In J. Valdes (Ed.), *Culture Bound: Bridging the Cultural Gap in Language Teaching* (pp. 64–76). Cambridge: Cambridge University Press.

Morcos, D. A. (1986). *A linguistic study of coordination and subordination in the writing of Arabic speaking ESL students.* Unpublished master's thesis, University of New Orleans, Louisiana.

Morrow, K. (1977). *Techniques of Evaluation for a Notional Syllabus.* University of Reading: Centre for Applied Language Studies.

Mosallem, E. A. (1984). English for police officers in Egypt. *The ESP Journal, 3*(2), 171–182.

Moxley, J. (1989). Responding to student writing: Goals, methods, alternatives. *Freshman English News, 17*, 3–11.

Munby, J. (1978). *Communicative Syllabus Design.* Cambridge: Cambridge University Press.

Murdoch, G. (1992). The neglected text: A fresh look at teaching literature. *English Teaching Forum, 30*(1), 2–9.

Murray, D. (1978). Write before writing. *College Composition and Communication, 29*, 375–382.

Murray, D. (1982). *Learning by Teaching.* Upper Montclair, NJ: Boynton/Cook.

Murray, D. (1985a). The essential delay: When the writer's block isn't. In M. Rose (Ed.), *When a Writer Can't Write: Studies in Writer's Block and Other Composing Process Problems* (pp. 219–226). New York: Guilford Press.

Murray, D. (1985b). *A Writing Teacher Teaches Writing* (2nd ed.). Boston: Houghton Mifflin.

Murray, D. (1988). The listening eyes: Reflections on the writing conference. In G. Tate and E. P. J. Corbett (Eds.), *The Writing Teacher's Sourcebook* (pp. 232–237). New York: Oxford University Press.

Murray, D. M. (1990). How the text instructs: Writing teaches writing. In D. A. Daiker and M. Morenberg (Eds.), *The Writing Teacher as Researcher: Essays in the Theory and Practice of Class-Based Research* (pp. 76–90). Portsmouth, NH: Boynton/Cook Heinemann.

Naiman, D. (1988). *Telecommunications and an Interactive Approach to Literacy in Disabled Students.* New York: New York University.

Nation, P. (1991). Dictation, dicto-comp, and related techniques. *English Teaching Forum, 29*(4), 12–14.

Nayar, P. B. (1986). Acculturation or enculturation: Foreign students in the United States. In P. Byrd (Ed.), *Teaching Across Cultures in the University ESL Program* (pp. 1–14). Washington, DC: NAFSA.

Neeld, E. C. (1986). *Writing* (2nd ed.). Glenview, IL: Scott, Foresman.

Neu, J. and Scarcella, R. (1991). Word processing in the ESL writing classroom: A survey of student attitudes. In P. Dunkel (Ed.), *Computer-Assisted Language Learning and Testing: Research Issues and Practice* (pp. 169–187). New York: Newbury/Harper Collins.

Neuman, R. (1977). *An attempt to define through error analysis an intermediate ESL level at UCLA.* Unpublished master's thesis, University of California, Los Angeles.

Newell, G. and MacAdam, P. (1987). Examining the source of writing problems: An instrument for measuring topic specific knowledge. *Written Communication, 9,* 156–174.

Nickel, G. (1985). How "native" can (or should) an non-native speaker be? *ITL Review of Applied Linguistics, 67–68,* 141–160.

Nickel, G. (1989). Some controversies in present-day error analysis: "Contrastive" vs. "non-contrastive." *International Review of Applied Linguistics in Language Teaching, 27*(4), 293–305.

Nunan, D. (1988). *The Learner-Centered Curriculum.* Cambridge: Cambridge University Press.

Nunan, D. (1989a). Investigating learner behavior in the classroom. *The Language Teacher, 13*(12), 11–18.

Nunan, D. (1989b). *Syllabus Design.* Oxford: Oxford University Press.

Nunan, D. (1989c). *Understanding Language Classrooms: A Guide for Teacher Initiated Action.* New York: Prentice Hall International.

Nunan, D. (1990). The questions teachers ask. *JALT Journal, 12*(2), 187–202.

Nystrand, M. (1990). Sharing words: The effects of readers on developing writers. *Written Communication, 7*(1), 3–24.

O'Brien, L. (1989). Learning styles: Make the student aware. *National Association of Secondary School Principals' Bulletin, 73,* 85–89.

O'Malley, J. M. (1985). Learning strategy applications to content instruction in second language development. In *Issues in English Language Development* (pp. 69–73). Wheaton, MD: National Clearinghouse for Bilingual Education.

O'Malley, J. M., Chamot, A. U., and Küpper, L. (1986). *The Role of Learning Strategies and Cognition in Second Language Acquisition: A Study of Strategies for Listening Comprehension Used by Students of English as a Second Language.* Rosslyn, VA: InterAmerica Research Associates.

O'Malley, J. M., Chamot, A. U., Stewner-Manzanares, G., Küpper, L., and Russo, R. P. (1985). Learning strategies used by beginning and intermediate ESL students. *Language Learning, 35*(1), 21–46.

Odell, L. and Goswami, D. (1982). Writing in a non-academic setting. *Research in the Teaching of English, 16,* 201–223.

Oller, J. W. J. and Richard-Amato, P. A. (Eds.). (1983). *Methods that Work.* New York: Harper and Row.

Olsen, G. (Ed.). (1984). *Writing Centers: Theory and Administration.* Urbana, IL: NCTE.

O'Neil, J. (1990). Making sense of style. *Educational Leadership, 48*(2), 4–9.

Oster, J. (1989). Seeing with different eyes: Another view of literature in the ESL class. *TESOL Quarterly, 23*(3), 557–584.

Ostler, S. (1980). A survey of academic needs for advanced ESL. *TESOL Quarterly, 14*(4), 489–502.

Ostler, S. (1987). A study in the contrastive rhetoric of Arabic, English, Japanese, and Spanish. Unpublished doctoral dissertation, University of Southern California.

Ouaouicha, D. (1986). Contrastive rhetoric and the structure of learner-produced argumentative in Arabic and English. Unpublished doctoral dissertation, University of Texas/Austin.

Oxford, R. (1992). Individual learner differences and their impact on teacher roles and responsibilities. Paper presented at the International TESOL Convention, Vancouver, B.C. (March).

Oxford, R. L. (1990). *Language Learning Strategies: What Every Teacher Should Know*. New York: Newbury House/Harper and Row.

Pack, A. and Hendrichsen, L. (1981). *Sentence Combination: Writing and Combining Standard English Sentences*. Rowley, MA.: Newbury House.

Pak, J. (1986). *Find Out How You Teach*. Adelaide, Australia: National Curriculum Resource Centre: Adult Migrant Education Program Australia.

Park, Y. M. (1988). Academic and ethnic background as factors affecting writing performance. In A. Purves (Ed.), *Writing Across Languages and Cultures: Issues in Contrastive Rhetoric* (pp. 261–272). Newbury Park, CA: Sage Publishers.

Parkhurst, C. (1984). Using CALL to teach composition. In P. Larson, E. Judd, and D. Messerschmitt (Eds.), *On TESOL '84* (pp. 255–60). Washington, DC: TESOL.

Parsons, L. (1989). *Response Journals*. Portsmouth, NH: Heinemann.

Pask, G. (1988). Learning strategies, teaching strategies, and conceptual or learning styles. In R. R. Schmeck (Ed.), *Learning Strategies and Learning Styles* (pp. 83–100). New York: Plenum Press.

Paulston, C. (1972). Teaching writing in the ESOL classroom: Techniques of controlled composition. *TESOL Quarterly, 6*(1), 33–59.

Paulston, C. B. and Dykstra, G. (1973). *Controlled Composition in English as a Second Language*. New York: Regents.

Pearson, C. (1981). Advanced academic skills in the low-level ESL class. *TESOL Quarterly, 15*(4), 413–23.

Peck, S. (1991). Recognizing and meeting the needs of ESL students. In M. Celce-Murcia (Ed.), *Teaching English as a Second or Foreign Language* (2nd ed.) (pp. 363–372). New York: Newbury House/Harper Collins.

Perl, S. (1980). Understanding composing. *College Composition and Communication, 31*, 363–369.

Peyton, J., Staton, J., Richardson, G., and Wofram, W. (1990). The influence of writing task on ESL students' written production. *Research in the Teaching of English, 24*(2), 142–171.

Peyton, J. K. (Ed.). (1990). *Students and Teachers Writing Together*. Alexandria, VA: TESOL.

Peyton, J. K. and Reed, L. (Eds.). (1991). *Dialogue Journal Writing with Nonnative English Speakers: A Handbook for Teachers*. Alexandria, VA: TESOL.

Peyton, J. K. and Staton, J. (1991). *Writing Our Lives: Reflections on Dialogue Journal Writing with Adults Learning English.* Englewood Cliffs, NJ: Center for Applied Linguistics and Prentice Hall Regents.

Pica, T., Young, R., and Doughty, C. (1987). The impact of interaction on comprehension. *TESOL Quarterly, 21*(4), 737–758.

Picus, M. (1983). When Asians write: What to expect in grammar. *TECFORS, 6*(5), 1–3.

Poole, M. and Field, T. W. (1976). A comparison of oral and written code elaboration. *Language and Speech, 19,* 305–311.

Porat, M. (1988). Dialogue journals—A new and practical way of combining the teaching of writing and reading with getting to know your students. *English Teachers' Journal, 36,* 84–86.

Porter, P., Goldstein, L. M., Leatherman, J., and Conrad, S. (1990). Learning logs for teacher preparation. In J. Richards and D. Nunan (Eds.), *Second Language Teacher Education* (pp. 227–240). New York: Cambridge University Press.

Porter, R. E. and Samovar, L. A. (1991). Basic principles of intercultural communication. In L. A. Samovar and R. A. Porter (Eds.), *Intercultural Communication: A Reader* (6th ed.) (pp. 5–22). Belmont, CA: Wadsworth.

Powell, D. (1981). *What Can I Write About? 7000 Topics for High School Students.* Urbana, IL: NCTE.

Powers, J. (Forthcoming). Diversifying the model conference for the ESL writer. *Writing Lab Newsletter.*

Prapphal, K. (1987). Communication as the ultimate goal of English learning for Spanish, Chinese, Japanese, and Thai students. *BABEL, 22*(3), 40–44.

Prator, C. (1991). Cornerstones of method and names for the profession. In M. Celce-Murcia (Ed.), *Teaching English as a Second or Foreign Language* (2nd ed.) (pp. 11–22). New York: Newbury/Harper Collins.

Pritchard, R. H. (1990). The effects of cultural schemata on reading process strategies. *Reading Research Quarterly, 25*(4), 273–295.

Pritchard, R. J. (1987). Effects on student writing of teacher training in the National Writing Project model. *Written Communication, 9,* 51–67.

Prodromou, L. (1991). The good language teacher. *English Teaching Forum, 29*(2–3).

Prodromou, L. (1992). What culture? Which culture? Cross-cultural factors in language learning. *ESL Journal, 46*(1), 39–50.

Purves, A. (1988). The aesthetic mind of Louise Rosenblatt. *Reader, 20,* 68–76.

Purves, A. and Purves, W. (1986). On the nature and formation of interpretive and rhetorical communities. In T. N. Postlethwaite (Ed.), *International Education Research: Papers in Honor of Torstern Husen* (pp. 45–64). Oxford: Pergamon.

Pusch, M.D. (1979). *Multiculltural Education: A Cross-Cultural Training Approach.* La Grange Park, IL: Intercultural Network.

Pusch, M. D. (1981). Cross-cultural training. In G. Althen (Ed.), *Learning Across Cultures: Intercultural Communication and International Educational Exchange* (pp. 72–103). Washington, DC: NAFSA.

Purves, A. (1992). Reflections on research and assessment in written composition. *Research in the Teaching of English, 26*(1), 108–122.

Pytlik, B. P. (1991). Teaching the teaching of composition: Evaluating theories. *The Writing Instructor, 11*(1), 39–50.

Radecki, P. M. and Swales, J. M. (1988). ESL student reaction to written comments on their written work. *System, 16*, 355–365.

Raimes, A. (1978). Controlled by the teacher, free for the students. *English Teaching Forum, 16*(1), 2–7.

Raimes, A. (1983). *Techniques in Teaching Writing.* New York: Oxford University Press.

Raimes, A. (1985). What unskilled ESL students do as they write: A classroom study of composing. *TESOL Quarterly, 19*(2), 229–258.

Raimes, A. (1987a). *Exploring Through Writing: A Process Approach to ESL Composition.* New York: St. Martin's Press.

Raimes, A. (1987b). Language proficiency, writing ability and composing strategies: A study of ESL college student writers. *Language Learning, 37*(3), 439–468.

Raimes, A. (1990). The TOEFL Test of Written English: Causes for concern. *TESOL Quarterly, 24*(3), 427–442.

Raimes, A. (1991). Errors: Windows into the mind. *College ESL, 1*(2), 55–64.

Rainsbury, R. (1977). *Introduction for Beginning Students of English as a Second Language.* Englewood Cliffs, NJ: Prentice-Hall, Inc.

Rankin, E. (1990). From simple to complex: Ideas of order in assignment sequences. *Journal of Advanced Composition, 10*(1), 126–135.

Redd-Boyd, T. and Slater, W. M. (1989). The effects of audience specification on undergraduates' attitudes, strategies and writing. *Research in the Teaching of English, 23*(1), 77–108.

Reid, E. S. (1991). Personal communication.

Reid, J. (1982). *The Process of Composition.* Englewood Cliffs, NJ: Prentice-Hall.

Reid, J. (1987a). The learning style preferences of ESL students. *TESOL Quarterly, 21*(1), 87–111.

Reid, J. (1987b). The Writer's Workbench and ESL composition. *Computers and Composition, 4*(3), 53–63.

Reid, J. (1989). ESL expectations in higher education: The expectations of the academic audience. In D. Johnson and D. Roen (Eds.), *Richness in Writing: Empowering ESL Students* (pp. 220–234). New York: Longman.

Reid, J. (1990). Multiple audiences for ESL writers: The peer editor program. Paper presented at the Wyoming Conference on English, Laramie, WY (July).

Reid, J. (1991a). The impact of change in the ESL classroom. *TESL Ontario Journal, 17*(1), 1–3.

Reid, J. (1991b). Language learning: Strategies, expectations and change. Paper presented at the California TESOL Convention (CATESOL), Santa Clara (April).

Reid, J. (1992). Writers, readers, and second sentences. Unpublished manuscript.

Reid., J. (1993). *The Process of Paragraph Writing* (2nd ed.). Englewood Cliffs, NJ: Prentice Hall.

Reid, J. (Forthcoming). Historical perspectives on reading and writing in the ESL classroom. In I. Leki and J. Carson (Eds.), *Second Language Perspectives on Reading in the Composition Classroom*. New York: Newbury House/Heinle and Heinle.

Reid, J., Lindstrom, M., McCaffrey, M., and Larson, D. (1983). Computer-assisted text analysis for ESL students. *CALICO Journal, 1*(3), 40–46.

Reid, J. and Powers, J. (Forthcoming). Extending the benefits of collaborative learning to ESL students. *TESOL Journal*.

Reid, S. (1991). *The Prentice-Hall Guide to College Writing* (Annotated Instructor's Ed.). Englewood Cliffs, NJ: Prentice Hall.

Reid, S. (1992a). *The Prentice Hall Guide for College Writers* (2nd ed.). Englewood Cliffs, NJ: Prentice Hall.

Reid, S. (1992b). *The Prentice Hall Guide to College Writing* (Teacher's Manual). Englewood Cliffs, NJ: Prentice Hall.

Reid, S. and Findlay, G. (1986). Writer's Workbench analysis of holistically scored essays. *Computers and Composition, 3*(2), 6–32.

Reither, J. A. (1988). Writing and knowing: Toward redefining the writing process. In G. Tate and E. P. J. Corbett (Eds.), *The Writing Teacher's Sourcebook* (pp. 140–148). Oxford: Oxford University Press.

Reyes, M. de. la. Luz. (1991). A process approach to literacy: Using dialogue journals and literature logs with second language learners. *Research in the Teaching of English, 25*(3), 291–313.

Rice, M. K. and Burns, J. U. (1986). *Thinking/Writing*. Englewood Cliffs, NJ: Prentice-Hall.

Ricento, T. (1986). Comments on Bernard Mohan and Winnie Au-Yeung Lo's "Academic writing and Chinese students: transfer and developmental factors." *TESOL Quarterly, 20*(3), 565–568.

Ricento, T. (1987). *Aspects of coherence in English and Japanese expository prose.* Unpublished doctoral dissertation, University of California, Los Angeles.

Richard-Amato, P. (1988). *Making It Happen: Interaction in the Second Language Classroom*. New York: Longman.

Richard-Amato, P.A. and Snow, M.A. (Eds.). (1992). *The Multiculltural Classroom: Readings for Content-Area Teachers*. New York: Longman.

Richards, J. C. (1990a). The dilemma of teacher education in second language teaching. In J. C. Richards and D. Nunan (Eds.), *Second Language Teacher Education* (pp. 3–15). New York: Cambridge University Press.

Richards, J. C. (1990b). *The Language Teaching Matrix*. Cambridge: Cambridge University Press.

Richards, J. C. (1990c). What happened to methods? *The Language Teacher, 15*(6), 9–10.

Richards, J. C. and Lockhart, C. (1991–1992). Teacher development through peer observation. *TESOL Journal, 1*(2), 7–10.

Richards, J. C. and Nunan, D. (Eds.). (1990). *Second Language Teacher Education*. New York: Cambridge University Press.

Riley, P. (1975). The dicto-comp. In A. Newton (Ed.), *The Art of TESOL: Selected Articles from the English Teaching Forum* (pp. 238–240). Washington, DC: United States Information Agency.

Rinkerman, G. and Moody, L. (1992). Beat not the poor computer: Interactive composition. Paper presented at the International TESOL Convention, Vancouver, B.C. (March).

Rivers, W. (1964). *The Psychologist and the Foreign Language Teacher*. Chicago: University of Chicago Press.

Rivers, W. (1968). *Teaching Foreign Language Skills*. Chicago: University of Chicago Press.

Rivers, W. (1990). Interaction and communication in the language classroom in an age of technology. *Canadian Modern Language Review, 46*(2), 271–283.

Robb, T. (1991). Personal communication.

Robb, T., Ross, S., and Shortreed, I. (1986). Salience of feedback on error and its effect on EFL writing quality. *TESOL Quarterly, 20*, 83–95.

Robb, T. and Susser, B. (1989). Extensive reading vs. skills buildings in an EFL context. *Reading in a Foreign Language, 5*(2), 239–251.

Robinson, G. L. (1985). *Crosscultural Understanding: Processes and Approaches for Foreign Language, English as a Second Language, and Bilingual Education*. New York: Pergamon.

Robinson, G.L. (1991). Effective feedback strategies in CALL: Learning theory and empirical research. In P. Dunkel (Ed.), *Computer-Assisted Language Learning and Testing: Research Issues and Practice* (pp. 155–167). New York: Newbury/HarperCollins.

Robinson, T. (1985). Evaluating foreign students' compositions: The effects of rater background and handwriting, spelling and grammar. Unpublished doctoral dissertation, University of Texas at Austin.

Rodrigues, D. (1985). Computers and basic writers. *College Composition and Communication, 39*(2), 217–219.

Rodrigues, D. and Rodrigues, R. (1989). How word processing is changing our teaching: New technologies, new approaches, new challenges. *Computers and Composition, 31*(3), 13–25.

Roemer, M., Schultz, L.M., and Durst, R. (1991). Portfolios and the process of change. *College Composition and Communication, 42*(4), 455–469.

Roen, D. (1989). Developing effective assignments for second language writers. In D. Johnson and D. Roen (Eds.), *Richness in Writing: Empowering ESL Students* (pp. 193–206). New York: Longman.

Rohman, D. G. (1965). Pre-writing: The stage of discovery in the writing process. *College Composition and Communication, 16*, 106–112.

Rose, M. (1985a). The language of exclusion: Writing instruction at the university. *College English, 47*, 341–359.

Rose, M. (Ed.). (1985b). *When a Writer Can't Write: Studies in Writer's Block and Other Composing Process Problems*. New York: Guilford Press.

Rose, M. (1989). *Lives on the Boundaries*. New York: Penguin Books.

Rosenblatt, L. (1988). Writing and reading: The transactional theory. *Reader, 20*, 7–31.

Ross, J. (1968). Controlled writing: A transformational approach. *TESOL Quarterly*, *2*(4), 253–261.

Ross, S., Shortreed, I. M., and Robb, T. J. (1988). First language composition pedagogy in the second language classroom: A reassessment. *RELC Journal*, *19*(1), 29–48.

Rubin, J. (1987). Learner strategies: Theoretical assumptions, research, history, and typology. In A. Wenden and J. Rubin (Eds.), *Learner Strategies in Language Learning* (pp. 15–30). Englewood Cliffs, NJ: Prentice-Hall.

Russell, D. (1987). Writing across the curriculum and the communications movement: Some lessons from the past. *College Composition and Communication*, *38*(2), 184–194

Russell, D. (1990). Writing across the curriculum in historical perspective: Toward a social interpretation. *College English*, *52*(1), 52–73.

Ruth, L. and Murphy, S. (1984). Developing topics for writing assessments: Problems of meaning. *College Composition and Communication*, *35*, 410–42.

Ruth, L. and Murphy, S. (1987). *Designing Writing Tasks for the Assessment of Writing*. New York: Ablex.

Sage, H. (1987). *Incorporating Literature in ESL Instruction*. Englewood Cliffs, NJ: Prentice-Hall.

Salvatori, M. (1983). Reading and writing a text: Correlations between reading and writing. *College English*, *45*, 657–666.

Samovar, L. and Porter, R. (1991). *Intercultural Communication: A Reader* (6th ed.). Belmont, CA: Wadsworth.

Sampson, G. (1980). Teaching written language using a functional approach. *TESL Talk*, *2*(2), 38–44.

Santaña-Seda, O. (1974). A contrastive study in rhetoric: An analysis of the English and Spanish paragraphs written by native speakers of each language. Unpublished doctoral dissertation, New York University.

Santos, T. (1988). Professors' reactions to the academic writing of non-native speaking students. *TESOL Quarterly*, *18*(4), 671–688.

Santos, T. (1992). What do we teach when we teach ESL writing? Paper presented at the International TESOL Convention, Vancouver, B. C. (March).

Sarig, G. (1988). Composing a study-summary: A reading-writing encounter. Paper presented at the International TESOL Convention, Chicago (March).

Savignon, S. (1983). *Communicative Competence: Theory and Classroom Practice*. Reading, MA: Addison-Wesley.

Savova, L. and Donato, R. (1991). Group activities in the language classroom. *English Teaching Forum*, *29*(2), 12–15, 26.

Sayers, D. (1986). Sending messages: Across the classroom and around the world. *TESOL Newsletter (Supplement on computer-assisted language learning)*, *20*(1), 7–8.

Scarcella R. (1984a). Cohesion in the writing development of native and non-native writers. Unpublished doctoral dissertation, University of Southern California.

Scarcella, R. (1984b). How writers orient their readers in expository essays: A comparative study of native and non-native English writers. *TESOL Quarterly, 18*(4), 671–688.

Scarcella, R. (1986). Coming out of the cabbage page: Relying on what you've got—linguistic fallback. *TECFORS, 9*(4), 1–9.

Scarcella, R. (1988). How writers orient their readers in expository essays: A comparative study of native and non-native speakers of English writers. Paper presented at the International TESOL Convention, Chicago (March).

Scarcella, R. (1990). *Teaching Language Minority Students in the Multicultural Classroom.* Englewood Cliffs, NJ: Prentice Hall Regents.

Scarcella, R. and Oxford, R. (1992). *The Tapestry of Language Learning: The Individual in the Communicative Classroom.* Boston: Heinle and Heinle.

Schachter, J. (1974). An error in error analysis. *Language Learning, 24*(2), 205–214.

Schachter, J. (1990). Communicative competence revisited. In B. Harley, P. Allen, J. Cummins, and M. Swain (Eds.), *The Development of Second Language Proficiency* (pp. 39–49). London: Cambridge University Press.

Schafer, J. A. (1981). The linguistic analysis of spoken and written texts. In B. Kroll and R. Vann (Eds.), *Exploring Reading-Writing Relationships* (pp. 1–37). Urbana, IL: NCTE.

Schenk, M. J. (1988). *Read, Write, Revise: A Guide to Academic Writing.* New York: St. Martin's Press.

Schleppegrell, M. (1985). Economic input: An ESP program. *The ESP Journal, 4*(2), 11–20.

Schleppegrell, M. J. (1991). English for Specific Purposes: A program design model. *English Teaching Forum, 29*(4), 18–22.

Schlossberg, N. K. (1987). Taking the mystery out of change: By recognizing our strengths and building on them we can learn how to master transitions. *Psychology Today, 21,* 75–76.

Schriver, K.A. (1992). Teaching writers to anticipate readers' needs: A classroom-evaluated pedagogy. *Written Communication, 9*(2), 179–208.

Schwartz, H. (1985). *Interactive Writing: Composing on a Word Processor.* New York: Holt, Rinehart and Winston.

Schwartz, H. (1989). Creating writing activities with the word processor. In C. Selfe, D. Rodrigues, and W. Oates (Eds.), *Computers in English and the Language Arts* (pp. 197–203). Urbana, IL: NCTE.

Scollon, R. and Scollon, S. B. K. (1981). *Narrative, Literacy and Face in Interethnic Communication.* Norwood, NJ: Ablex.

Scott, M. S. and Tucker, G. R. (1974). Error analysis and English language strategies of Arab students. *Language Learning, 24,* 69–97.

Scovel, T. (1988). Multiple perspectives make singular teaching. In L. M. Beebe (Ed.), *Issues in Second Language Acquisition* (pp. 169–190). New York: Newbury/Harper and Row.

Scribner, S. and Cole, M. (1981). *The Psychology of Literacy.* Cambridge: Harvard University Press.

Seale, B. (1978). *Writing Efficiently.* Englewood Cliffs, NJ: Prentice-Hall.

Segal, M. K. and Pavlik, C. (1985). *Interactions II: A Writing Process Book* (2nd ed.). New York: Random House.

Selfe, C., Rodrigues, D., and Oates, W. (1989). *Computers in English and the Language Arts*. Urbana, IL: NCTE.

Semke, H. D. (1984). The effects of the red pen. *Foreign Language Annals, 17,* 7–31.

Severino, C. (1992). Where the cultures of basic writing and academia intersect: Cultivating the common ground. *Journal of Basic Writing, 11*(1), 4–15.

Shang, S. (1991). Incorporating culturgrams into the EFL classroom. *English Teaching Forum, 29*(4), 39–40.

Shaughnessy, M. (1977). *Errors and Expectations: A Guide for the Teacher of Basic Writing*. New York: Oxford University Press.

Shen, F. (1989). The classroom and the wider culture: Identity as a key to learning composition. *College Composition and Communication, 40*(4), 459–466.

Sheorey, R. (1986). Error perceptions of native-speaking and non-native speaking teachers of ESL. *ELT Journal, 40*(4), 306–312.

Sheridan, D. (1991). Changing business as usual: Reader response in the classroom. *College English, 53,* 804–814.

Sherman, J. (1992). Your own thoughts in your own words. *ELT Journal, 46*(2), 190–198.

Shih. M. 1986. Content-based approaches to teaching academic writing. *TESOL Quarterly, 20*(1), 87–103.

Shih, M. (1992). Beyond comprehension exercises in the ESL academic reading class. *TESOL Quarterly, 26*(2), 289–318.

Shimazu, Y.-M. (1992). Advice for ESL/EFL teachers of Japanese students. *TESOL Journal, 1*(4), 26.

Shoemaker, C. (1985). *Write in the Corner Where You Are*. New York: Holt, Rinehart and Winston.

Shoemaker, C. and Shoemaker, F. (1991). *Interactive Techniques for the ESL Classroom*. New York: Newbury House/Harper Collins.

Shook, R. (1978). Sentence-combining: A theory and two reviews. *TESL Reporter, 2,* 4–7,12,15.

Shriner, D. K. and Rice, W. C. (1989). Computer conferencing and collaborative learning: A discourse community at work. *College Composition and Communication, 40*(472–478).

Shuy, R. W. and Robinson, D. G. (1990). The oral language process in writing: A real-life writing session. *Research in the Teaching of English, 24*(1), 88–100.

Silva, T. (1990). Second language composition instruction: Developments, issues and directions in ESL. In B. Kroll (Ed.), *Second Language Writing: Research Insights for the Classroom* (pp. 11–23). New York: Cambridge University Press.

Silva, T. (1992). Comparison of NES/ESL writing. Paper presented at the International TESOL Convention, Vancouver, B.C. (March).

Simon, A. and Byram, C. (1984). *You've Got to Reach 'Em to Teach 'Em*. Dallas, TX: Training Associate Press.

Simons, G. (1989). *Working Together: How to Become More Effective in a Multicultural Organization*. Los Altos, CA: Crisp Publications.

Skehan, P. (1989). *Individual Differences in Second Language Learning*. London: Edward Arnold/Hodder and Stoughton.

Skehan, P. (1991). Individual differences in second language learning. *Studies in Second Language Acquisition, 13*(2), 275–298.

Skierso, A. (1990). Textbook selection and evaluation. In M. Celce-Murcia (Ed.), *Teaching English as a Second or Foreign Language* (2nd ed.) (pp. 432–453). New York: Newbury House/Harper Collins.

Skow, L. and Samovar, L. A. (1991). Cultural patterns of the Masai. In L. A. Samovar and R. E. Porter (Eds.), *Intercultural Communication: A Reader* (pp. 87–96). Belmont, CA: Wadsworth.

Sloan, G. (1990). Frequency of errors in essays by college freshmen and by professional writers. *College Composition and Communication, 41*(3), 299–308.

Smagorinsky, P. (1991a). The aware audience: Role-playing peer-response groups. *English Journal, 80*(5), 35–40.

Smagorinsky, P. (1991b). The writer's knowledge and the writing process. *Research in the Teaching of English, 25*(3), 339–364.

Smit, D., Kolonsky, P., and Seltzer, K. (1991). Implementing a portfolio system. In P. Belanoff and M. Dickson (Eds.), *Portfolios: Process and Product* (pp. 46–56). Portsmouth, NH: Heinemann.

Smith, C. (in press). Text-analysis: Computer analysis for writing and writing instruction. In I. Lancashire, S. Hockey, M. Ide, and G. Holmes (Eds.), *Methodologies in Humanities Computing*. Philadelphia: University of Pennsylvania.

Smith, F. (1987). *Understanding Reading: A Psycholinguistic Analysis of Reading and Learning*. New York: Holt, Rinehart and Winston.

Smith, M. (1991). *The Macmillan Guide for Teachers of Writing*. New York: Macmillan.

Smoke, T. (1987). *A Writer's Workbook: An Interactive Writing Text for ESL Students*. New York: St. Martin's Press.

Snow, M. A. and Brinton, D. (1988). Content-based language instruction: Investigating the effectiveness of the adjunct model. *TESOL Quarterly, 22*(4), 553–574.

Sommers, N. (1980). Revision strategies of student writers and experienced adult writers. *College Composition and Communication, 31*, 378–388.

Sommers, N. (1982). Responding to student writers. *College Composition and Communication, 33*, 148–156.

Sommers, N. (1992). Between the drafts. *College Composition and Communication, 43*, 23–31.

Spack, R. (1984). Invention strategies and the ESL college composition student. *TESOL Quarterly, 18*(4), 649–670.

Spack, R. (1985). Literature, reading, writing and the ESL student. *TESOL Quarterly, 19*, 703–725.

Spack, R. (1988). Initiating ESL students into the academic discourse community: How far should we go? *TESOL Quarterly, 22*(1), 29–51.

Spack, R. (1990). *Guidelines: A Cross/Cultural Reading/Writing Text*. New York: St. Martin's Press.

Spack, R. and Sadow, C. (1983). Student-teacher working journals in ESL freshman composition. *TESOL Quarterly, 17*(4), 575–594.

Spandal, V. and Stiggins, R. (1990). *Creating Writers: Linking Assessment and Writing Instruction*. New York: Longman.

Spatt, B. (1987). *Writing From Sources* (2nd ed.). New York: St. Martin's Press.

Spear, K. (1988). *Sharing Writing: Peer Response Groups in the Classroom*. Portsmouth, NH: Boynton/Cook.

Sperling, M. and Freedman, S. W. (1987). A good girl writes like a good girl. *Written Communication, 4*, 343–369.

Spivey, N. (1987). Construing constructivism: Reading research in the United States. *Poetics, 16*, 169–182.

Spivey, N. (1990). Transforming texts: Construction processes in reading and writing. *Written Communication, 7*, 256–287.

Spivey, N. (1991). The shaping of meaning: Options in writing the comparison. *Research in the Teaching of English, 25*(4), 390–418.

St. John, M. J. (1987). Writing processes of Spanish scientists publishing in English. *English for Specific Purposes, 6*(2), 112–120.

Stall, J. (1988). ESL entry level students can write too. Paper presented at the International TESOL Convention, Chicago (March).

Stansfield, C. (1986). A history of the Test of Written English: The developmental year. *Language Testing, 3*, 224–234.

Steele, R. (1990). Culture in the foreign language classroom. *ERIC/CLL News Bulletin, 14*(1), 1, 4–5, 12.

Sternglass, M. (1986). Introduction. In B. T. Peterson (Ed.), *Convergences: Transactions in Reading and Writing* (pp. 1–11). Urbana, IL: NCTE.

Stevick, E. (1980). *Teaching Languages: A Way and Ways*. Rowley, MA: Newbury House.

Stevick, E. (1989). *Success with Foreign Languages*. Englewood Cliffs, NJ: Prentice-Hall International.

Stoller, F. (1990). Films and videotapes in the content-based ESL/EFL classroom. *English Teaching Forum, 28*(4), 10–14.

Stotsky, S. (1983). Research on reading/writing relationships: A synthesis and suggested directions. *Language Arts, 60*, 627–642.

Straw, S. (1990). Challenging communication. In D. Bogdan and S. Straw (Eds.), *Beyond Communication: Reading Comprehension and Criticism* (pp. 67–89). Portsmouth, NH: Boynton/Cook.

Strong, W. (1973). *Sentence Combining: A Composing Book*. New York: Random House.

Stuart, K. (1990). Developing extensive reading skills with culturally relevant folktales. *TESL Reporter, 23*(1), 3–4.

Subbiah, M. (1992). Adding a new dimension to the teaching of audience analysis: Cultural awareness. *IEEE Transactions of Professional Communication, 35*(1), 14–18.

Susser, B. and Robb, T. (1990). EFL extensive reading instruction: Research and procedure. *JALT Journal, 12*(2), 161–185.

Svendsen, C. and Krebs, K. (1984). Identifying English for the job: Examples from health care occupations. *The ESP Journal, 3*(2), 153–165.

Swales, J. (1990a). *Genre Analysis: English in Academic and Research Settings.* New York: Cambridge University Press.

Swales, J. (1990b). Nonnative speaker graduate engineering students and their introductions: Global coherence and local management. In U. Connor and A. Johns (Eds.), *Coherence in Writing* (pp. 187–207). Alexandria, VA: TESOL.

Swales, J. and Najar, N. (1987). The writing of research article introductions. *Written Communication, 4*(2), 175–191.

Tannen, D. (1982a). Oral and literate strategies in spoken and written narratives. *Language, 58*(1), 1–21.

Tannen, D. (Ed.). (1982b). *Spoken and Written Language: Exploring Orality and Literacy.* Norwood, NJ: Ablex.

Tannen, D. (Ed.). (1984a). *Coherence in Spoken and Written Discourse.* Norwood, NJ: Ablex.

Tannen, D. (1984b). Spoken and written narrative in English and Greek. In D. Tannen (Ed.), *Coherence in Spoken and Written Discourse* (pp. 21–41). Norwood, NJ: Ablex.

Tannen, D. (1986). *That's Not What I Meant! How Conversational Style Makes or Breaks Your Relations with Others.* New York: William Morrow.

Tannen, D. (1990). *You Just Don't Understand.* New York: William Morrow.

Tarone, E. and Yule, G. (1989). *Focus on the Language Learner.* Oxford: Oxford University Press.

Tarvers, J. K. (1990). The composing process: An overview. In L. Q. Troyka (Ed.), *The Simon and Schuster Handbook for Writers* (2nd ed.) Annotated Instructor's Edition. Englewood Cliffs, NJ: Prentice Hall.

Tate, G. and Corbett, E. P. J. (Eds.). (1988). *The Writing Teacher's Sourcebook.* New York: Oxford University Press.

Taylor, B. (1981). Content and written form: A two-way street. *TESOL Quarterly, 15*(1), 5–13.

Tebo-Messina, M. (1989). Authority and models of the writing workshop: All collaborative writing is not equal. *The Writing Instructor, 8*, 86–92.

Tedick, D. J. (1990). ESL writing assessment: The effects of subject-matter knowledge on performance. *The ESP Journal, 9*(2), 123–143.

Test of Written English Guide. (1990). Princeton, NJ: Educational Testing Service.

Thompson, D. P. (1989). Using a local network to teach computer revision. *Journal of Teaching Writing, 8*, 77–86.

Thompson-Panos, K. and Thomas-Ruzic (1983). The least you should know about Arabic. *TESOL Quarterly, 17*(4), 609–623.

Thury, E. (1988). Subordination patterns of remedial and average students. Unpublished manuscript, Drexel University.

Tierney, R. and Pearson, P. D. (1984). Toward a composing model of reading. In J. Jensen (Ed.), *Composing and Comprehending* (pp. 33–45). Urbana, IL: NCTE.

Tierney, R. and Leys, M. (1986). What is the value connecting reading and writing? In B. T. Petersen (Ed.), *Conferences: Transactions in Reading and Writing* (pp. 15–29). Urbana, IL: NCTE.

Tikunoff, W. J. (1985). *Applying Significant Bilingual Instruction Features in the Classroom*. Rosslyn, VA: National Clearinghouse for Bilingual Education.

Trimble, L. (1985). *English for Science and Technology*. Cambridge: Cambridge University Press.

Trimbur, J. (1989). Consensus and differences in collaborative learning. *College Learning, 51*(6), 602–616.

Troyka, L. (1993). *The Simon and Schuster Handbook for Writers (3rd ed.)*. Annotated Instructor's Edition. Englewood Cliffs, NJ: Prentice Hall.

Tyacke, M. (1991). Strategies for success: Bringing out the best in a learner. *TESL Canada Journal, 8*(2), 45–56.

Tyler, A. and Bro, J. (1992). Discourse structure in nonnative English discourse. *Studies in Second Language Acquisition, 14*(1), 71–85.

Tyler, L. V. (Ed.). (1985). *How to Develop and Creatively Use Culture Guides*. Provo Utah: Culturgram Series.

Under hill, A. (1992). The role of groups in developing teacher awareness. *ELT Journal, 46*(1), 71–74.

Ur, P. (1992). Teacher learning. *ELT Journal, 46*(1), 56–61.

Valdes, J. M. (Ed.). (1986). *Culture Bound: Bridging the Cultural Gap in Language Teaching*. Cambridge: Cambridge University Press.

Van Ek, J. and Alexander, L. (1980). *Threshold Level English*. Oxford: Pergamon.

Vann, R. and Abraham, R. (1990). Strategies of unsuccessful language learners. *TESOL Quarterly, 24*(2), 177–198.

Vann, R., Lorenz, F. D., and Meyer, D. E. (1991). Error gravity: Faculty response to error in the written discourse of non-native speakers of English. In L. Hamp-Lyons (Ed.), *Assessing ESL Writing in Academic Contexts* (pp. 181–195). Norwood, NJ: Ablex.

Vann, R., Meyer, D. E., and Lorenz, F. D. (1984). Error gravity: A study of faculty opinion of ESL errors. *TESOL Quarterly, 18*(3), 427–440.

Varone, S. D. and D'Agostino, K. N. (1990). Beyond software: Computers and the composition curriculum. *Composition Chronicle, 2*(9), 4–6.

Vataloro, P. (1990). Putting students in charge of review. *Journal of Teaching Writing, 9*(1), 21–29.

Vaughn, C. (1992). Holistic assessments: What goes on in our minds? In L. Hamp-Lyons (Ed.), *Assessing ESL Writing in Academic Contexts* (pp. 111–125). Norwood, NJ: Ablex.

Wallace, C. (1988). *Learning to Read in a Multicultural Society: The Social Context of Second Language Literacy*. New York: Prentice-Hall International.

Walvoord, B.E. and McCarthy, L.P. (1991). *Thinking and Writing in College: A Naturalistic Study of Students in Four Disciplines*. Urbana, IL: NCTE.

Walworth, M. (1990). Interactive teaching of reading: A model. In J. K. Peyton (Ed.), *Students and Teachers Writing Together: Perspectives on Journal Writing* (pp. 35–48). Alexandria, VA: TESOL.

Wanning, E. (1991). *Culture Shock USA*. Singapore: Times Books International.

Wederspahn, A. and Barger, N. (1985). Learning strategies. *TESOL Newsletter*, *19*(5), 1,7.

Weiner, H. (1986). Collaborative learning in the classroom: A guide to evaluation. *College English*, *48*(1), 52–61.

Wenden, A. (1985). Learner strategies. *TESOL Newsletter*, *19*(5), 1,7.

Wenden, A. (1987). Conceptual background and utility. In A. Wenden and S. Rubin (Eds.), *Learner Strategies in Language Learning* (pp. 3–13). Englewood Cliffs, NJ: Prentice-Hall.

Wenden, A. and Rubin, J. (Eds.). (1987). *Learner Strategies in Language Learning*. Englewood Cliffs, NJ: Prentice-Hall.

West, G. K. and Byrd, P. (1982). Technical writing required of graduate engineering students. *Journal of Technical Writing and Communication*, *12*, 1–6.

White, E. M. (1986). *Teaching and Assessing Writing*. San Francisco: Jossey.

White, E. M. (1990). Language and reality in writing assessment. *College Composition and Communication*, *41*(5), 397–425.

White, R. V. (1987). *Writing Advanced*. Oxford: Oxford University Press.

Widdowson, H. (1987). Forward. In U. Connor and R. B. Kaplan (Eds.), *Writing Across Languages: Analysis of L2 Text* (pp. iii–iv). Reading, MA: Addison-Wesley.

Widdowson, H. G. (1978). *Teaching Language as Communication*. Oxford: Oxford University Press.

Wilkins, D. (1976). *Notional Syllabus*. Oxford: Oxford University Press.

Williams, K. L. (1990). Three new tests for overseas students entering post graduate and vocational training courses. *ELT Journal*, *44*(1), 55.

Williamson, J. (1991–1992). A culture capsule that works: Presenting proverbs in the advanced ESOL classroom. *TESOL Journal*, *1*(2), 32.

Willig, K. (1988). *Learning Styles in Adult Migrant Education*. Adelaide: National Curriculum Resource Centre.

Willig, K. (1991). Learning-how-to-learn: A review of current learner strategies publications. *Prospect*, *6*(2), 51–57.

Willoquet-Mariondi, P. (1991–1992). Integrating ESOL skills through literature. *TESOL Journal*, *1*(2), 11–14.

Witkin, H. A. (1976). Cognitive style in academic performance and in teacher-student relations. In T. Messick and Associates (Eds.), *Individuality in Learning* (pp. 38–72). San Fransisco: Jossey-Bass.

Witte, S. P. (1987). Pre-text and composing. *College Composition and Communication*, *38*(5), 397–425.

Wohl, M. (1985). *Techniques for Writing: Composition* (2nd ed.). Rowley, MA: Newbury House.

Wolfson, N. (1986). Compliments in cross-cultural perspective. In J. Valdes (Ed.), *Cultural Bound: Bridging the Cultural Gap in Language Teaching* (pp. 123–129). Cambridge: Cambridge University Press.

Wong, C. (1988). What we do and don't know about Chinese learners of English: A critical review of selected research. *RELC Journal, 19*(1), 1–20.

Wong, S.-L. C. (1984). Applying error analysis to material development for advanced ESL writers. Paper presented at the International TESOL Convention, Toronto (March).

Wresch, W. (Ed.). (1984). *A Writer's Tool: The Computer in Composition Instruction*. Urbana, IL: NCTE.

Yancey, K.B. (Ed.). (1992). *Portfolios in the Writing Classroom: An Introduction*. Urbana, IL: NCTE.

Yorio, C. (1989). The other side of the looking glass. *Journal of Basic Writing, 8*, 32–45.

Young, R., Becker, A., and Pike, K. (1970). *Rhetoric: Discovery of Change*. New York: Harcourt Brace Jovanovich.

Zak, F. (1990). Exclusively positive responses to student writing. *Journal of Basic* 9(2), 40–53.

Zamel, V. (1976). Teaching composition in the ESL classroom: What we can learn from research in the teaching of English. *TESOL Quarterly, 10*, 67–76.

Zamel, V. (1980). Re-evaluating sentence-combining practice. *TESOL Quarterly, 14*(1), 81–90.

Zamel, V. (1982). Writing: The process of discovering meaning. *TESOL Quarterly, 16*(2), 195–209.

Zamel, V. (1983). The composing processes of advanced ESL students: Six case studies. *TESOL Quarterly, 17*(2), 165–187.

Zamel, V. (1985). Responding to student writing. *TESOL Quarterly, 19*(1), 79–102.

Zamel, V. (1987). Recent research on writing pedagogy. *TESOL Quarterly, 21*(4), 697–715.

Zamel, V. (1990). Through students' eyes: The experiences of three ESL writers. *Journal of Basic Writing, 9*(2), 83–98.

Zamel, V. (1991). Acquiring language, literacy, and academic discourse: Entering new conversations. *College ESL, 1*(1), 10–18.

Zamel, V. (1992). Writing one's way into reading. *TESOL Quarterly, 26*(3), 463–485.

Zebroski, J. T. (1986). The uses of theory: A Vygotskian approach to composition. *The Writing Instructor, 5*, 56–57.

Zhang, S. and Jacobs, G. (1989). The effectiveness of peer feedback in the ESL writing class. Unpublished manuscript, University of Hawaii at Manoa.

INDEX

Accuracy, 229–232
   in the ALM, 21–23
   in the language-based curriculum,
     74–75
Action research, 265
Affective learning styles, 56
ALM, 21–23
Alternative audiences, 214–216
   peer editors, 215–216
   tutorials, 215–216
   writing center, 214–215
Analytic scoring, 235–237
Annotated bibliography, 293–304
Audio-lingual method, 21–23

Basic writers, 8–9

CAI, 42–44
C.A.L.L., 42–44
Case study research, 8
Caveats
   collaboration, 156–157
   conferencing, 224–225
   cultural informant, 55
   group projects, 173
   group work, 135–136, 156–157,
     158–159
   journals, 163
   peer review, 213–217
   peer review groups, 208–209
   warm-ups, 154
Change, 124, 139–141, 229
   student resistance to, 139
Classroom activities
   collaborative, 155–157
   cross-cultural, 166
   design criteria for, 151
   start-up, 152–154
Classroom community, 109, 111,
    133–135, 150, 207
Classroom culture, 111
Classroom pacing, 138
Classroom structure, 120
Clustering, 6
Cognitive approach, 5, 260–261
Cognitive learning styles, 56
Coherence, 36–37

Cohesion, 36–37
Collaboration (*See* Group work)
   caveats about, 156–157
Collaborative activities, 155–161
   analysis of advertisements,
     160–161
   culturgrams, 161
   curiosity lists, 159
   group problem-solving, 160
   group summaries, 159
   newspaper headlines, 159
   outrageous claim, 161
   round-robin brainstorming, 160
   sentence combining, 160
   shared notes, 159
Collaborative learning, 16, 41–42
Combination-based curriculum, 76–
    77
Communicative competence, 30, 38-
    41
Composing processes, 34–35
Computer-Assisted Instruction (CAI),
    42–44
Computer-Assisted Language
    Learning (CALL), 42
Computers and composition, 13–14
Conferencing, 220–224
   student roles, 221–222
   teacher roles, 220–221
   worksheets, 222–223
Content-based syllabus, 92
Contrastive analysis, 35
Contrastive rhetoric, 60–62
Controlling writing, 23–24
Criteria for evaluation, 245–246
Cross-cultural activities, 167–171
   essay assignments, 168, 169–171
   group project, 168
   journal entries, 167–168
   newspapers, 171
   nonverbal communication,
     168–169
   proverbs, 170
   vice-virtue words, 171
Cross-cultural classroom, the, 51–53
Cross-cultural communication, 49–55
Cultural informant, 53